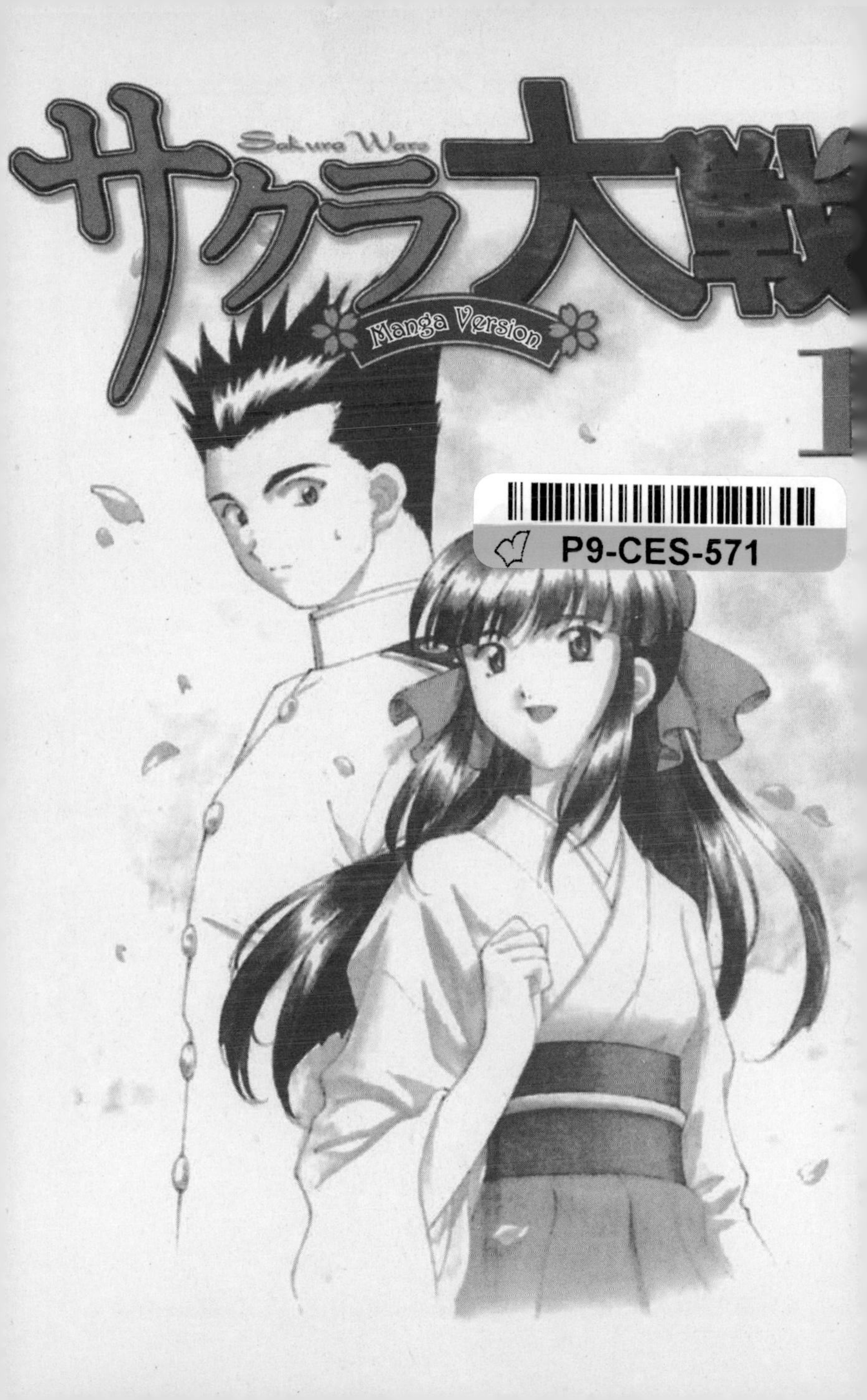
サクラ大戦
Sakura Wars
Manga Version
1

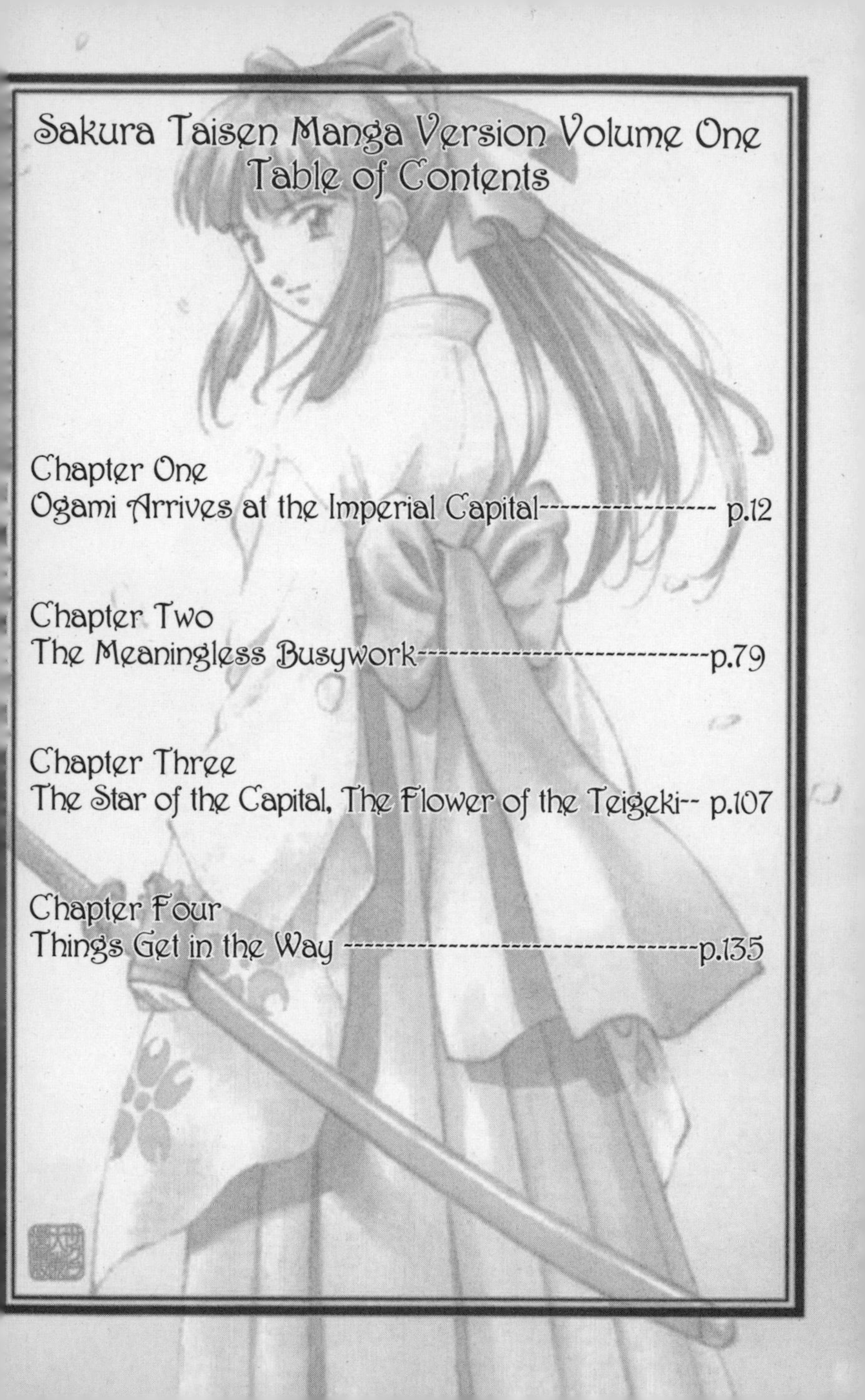

Sakura Taisen Manga Version Volume One
Table of Contents

Vol. 1

Story by
Ohji Hiroi

Art by
Ikku Masa

Characters by
Kosuke Fujishima

HAMBURG // LONDON // LOS ANGELES // TOKYO

Sakura Taisen Vol. 1
Story by Ohji Hiroi
Art by Ikku Masa
Characters by Kosuke Fujishima

Translation - Yuko Fukami
Retouch and Lettering - Irene Woori Choi
Production Artist - James Lee
Cover Design - Jorge Negrete

Editor - Lillian Diaz-Przybyl
Digital Imaging Manager - Chris Buford
Pre-Press Manager - Antonio DePietro
Production Managers - Jennifer Miller and Mutsumi Miyazaki
Art Director - Matt Alford
Managing Editor - Jill Freshney
VP of Production - Ron Klamert
Editor-in-Chief - Mike Kiley
President and C.O.O. - John Parker
Publisher and C.E.O. - Stuart Levy

A  Manga

TOKYOPOP Inc.
5900 Wilshire Blvd. Suite 2000
Los Angeles, CA 90036

E-mail: info@TOKYOPOP.com
Come visit us online at www.TOKYOPOP.com

ISBN: 1-59532-942-0

First TOKYOPOP printing: July 2005
10 9 8 7 6 5 4 3 2 1
Printed in the USA

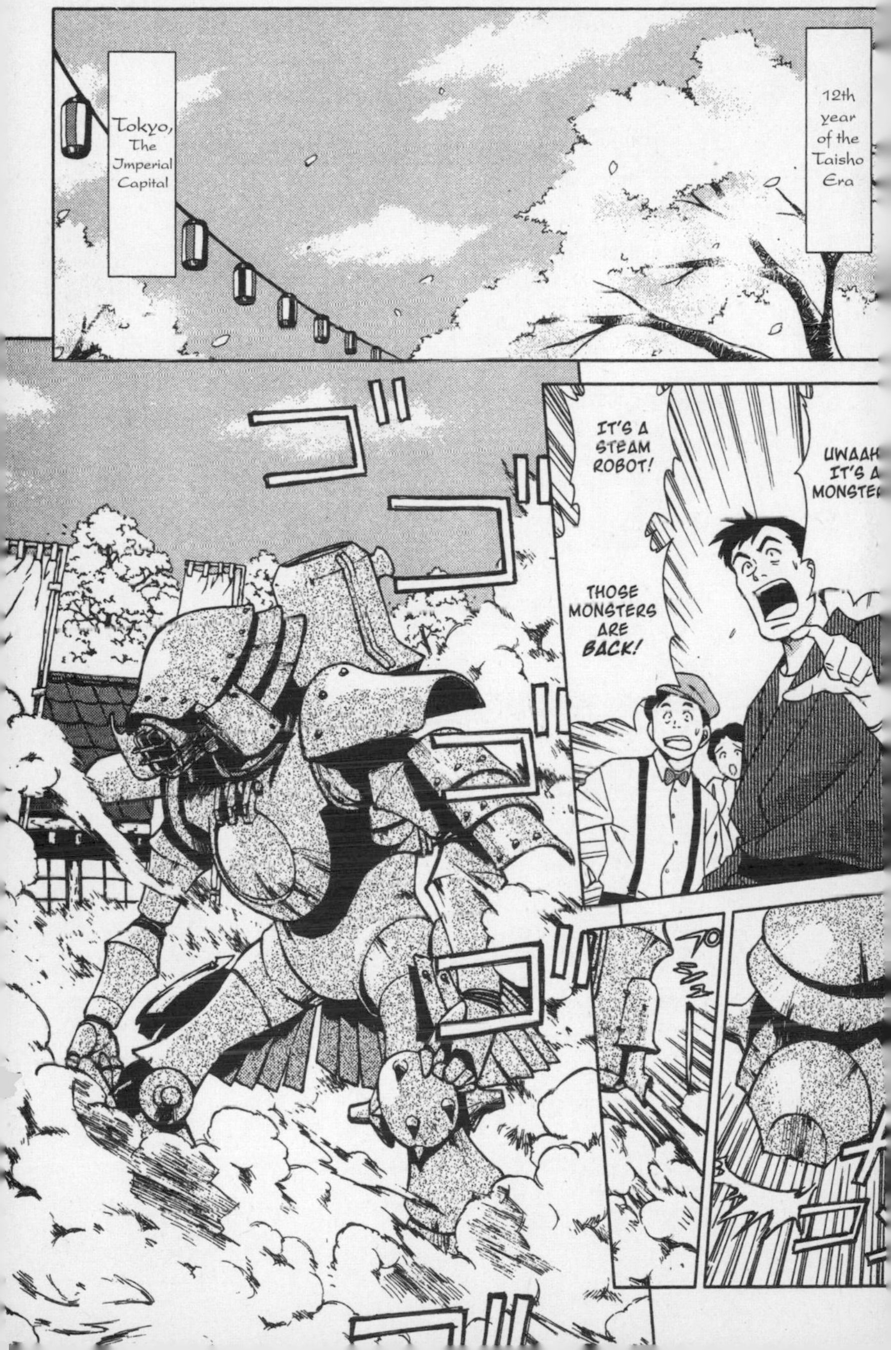
12th year of the Taisho Era
Tokyo, The Imperial Capital
UWAAH IT'S A MONSTE
IT'S A STEAM ROBOT!
THOSE MONSTERS ARE BACK!

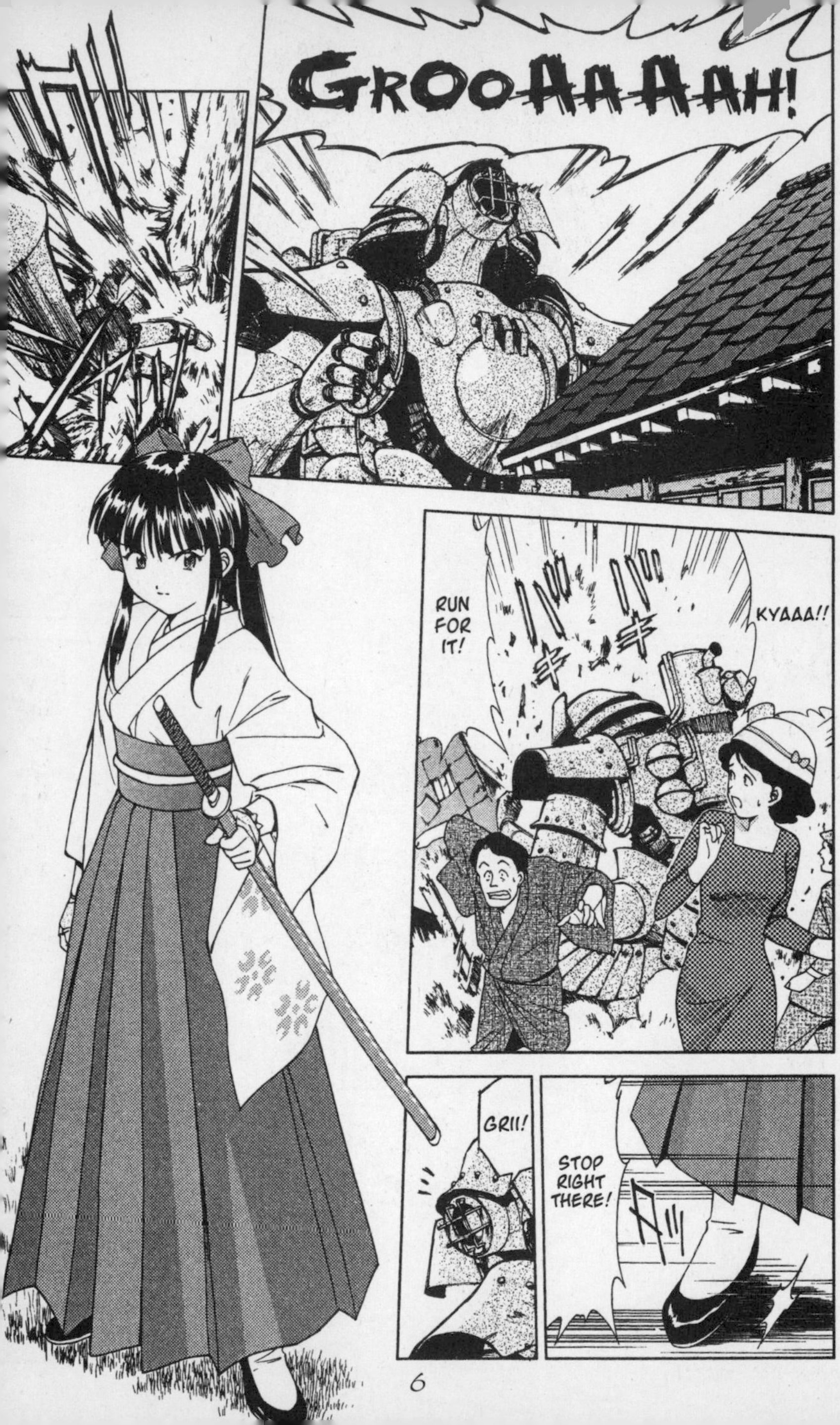
GROOAAAAH!
KYAAA!!
RUN FOR IT!
STOP RIGHT THERE!
GRII!

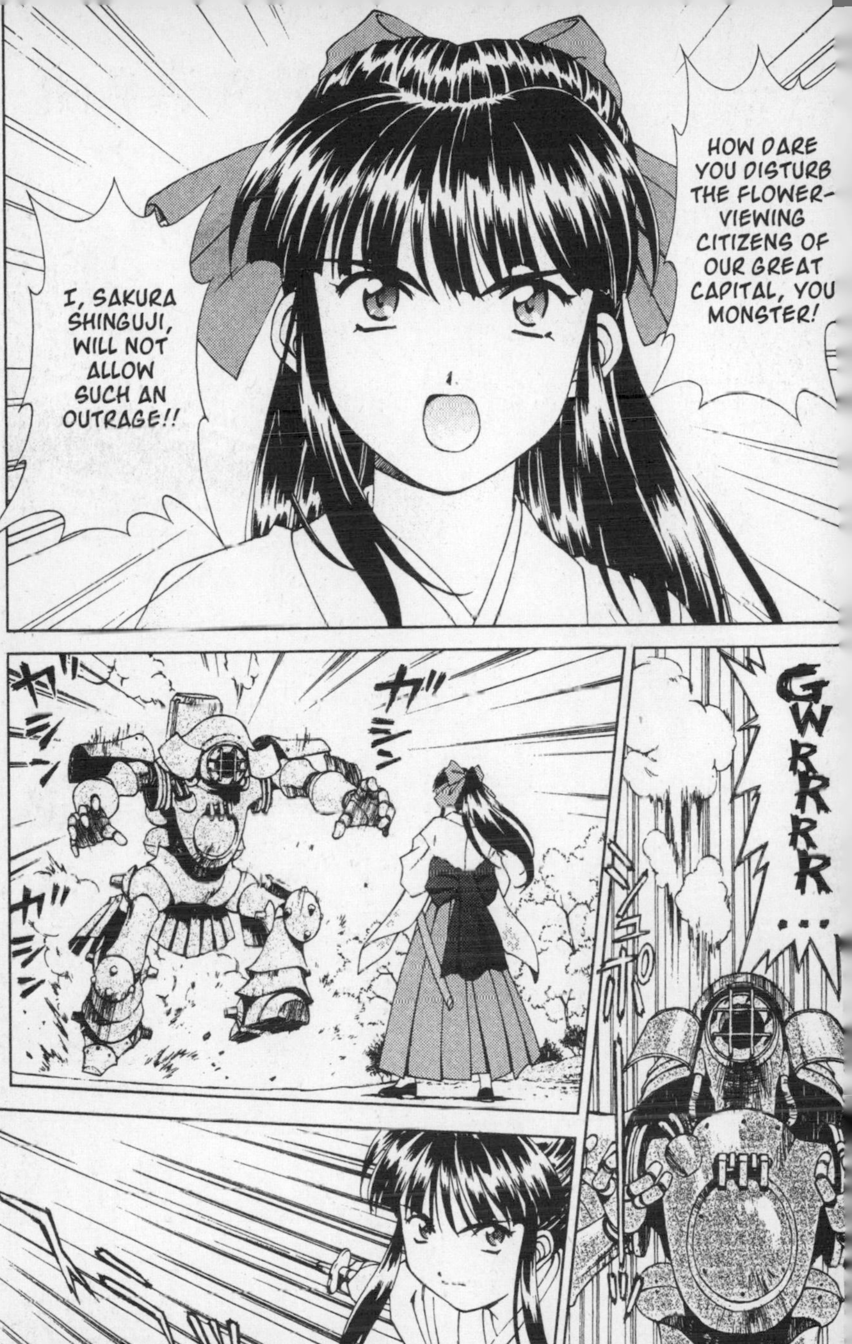
HOW DARE YOU DISTURB THE FLOWER-VIEWING CITIZENS OF OUR GREAT CAPITAL, YOU MONSTER!
I, SAKURA SHINGUJI, WILL NOT ALLOW SUCH AN OUTRAGE!!
GWRRRR...

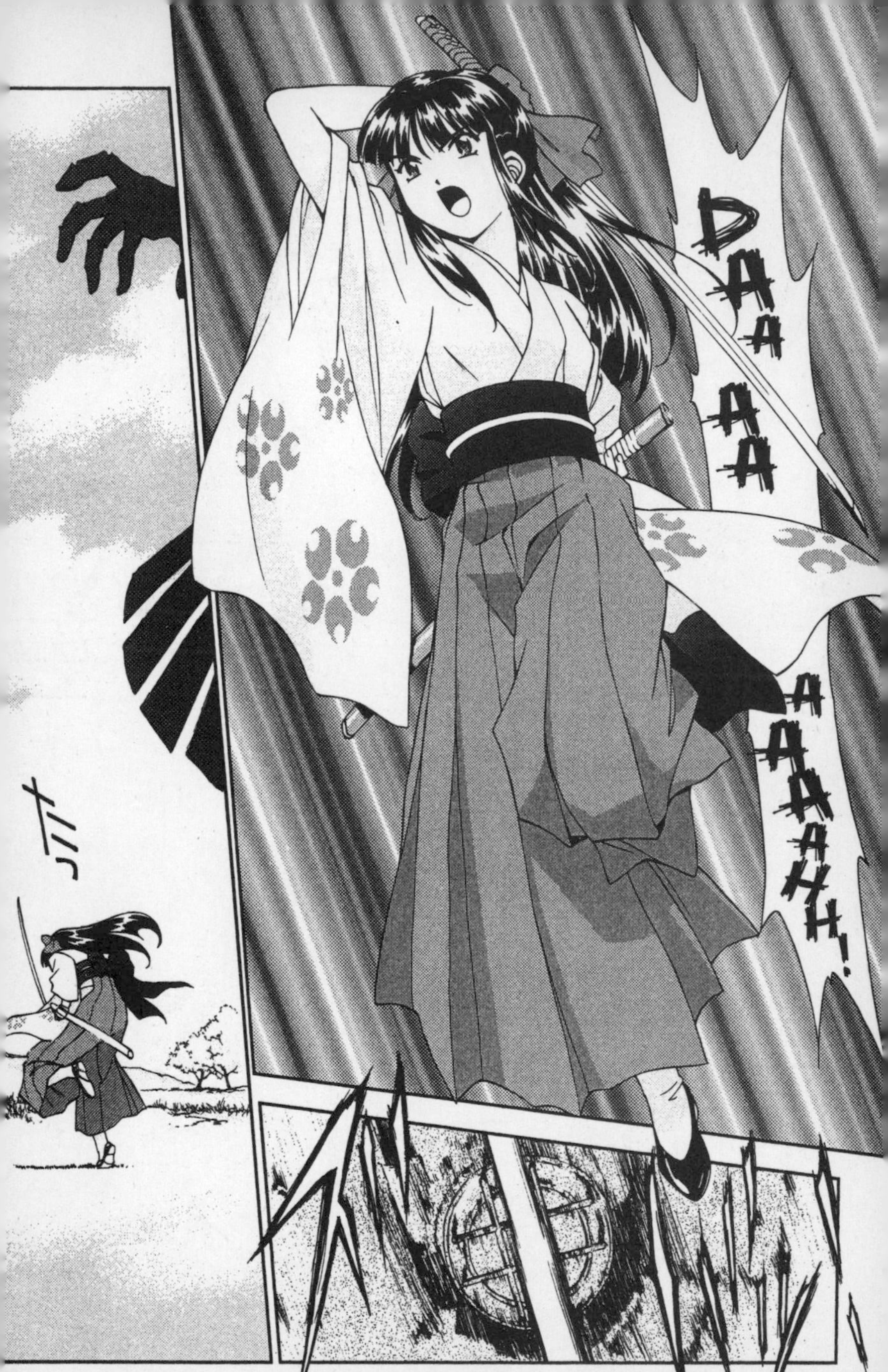
DAAAAAAAAAHH!
ザッ

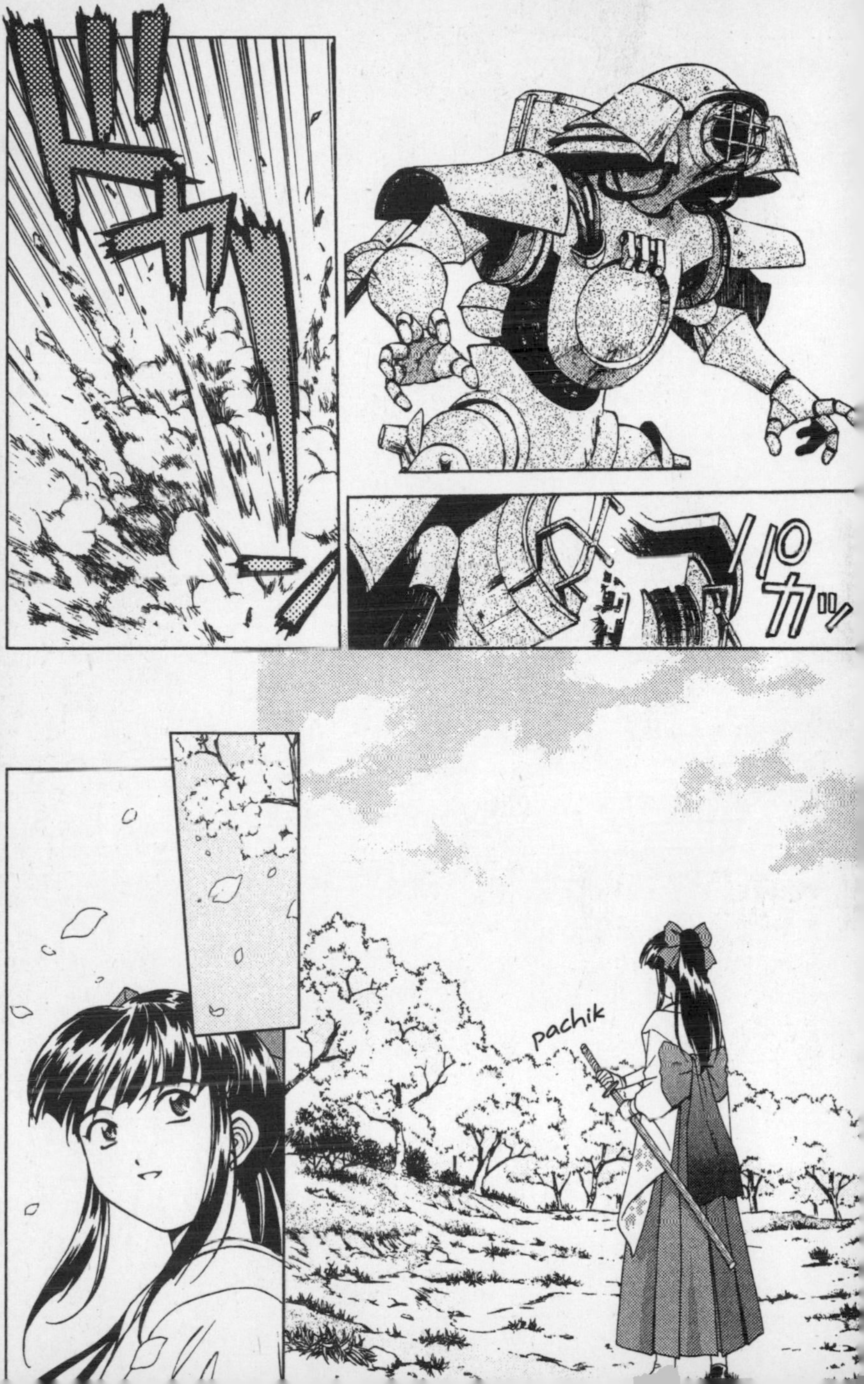
パカッ
ドカ!!
pachik

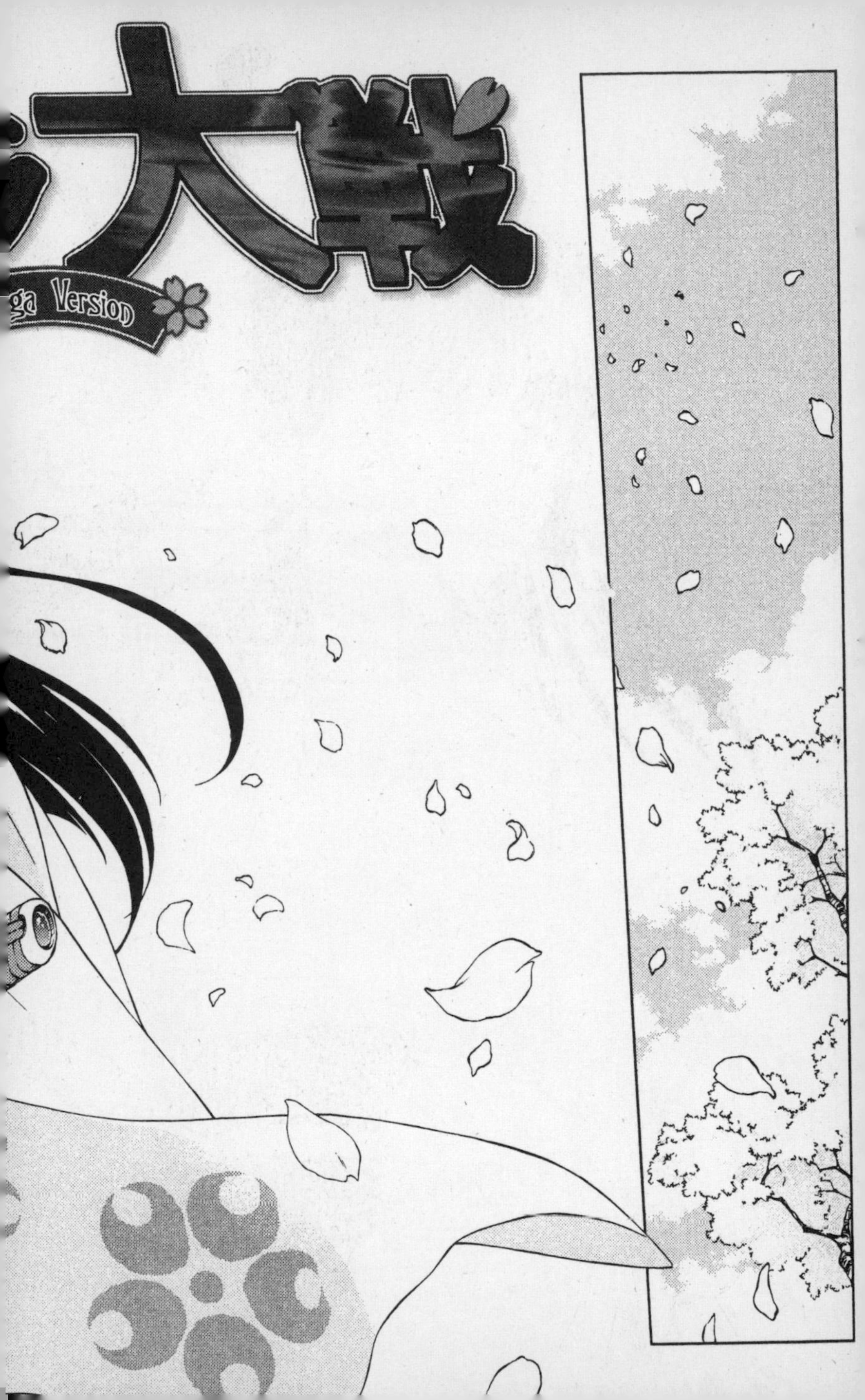
大戦
ga Version

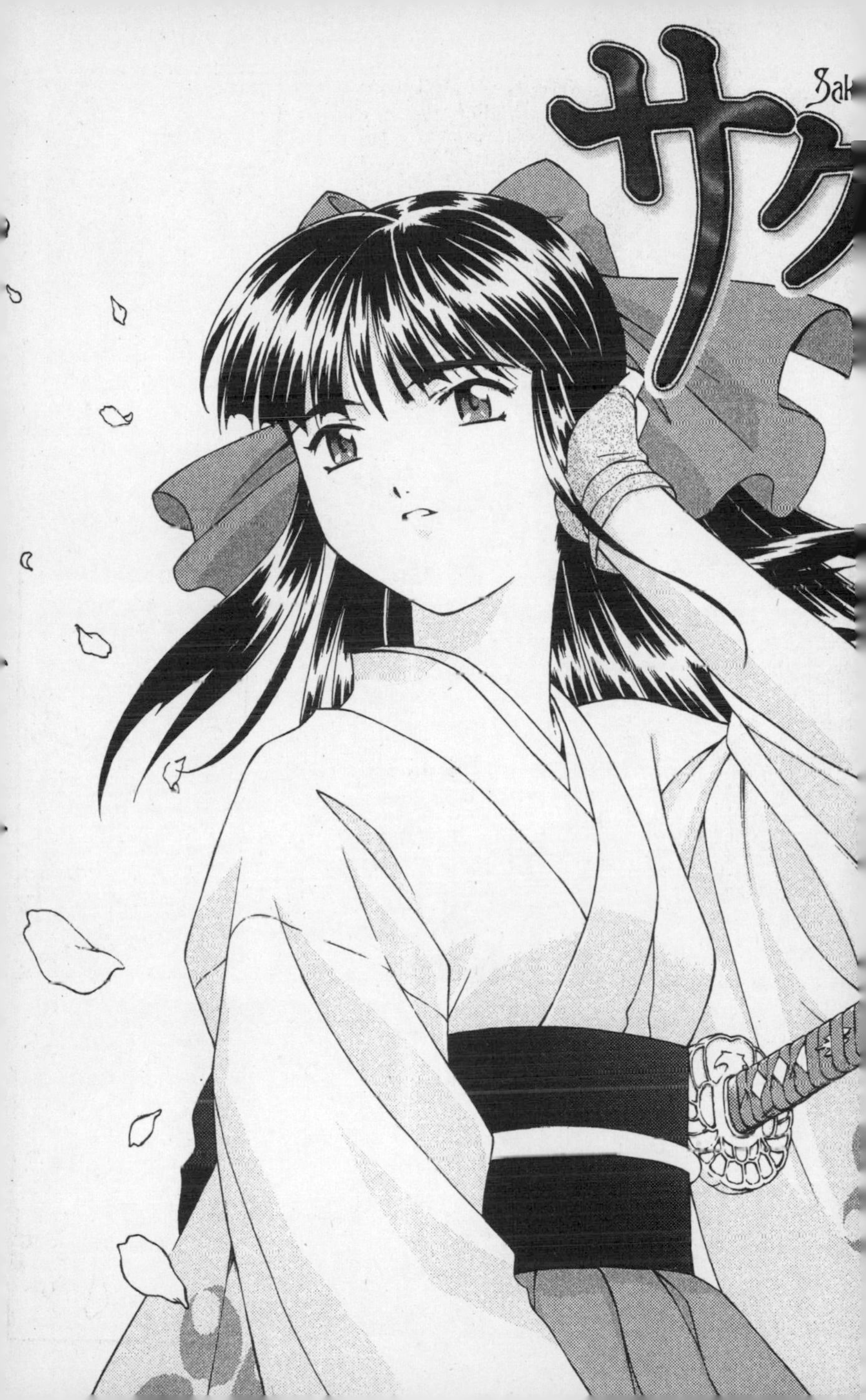
サク
Sak

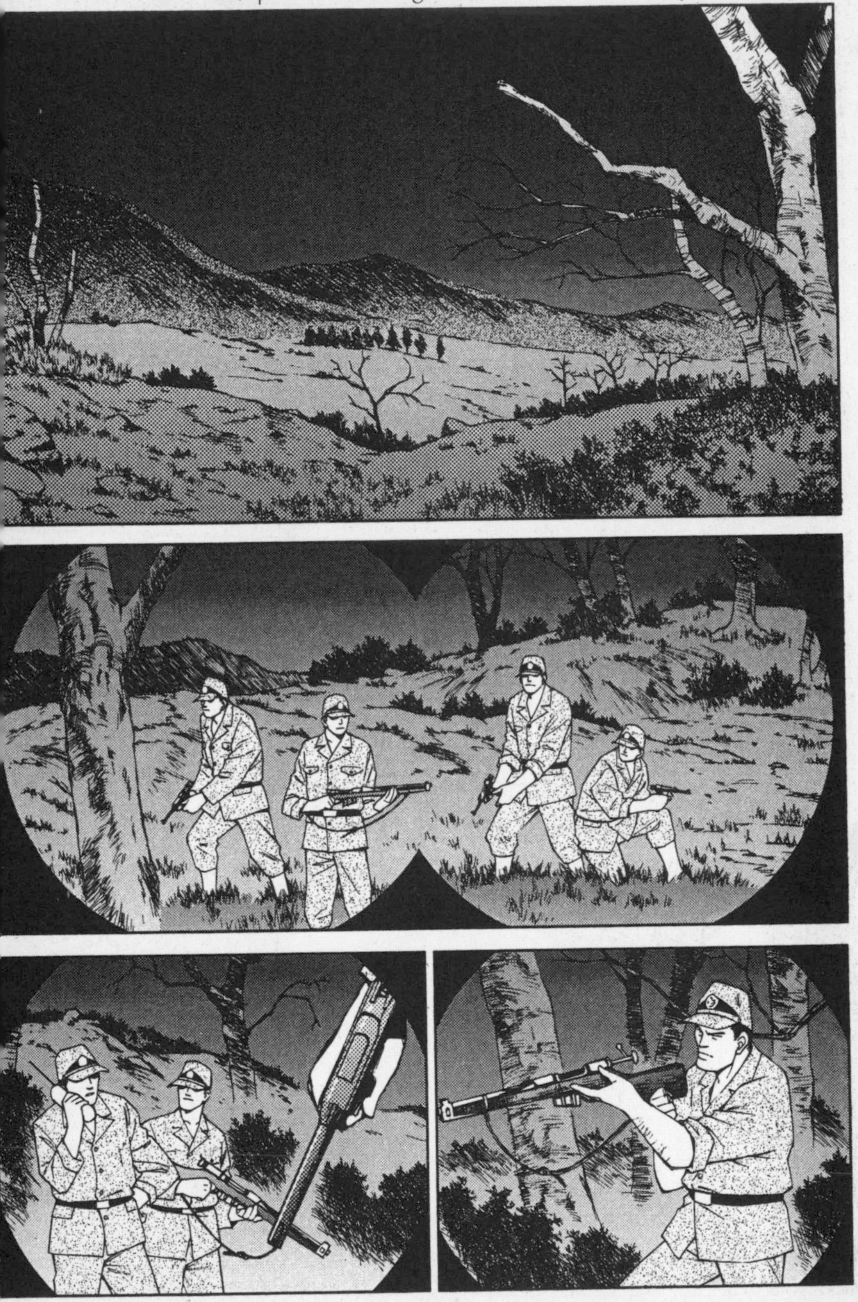

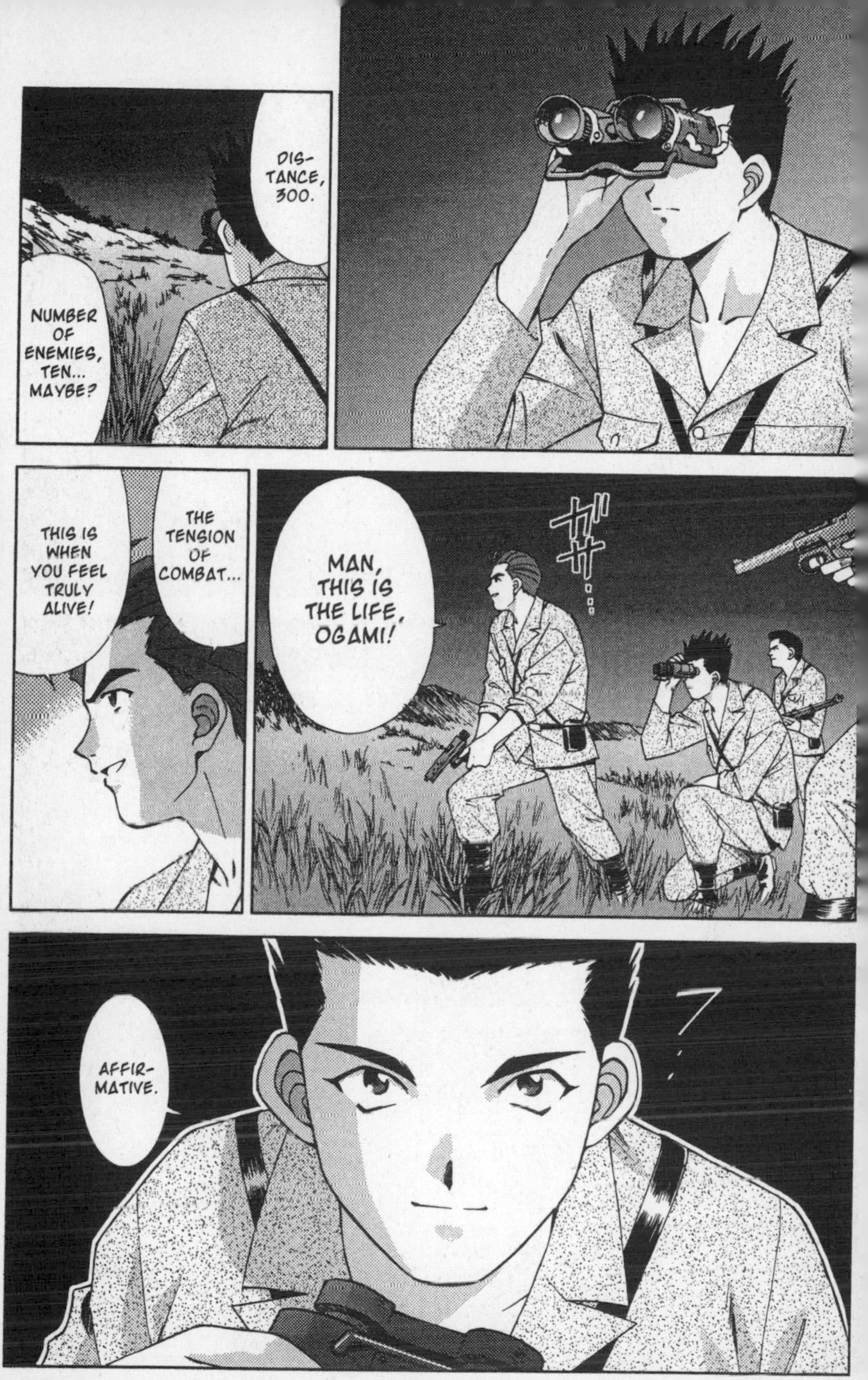
DIS-TANCE, 300.
NUMBER OF ENEMIES, TEN... MAYBE?
MAN, THIS IS THE LIFE, OGAMI!
THE TENSION OF COMBAT...
THIS IS WHEN YOU FEEL TRULY ALIVE!
AFFIR-MATIVE.

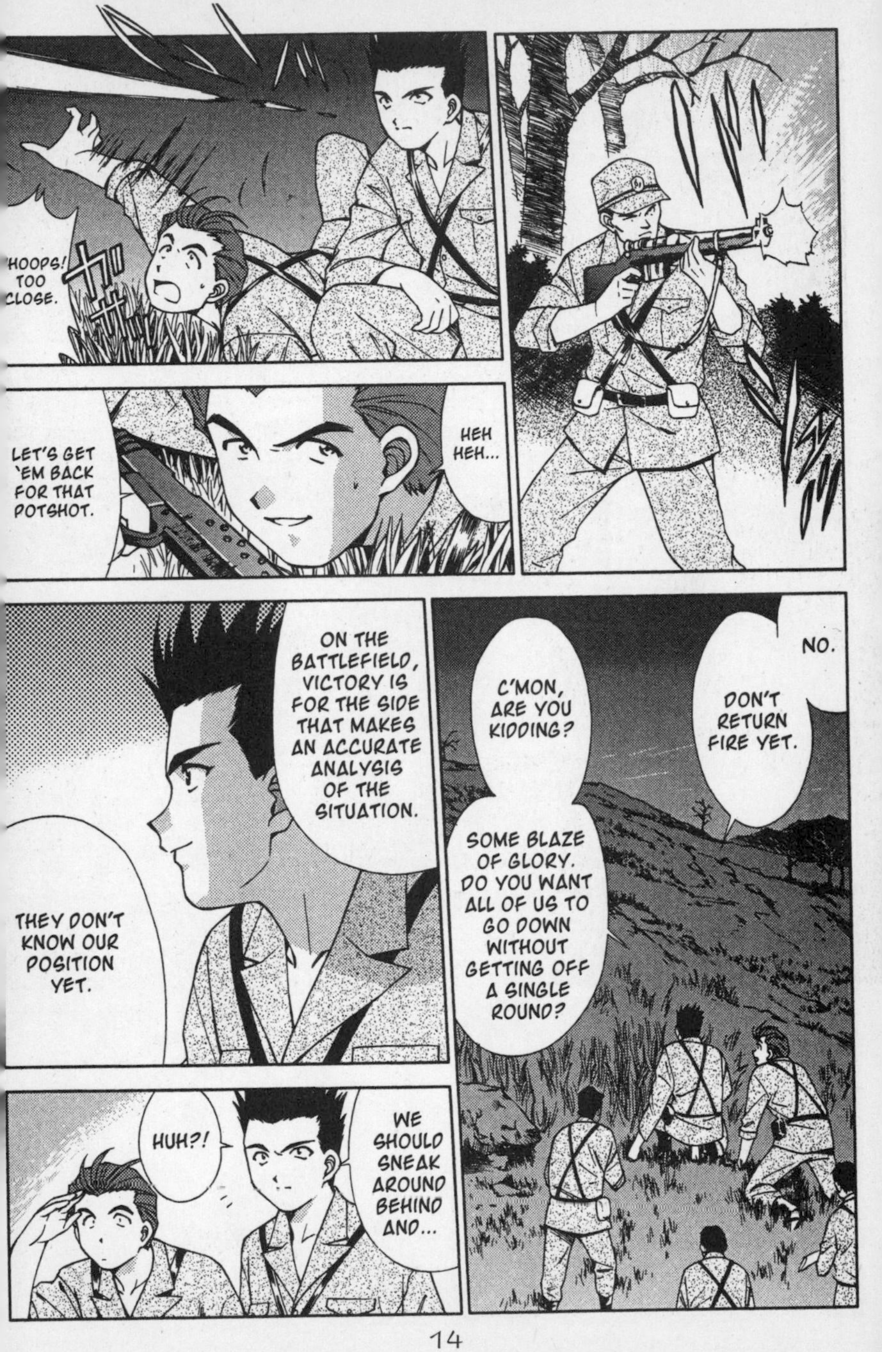

HOOPS! TOO CLOSE.
HEH HEH...
LET'S GET 'EM BACK FOR THAT POTSHOT.
NO.
DON'T RETURN FIRE YET.
C'MON, ARE YOU KIDDING?
SOME BLAZE OF GLORY. DO YOU WANT ALL OF US TO GO DOWN WITHOUT GETTING OFF A SINGLE ROUND?
ON THE BATTLEFIELD, VICTORY IS FOR THE SIDE THAT MAKES AN ACCURATE ANALYSIS OF THE SITUATION.
THEY DON'T KNOW OUR POSITION YET.
WE SHOULD SNEAK AROUND BEHIND AND...
HUH?!

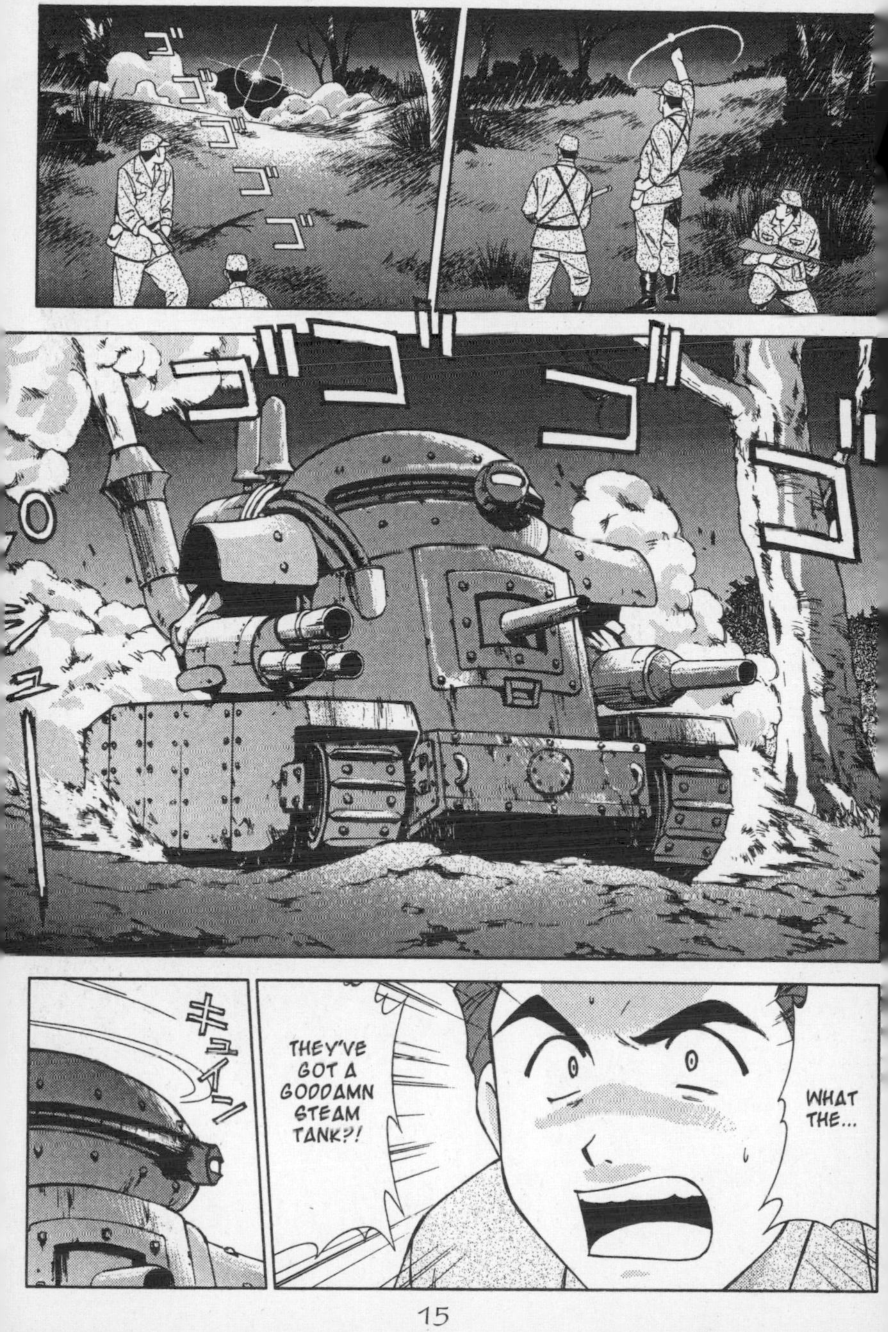
ゴゴゴゴゴ
ゴゴゴゴ
WHAT THE...
THEY'VE GOT A GODDAMN STEAM TANK?!
キュイーン

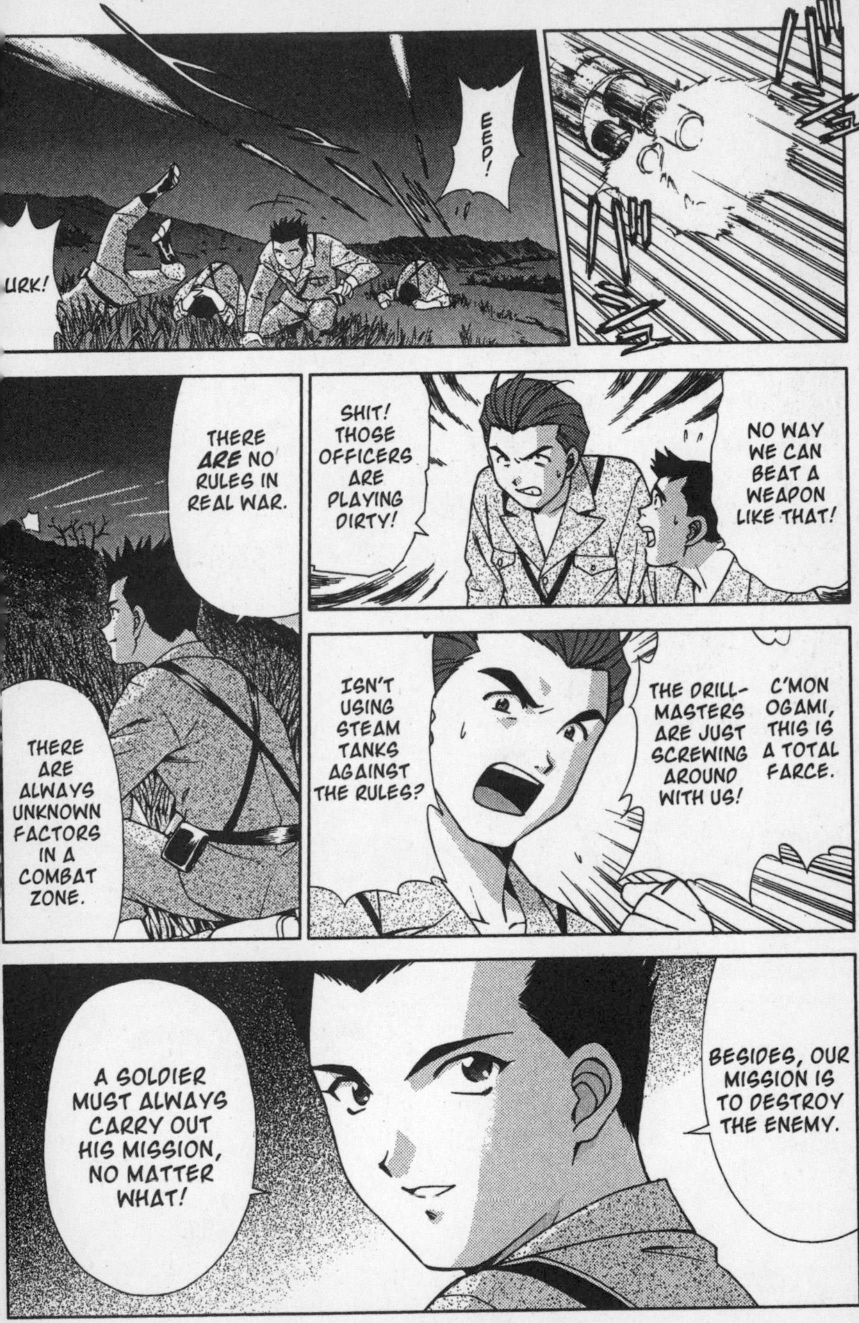
EEP!
URK!
NO WAY WE CAN BEAT A WEAPON LIKE THAT!
SHIT! THOSE OFFICERS ARE PLAYING DIRTY!
C'MON OGAMI, THIS IS A TOTAL FARCE.
THE DRILL-MASTERS ARE JUST SCREWING AROUND WITH US!
ISN'T USING STEAM TANKS AGAINST THE RULES?
THERE *ARE* NO RULES IN REAL WAR.
THERE ARE ALWAYS UNKNOWN FACTORS IN A COMBAT ZONE.
BESIDES, OUR MISSION IS TO DESTROY THE ENEMY.
A SOLDIER MUST ALWAYS CARRY OUT HIS MISSION, NO MATTER WHAT!

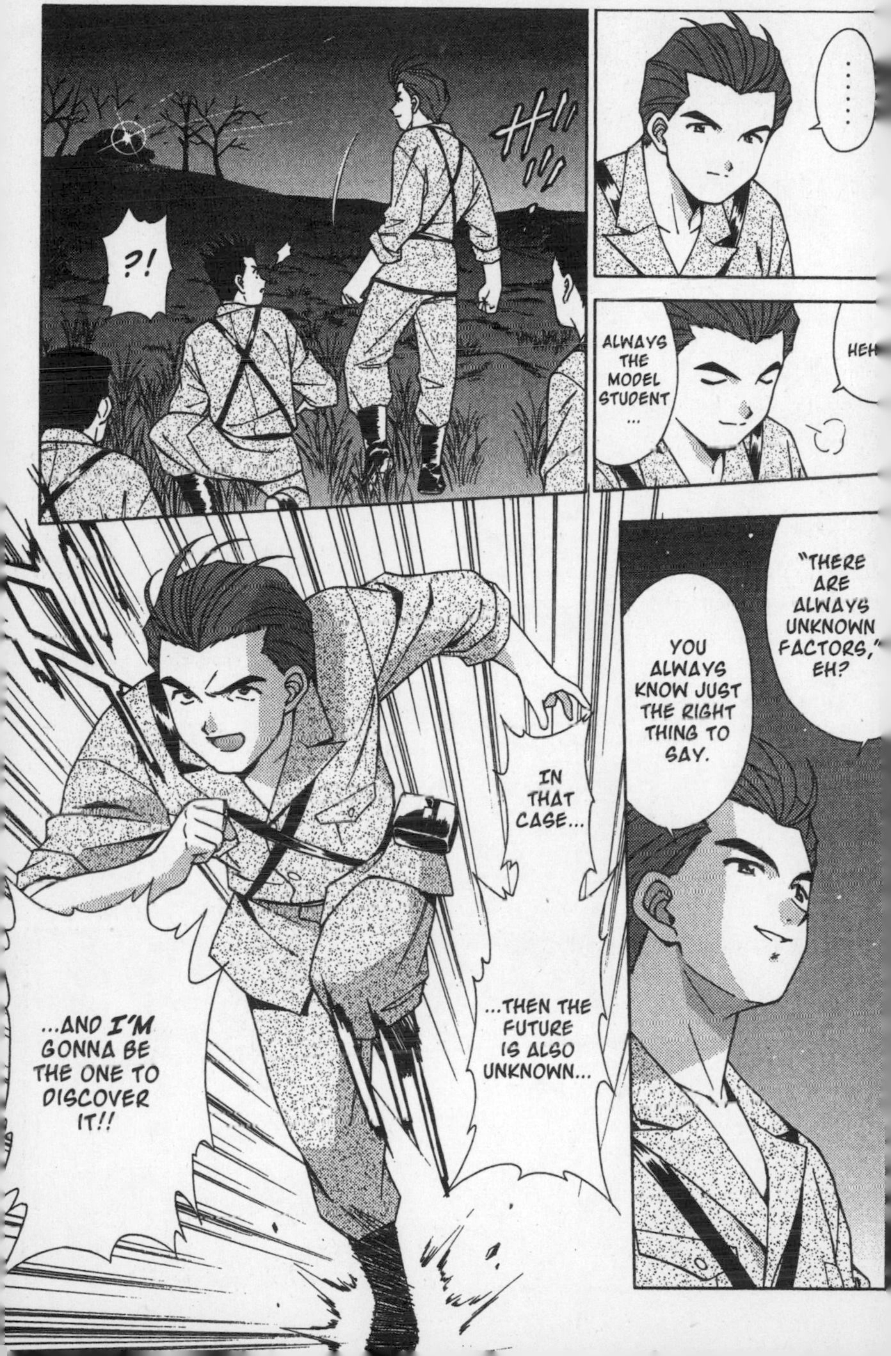
......
HEH
ALWAYS THE MODEL STUDENT ...
?!
"THERE ARE ALWAYS UNKNOWN FACTORS," EH?
YOU ALWAYS KNOW JUST THE RIGHT THING TO SAY.
IN THAT CASE...
...THEN THE FUTURE IS ALSO UNKNOWN...
...AND I'M GONNA BE THE ONE TO DISCOVER IT!!

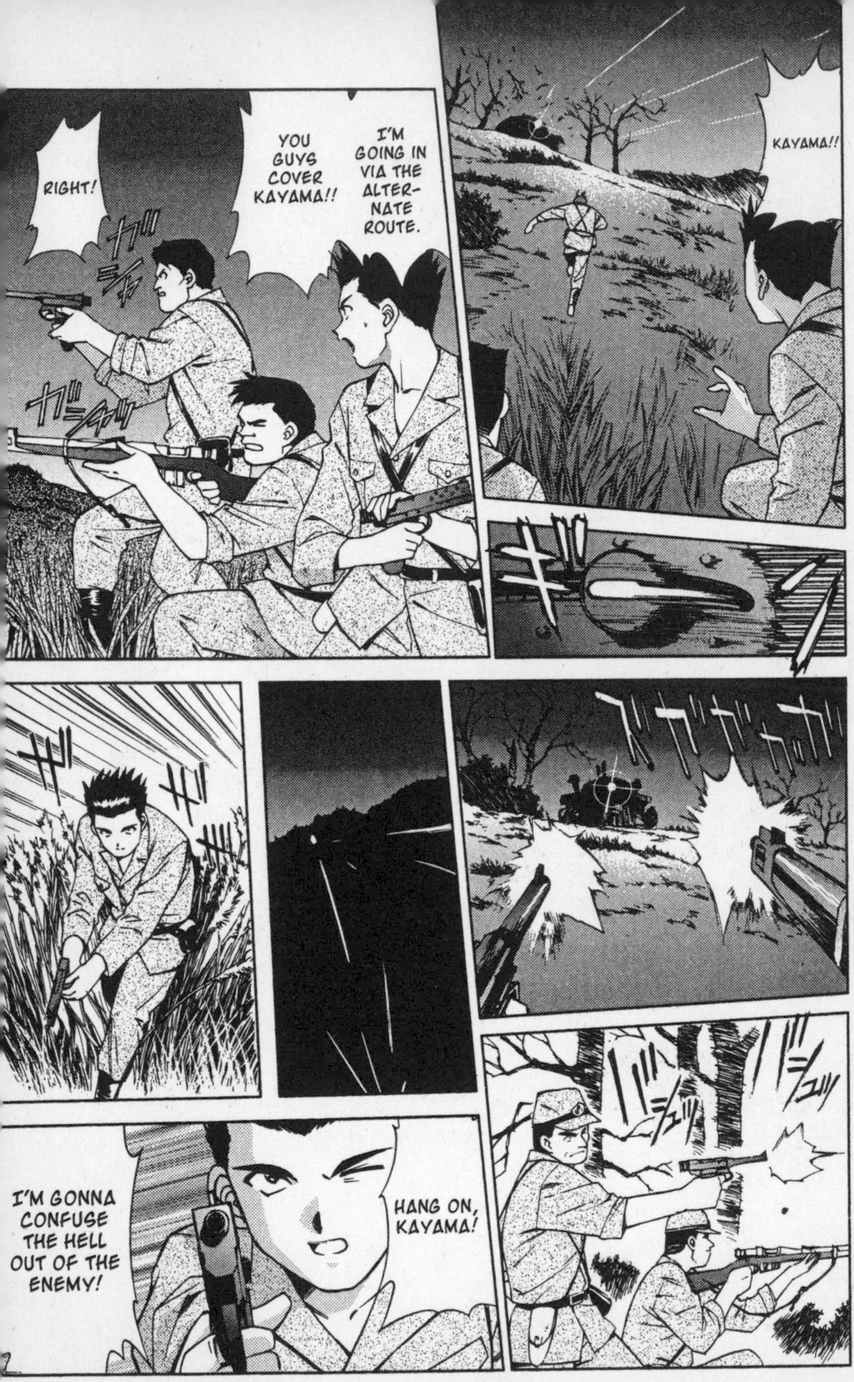
KAYAMA!!
I'M GOING IN VIA THE ALTERNATE ROUTE.
YOU GUYS COVER KAYAMA!!
RIGHT!
HANG ON, KAYAMA!
I'M GONNA CONFUSE THE HELL OUT OF THE ENEMY!

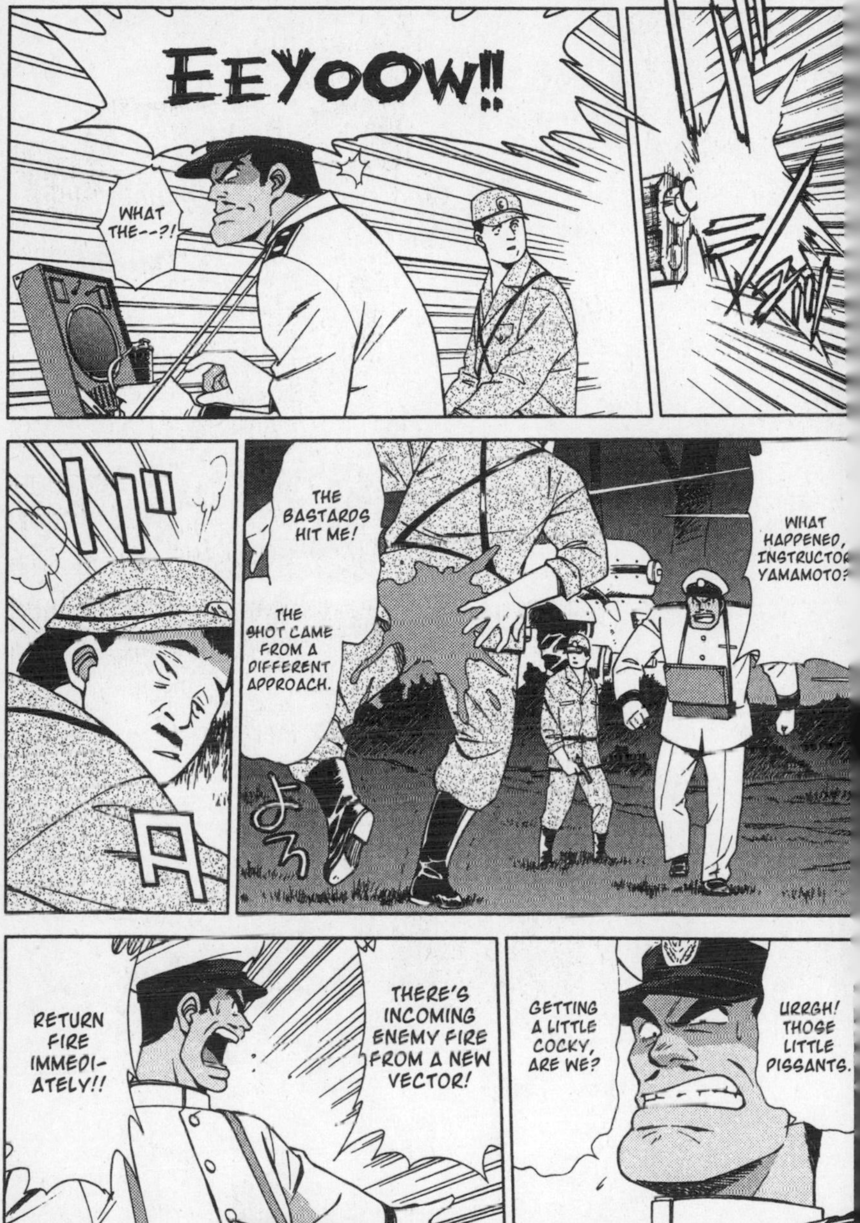
EEYOOW!!
WHAT THE--?!
WHAT HAPPENED, INSTRUCTOR YAMAMOTO?
THE BASTARDS HIT ME!
THE SHOT CAME FROM A DIFFERENT APPROACH.
よろ
URRGH! THOSE LITTLE PISSANTS.
GETTING A LITTLE COCKY, ARE WE?
THERE'S INCOMING ENEMY FIRE FROM A NEW VECTOR!
RETURN FIRE IMMEDI-ATELY!!

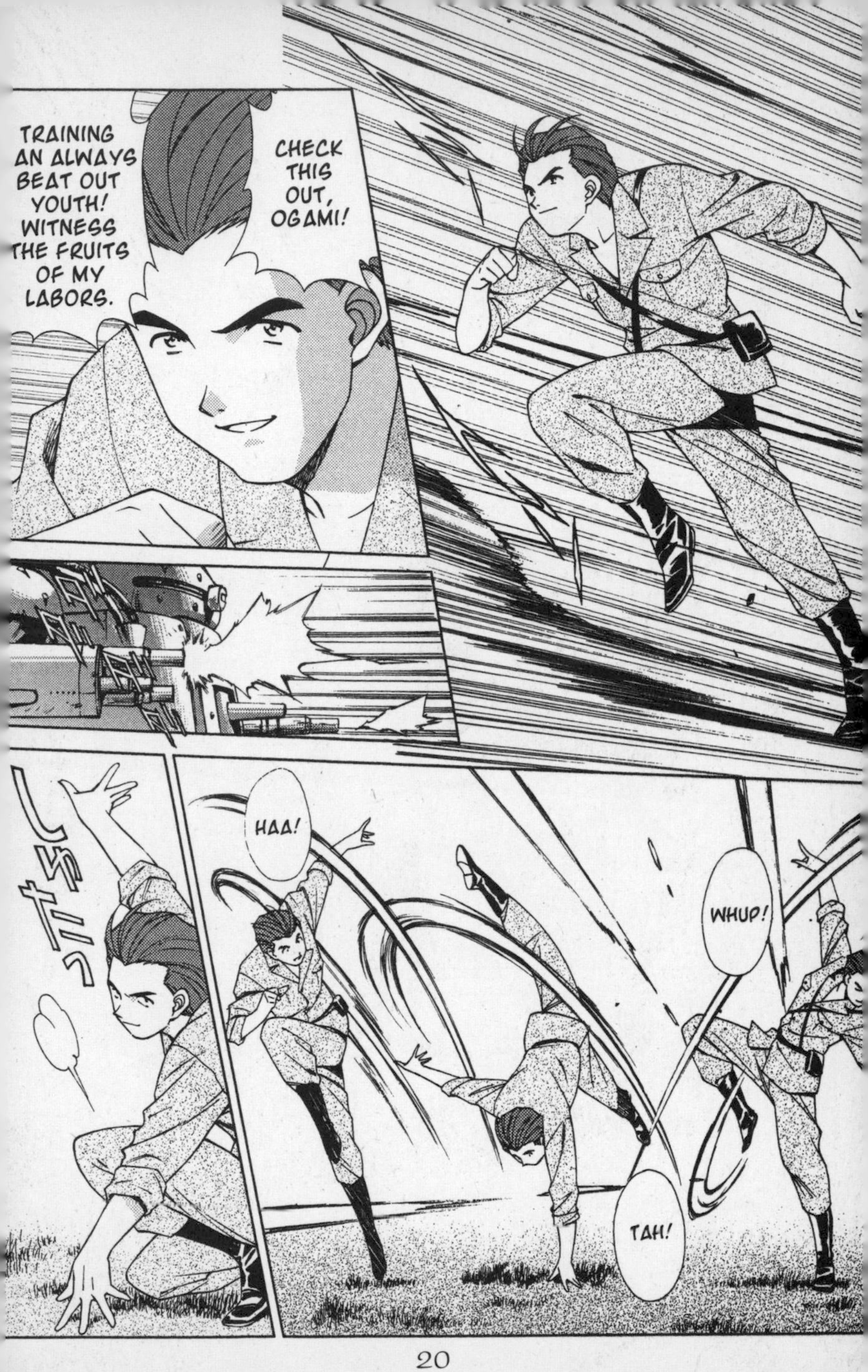
CHECK THIS OUT, OGAMI!
TRAINING AN ALWAYS BEAT OUT YOUTH! WITNESS THE FRUITS OF MY LABORS.
HAA!
WHUP!
TAH!

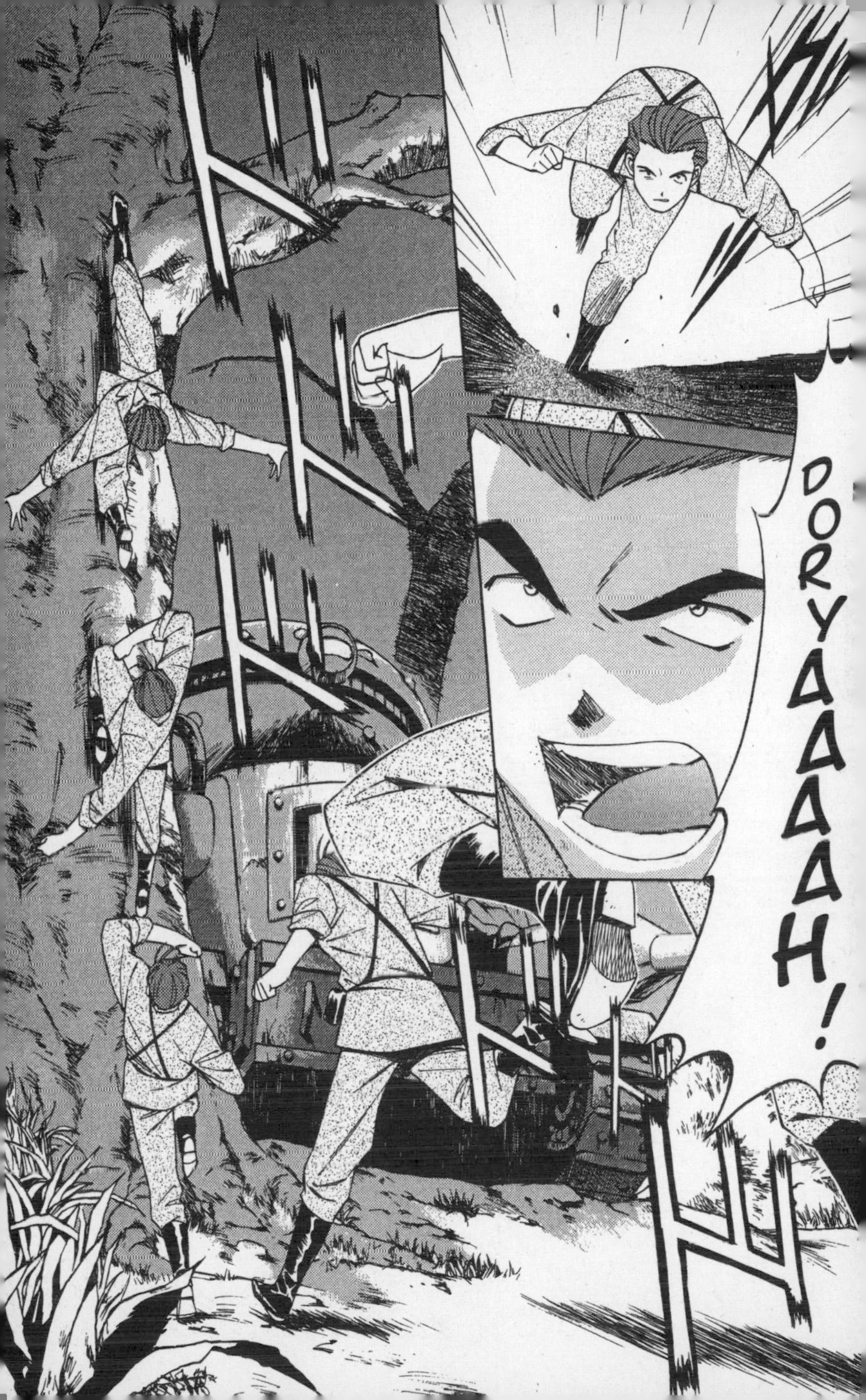
DORYAAAAH!

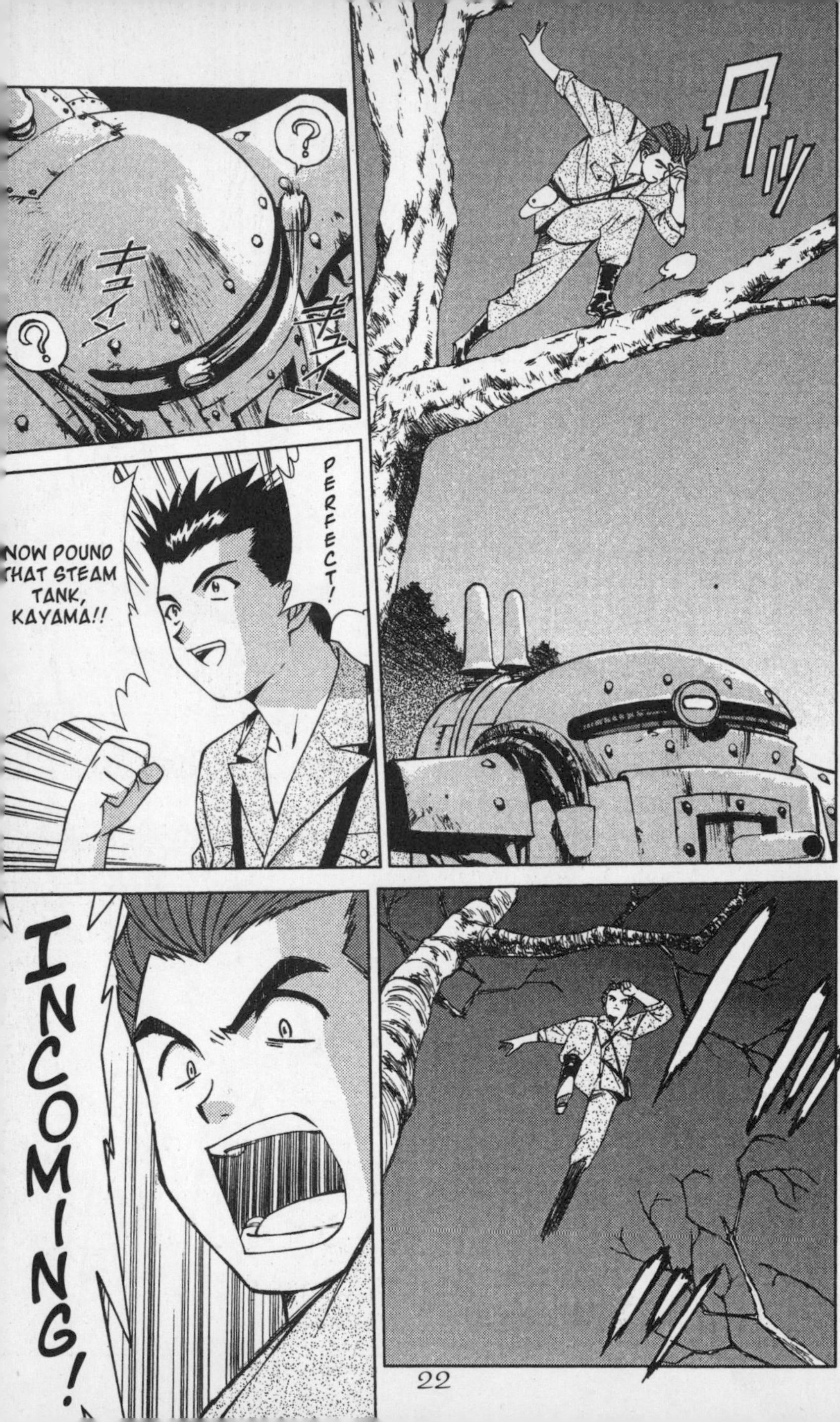
?
?
PERFECT!
NOW POUND THAT STEAM TANK, KAYAMA!!
INCOMING!

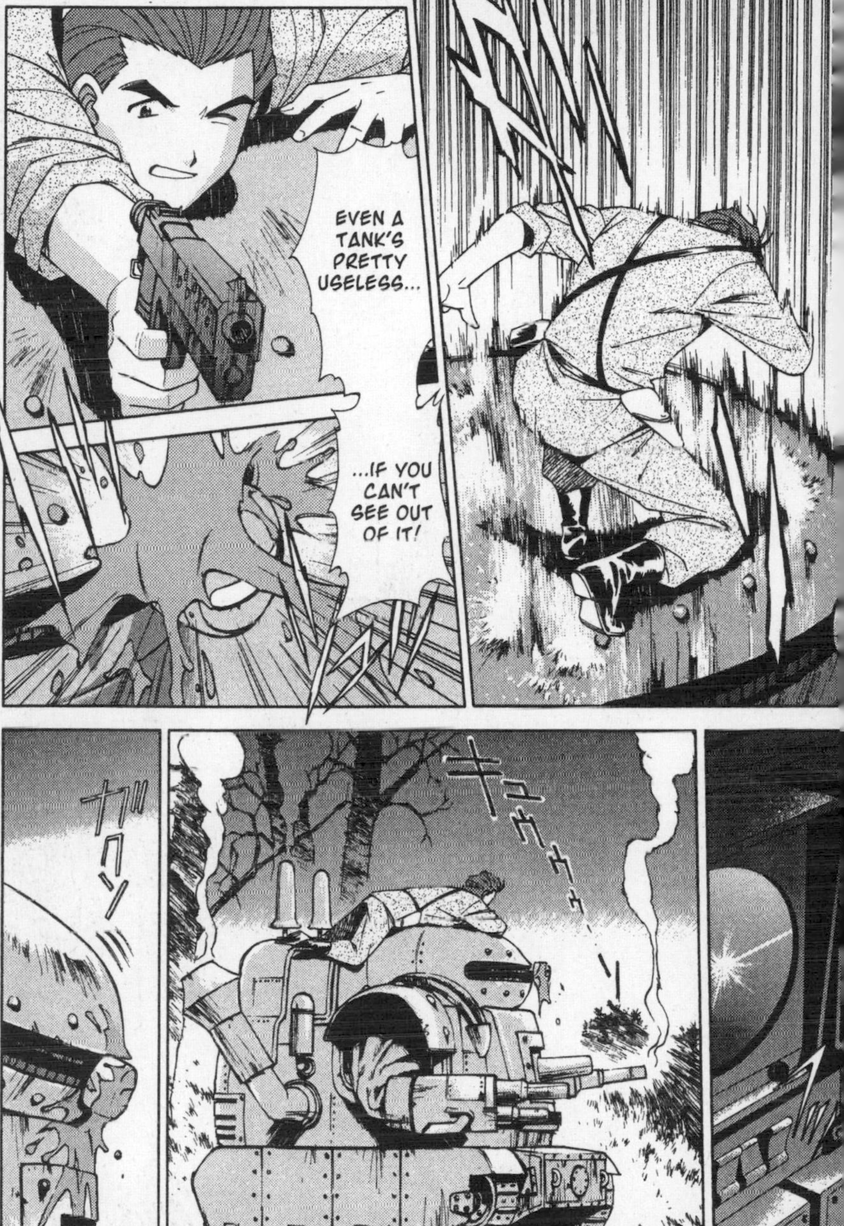
EVEN A TANK'S PRETTY USELESS...
...IF YOU CAN'T SEE OUT OF IT!

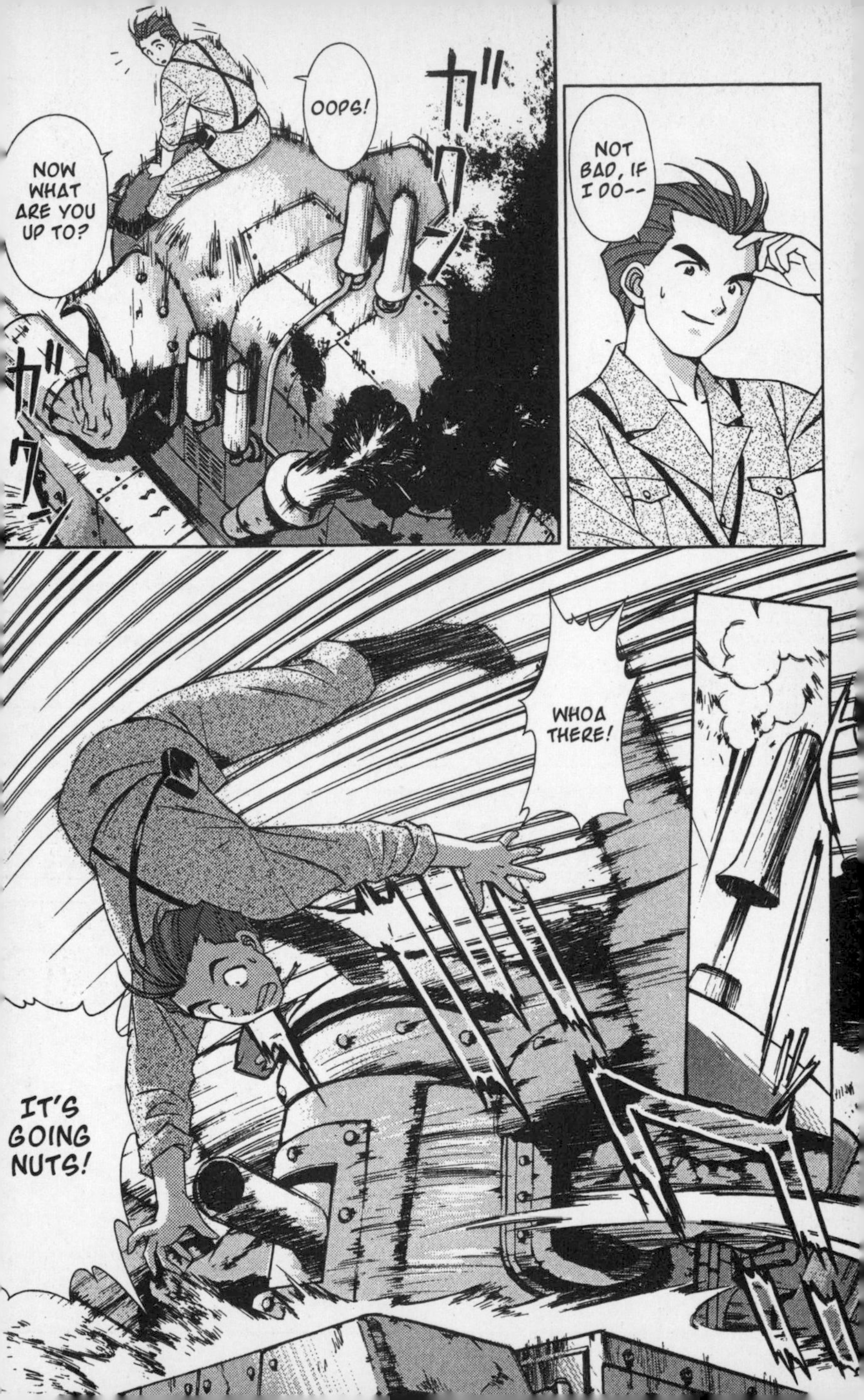
NOT BAD, IF I DO--
ガク
OOPS!
NOW WHAT ARE YOU UP TO?
ガク
WHOA THERE!
IT'S GOING NUTS!

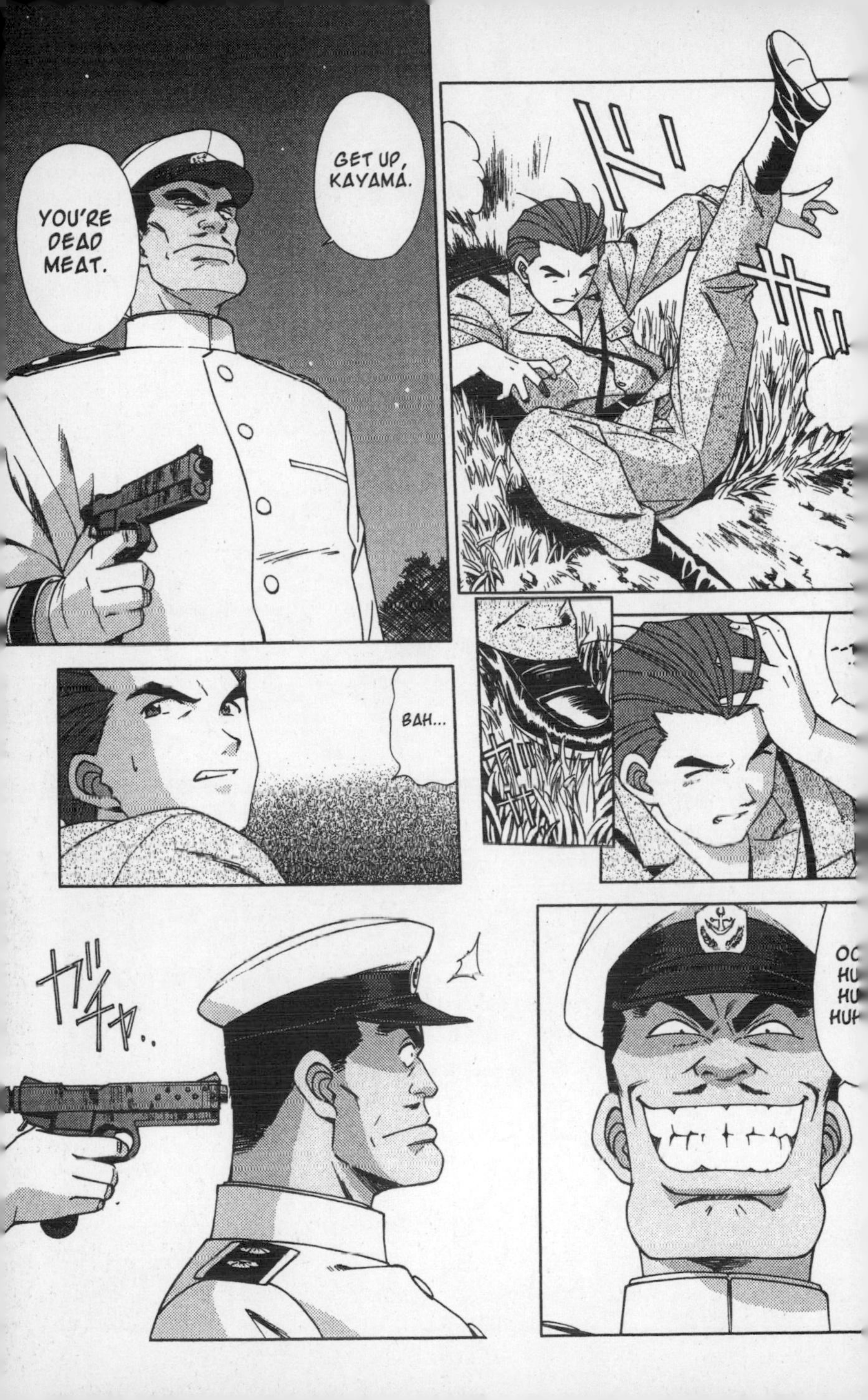
GET UP, KAYAMA.
YOU'RE DEAD MEAT.
BAH...
ガチャ..

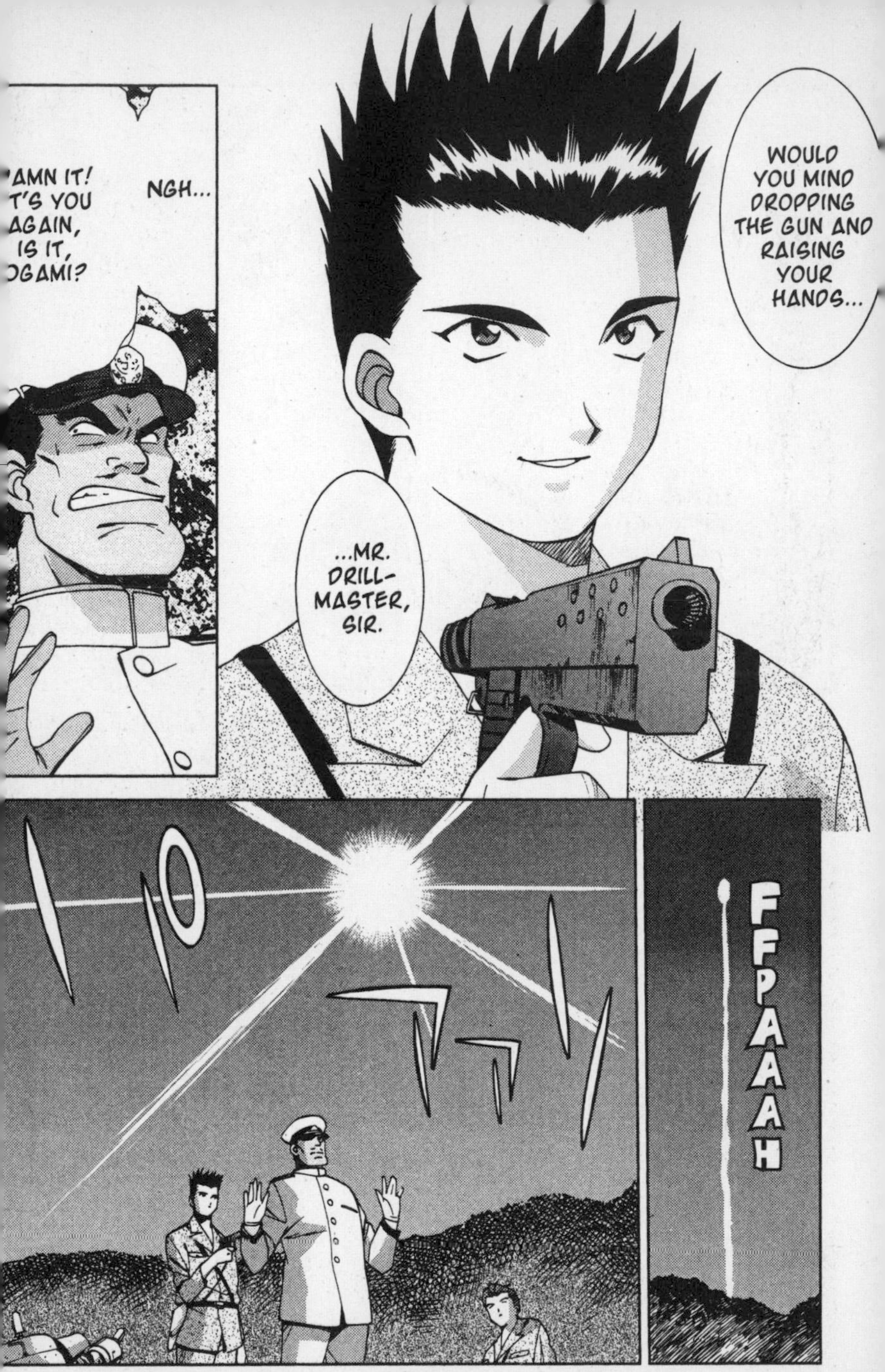
WOULD YOU MIND DROPPING THE GUN AND RAISING YOUR HANDS...
...MR. DRILL-MASTER, SIR.
NGH...
AMN IT! T'S YOU AGAIN, IS IT, OGAMI?
FFPAAAAH

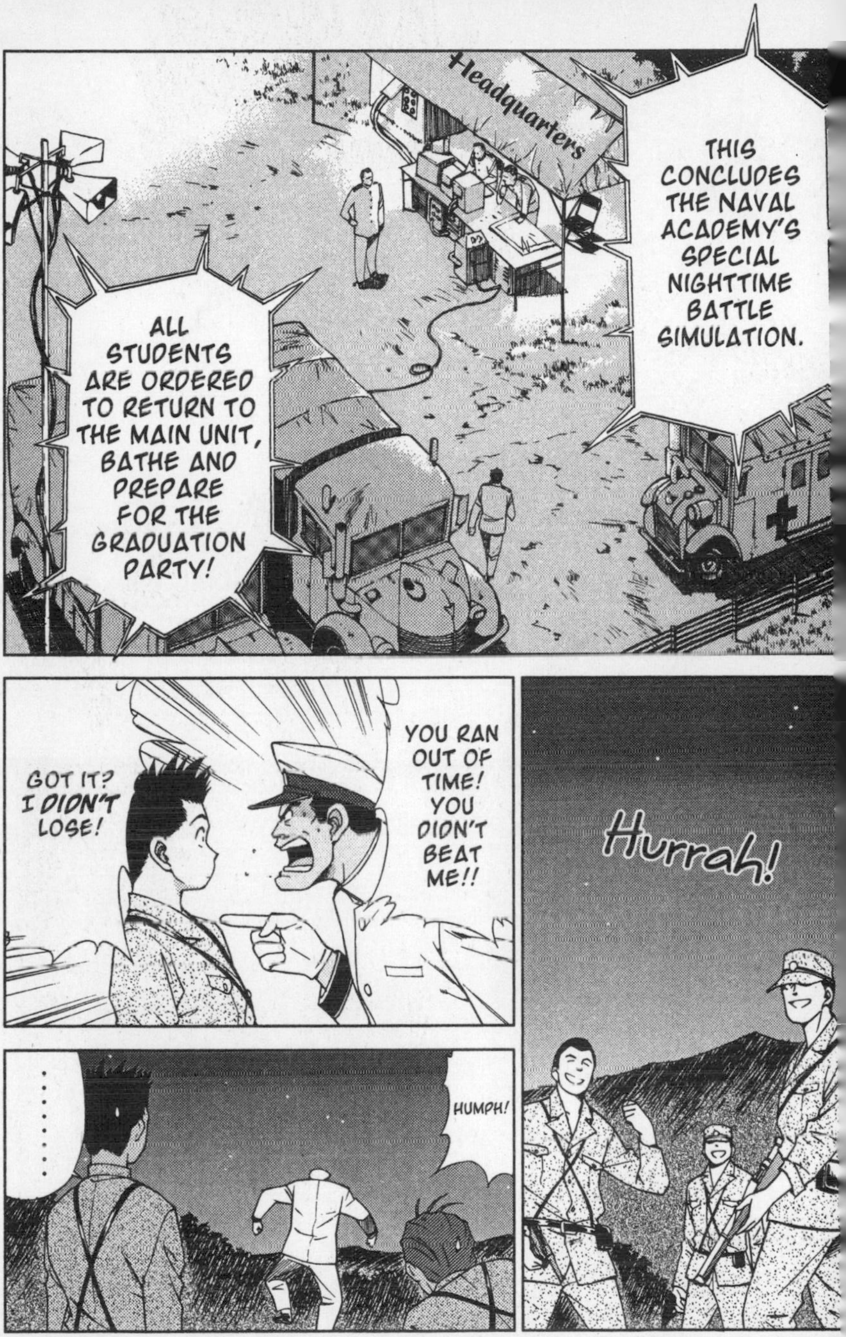
Headquarters
THIS CONCLUDES THE NAVAL ACADEMY'S SPECIAL NIGHTTIME BATTLE SIMULATION.
ALL STUDENTS ARE ORDERED TO RETURN TO THE MAIN UNIT, BATHE AND PREPARE FOR THE GRADUATION PARTY!
Hurrah!
YOU RAN OUT OF TIME! YOU DIDN'T BEAT ME!!
GOT IT? I DIDN'T LOSE!
HUMPH!
......

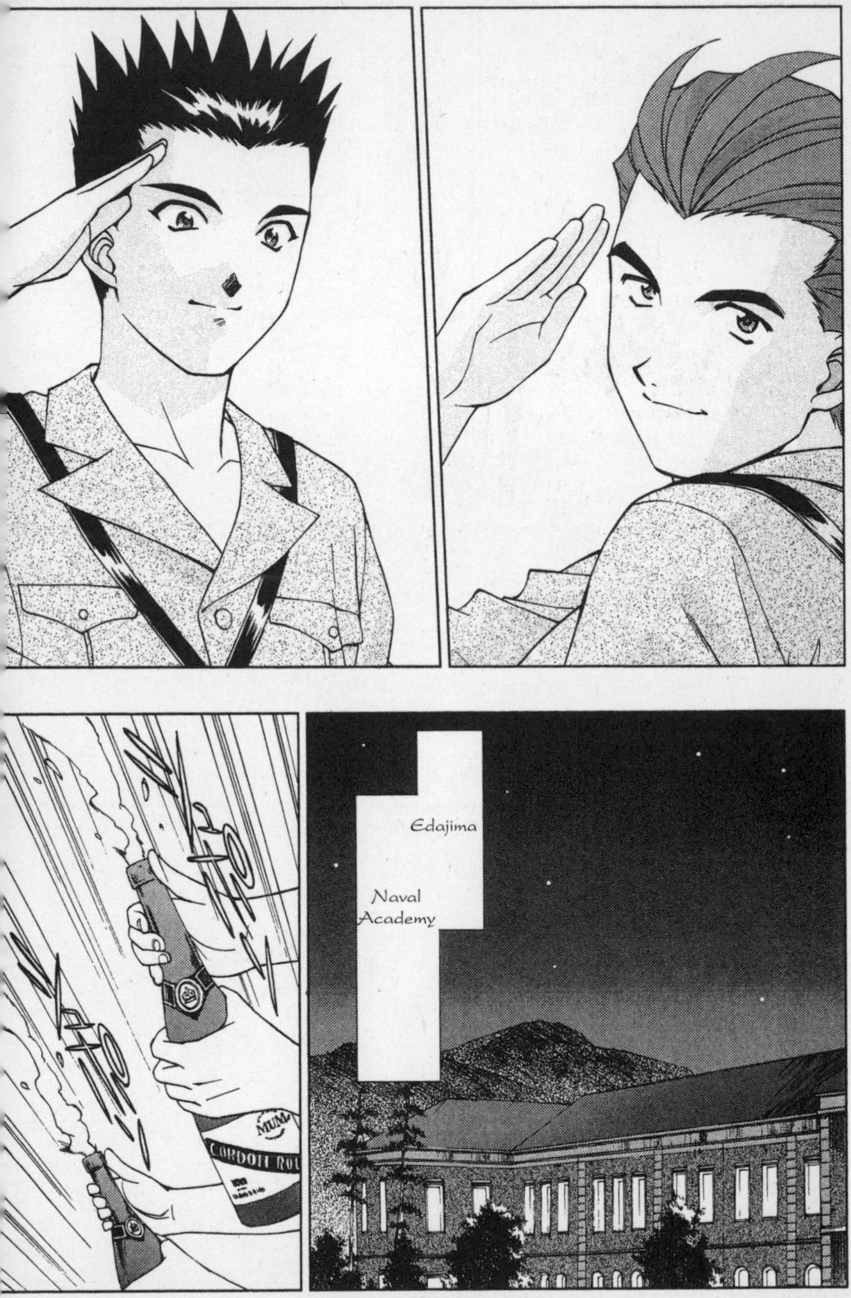
Edajima
Naval Academy

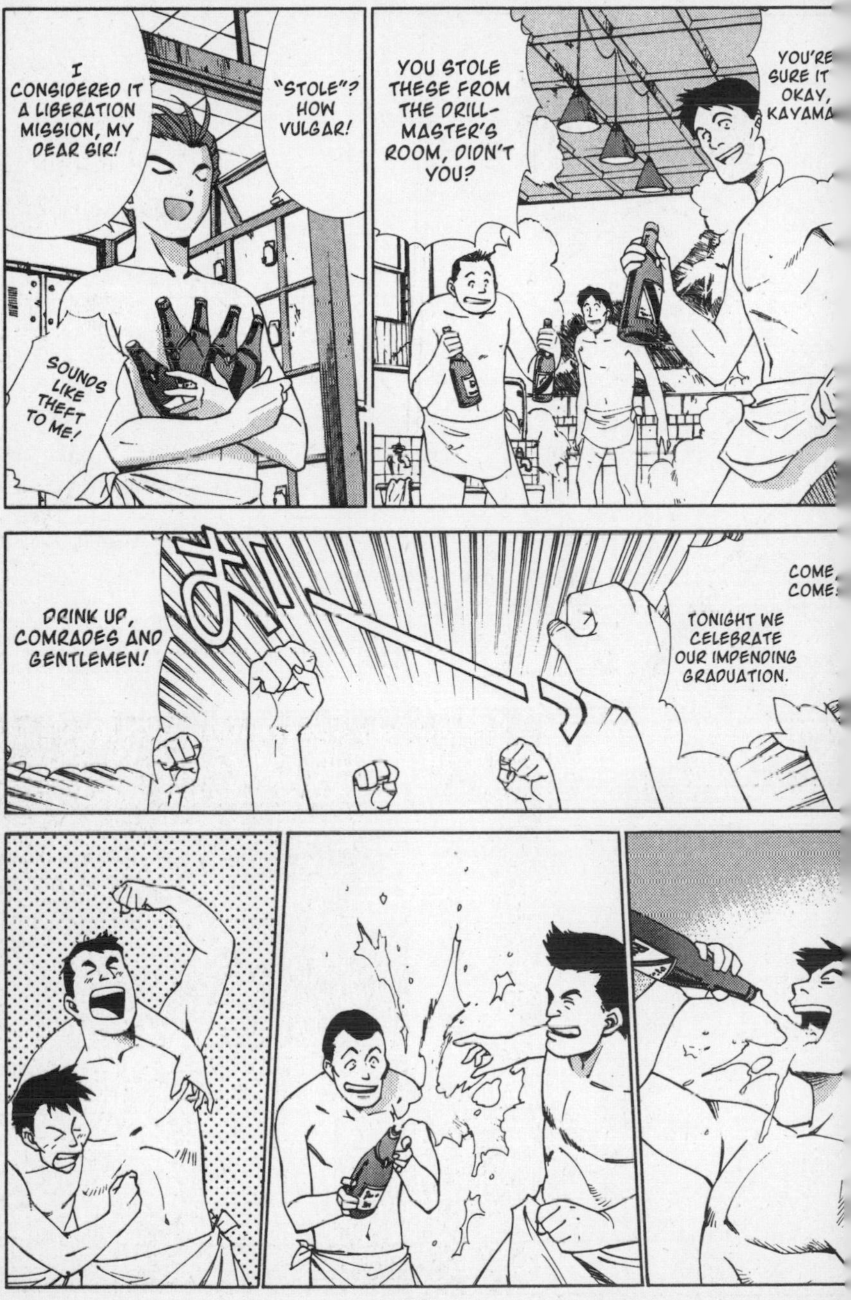
YOU'RE SURE IT OKAY, KAYAMA
YOU STOLE THESE FROM THE DRILL-MASTER'S ROOM, DIDN'T YOU?
"STOLE"? HOW VULGAR!
I CONSIDERED IT A LIBERATION MISSION, MY DEAR SIR!
SOUNDS LIKE THEFT TO ME!
COME, COME!
TONIGHT WE CELEBRATE OUR IMPENDING GRADUATION.
お
DRINK UP, COMRADES AND GENTLEMEN!

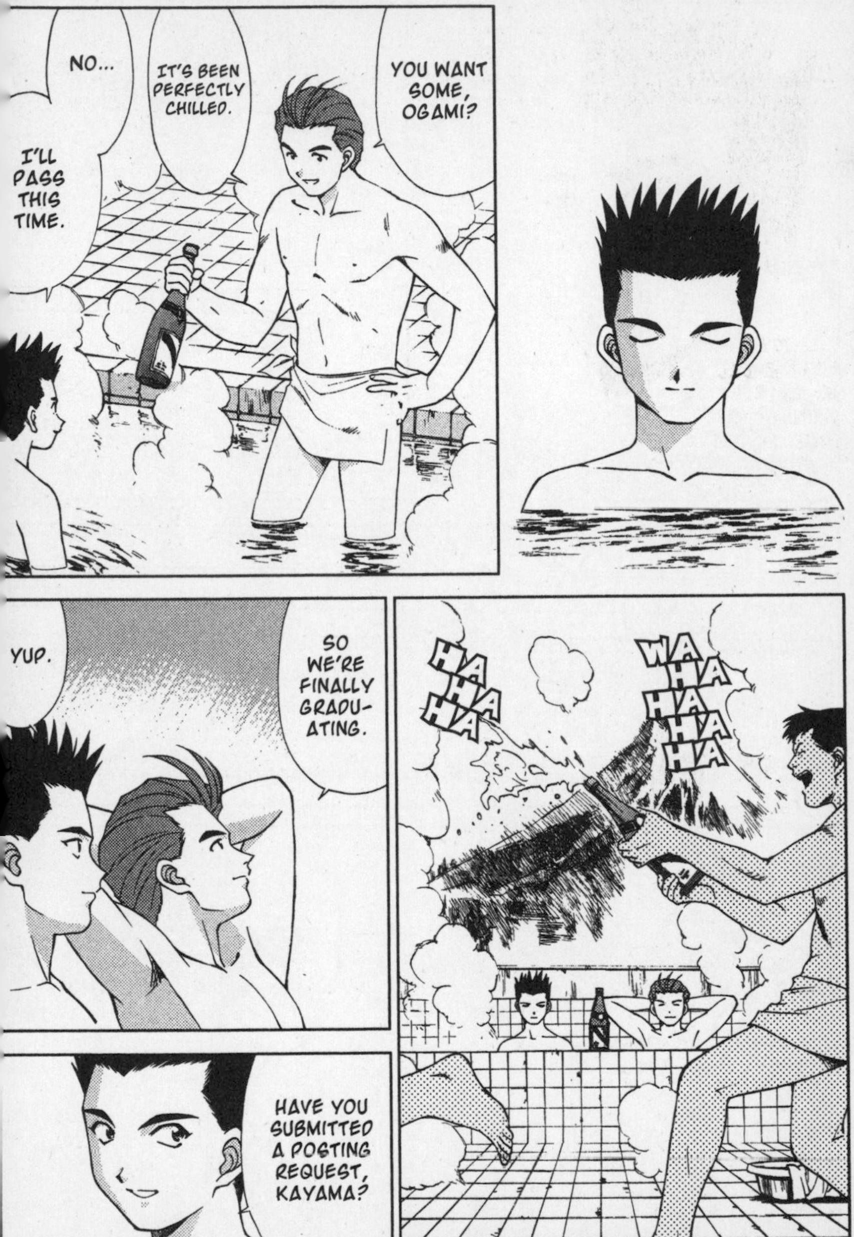
YOU WANT SOME, OGAMI?
IT'S BEEN PERFECTLY CHILLED.
NO...
I'LL PASS THIS TIME.
WAHAHAHAHAHA
HAHAHA
SO WE'RE FINALLY GRADU-ATING.
YUP.
HAVE YOU SUBMITTED A POSTING REQUEST, KAYAMA?

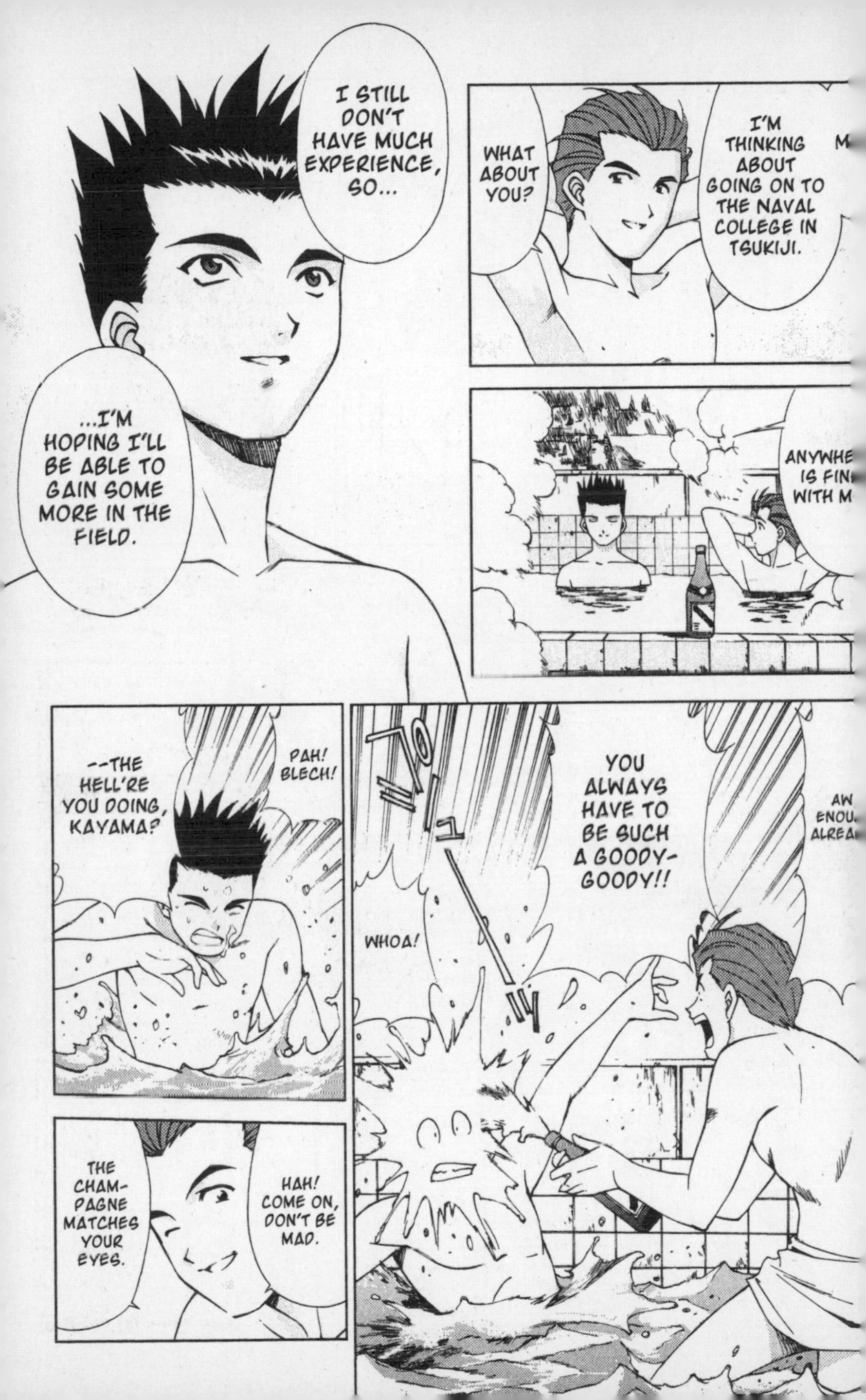
I'M THINKING ABOUT GOING ON TO THE NAVAL COLLEGE IN TSUKIJI.
WHAT ABOUT YOU?
I STILL DON'T HAVE MUCH EXPERIENCE, SO...
...I'M HOPING I'LL BE ABLE TO GAIN SOME MORE IN THE FIELD.
YOU ALWAYS HAVE TO BE SUCH A GOODY-GOODY!!
WHOA!
PAH! BLECH!
--THE HELL'RE YOU DOING, KAYAMA?
HAH! COME ON, DON'T BE MAD.
THE CHAMPAGNE MATCHES YOUR EYES.

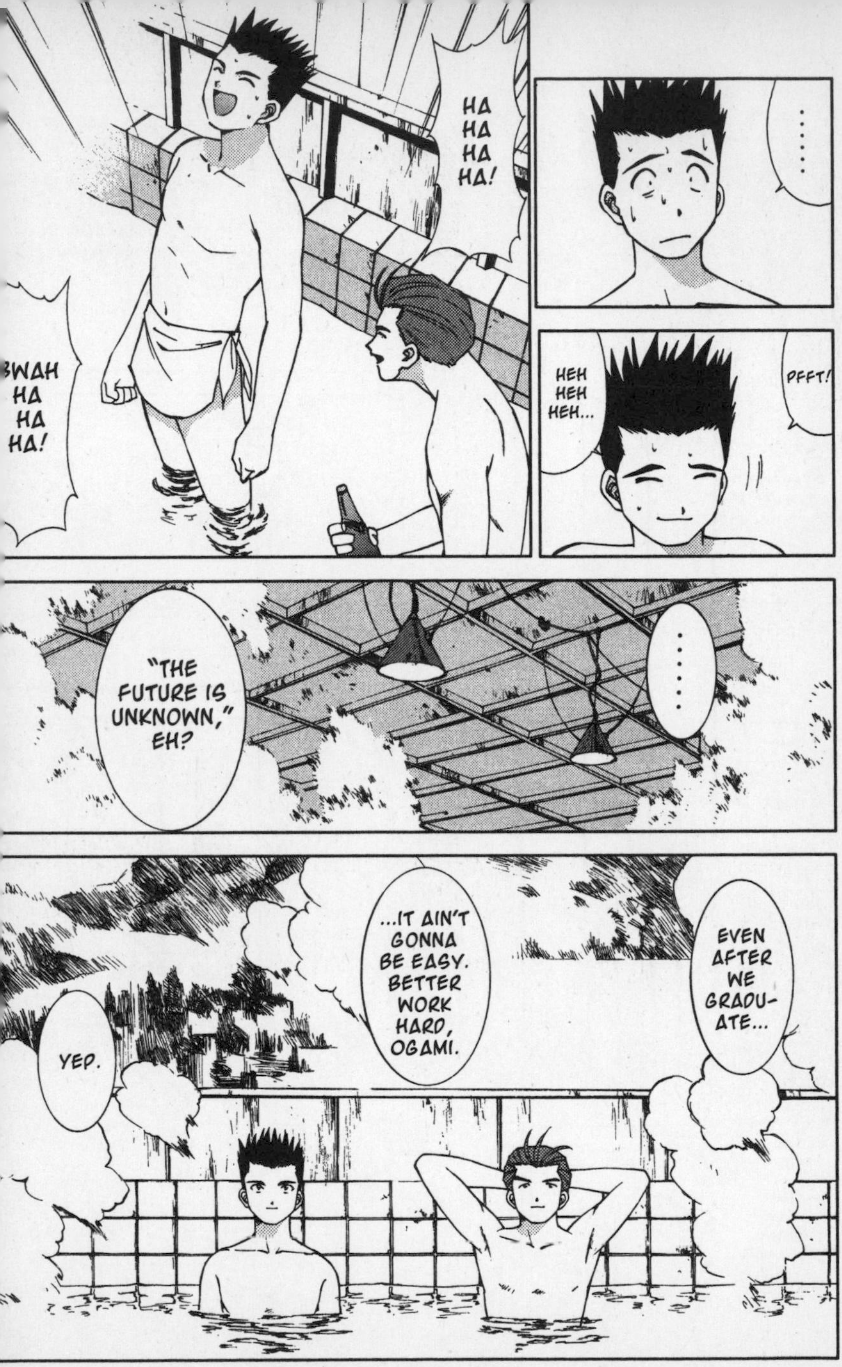
......
PFFT!
HEH HEH HEH...
HA HA HA HA!
BWAH HA HA HA!
......
"THE FUTURE IS UNKNOWN," EH?
EVEN AFTER WE GRADUATE...
...IT AIN'T GONNA BE EASY. BETTER WORK HARD, OGAMI.
YEP.

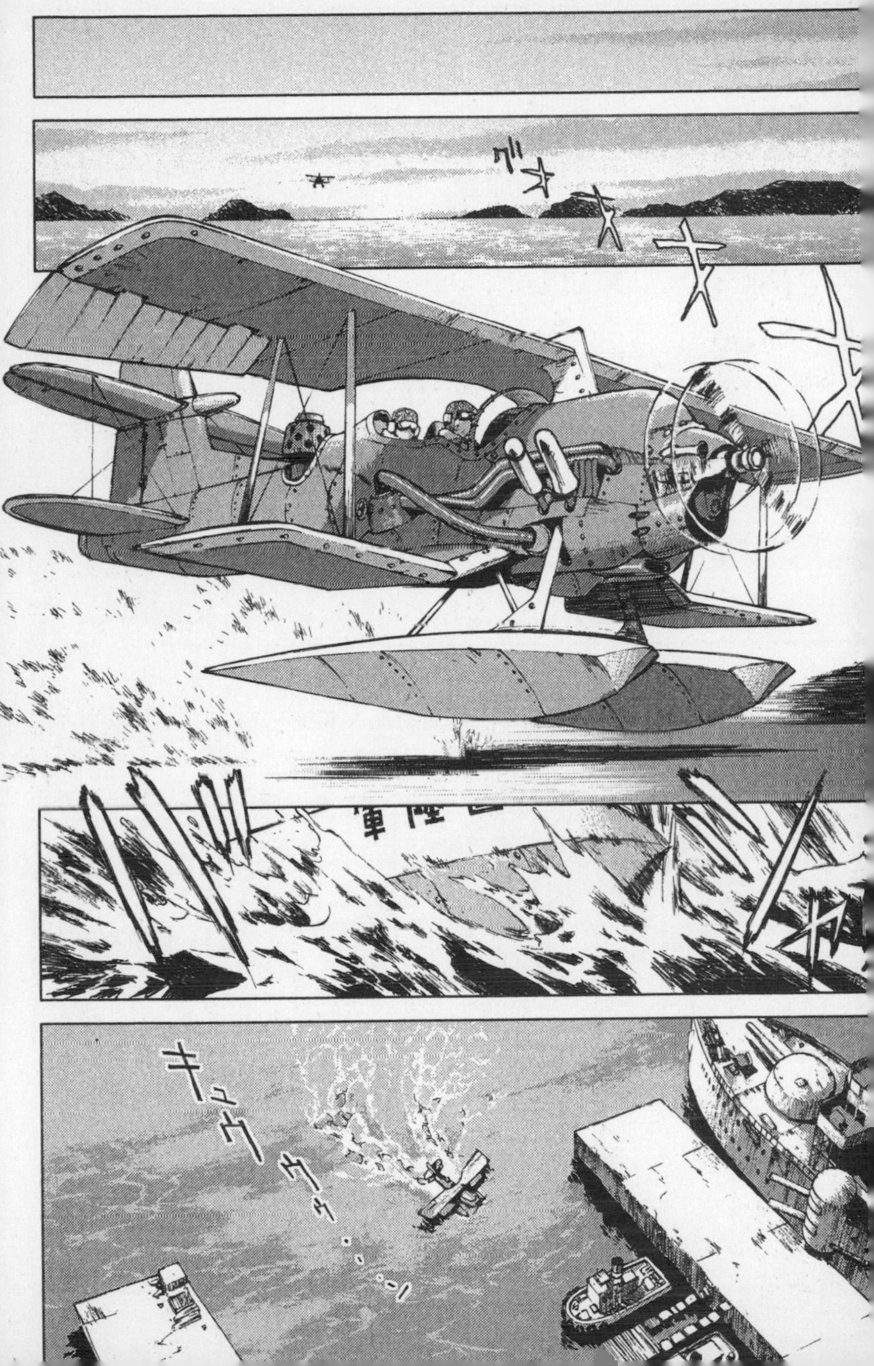
グォオオオ
キュウーウゥ・・・ン

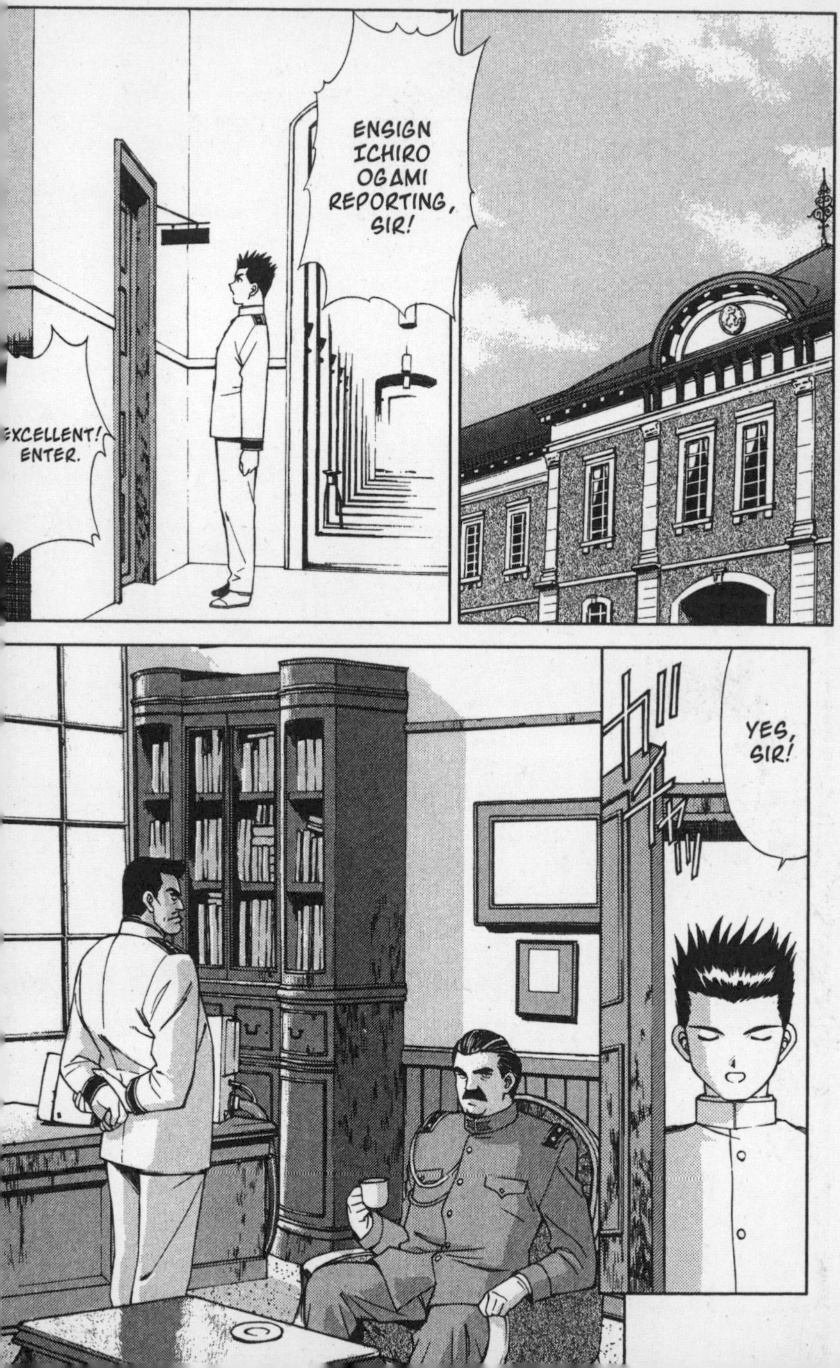
ENSIGN ICHIRO OGAMI REPORTING, SIR!
EXCELLENT! ENTER.
YES, SIR!

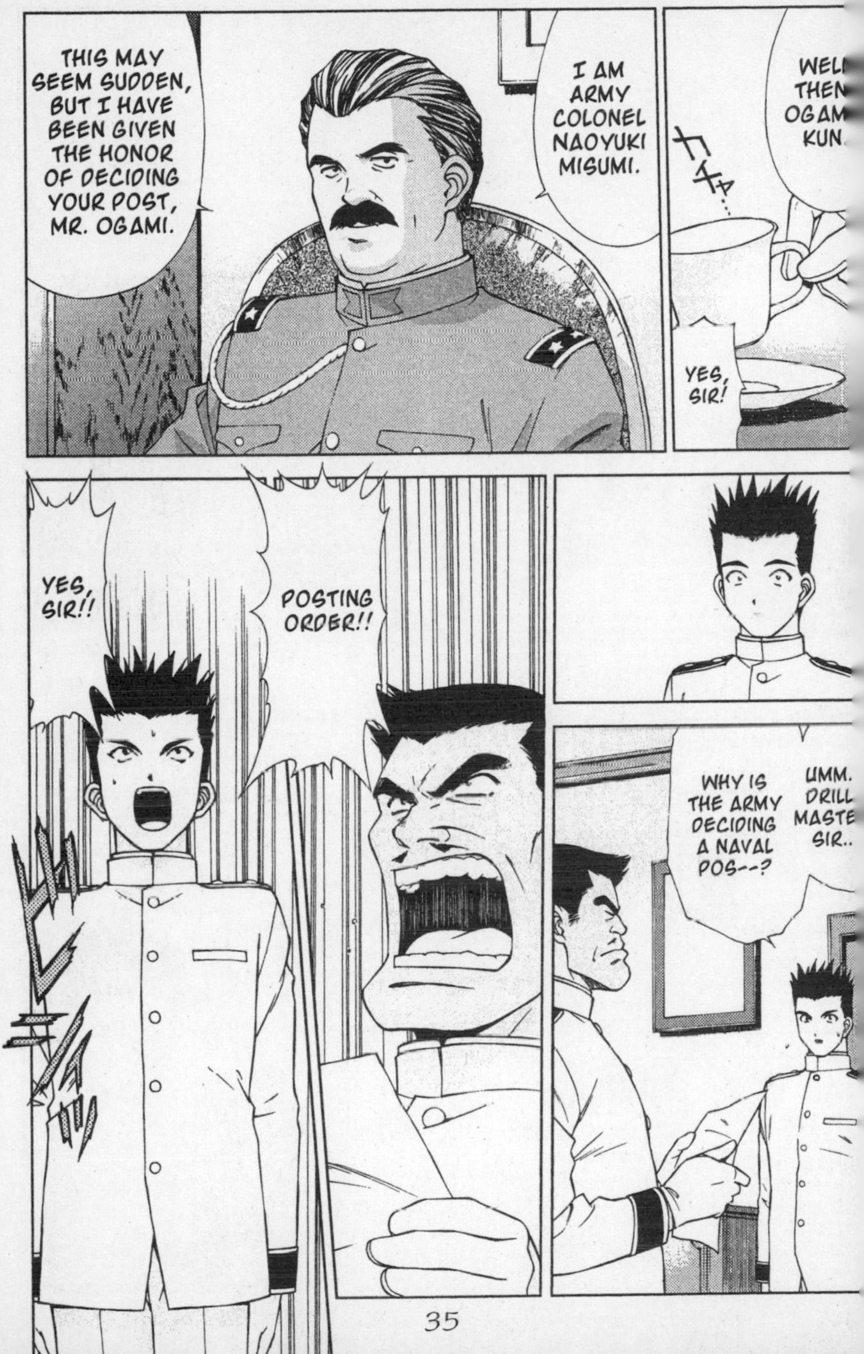
WELL THEN OGAM KUN.
カチャ…
YES, SIR!
I AM ARMY COLONEL NAOYUKI MISUMI.
THIS MAY SEEM SUDDEN, BUT I HAVE BEEN GIVEN THE HONOR OF DECIDING YOUR POST, MR. OGAMI.
UMM. DRILL MASTE SIR..
WHY IS THE ARMY DECIDING A NAVAL POS--?
POSTING ORDER!!
YES, SIR!!

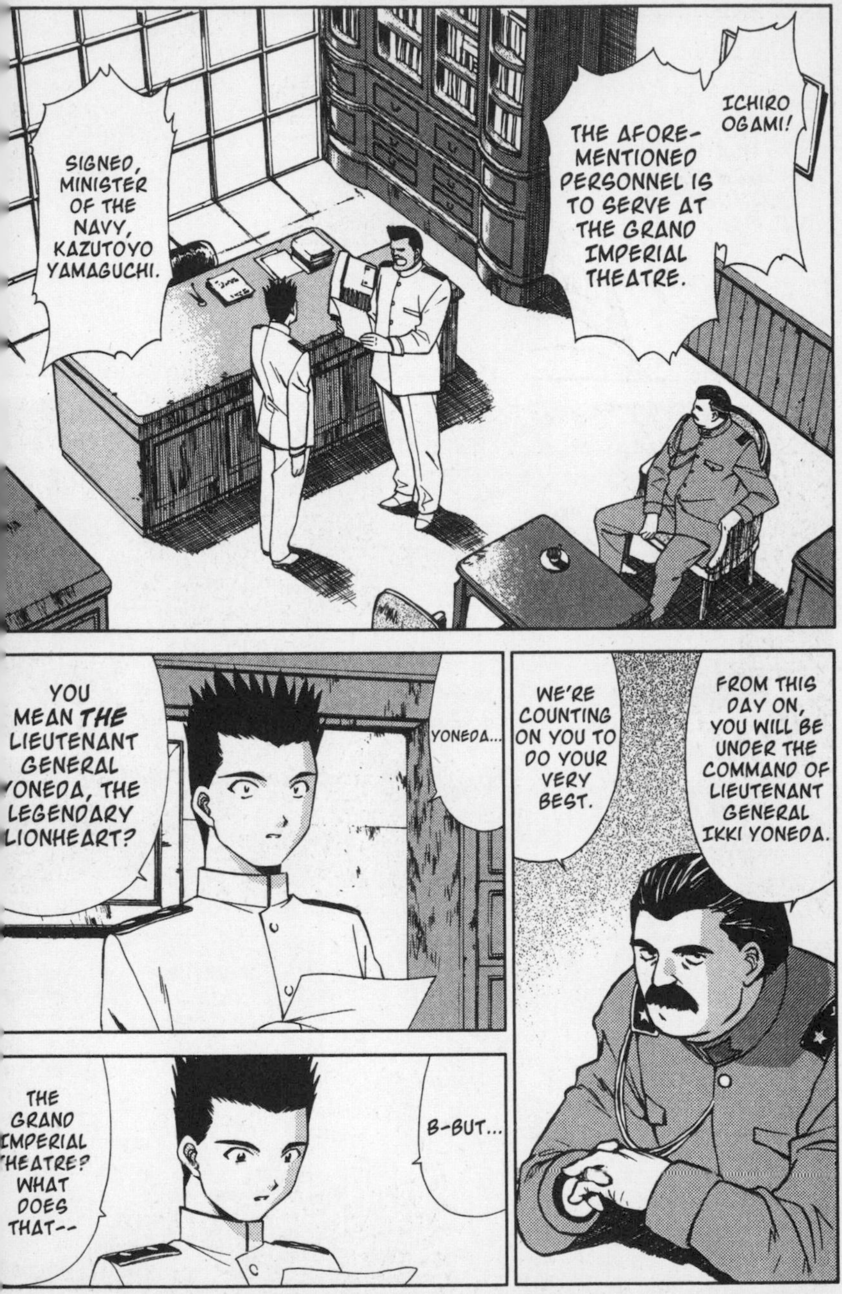
ICHIRO OGAMI!
THE AFORE-MENTIONED PERSONNEL IS TO SERVE AT THE GRAND IMPERIAL THEATRE.
SIGNED, MINISTER OF THE NAVY, KAZUTOYO YAMAGUCHI.
FROM THIS DAY ON, YOU WILL BE UNDER THE COMMAND OF LIEUTENANT GENERAL IKKI YONEDA.
WE'RE COUNTING ON YOU TO DO YOUR VERY BEST.
YONEDA...
YOU MEAN *THE* LIEUTENANT GENERAL YONEDA, THE LEGENDARY LIONHEART?
B-BUT...
THE GRAND IMPERIAL THEATRE? WHAT DOES THAT--

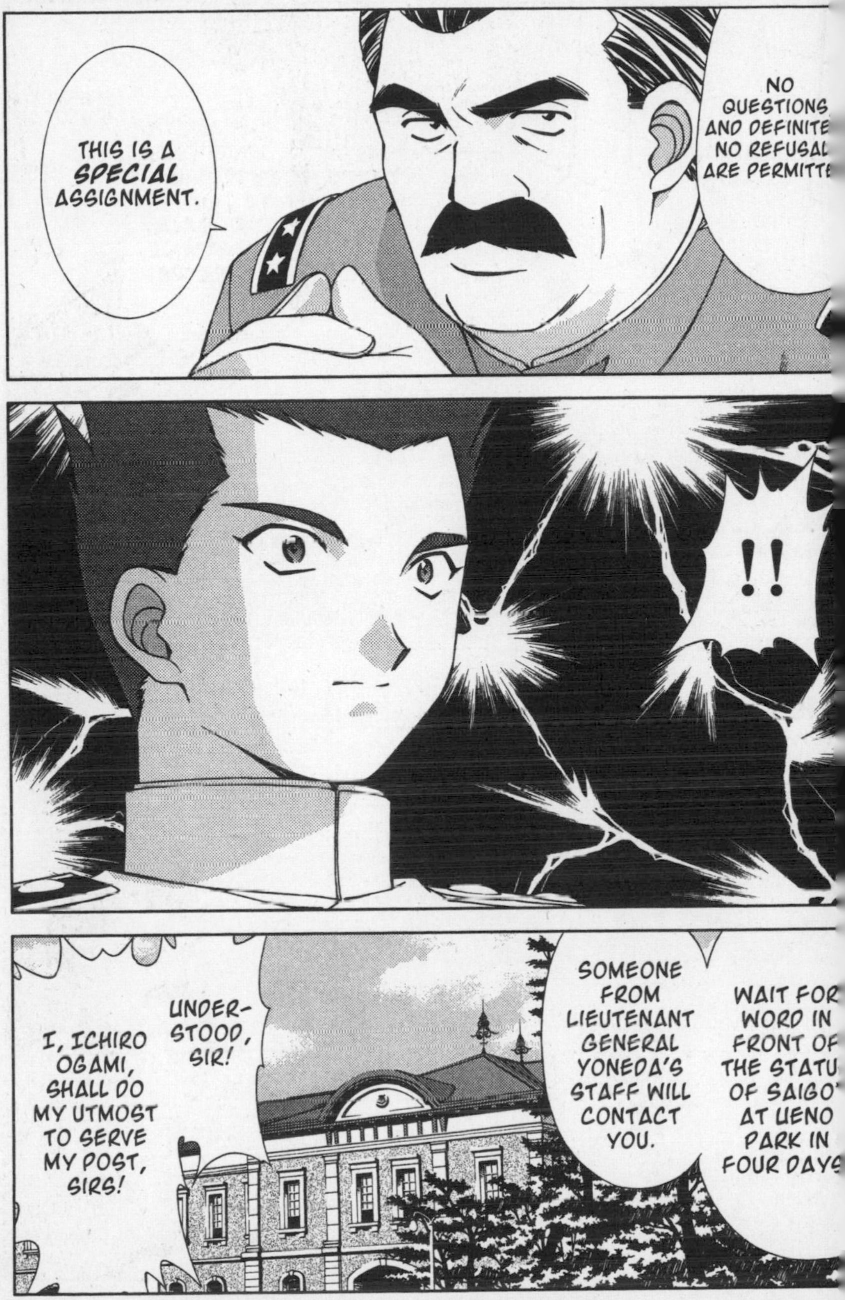
NO QUESTIONS AND DEFINITE NO REFUSAL ARE PERMITTE
THIS IS A SPECIAL ASSIGNMENT.
!!
WAIT FOR WORD IN FRONT OF THE STATU OF SAIGO* AT UENO PARK IN FOUR DAYS
SOMEONE FROM LIEUTENANT GENERAL YONEDA'S STAFF WILL CONTACT YOU.
UNDER-STOOD, SIR!
I, ICHIRO OGAMI, SHALL DO MY UTMOST TO SERVE MY POST, SIRS!

*A FAMOUS SAMURAI WARRIOR FROM THE END OF THE MEIJI ERA.

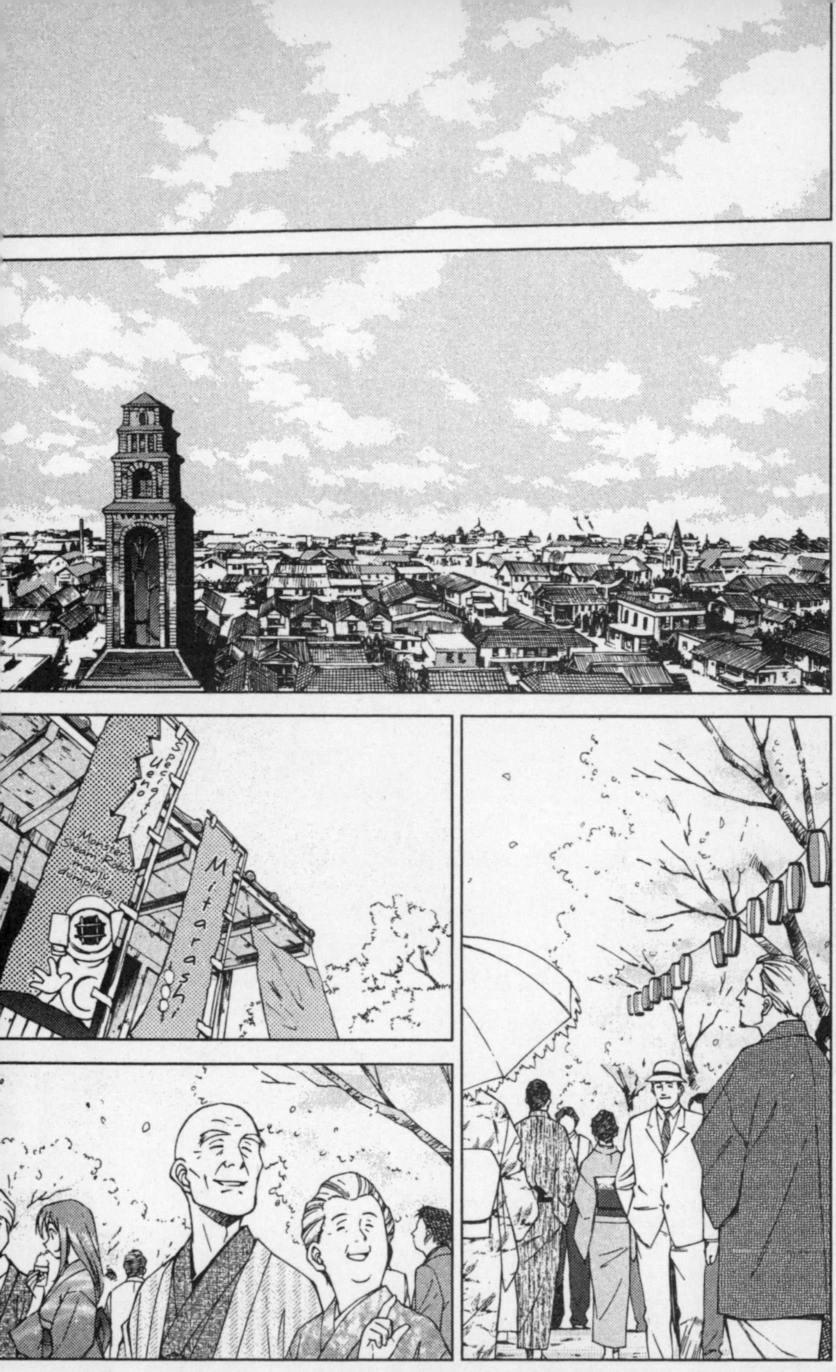
Ueno Specialty!
Mitarashi
Monster Steam Robot manju dumpling

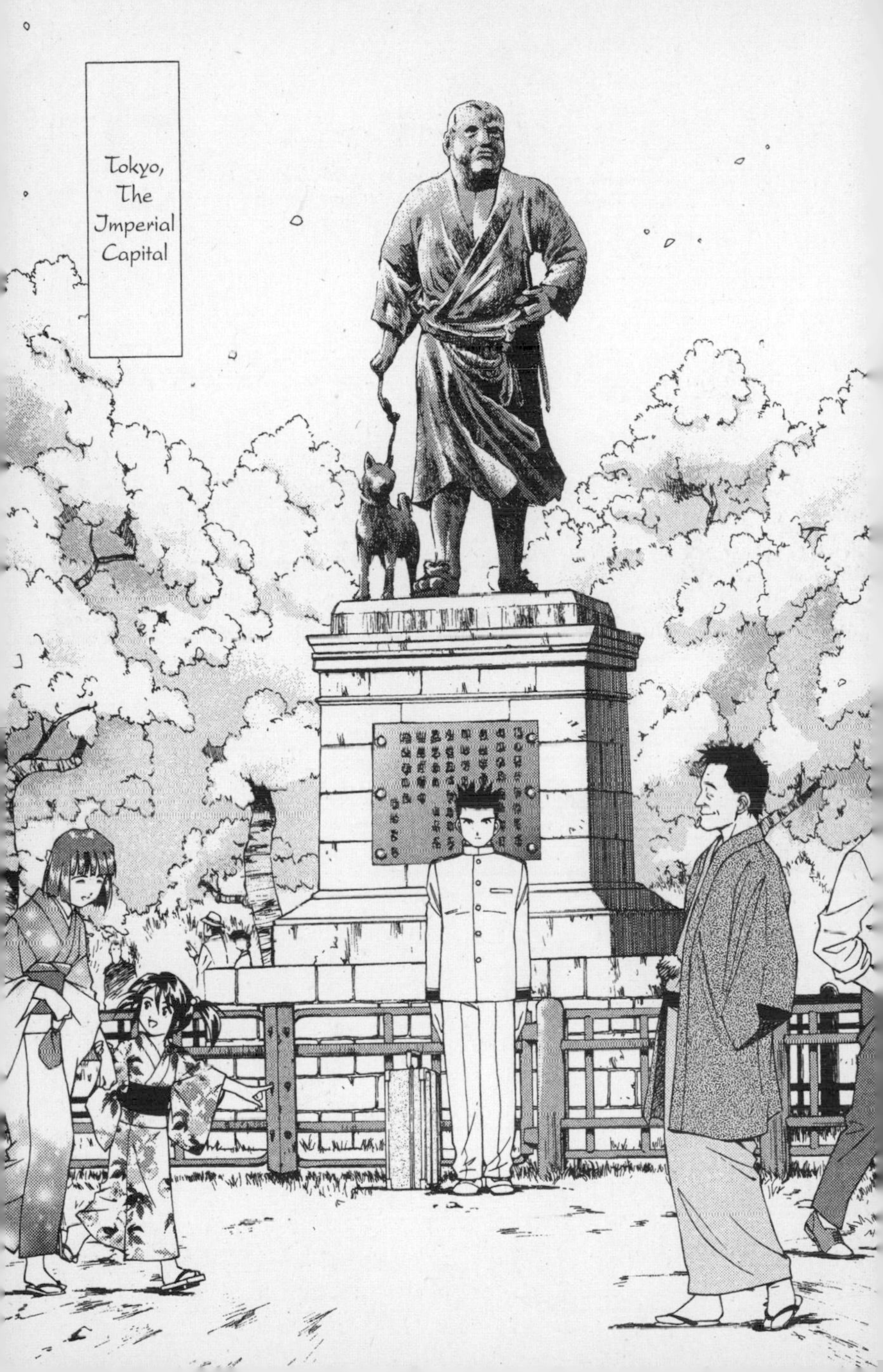
Tokyo, The Imperial Capital

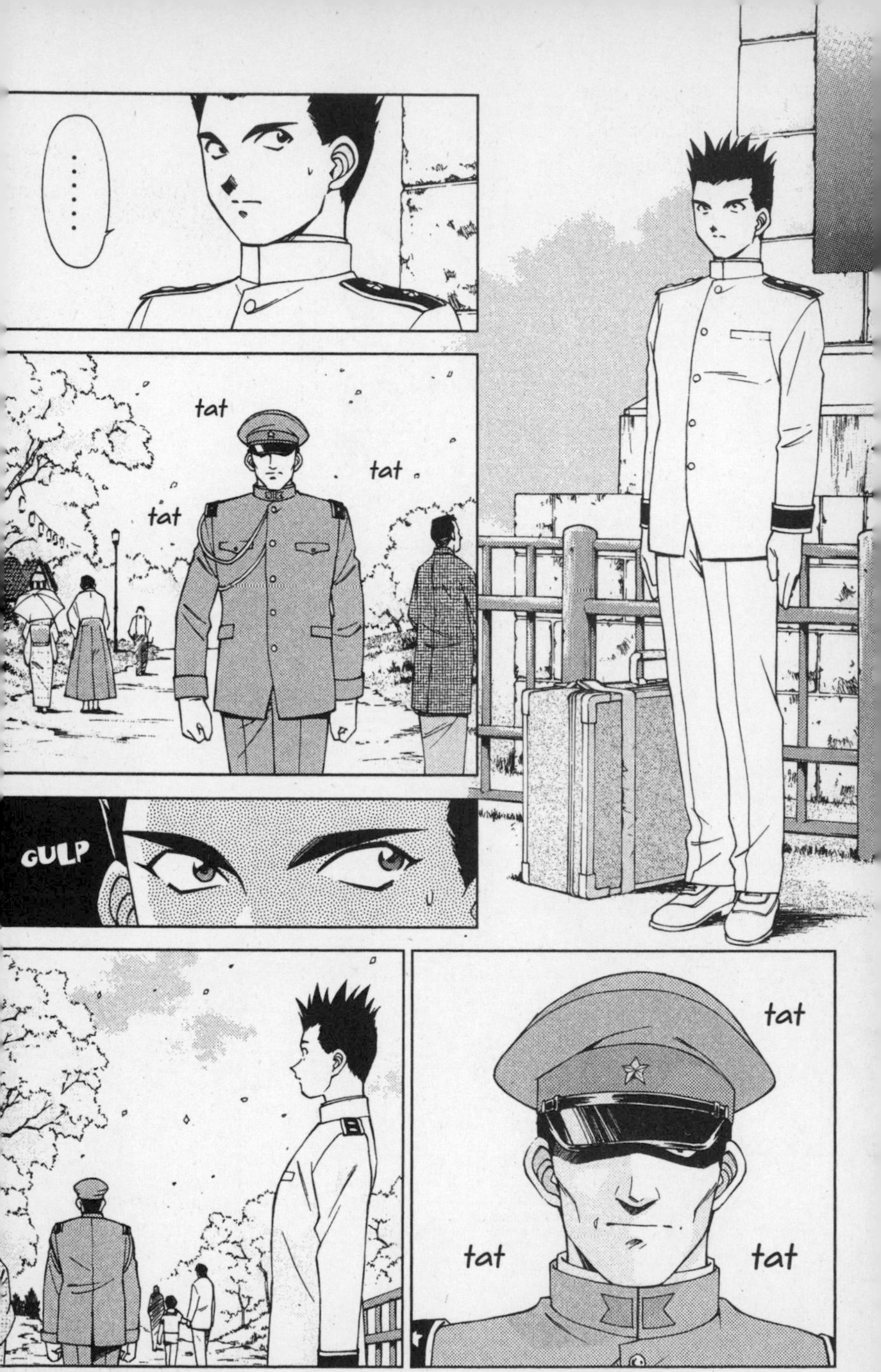

......
tat
tat
tat
GULP
tat
tat
tat

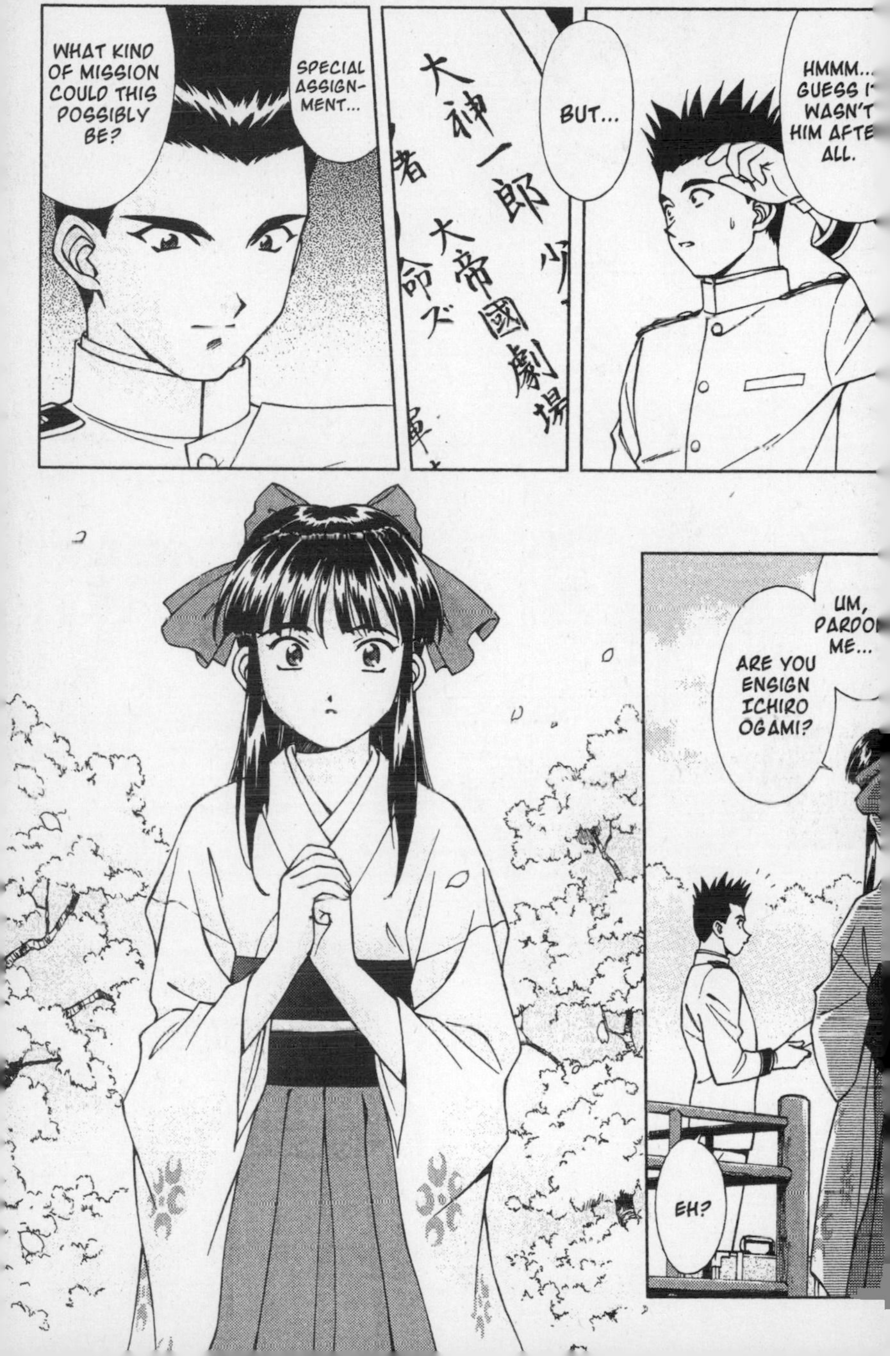
HMMM... GUESS I WASN'T HIM AFTE ALL.
BUT...
大神一郎
大帝國劇場
者
命ズ
SPECIAL ASSIGN-MENT...
WHAT KIND OF MISSION COULD THIS POSSIBLY BE?
UM, PARDO ME...
ARE YOU ENSIGN ICHIRO OGAMI?
EH?

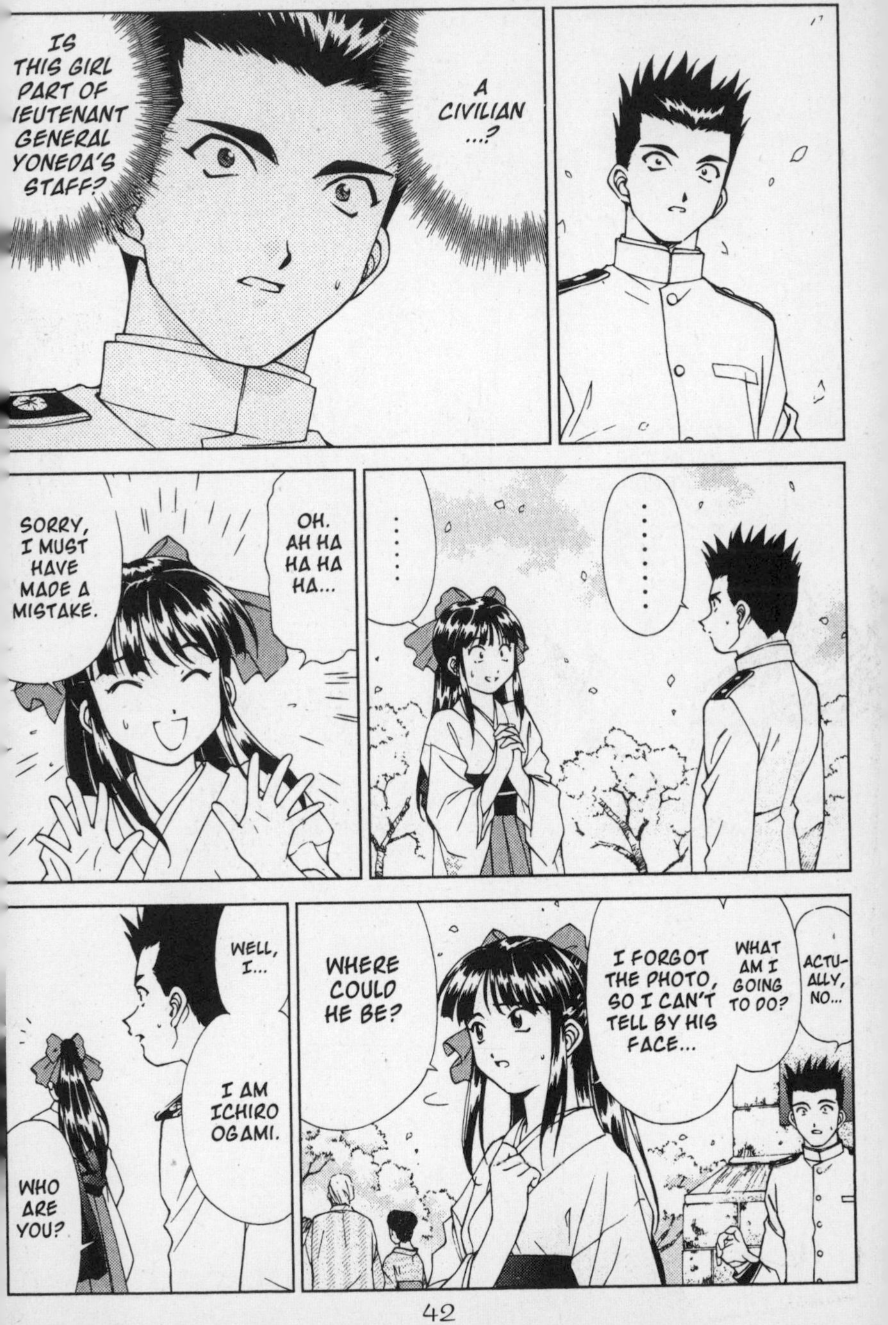
A CIVILIAN ...?
IS THIS GIRL PART OF IEUTENANT GENERAL YONEDA'S STAFF?
......
......
OH. AH HA HA HA HA...
SORRY, I MUST HAVE MADE A MISTAKE.
ACTU- ALLY, NO...
WHAT AM I GOING TO DO?
I FORGOT THE PHOTO, SO I CAN'T TELL BY HIS FACE...
WHERE COULD HE BE?
WELL, I...
I AM ICHIRO OGAMI.
WHO ARE YOU?

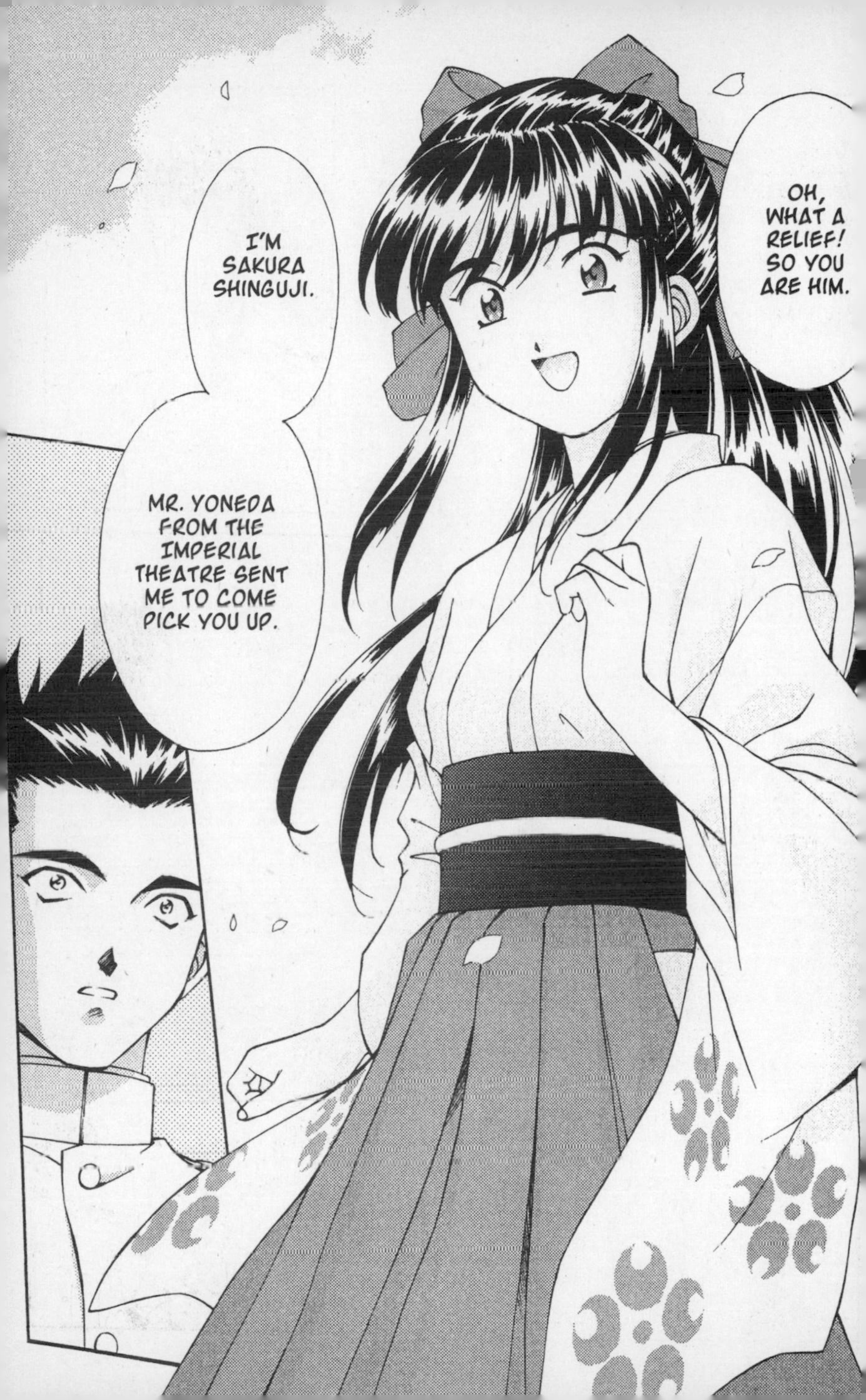
OH, WHAT A RELIEF! SO YOU ARE HIM.
I'M SAKURA SHINGUJI.
MR. YONEDA FROM THE IMPERIAL THEATRE SENT ME TO COME PICK YOU UP.

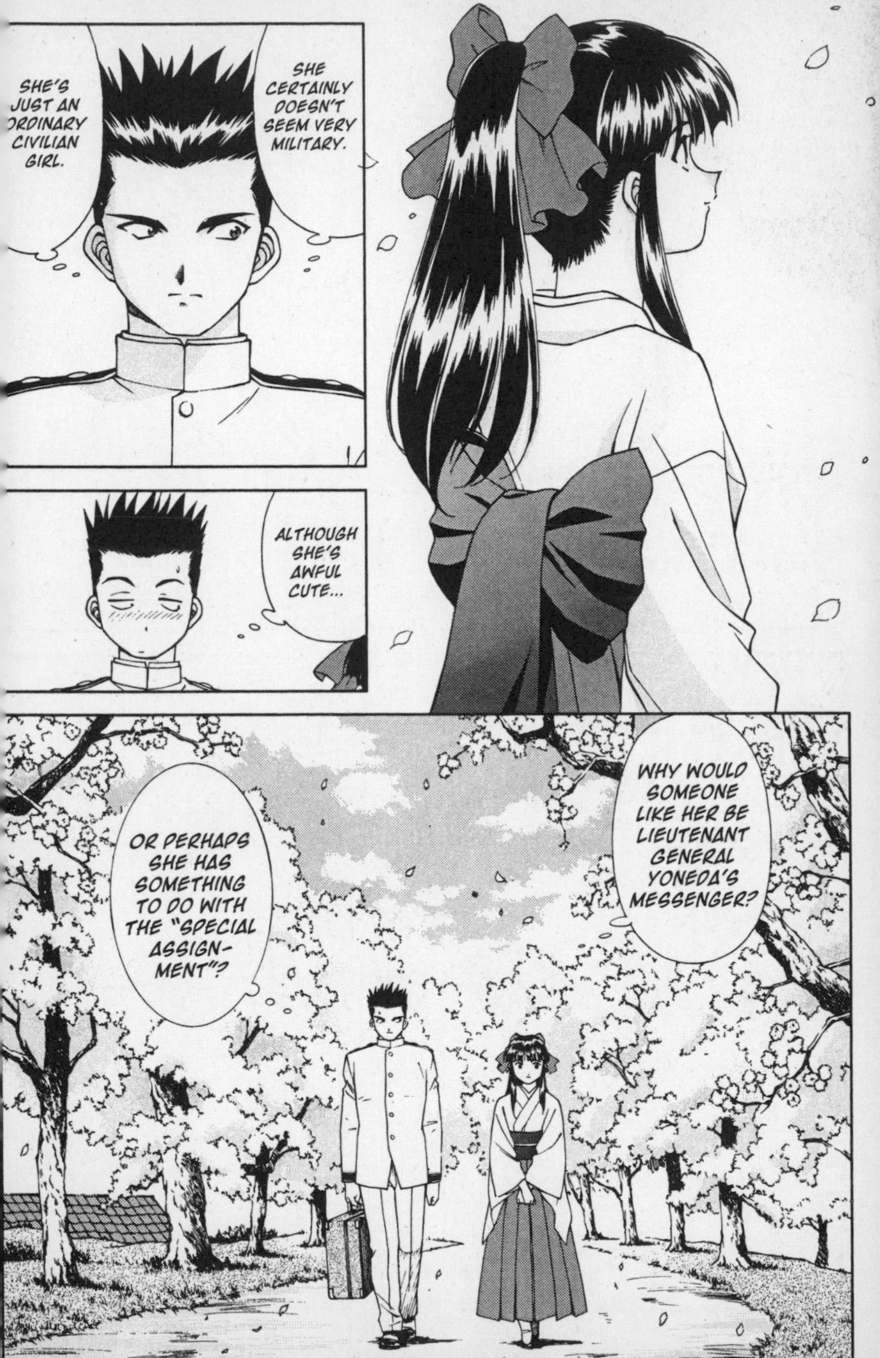
SHE CERTAINLY DOESN'T SEEM VERY MILITARY.
SHE'S JUST AN ORDINARY CIVILIAN GIRL.
ALTHOUGH SHE'S AWFUL CUTE...
WHY WOULD SOMEONE LIKE HER BE LIEUTENANT GENERAL YONEDA'S MESSENGER?
OR PERHAPS SHE HAS SOMETHING TO DO WITH THE "SPECIAL ASSIGNMENT"?

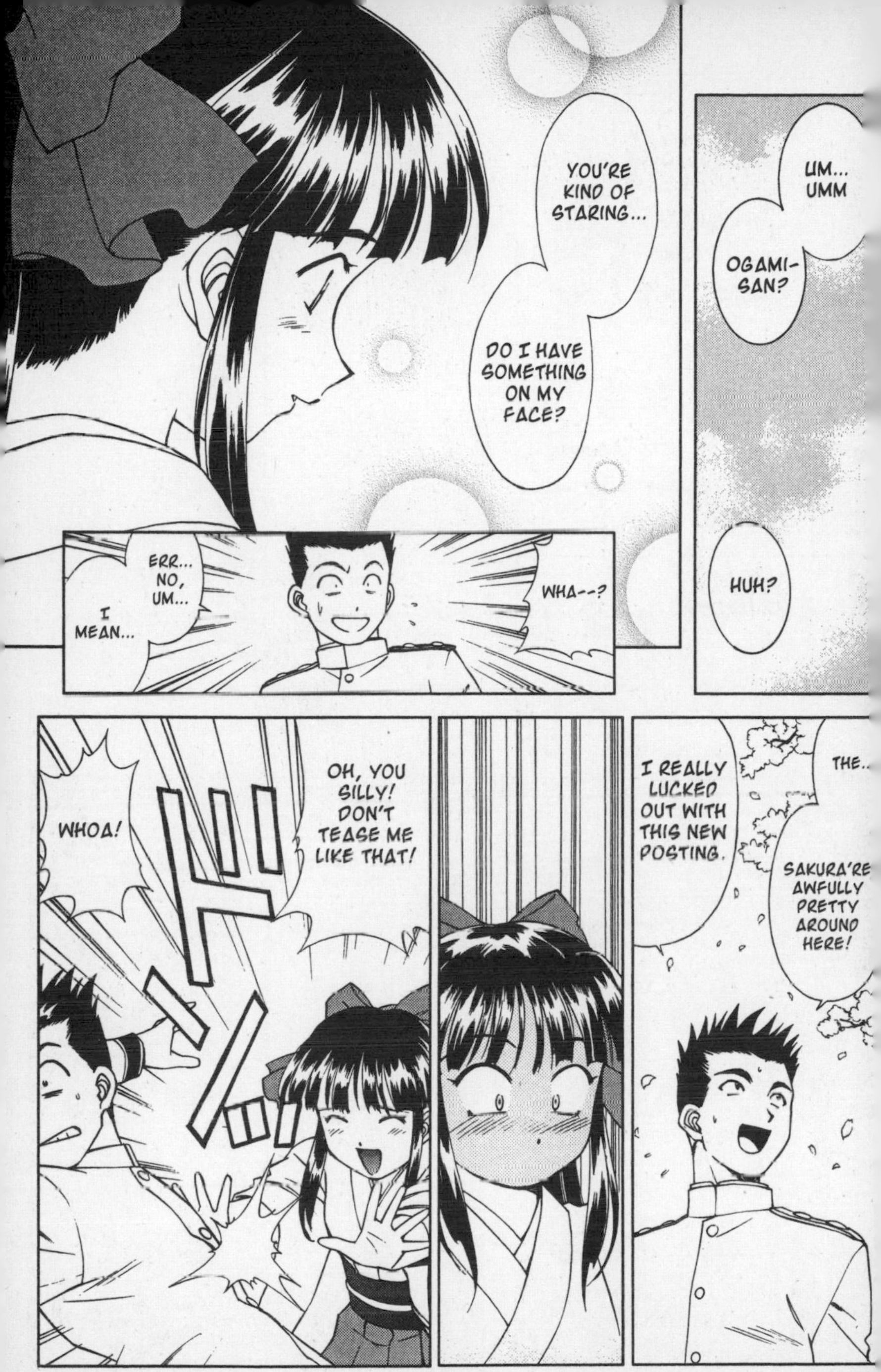
UM... UMM
OGAMI-SAN?
HUH?
YOU'RE KIND OF STARING...
DO I HAVE SOMETHING ON MY FACE?
WHA--?
ERR... NO, UM...
I MEAN...
THE...
SAKURA'RE AWFULLY PRETTY AROUND HERE!
I REALLY LUCKED OUT WITH THIS NEW POSTING.
OH, YOU SILLY! DON'T TEASE ME LIKE THAT!
WHOA!

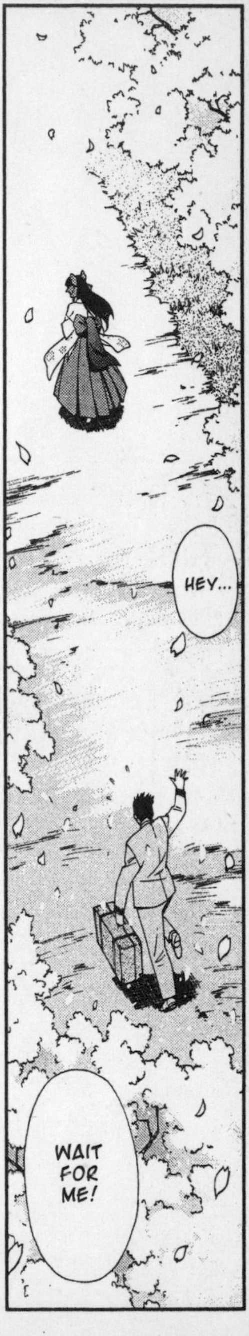
HEY...
WAIT FOR ME!

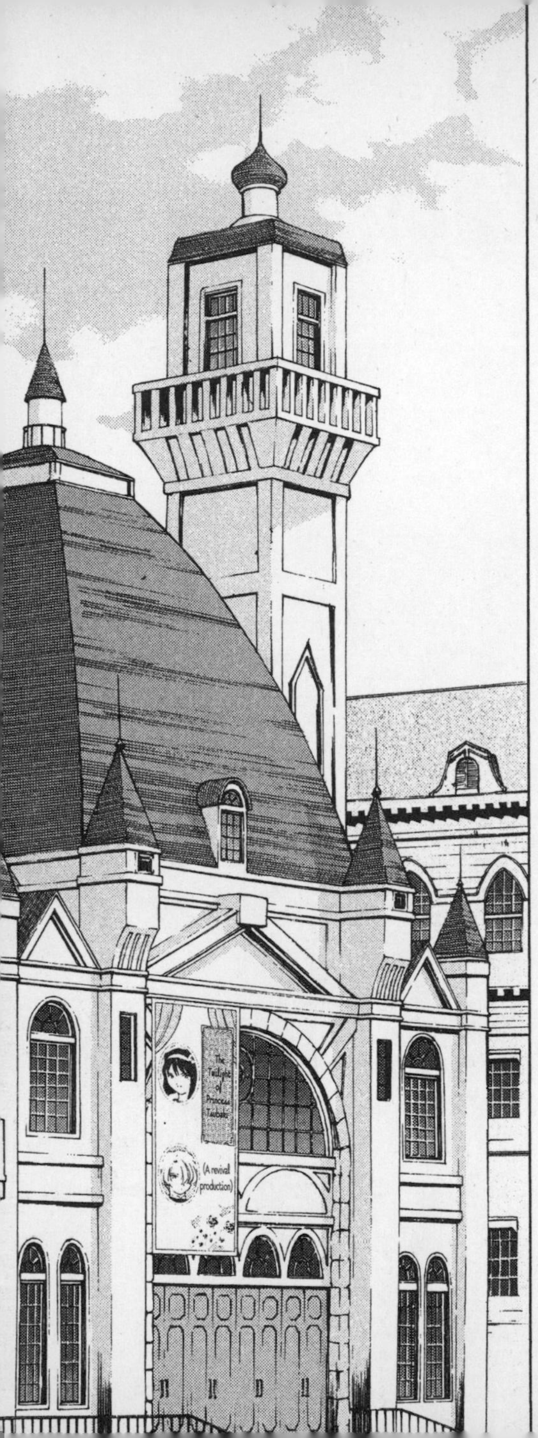
The Twilight of Princess Tsubaki
(A revival production)

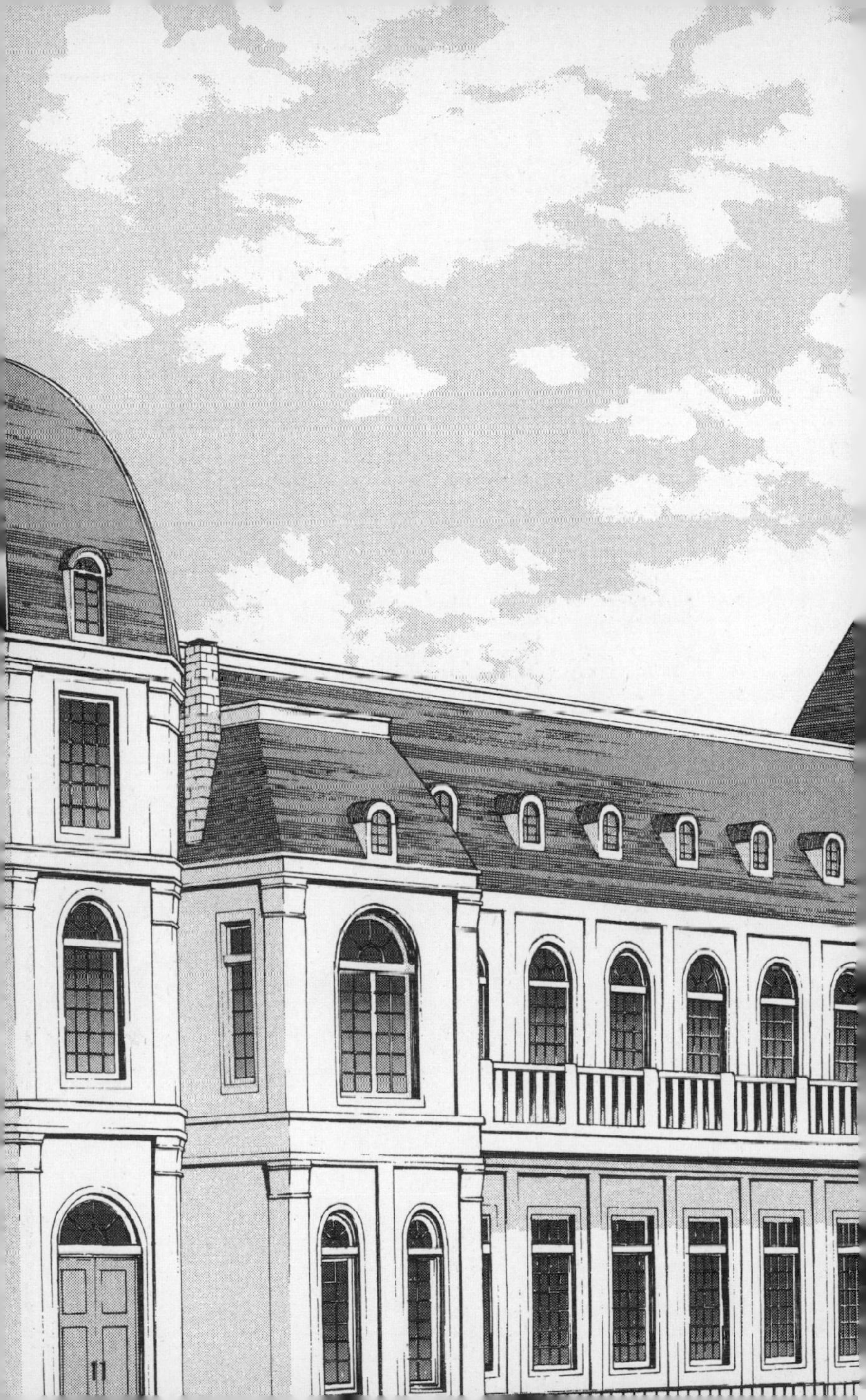

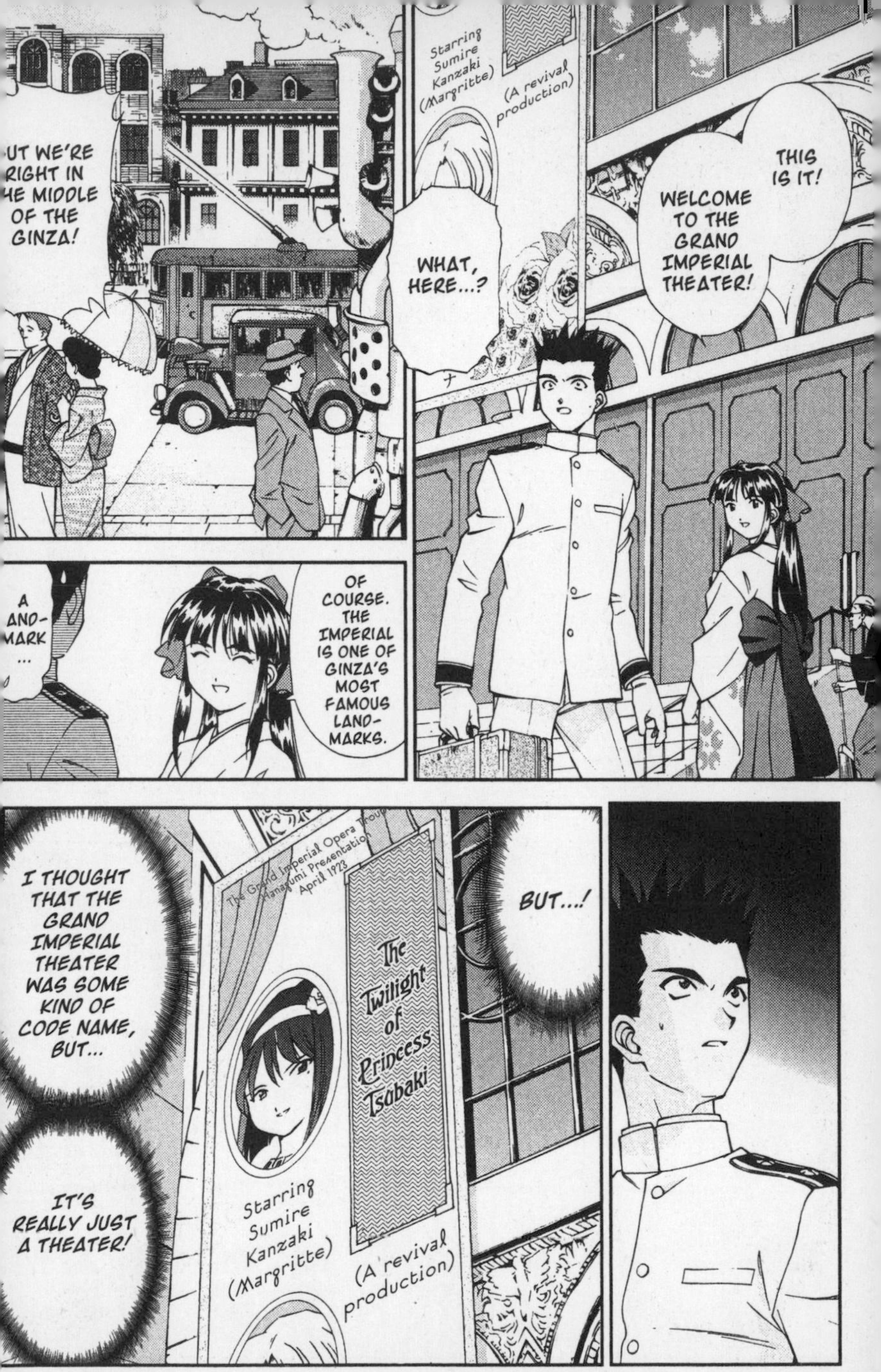
Starring Sumire Kanzaki (Margritte)
(A revival production)
THIS IS IT!
WELCOME TO THE GRAND IMPERIAL THEATER!
WHAT, HERE...?
UT WE'RE RIGHT IN HE MIDDLE OF THE GINZA!
OF COURSE. THE IMPERIAL IS ONE OF GINZA'S MOST FAMOUS LAND-MARKS.
A ANDMARK ...
BUT...!
The Grand Imperial Opera Trou
Hanagumi Presentation
April 1923
The Twilight of Princess Tsubaki
Starring Sumire Kanzaki (Margritte)
(A revival production)
I THOUGHT THAT THE GRAND IMPERIAL THEATER WAS SOME KIND OF CODE NAME, BUT...
IT'S REALLY JUST A THEATER!

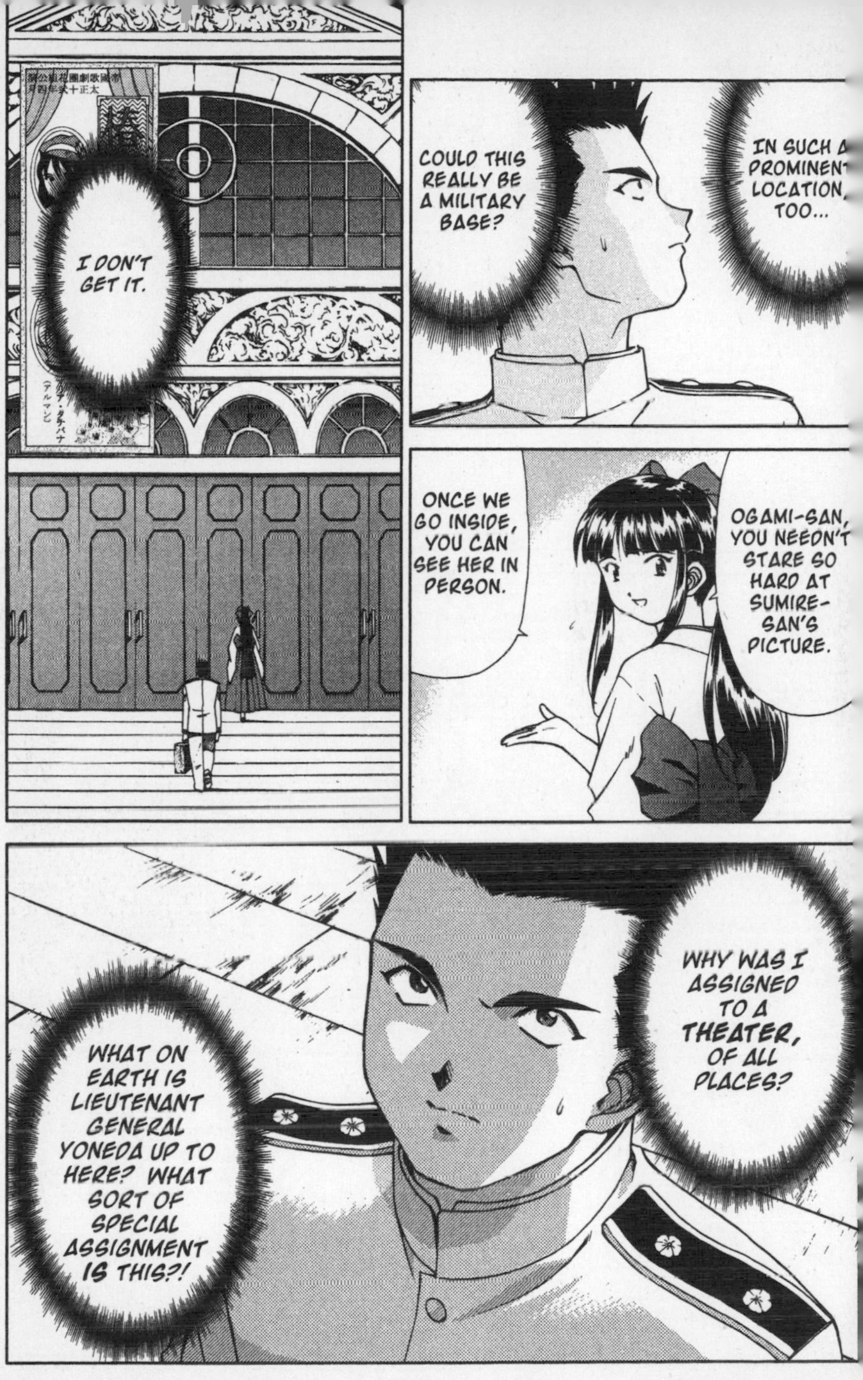
IN SUCH A PROMINENT LOCATION, TOO...
COULD THIS REALLY BE A MILITARY BASE?
I DON'T GET IT.
OGAMI-SAN, YOU NEEDN'T STARE SO HARD AT SUMIRE-SAN'S PICTURE.
ONCE WE GO INSIDE, YOU CAN SEE HER IN PERSON.
WHY WAS I ASSIGNED TO A THEATER, OF ALL PLACES?
WHAT ON EARTH IS LIEUTENANT GENERAL YONEDA UP TO HERE? WHAT SORT OF SPECIAL ASSIGNMENT IS THIS?!

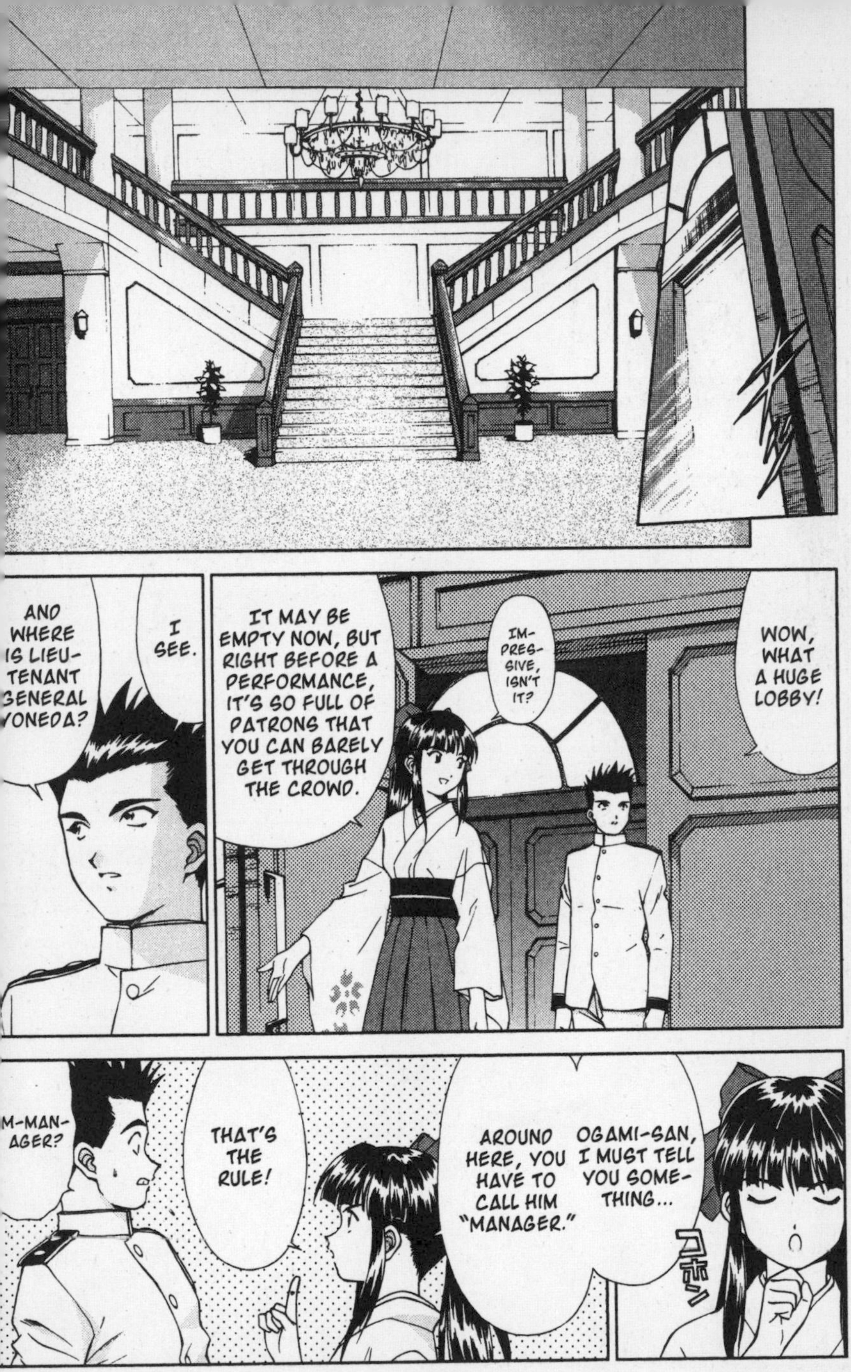
WOW, WHAT A HUGE LOBBY!
IM-PRES-SIVE, ISN'T IT?
IT MAY BE EMPTY NOW, BUT RIGHT BEFORE A PERFORMANCE, IT'S SO FULL OF PATRONS THAT YOU CAN BARELY GET THROUGH THE CROWD.
I SEE.
AND WHERE IS LIEU-TENANT GENERAL YONEDA?
OGAMI-SAN, I MUST TELL YOU SOME-THING...
コホン
AROUND HERE, YOU HAVE TO CALL HIM "MANAGER."
THAT'S THE RULE!
M-MAN-AGER?

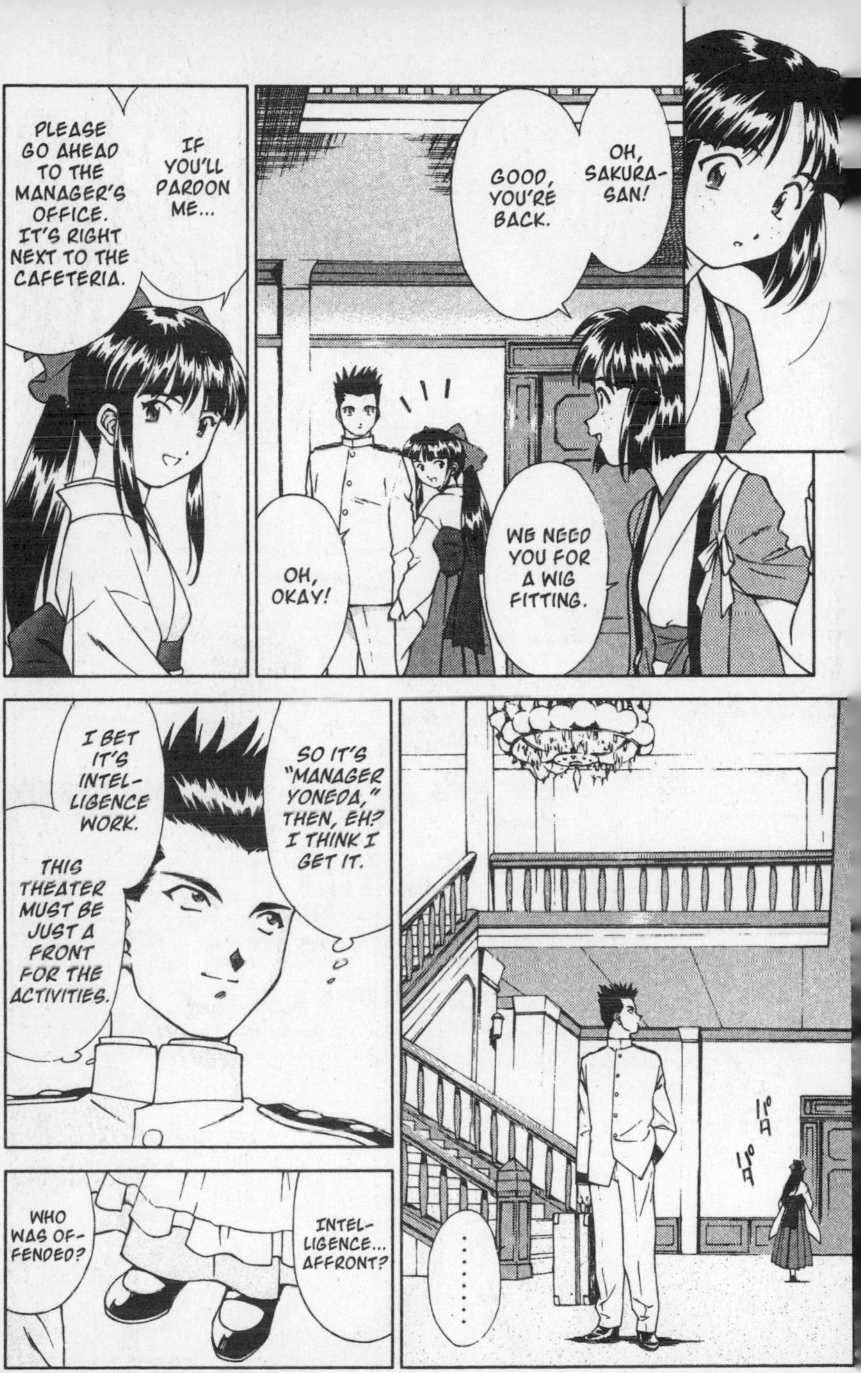
OH, SAKURA-SAN!
GOOD, YOU'RE BACK.
WE NEED YOU FOR A WIG FITTING.
OH, OKAY!
IF YOU'LL PARDON ME...
PLEASE GO AHEAD TO THE MANAGER'S OFFICE. IT'S RIGHT NEXT TO THE CAFETERIA.
......
SO IT'S "MANAGER YONEDA," THEN, EH? I THINK I GET IT.
I BET IT'S INTEL-LIGENCE WORK.
THIS THEATER MUST BE JUST A FRONT FOR THE ACTIVITIES.
INTEL-LIGENCE... AFFRONT?
WHO WAS OF-FENDED?

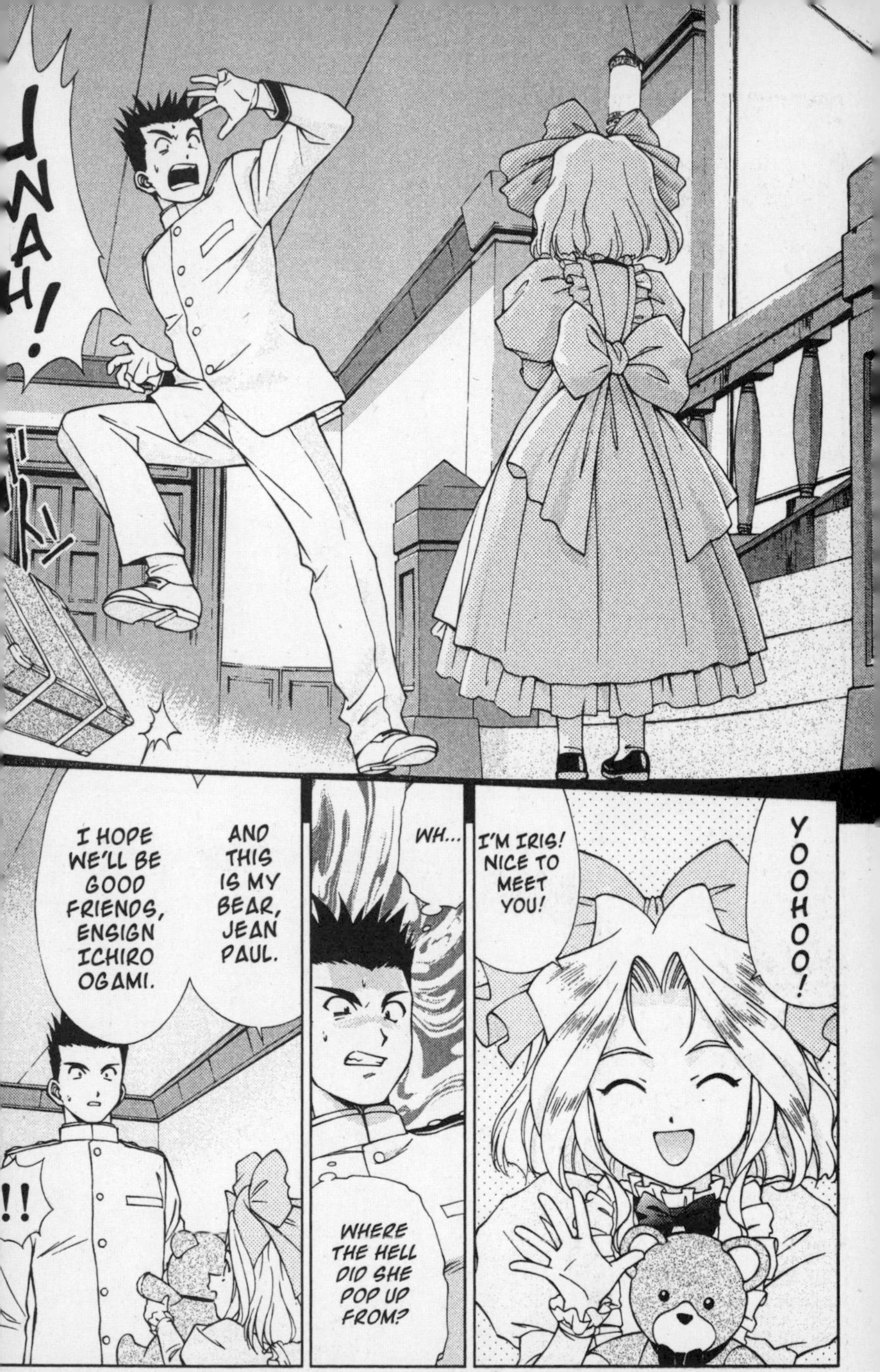
WAH!
YOOHOO!
I'M IRIS! NICE TO MEET YOU!
WH...
WHERE THE HELL DID SHE POP UP FROM?
AND THIS IS MY BEAR, JEAN PAUL.
I HOPE WE'LL BE GOOD FRIENDS, ENSIGN ICHIRO OGAMI.
!!

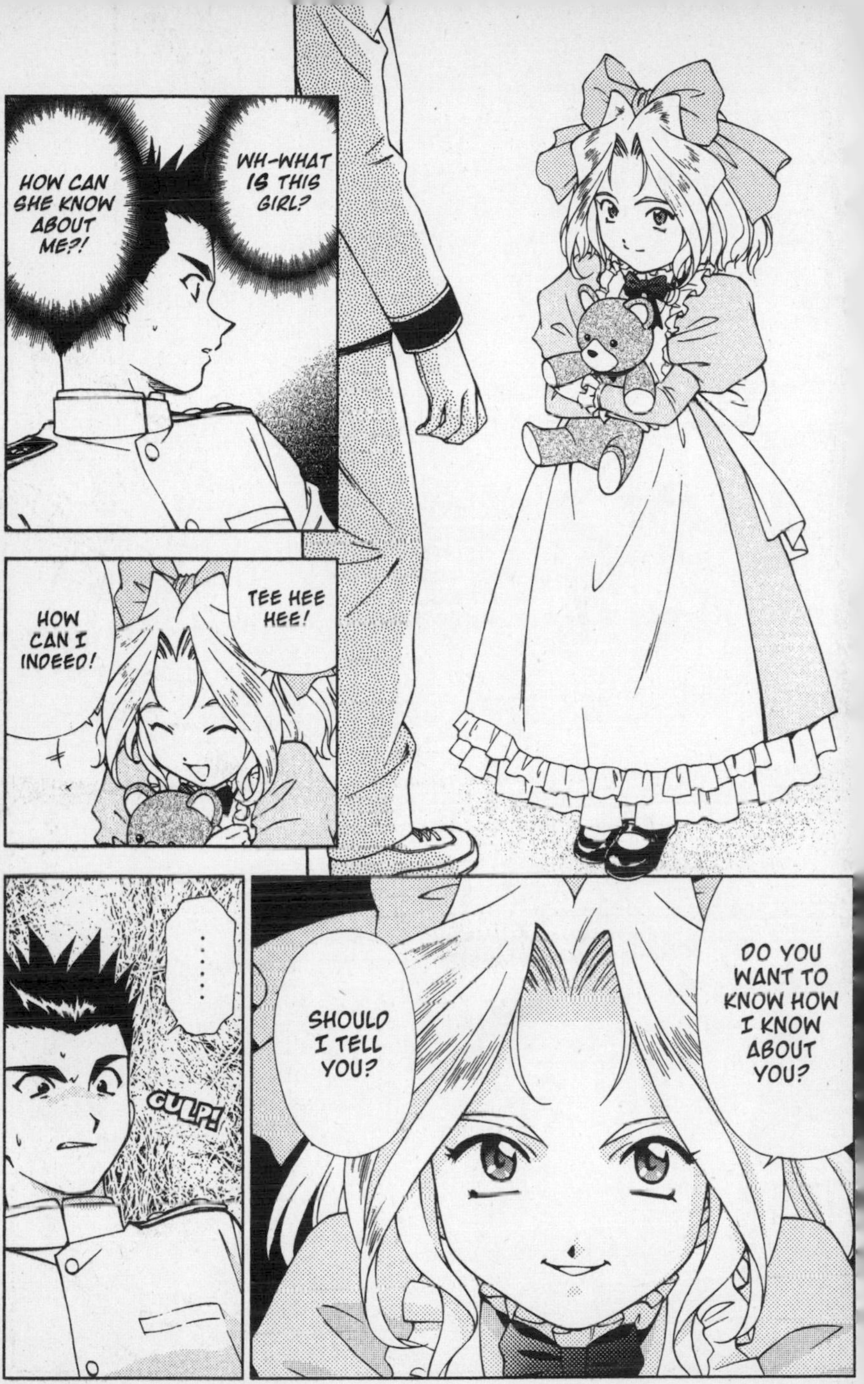
WH-WHAT IS THIS GIRL?
HOW CAN SHE KNOW ABOUT ME?!
TEE HEE HEE!
HOW CAN I INDEED!
DO YOU WANT TO KNOW HOW I KNOW ABOUT YOU?
SHOULD I TELL YOU?
......
GULP!

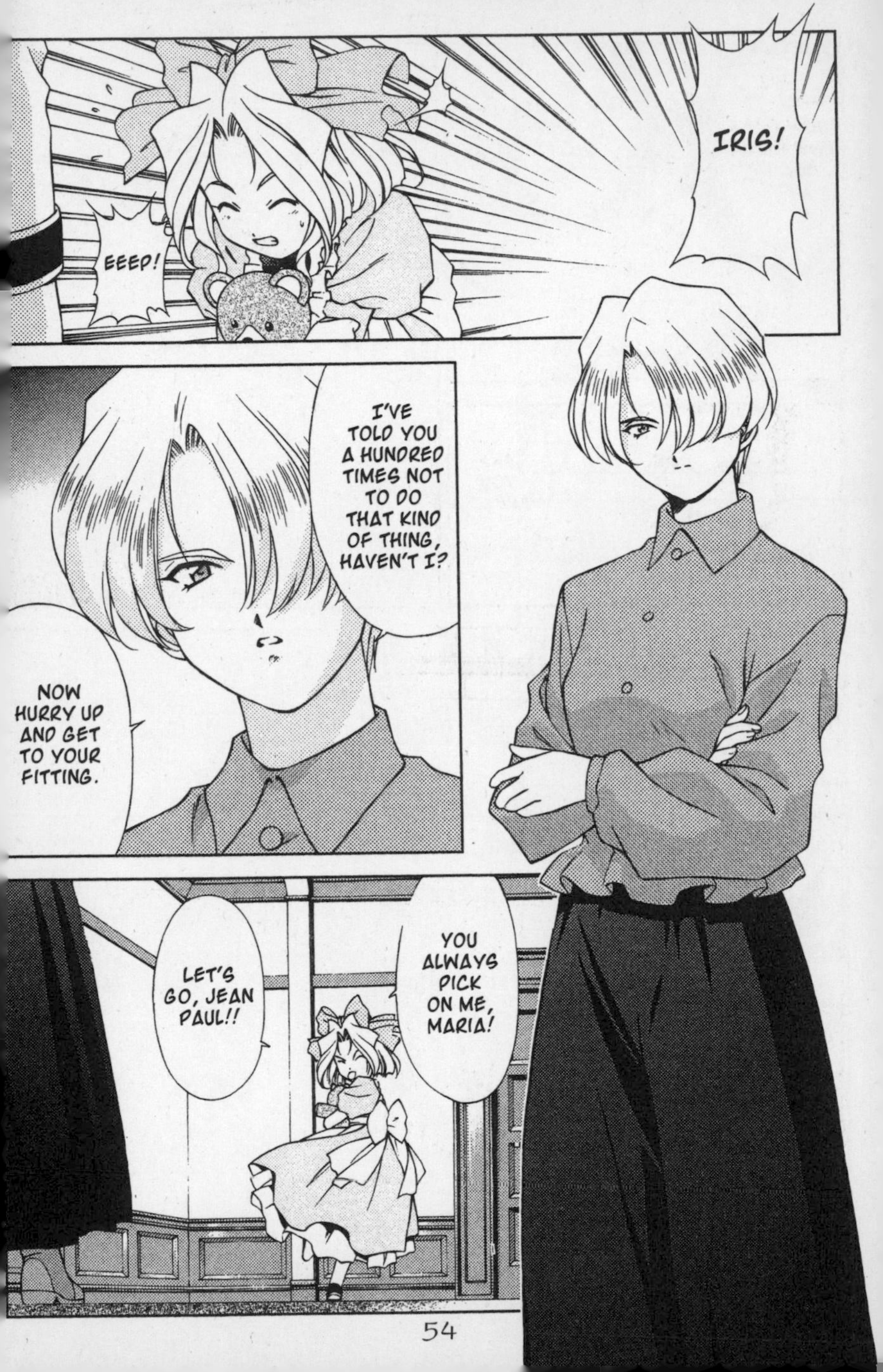
IRIS!
EEEP!
I'VE TOLD YOU A HUNDRED TIMES NOT TO DO THAT KIND OF THING, HAVEN'T I?
NOW HURRY UP AND GET TO YOUR FITTING.
YOU ALWAYS PICK ON ME, MARIA!
LET'S GO, JEAN PAUL!!

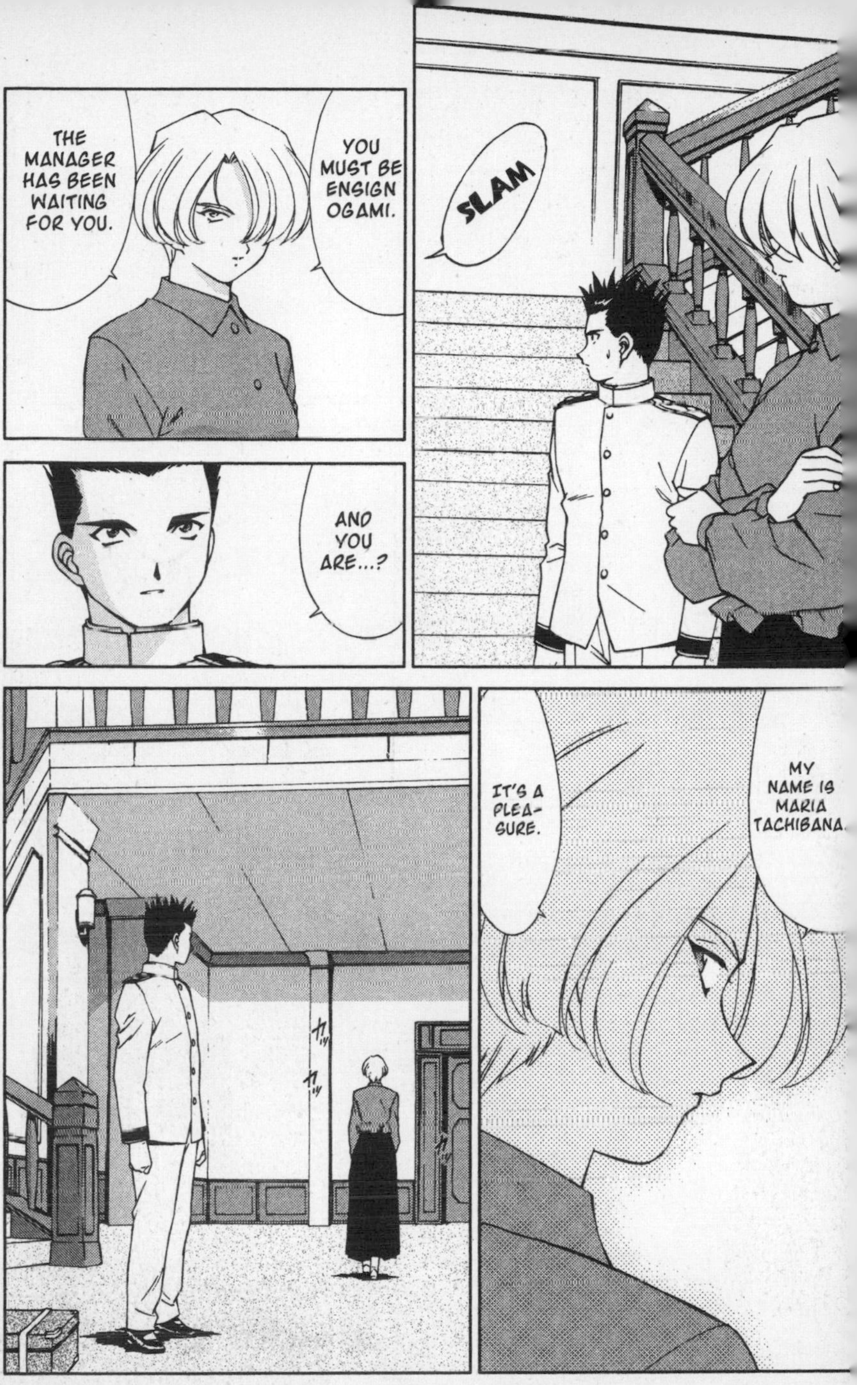
SLAM
YOU MUST BE ENSIGN OGAMI.
THE MANAGER HAS BEEN WAITING FOR YOU.
AND YOU ARE...?
MY NAME IS MARIA TACHIBANA.
IT'S A PLEASURE.

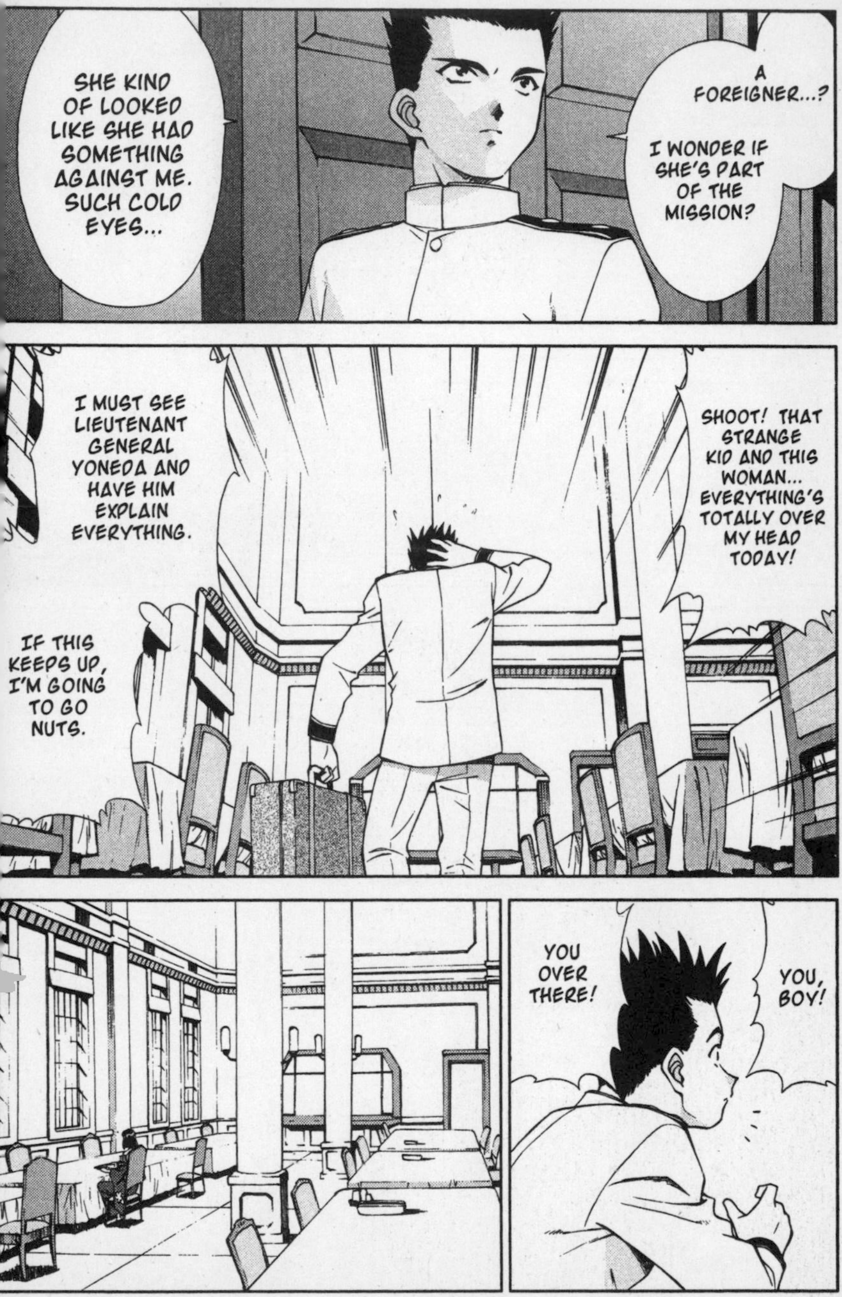
A FOREIGNER...?
I WONDER IF SHE'S PART OF THE MISSION?
SHE KIND OF LOOKED LIKE SHE HAD SOMETHING AGAINST ME. SUCH COLD EYES...
SHOOT! THAT STRANGE KID AND THIS WOMAN... EVERYTHING'S TOTALLY OVER MY HEAD TODAY!
I MUST SEE LIEUTENANT GENERAL YONEDA AND HAVE HIM EXPLAIN EVERYTHING.
IF THIS KEEPS UP, I'M GOING TO GO NUTS.
YOU, BOY!
YOU OVER THERE!

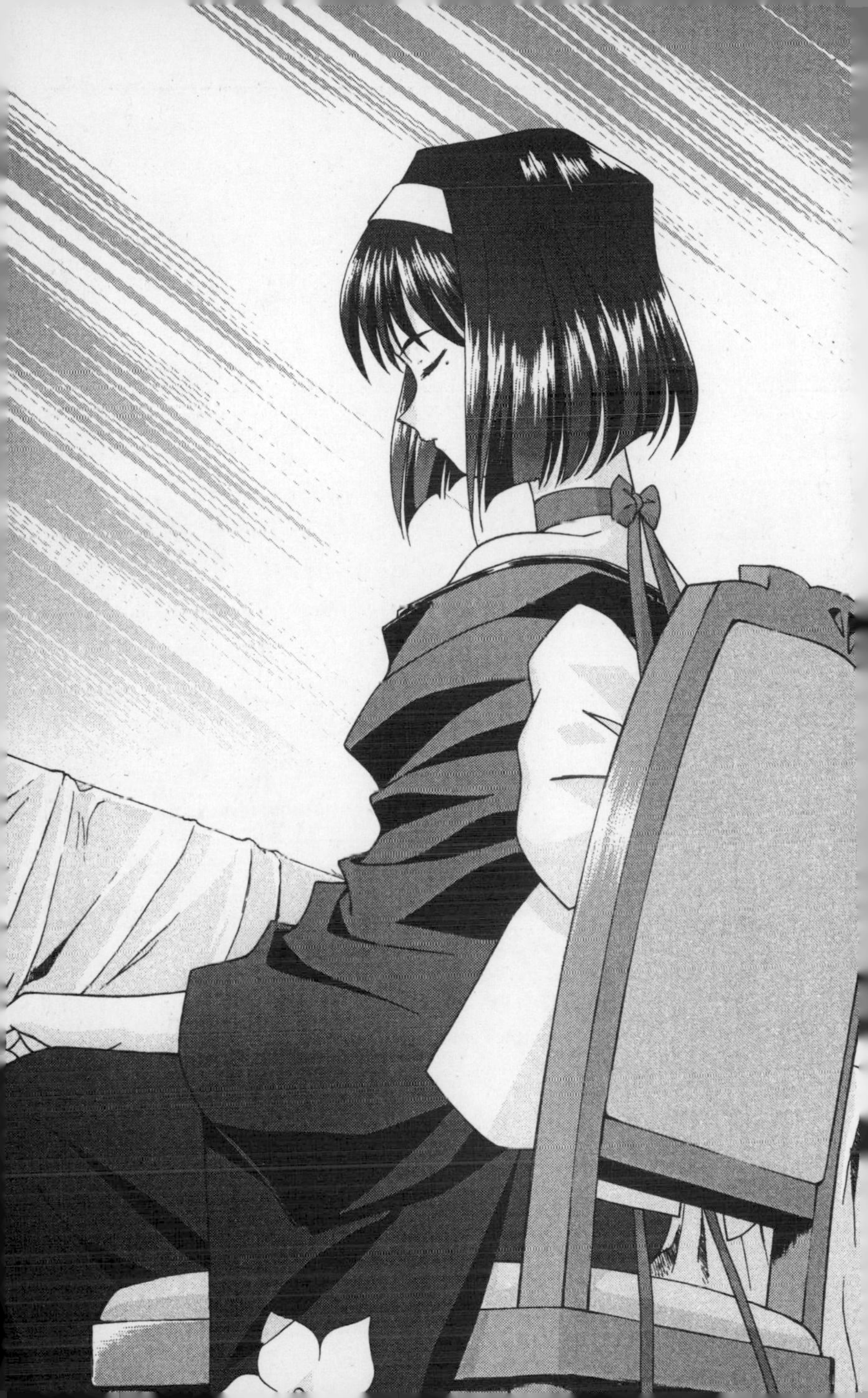

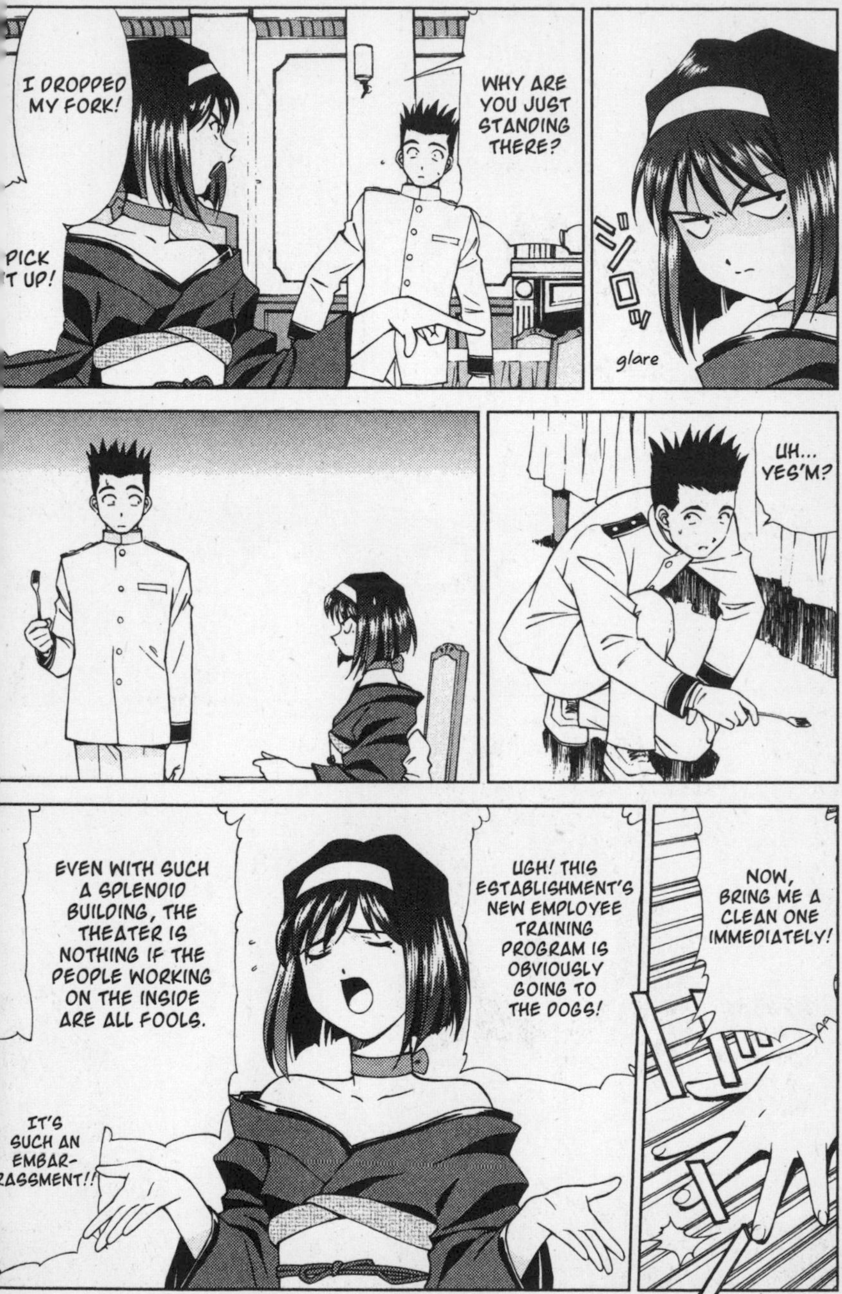
glare
WHY ARE YOU JUST STANDING THERE?
I DROPPED MY FORK!
PICK T UP!
UH... YES'M?
NOW, BRING ME A CLEAN ONE IMMEDIATELY!
UGH! THIS ESTABLISHMENT'S NEW EMPLOYEE TRAINING PROGRAM IS OBVIOUSLY GOING TO THE DOGS!
EVEN WITH SUCH A SPLENDID BUILDING, THE THEATER IS NOTHING IF THE PEOPLE WORKING ON THE INSIDE ARE ALL FOOLS.
IT'S SUCH AN EMBAR-RASSMENT!!

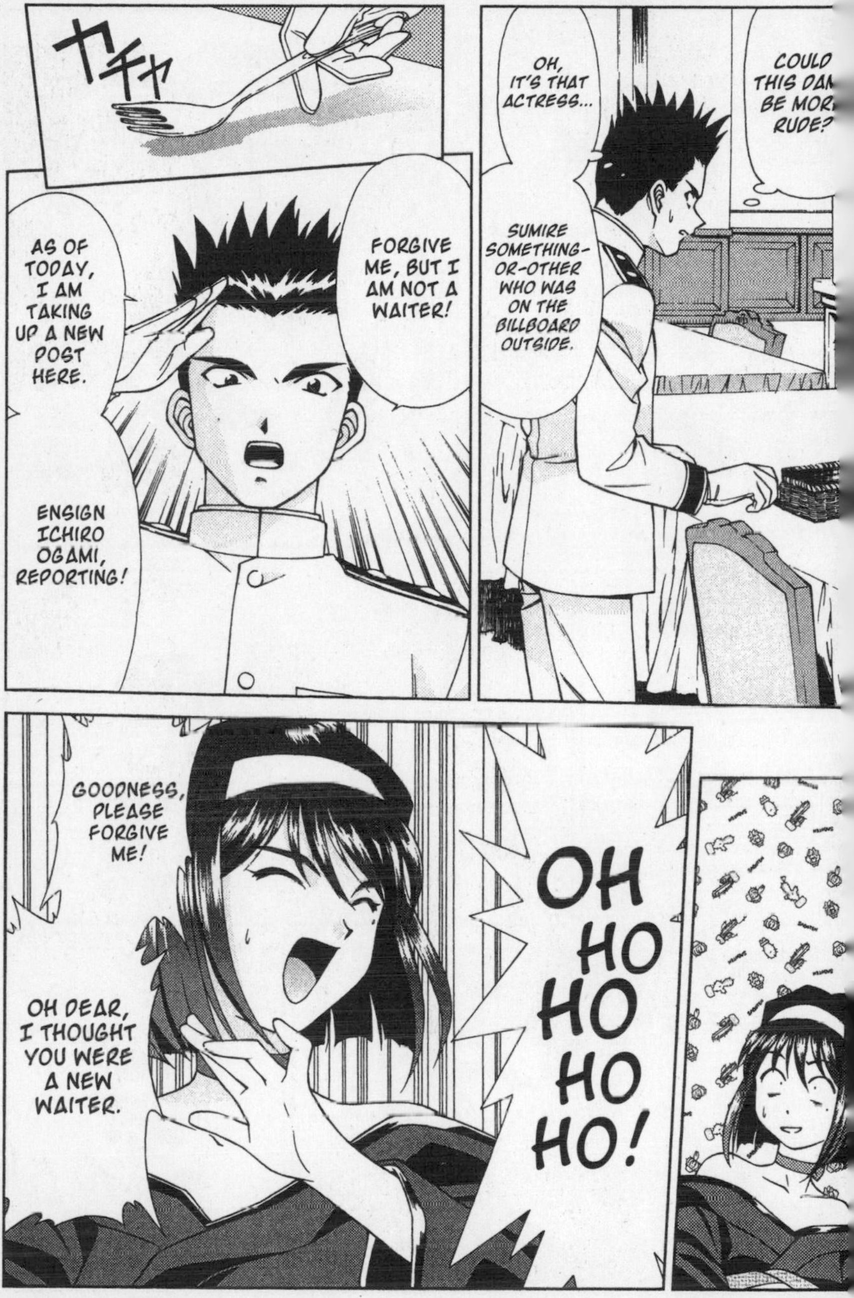
COULD THIS DAM BE MOR RUDE?
OH, IT'S THAT ACTRESS...
SUMIRE SOMETHING-OR-OTHER WHO WAS ON THE BILLBOARD OUTSIDE.
ヤチャ
FORGIVE ME, BUT I AM NOT A WAITER!
AS OF TODAY, I AM TAKING UP A NEW POST HERE.
ENSIGN ICHIRO OGAMI, REPORTING!
OH HO HO HO HO HO!
GOODNESS, PLEASE FORGIVE ME!
OH DEAR, I THOUGHT YOU WERE A NEW WAITER.

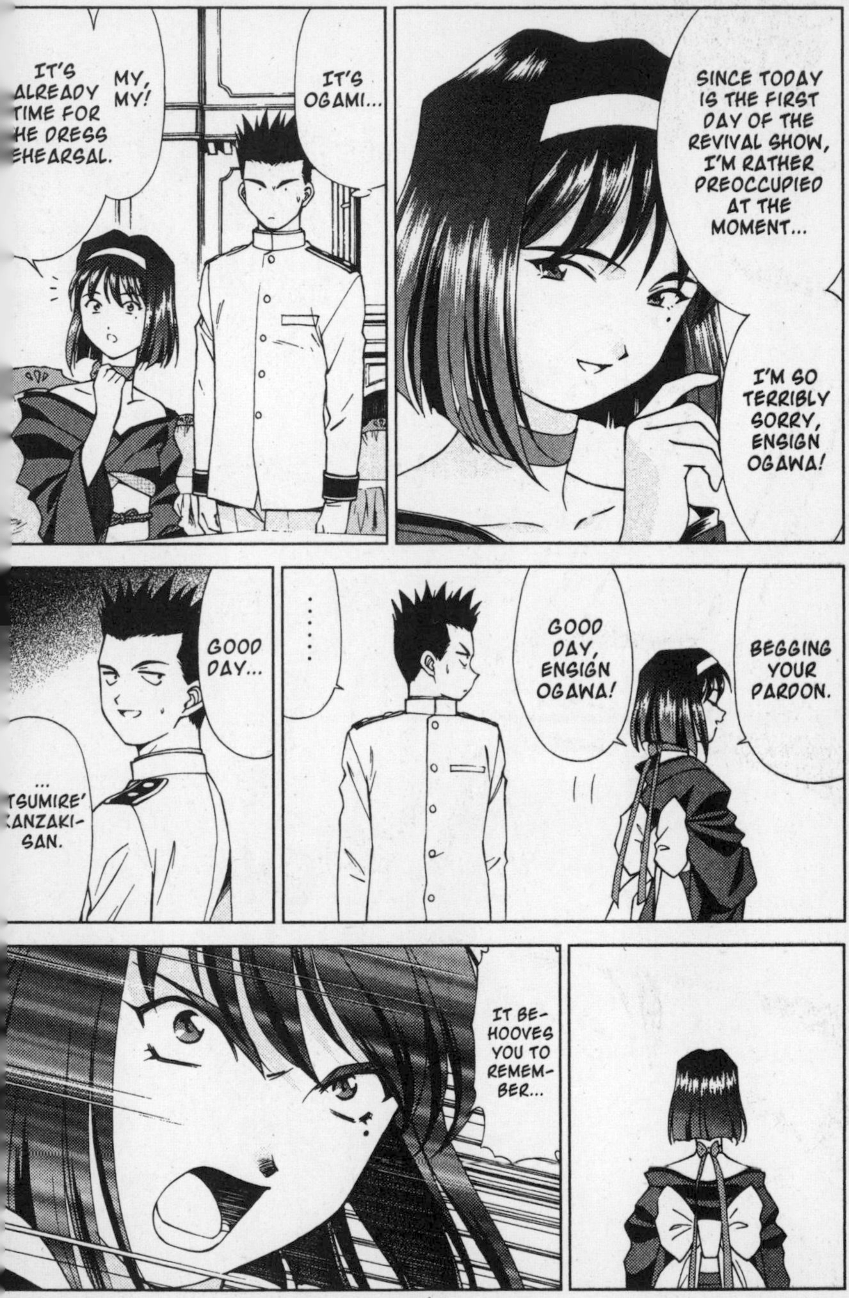

SINCE TODAY IS THE FIRST DAY OF THE REVIVAL SHOW, I'M RATHER PREOCCUPIED AT THE MOMENT...
I'M SO TERRIBLY SORRY, ENSIGN OGAWA!
IT'S OGAMI...
MY, MY!
IT'S ALREADY TIME FOR HE DRESS EHEARSAL.
BEGGING YOUR PARDON.
GOOD DAY, ENSIGN OGAWA!
......
GOOD DAY...
... TSUMIRE' ANZAKI-SAN.
IT BE-HOOVES YOU TO REMEM-BER...

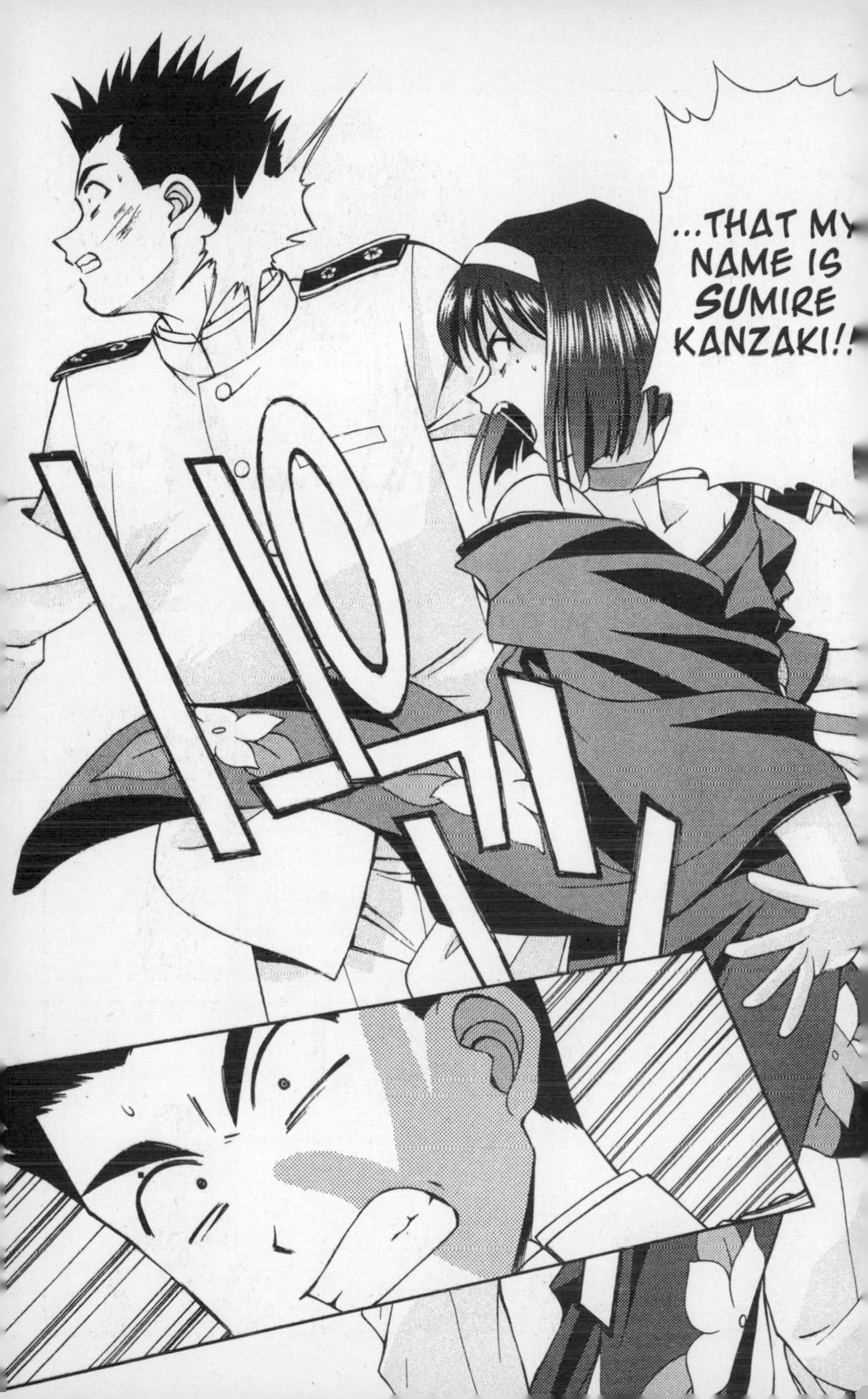
...THAT MY NAME IS SUMIRE KANZAKI!!

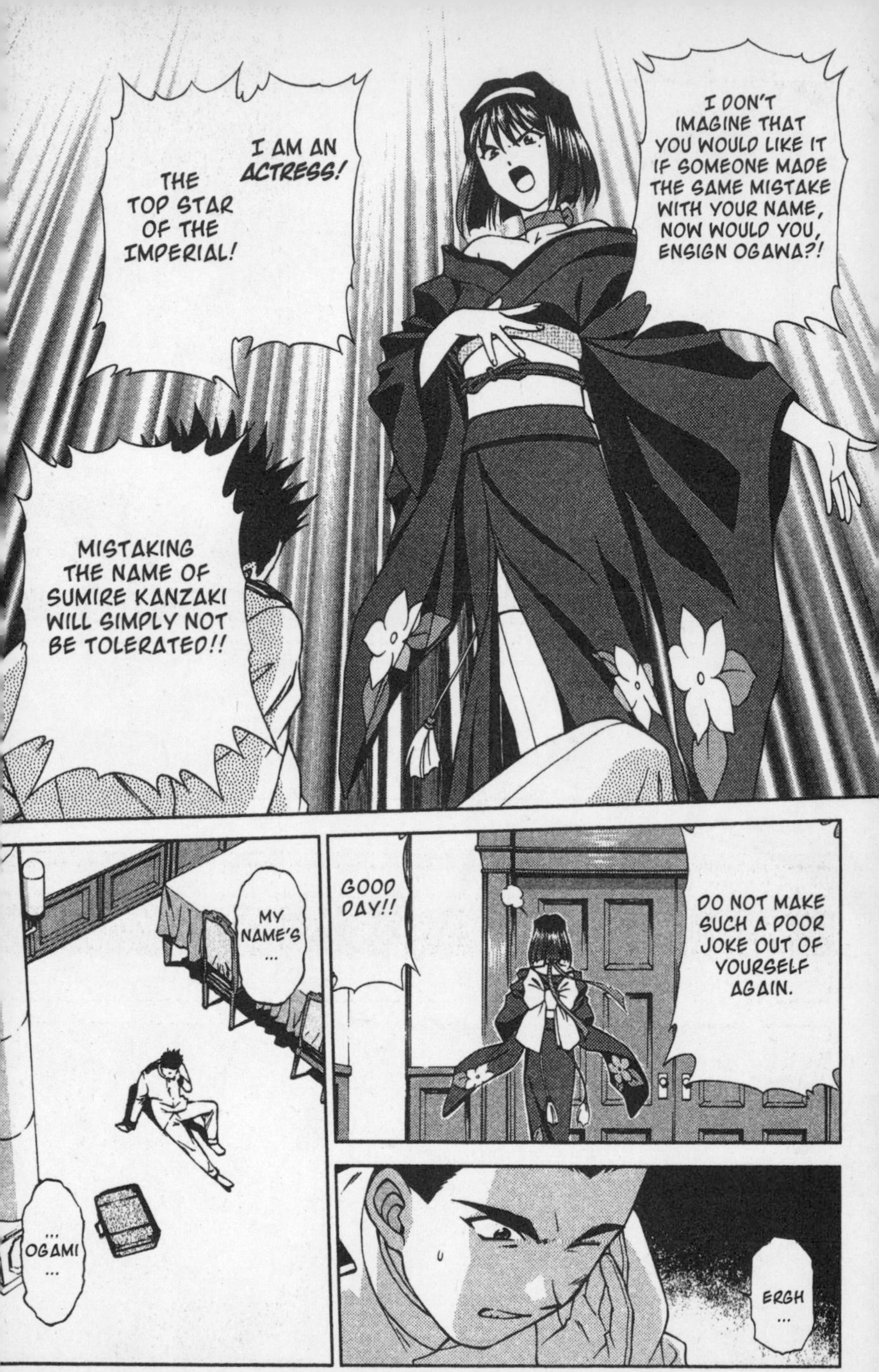
I DON'T IMAGINE THAT YOU WOULD LIKE IT IF SOMEONE MADE THE SAME MISTAKE WITH YOUR NAME, NOW WOULD YOU, ENSIGN OGAWA?!
I AM AN ACTRESS!
THE TOP STAR OF THE IMPERIAL!
MISTAKING THE NAME OF SUMIRE KANZAKI WILL SIMPLY NOT BE TOLERATED!!
DO NOT MAKE SUCH A POOR JOKE OUT OF YOURSELF AGAIN.
GOOD DAY!!
ERGH ...
MY NAME'S ...
... OGAMI ...

RUMBLE

RUMBLE

RUMBLE

Manager's Office

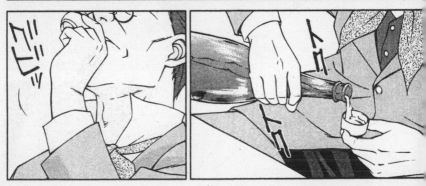

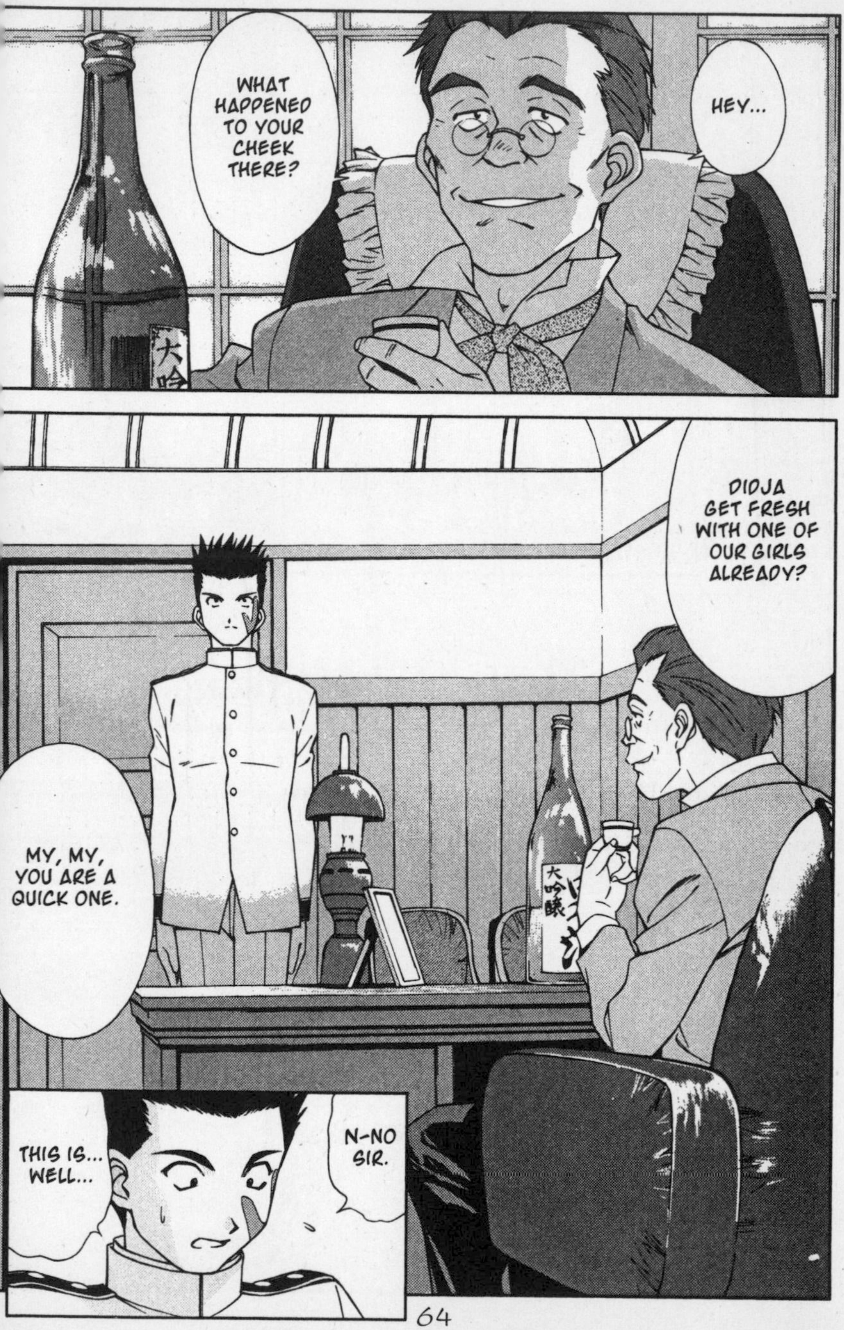
HEY...
WHAT HAPPENED TO YOUR CHEEK THERE?
大吟
DIDJA GET FRESH WITH ONE OF OUR GIRLS ALREADY?
MY, MY, YOU ARE A QUICK ONE.
大吟醸
N-NO SIR.
THIS IS... WELL...

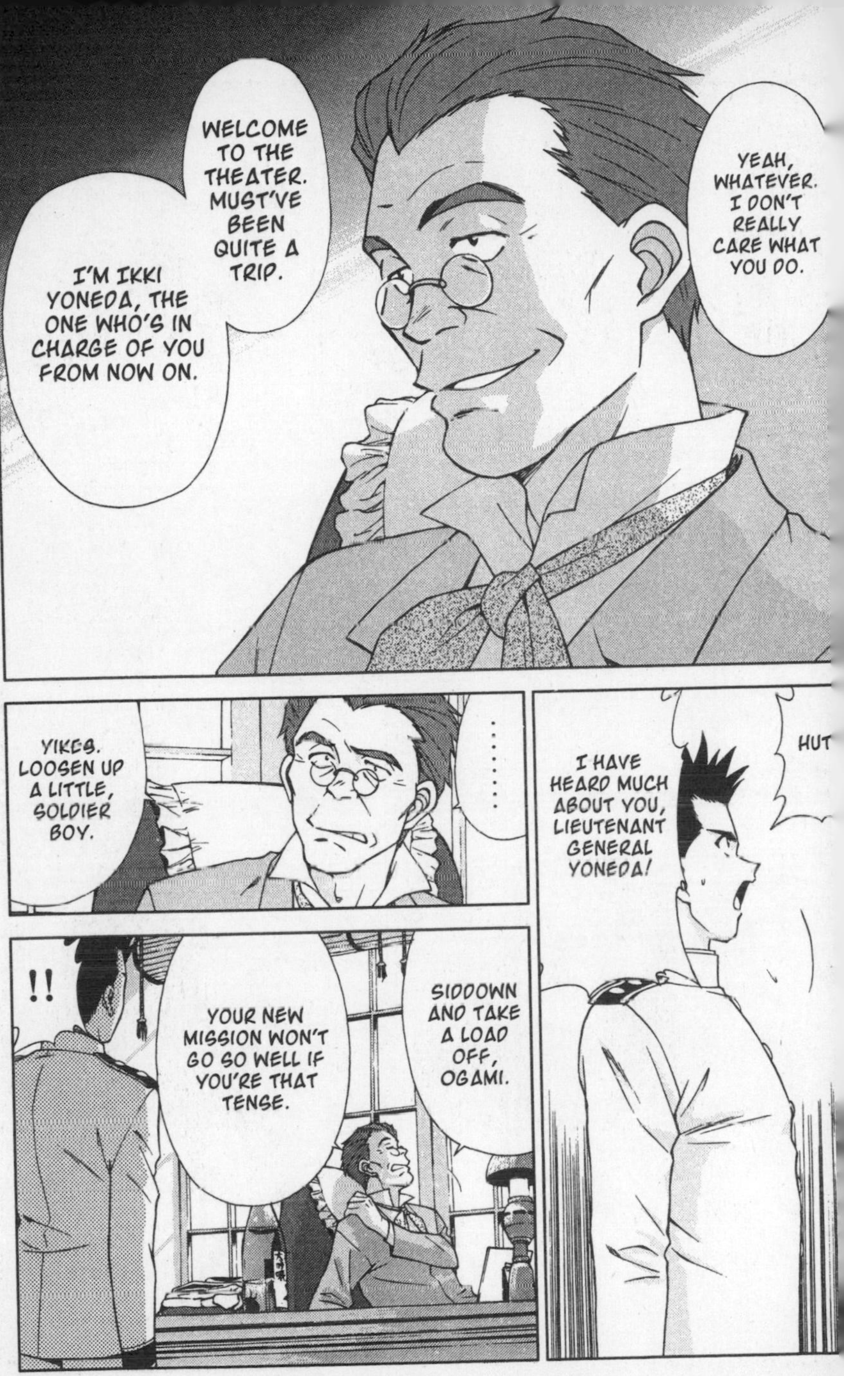
YEAH, WHATEVER. I DON'T REALLY CARE WHAT YOU DO.
WELCOME TO THE THEATER. MUST'VE BEEN QUITE A TRIP.
I'M IKKI YONEDA, THE ONE WHO'S IN CHARGE OF YOU FROM NOW ON.
HUT
I HAVE HEARD MUCH ABOUT YOU, LIEUTENANT GENERAL YONEDA!
......
YIKES. LOOSEN UP A LITTLE, SOLDIER BOY.
SIDDOWN AND TAKE A LOAD OFF, OGAMI.
YOUR NEW MISSION WON'T GO SO WELL IF YOU'RE THAT TENSE.
!!

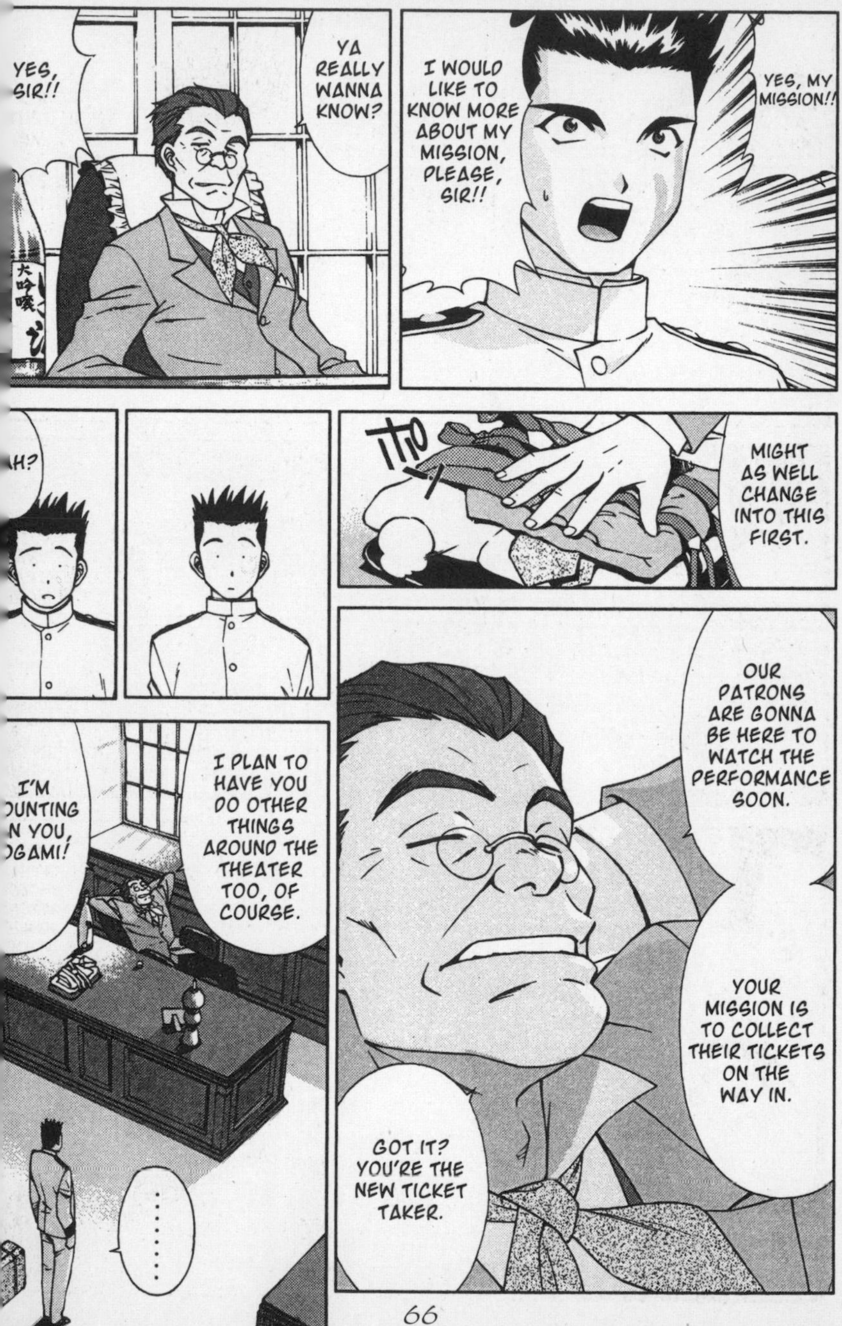
YES, MY MISSION!!
I WOULD LIKE TO KNOW MORE ABOUT MY MISSION, PLEASE, SIR!!
YA REALLY WANNA KNOW?
YES, SIR!!
MIGHT AS WELL CHANGE INTO THIS FIRST.
AH?
OUR PATRONS ARE GONNA BE HERE TO WATCH THE PERFORMANCE SOON.
YOUR MISSION IS TO COLLECT THEIR TICKETS ON THE WAY IN.
GOT IT? YOU'RE THE NEW TICKET TAKER.
I PLAN TO HAVE YOU DO OTHER THINGS AROUND THE THEATER TOO, OF COURSE.
I'M OUNTING N YOU, OGAMI!
......

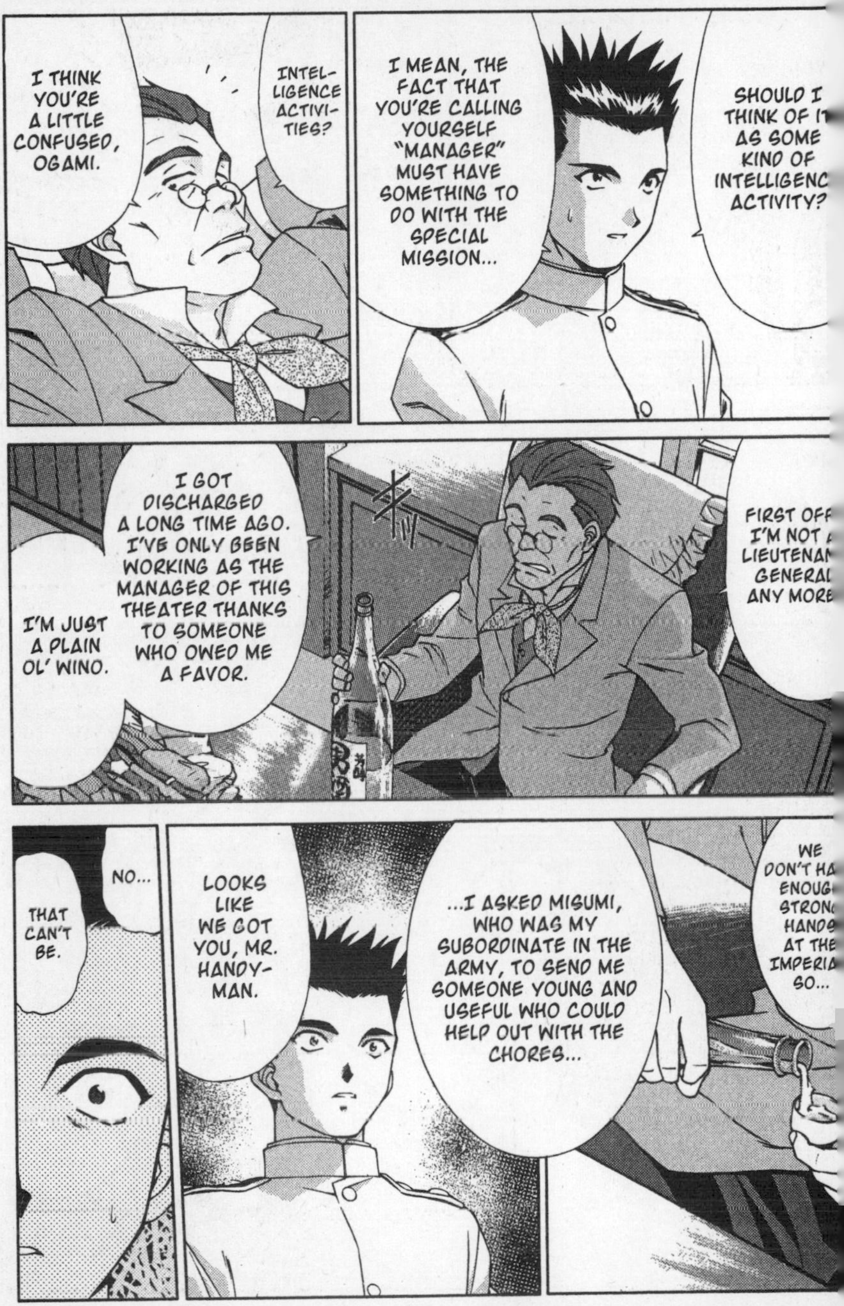
SHOULD I THINK OF IT AS SOME KIND OF INTELLIGENC ACTIVITY?
I MEAN, THE FACT THAT YOU'RE CALLING YOURSELF "MANAGER" MUST HAVE SOMETHING TO DO WITH THE SPECIAL MISSION...
INTEL-LIGENCE ACTIVI-TIES?
I THINK YOU'RE A LITTLE CONFUSED, OGAMI.
FIRST OFF I'M NOT A LIEUTENAN GENERAL ANY MORE
I GOT DISCHARGED A LONG TIME AGO. I'VE ONLY BEEN WORKING AS THE MANAGER OF THIS THEATER THANKS TO SOMEONE WHO OWED ME A FAVOR.
I'M JUST A PLAIN OL' WINO.
WE DON'T HA ENOUG STRON HANDS AT THE IMPERIA SO...
...I ASKED MISUMI, WHO WAS MY SUBORDINATE IN THE ARMY, TO SEND ME SOMEONE YOUNG AND USEFUL WHO COULD HELP OUT WITH THE CHORES...
LOOKS LIKE WE GOT YOU, MR. HANDY-MAN.
NO...
THAT CAN'T BE.

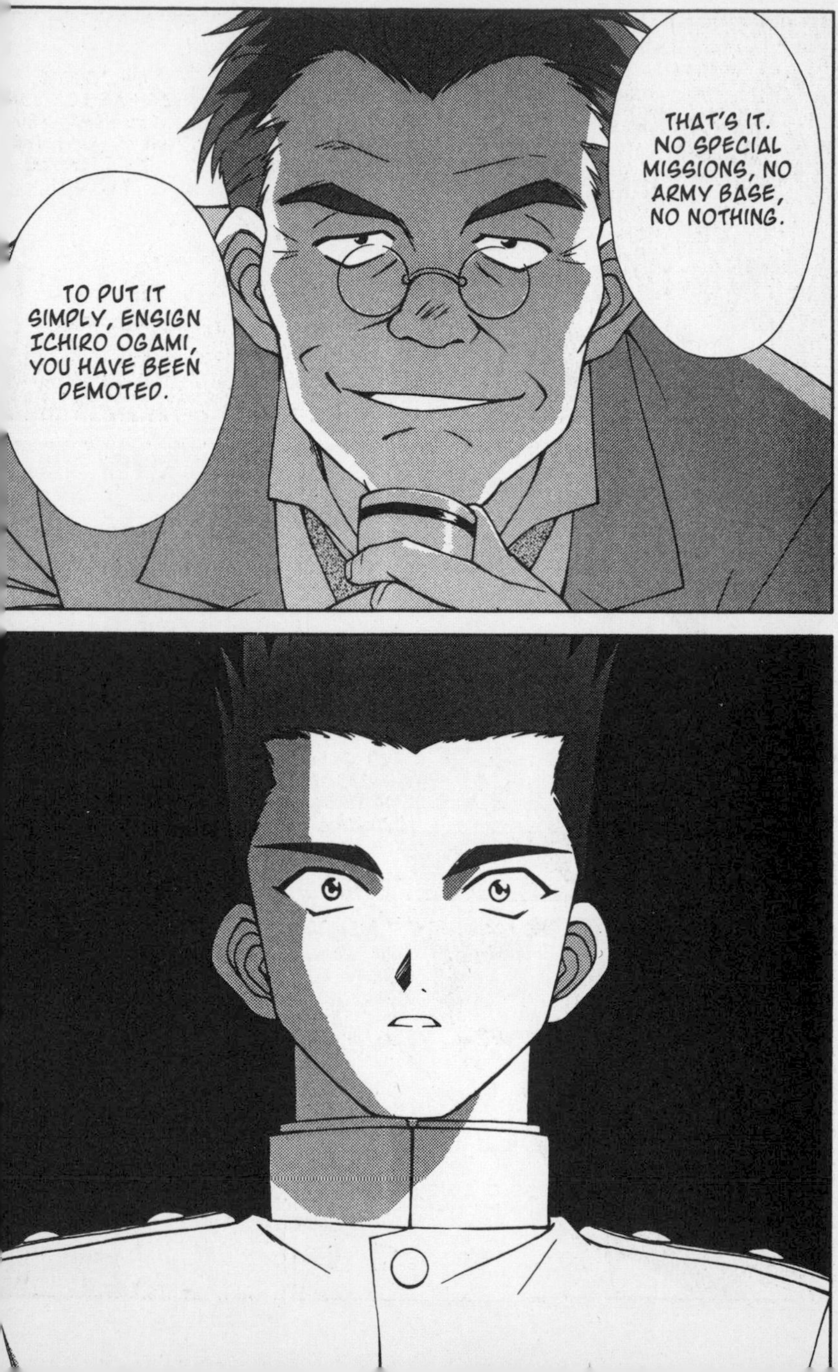
TO PUT IT SIMPLY, ENSIGN ICHIRO OGAMI, YOU HAVE BEEN DEMOTED.
THAT'S IT. NO SPECIAL MISSIONS, NO ARMY BASE, NO NOTHING.

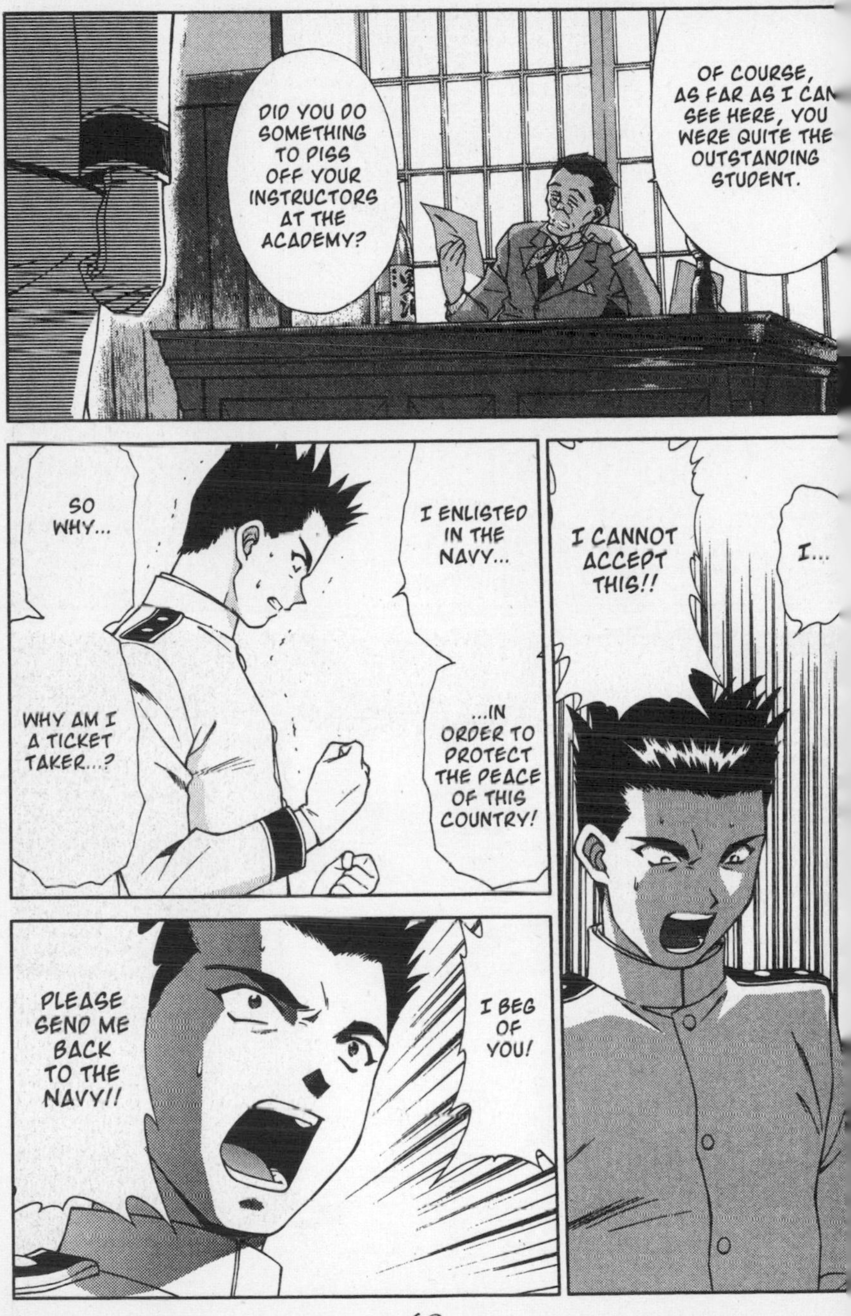
DID YOU DO SOMETHING TO PISS OFF YOUR INSTRUCTORS AT THE ACADEMY?
OF COURSE, AS FAR AS I CAN SEE HERE, YOU WERE QUITE THE OUTSTANDING STUDENT.
SO WHY...
WHY AM I A TICKET TAKER...?
I ENLISTED IN THE NAVY...
...IN ORDER TO PROTECT THE PEACE OF THIS COUNTRY!
I CANNOT ACCEPT THIS!!
I...
PLEASE SEND ME BACK TO THE NAVY!!
I BEG OF YOU!

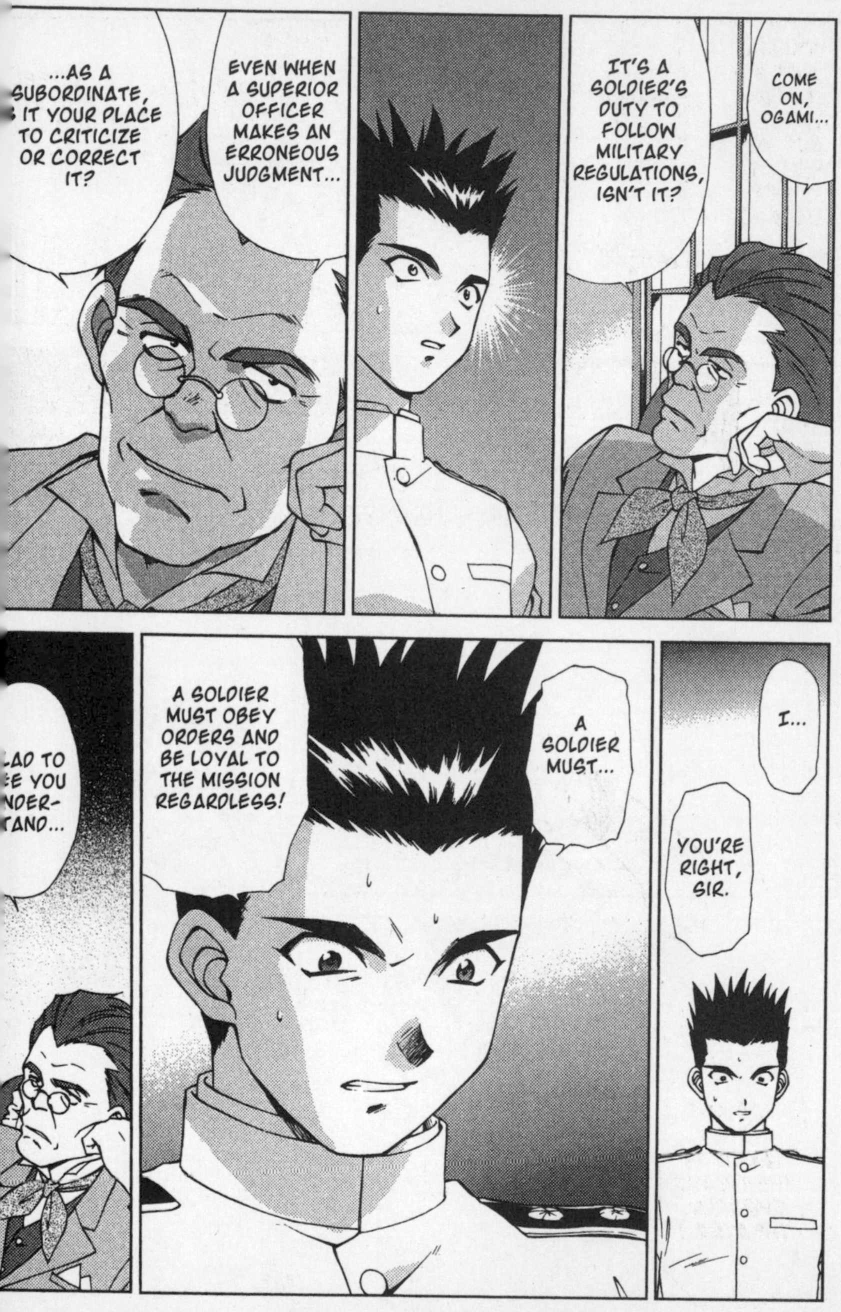
COME ON, OGAMI...
IT'S A SOLDIER'S DUTY TO FOLLOW MILITARY REGULATIONS, ISN'T IT?
EVEN WHEN A SUPERIOR OFFICER MAKES AN ERRONEOUS JUDGMENT...
...AS A SUBORDINATE, S IT YOUR PLACE TO CRITICIZE OR CORRECT IT?
I...
YOU'RE RIGHT, SIR.
A SOLDIER MUST...
A SOLDIER MUST OBEY ORDERS AND BE LOYAL TO THE MISSION REGARDLESS!
LAD TO EE YOU NDER- TAND...

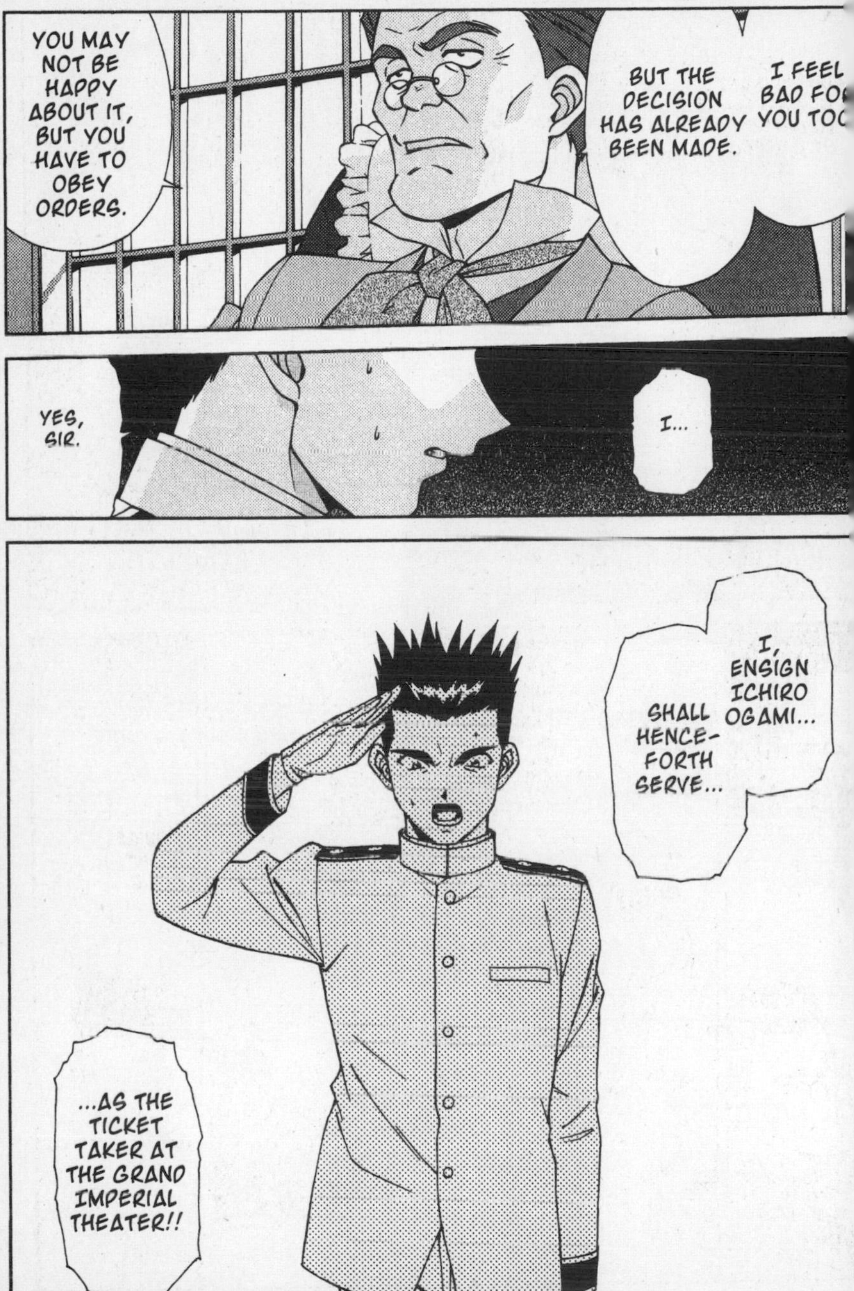

I FEEL BAD FO YOU TO
BUT THE DECISION HAS ALREADY BEEN MADE.
YOU MAY NOT BE HAPPY ABOUT IT, BUT YOU HAVE TO OBEY ORDERS.
I...
YES, SIR.
I, ENSIGN ICHIRO OGAMI...
SHALL HENCE-FORTH SERVE...
...AS THE TICKET TAKER AT THE GRAND IMPERIAL THEATER!!

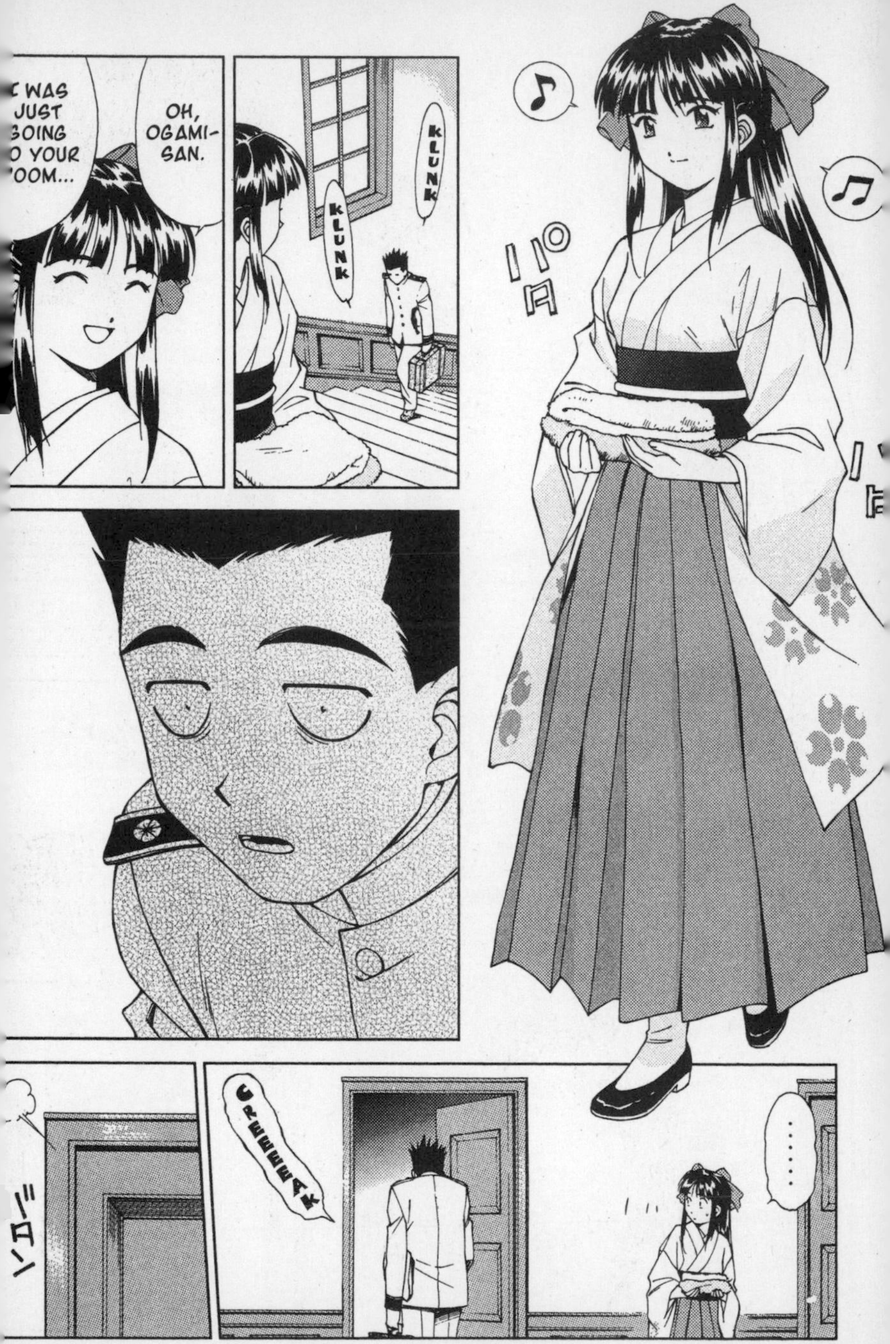
KLUNK
KLUNK
OH, OGAMI-SAN.
WAS JUST GOING O YOUR OOM...
CREEEEAK
......

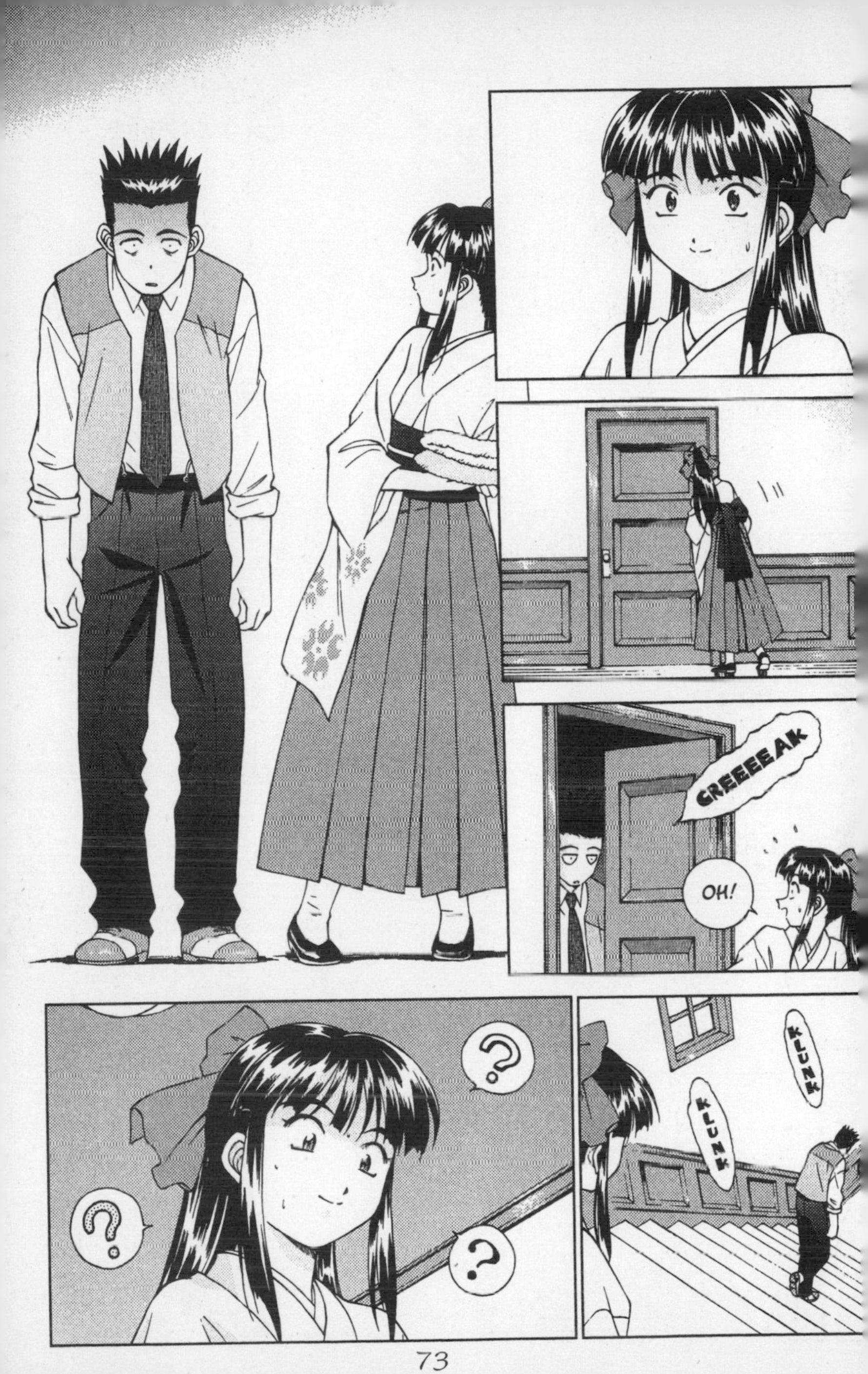
GREEEEAK
OH!
KLUNK
KLUNK
?
?
?

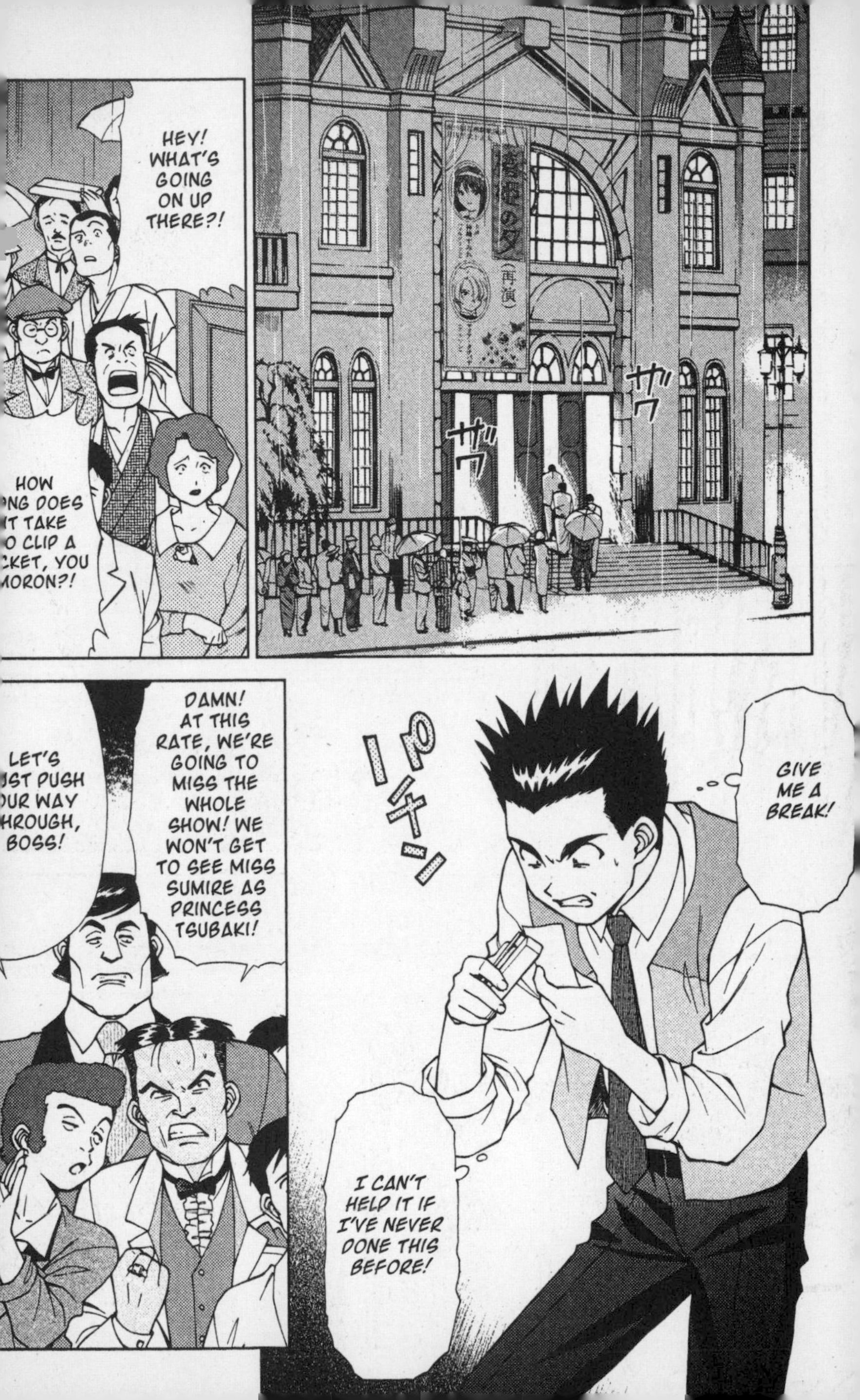
ザワ
ザワ
HEY! WHAT'S GOING ON UP THERE?!
HOW
ONG DOES
T TAKE
O CLIP A
CKET, YOU
MORON?!
GIVE ME A BREAK!
I CAN'T HELP IT IF I'VE NEVER DONE THIS BEFORE!
DAMN! AT THIS RATE, WE'RE GOING TO MISS THE WHOLE SHOW! WE WON'T GET TO SEE MISS SUMIRE AS PRINCESS TSUBAKI!
LET'S
UST PUSH
OUR WAY
HROUGH,
BOSS!

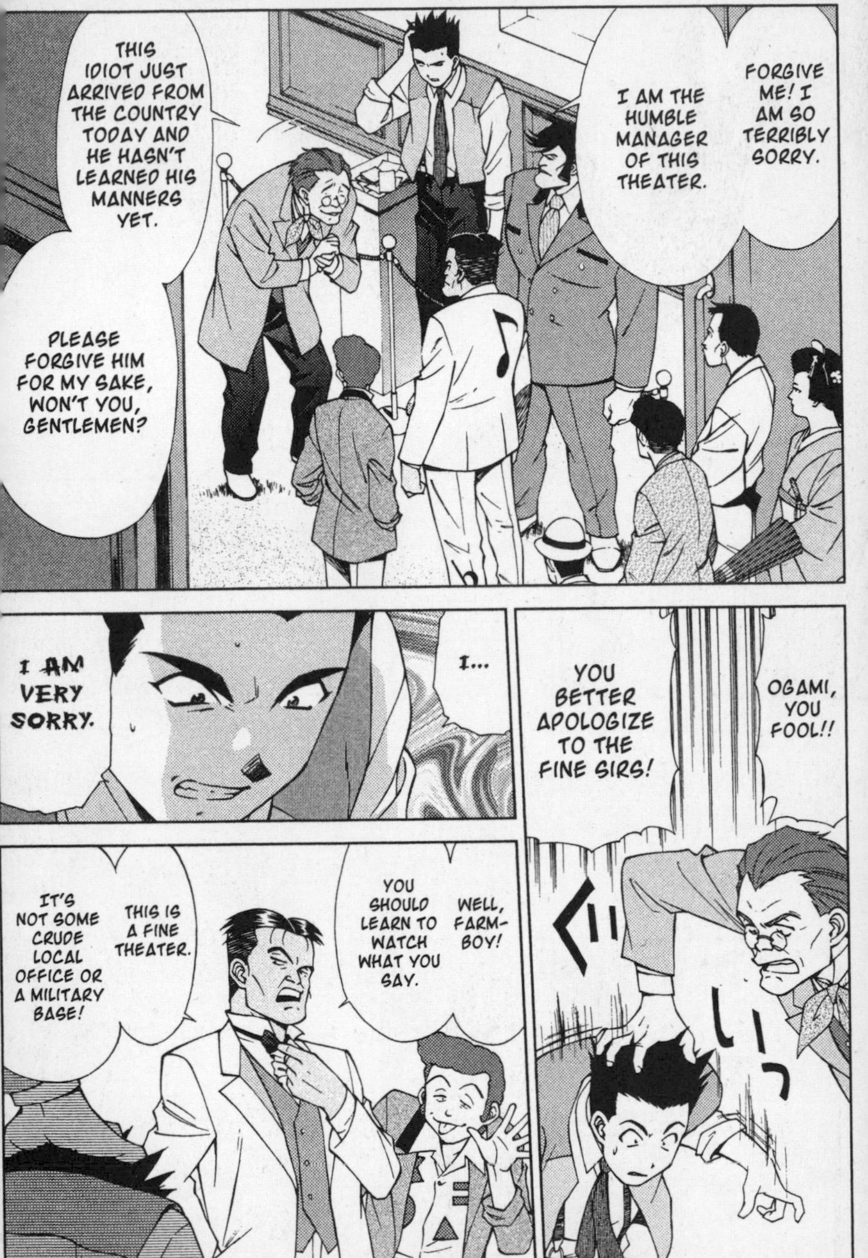
FORGIVE ME! I AM SO TERRIBLY SORRY.
I AM THE HUMBLE MANAGER OF THIS THEATER.
THIS IDIOT JUST ARRIVED FROM THE COUNTRY TODAY AND HE HASN'T LEARNED HIS MANNERS YET.
PLEASE FORGIVE HIM FOR MY SAKE, WON'T YOU, GENTLEMEN?
OGAMI, YOU FOOL!!
YOU BETTER APOLOGIZE TO THE FINE SIRS!
I...
I AM VERY SORRY.
WELL, FARM-BOY!
YOU SHOULD LEARN TO WATCH WHAT YOU SAY.
THIS IS A FINE THEATER.
IT'S NOT SOME CRUDE LOCAL OFFICE OR A MILITARY BASE!

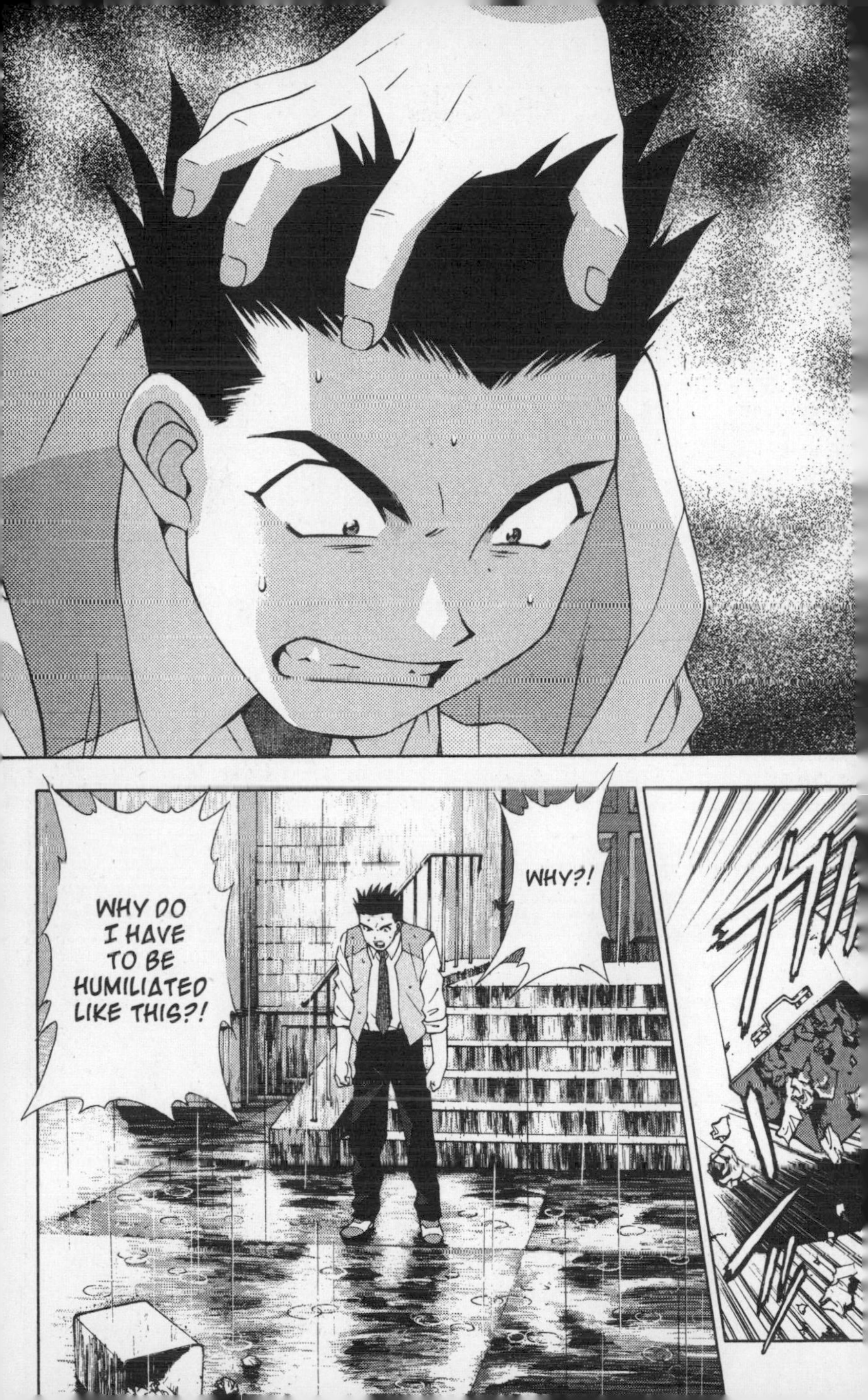
WHY?!
WHY DO I HAVE TO BE HUMILIATED LIKE THIS?!

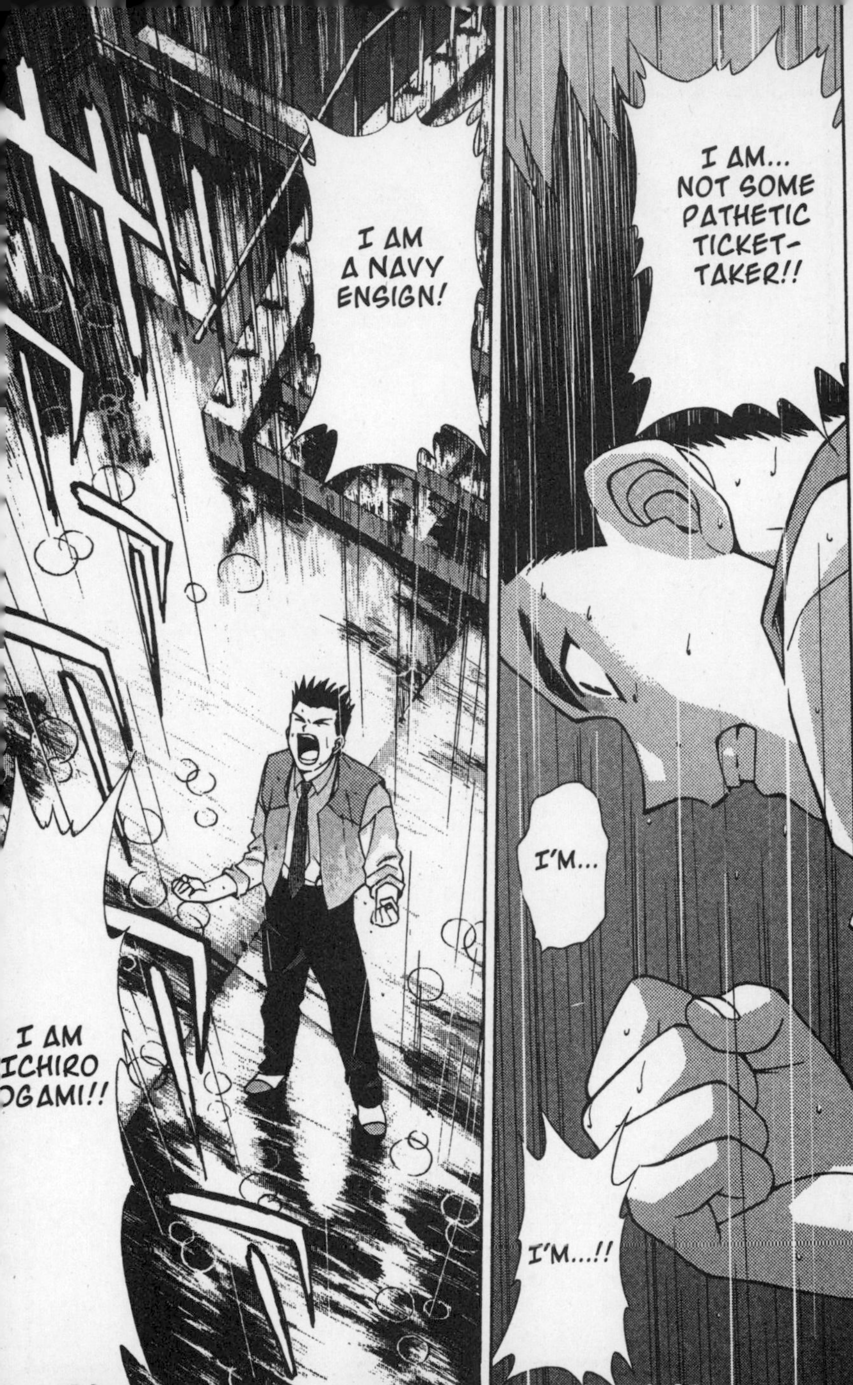
I AM... NOT SOME PATHETIC TICKET-TAKER!!
I'M...
I'M...!!
I AM A NAVY ENSIGN!
I AM ICHIRO OGAMI!!

Ogami Arrives at the Imperial Capital--End of Act

帝 国 華 撃 団

Imperial Fighting Troupe

Teikoku Kagekidan

T E I G E K I

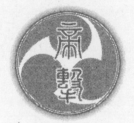

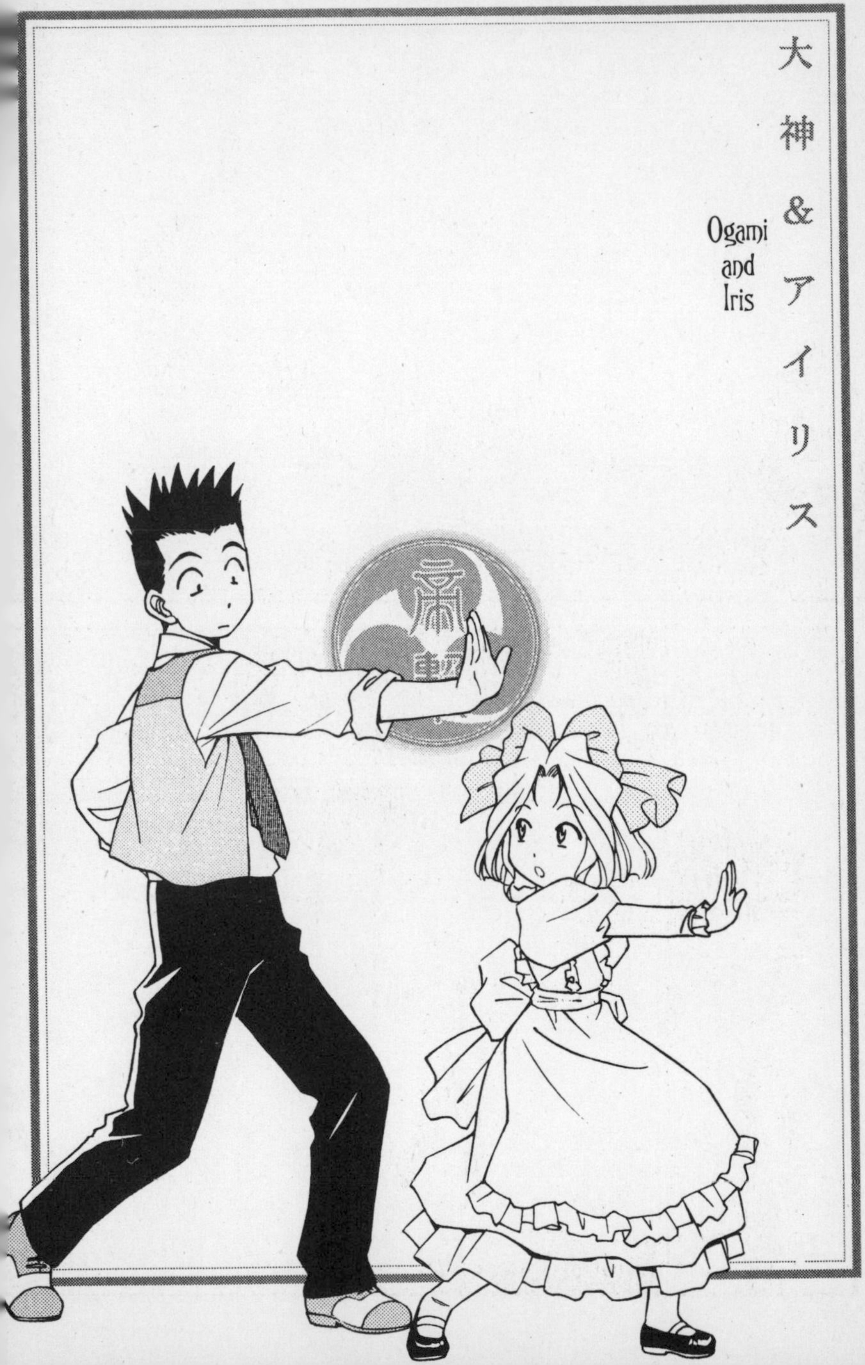
大神&アイリス
Ogami and Iris

Chapter Two–The Meaningless Busywork

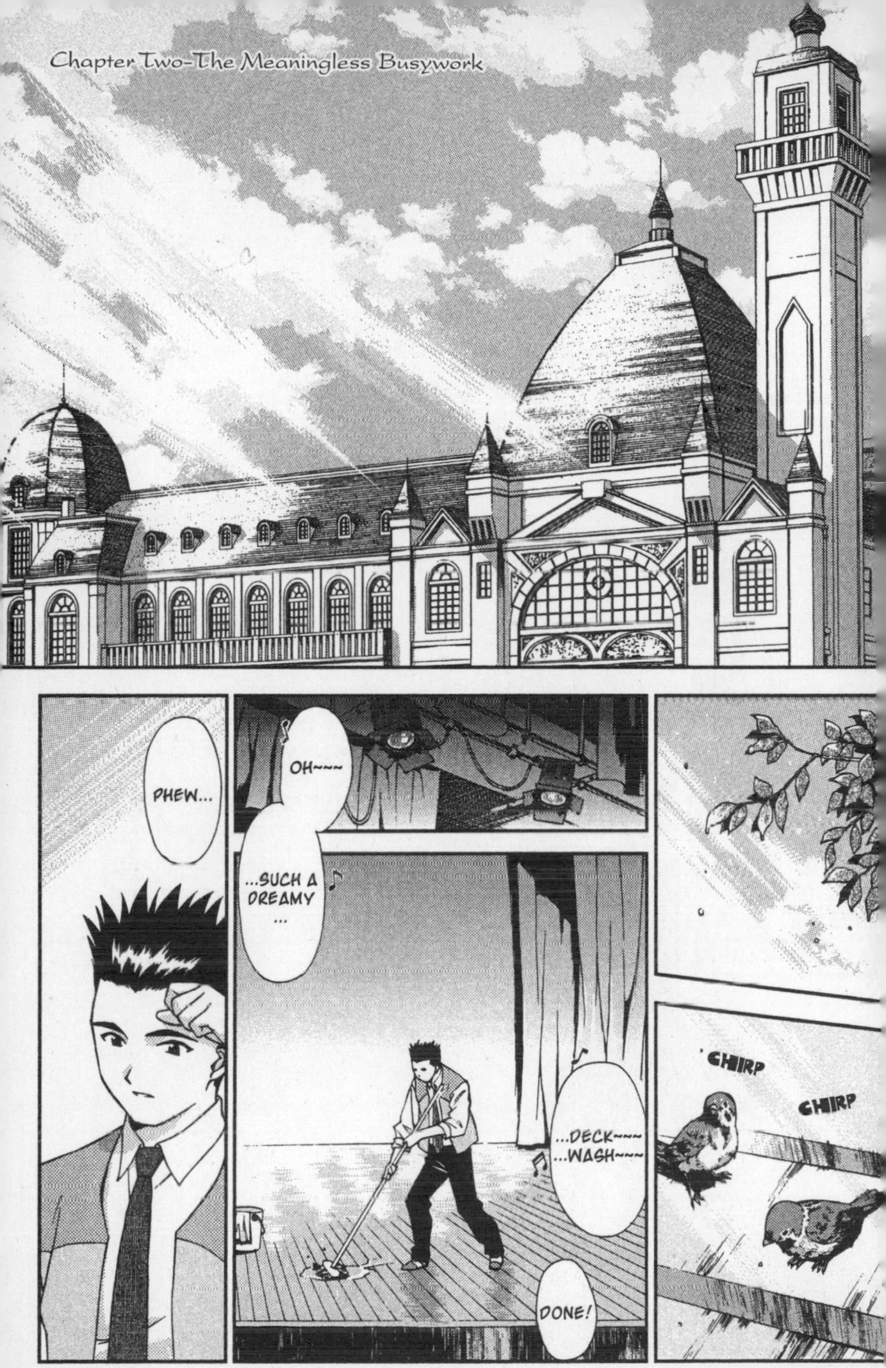
CHIRP
CHIRP
OH~~~
...SUCH A DREAMY ...
...DECK~~~ ...WASH~~~
DONE!
PHEW...

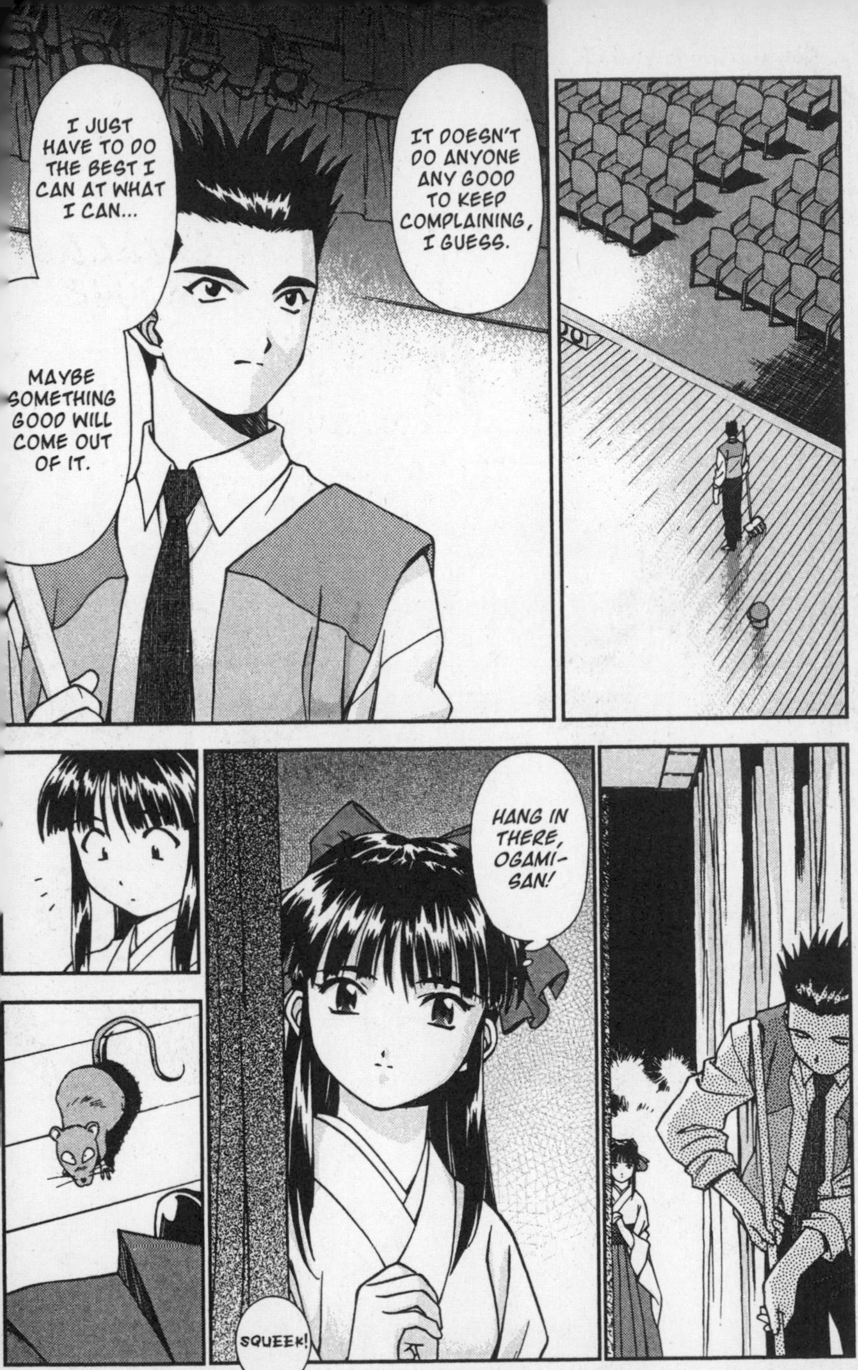
IT DOESN'T DO ANYONE ANY GOOD TO KEEP COMPLAINING, I GUESS.
I JUST HAVE TO DO THE BEST I CAN AT WHAT I CAN...
MAYBE SOMETHING GOOD WILL COME OUT OF IT.
HANG IN THERE, OGAMI-SAN!
SQUEEK!

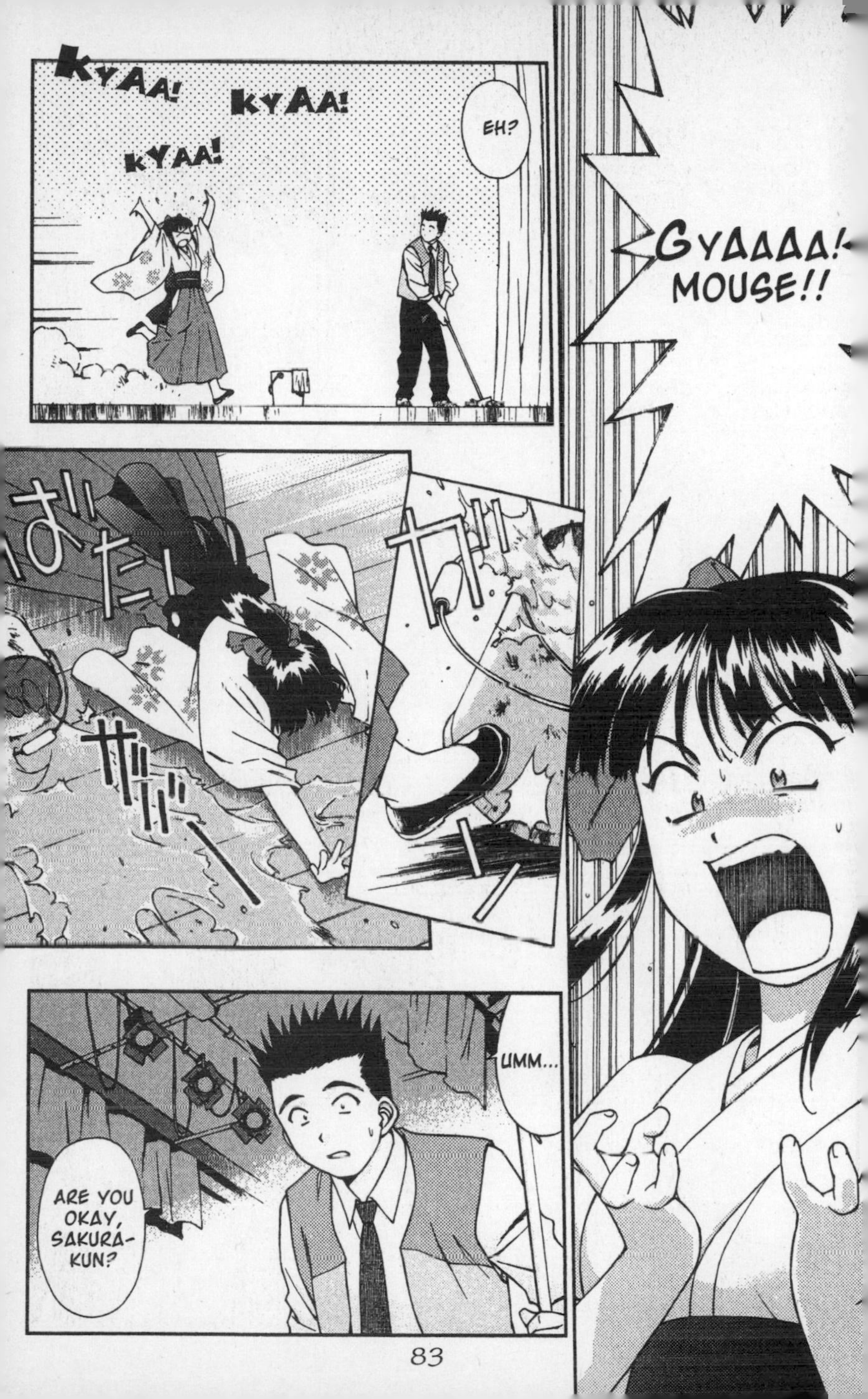
GYAAAA! MOUSE!!
KYAA! KYAA! KYAA!
EH?
UMM...
ARE YOU OKAY, SAKURA-KUN?

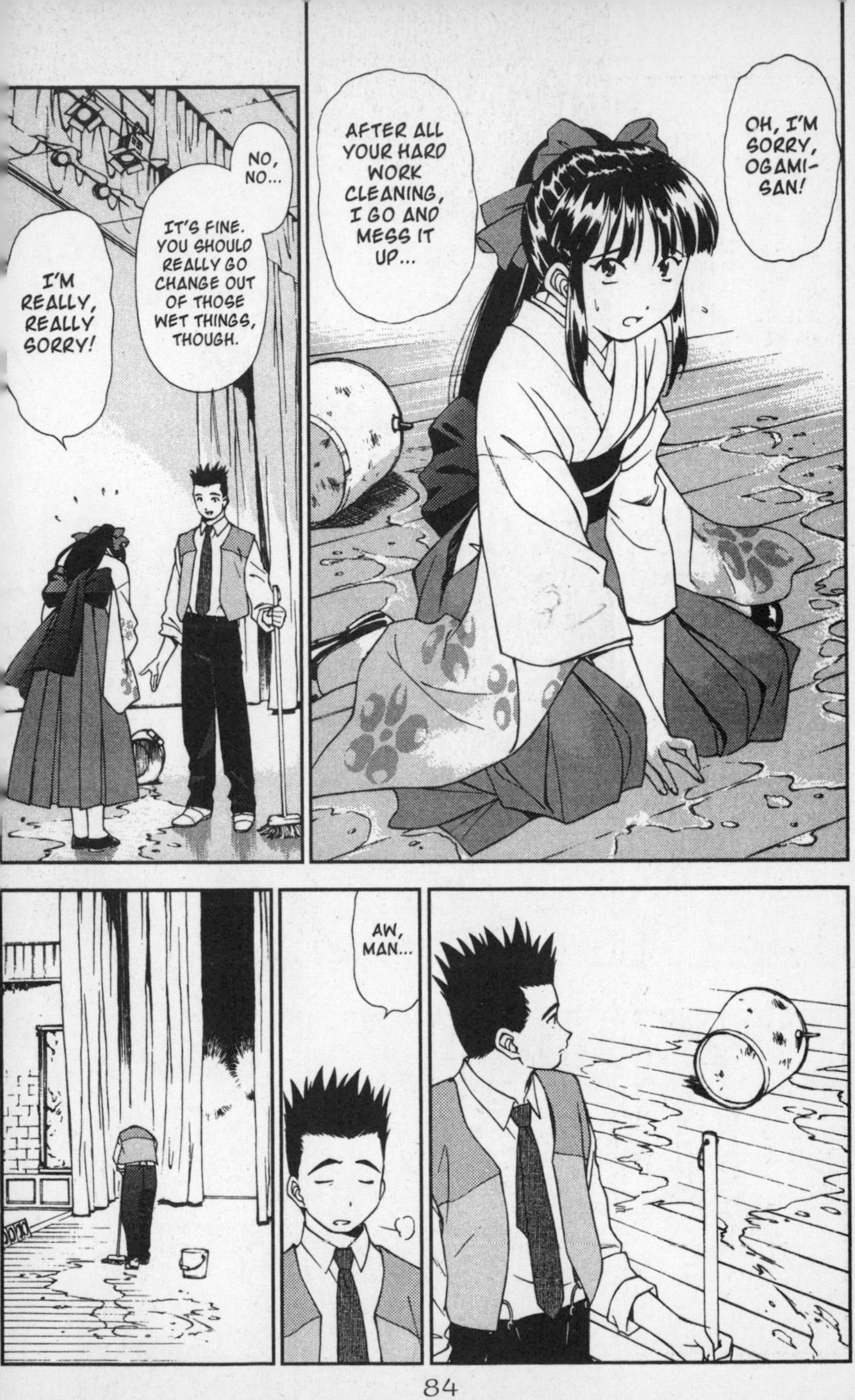
OH, I'M SORRY, OGAMI-SAN!
AFTER ALL YOUR HARD WORK CLEANING, I GO AND MESS IT UP...
NO, NO...
IT'S FINE. YOU SHOULD REALLY GO CHANGE OUT OF THOSE WET THINGS, THOUGH.
I'M REALLY, REALLY SORRY!
AW, MAN...

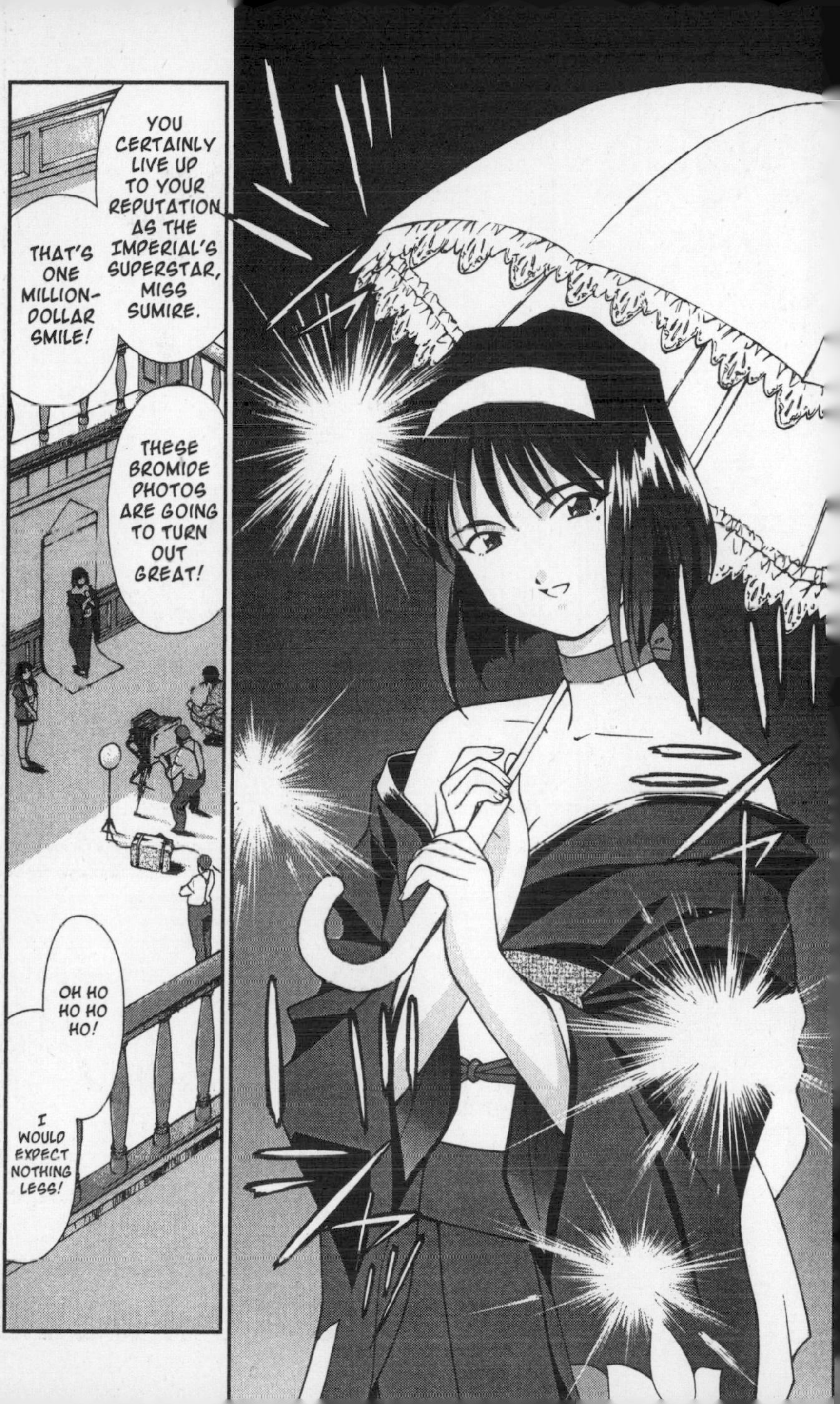
YOU CERTAINLY LIVE UP TO YOUR REPUTATION AS THE IMPERIAL'S SUPERSTAR, MISS SUMIRE.
THAT'S ONE MILLION-DOLLAR SMILE!
THESE BROMIDE PHOTOS ARE GOING TO TURN OUT GREAT!
OH HO HO HO HO!
I WOULD EXPECT NOTHING LESS!

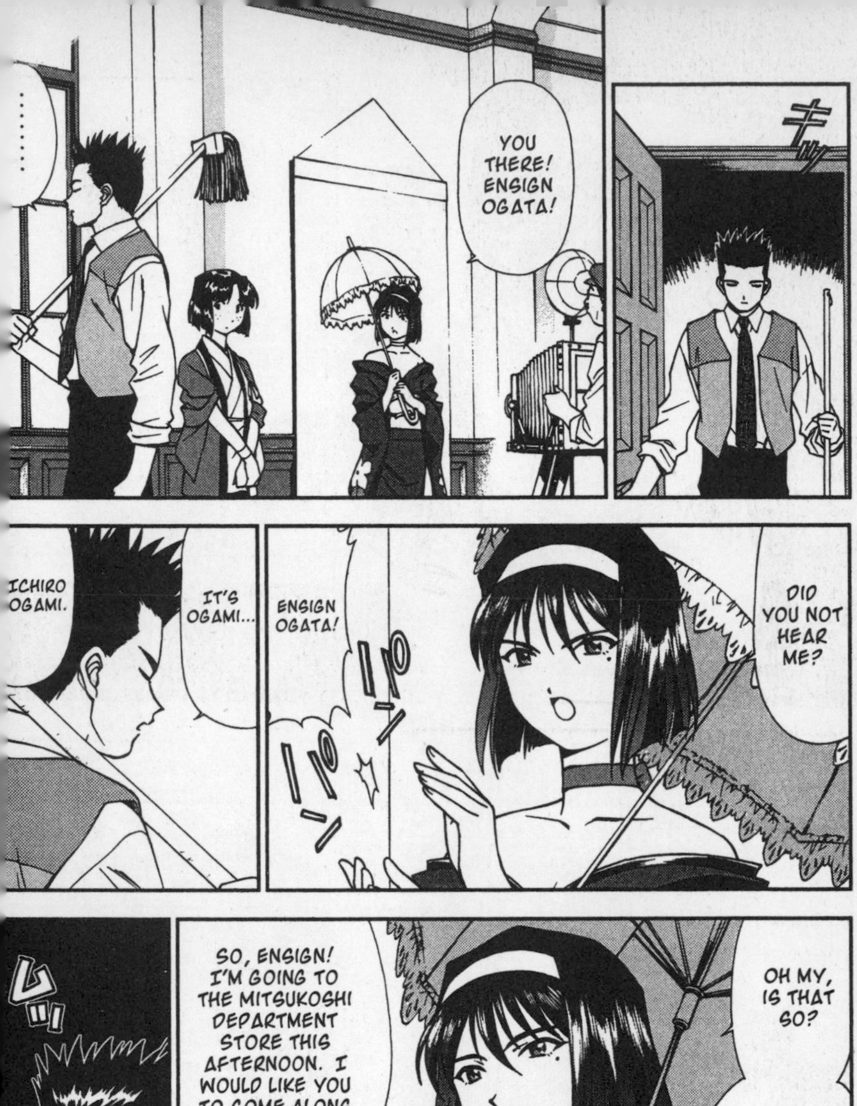

YOU THERE! ENSIGN OGATA!
......
DID YOU NOT HEAR ME?
ENSIGN OGATA!
IT'S OGAMI...
ICHIRO OGAMI.
OH MY, IS THAT SO?
FINE. FROM NOW ON, I SHALL SIMPLY CALL YOU "ENSIGN" TO AVOID ANY CONFUSION, THEN!
SO, ENSIGN! I'M GOING TO THE MITSUKOSHI DEPARTMENT STORE THIS AFTERNOON. I WOULD LIKE YOU TO COME ALONG TO CARRY MY THINGS.

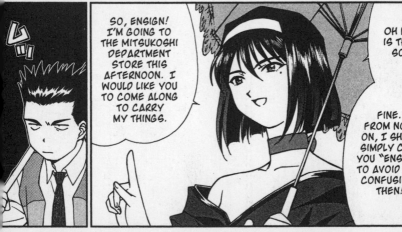

HOW DARE YOU!!

I AM NOT YOUR SERVANT!

I DECLINE

WHA--

I JUST HAVE A HARD TIME DEALING WITH HER.

S-SORRY.

YOU HAVE TO BE MORE POLITE TO SUMIRE-SAN! SHE'S THE STAR OF THE IMPERIAL!

COME ON, OGAMI-SAN!

OH HO HO HO!

OH MY!

ALL RIGHT...

WHEN SUMIRE-SAN GETS UPSET, WE ALL SUFFER, YOU KNOW!

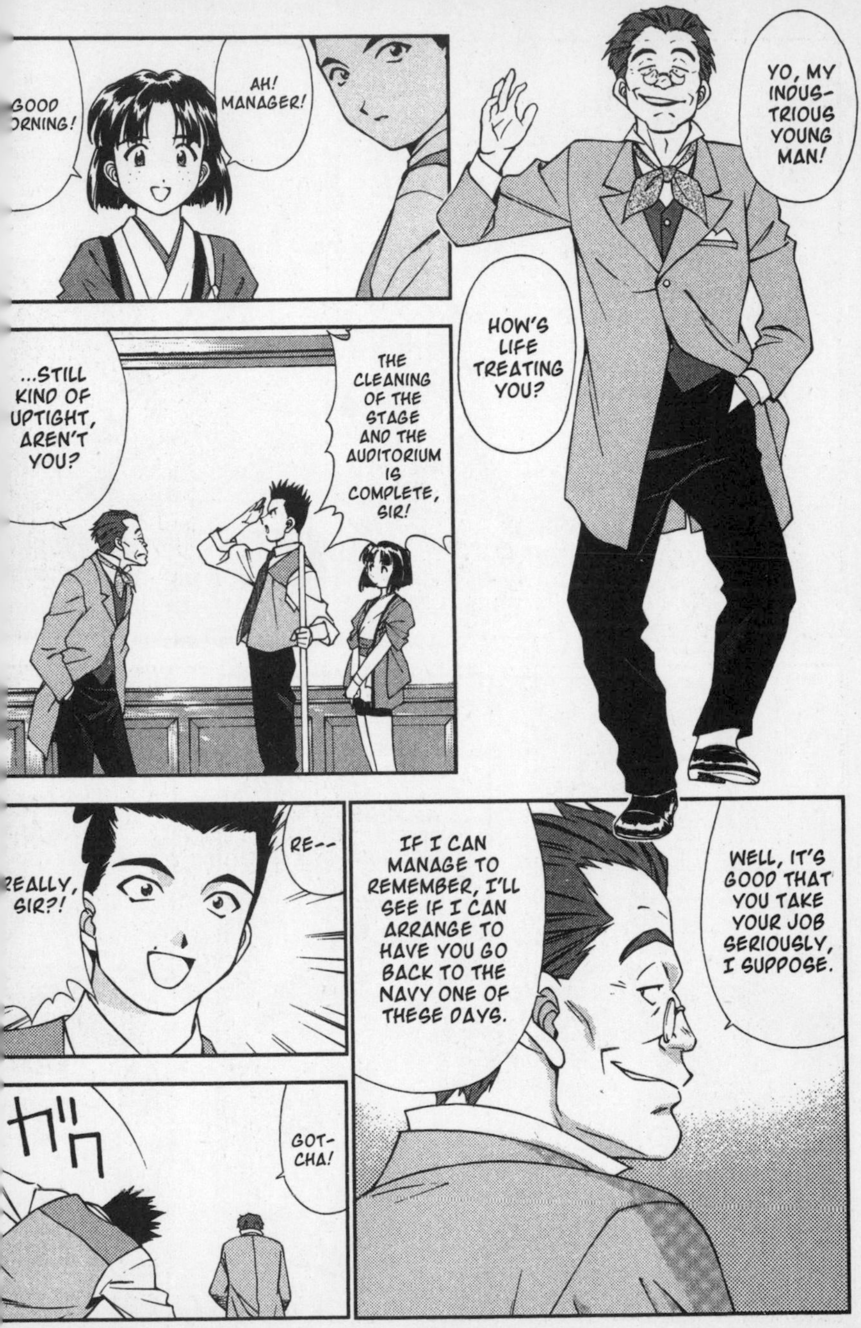

YO, MY INDUS-TRIOUS YOUNG MAN!
HOW'S LIFE TREATING YOU?
AH! MANAGER!
GOOD ORNING!
THE CLEANING OF THE STAGE AND THE AUDITORIUM IS COMPLETE, SIR!
...STILL KIND OF UPTIGHT, AREN'T YOU?
WELL, IT'S GOOD THAT YOU TAKE YOUR JOB SERIOUSLY, I SUPPOSE.
IF I CAN MANAGE TO REMEMBER, I'LL SEE IF I CAN ARRANGE TO HAVE YOU GO BACK TO THE NAVY ONE OF THESE DAYS.
RE--
REALLY, SIR?!
GOT-CHA!
ガク

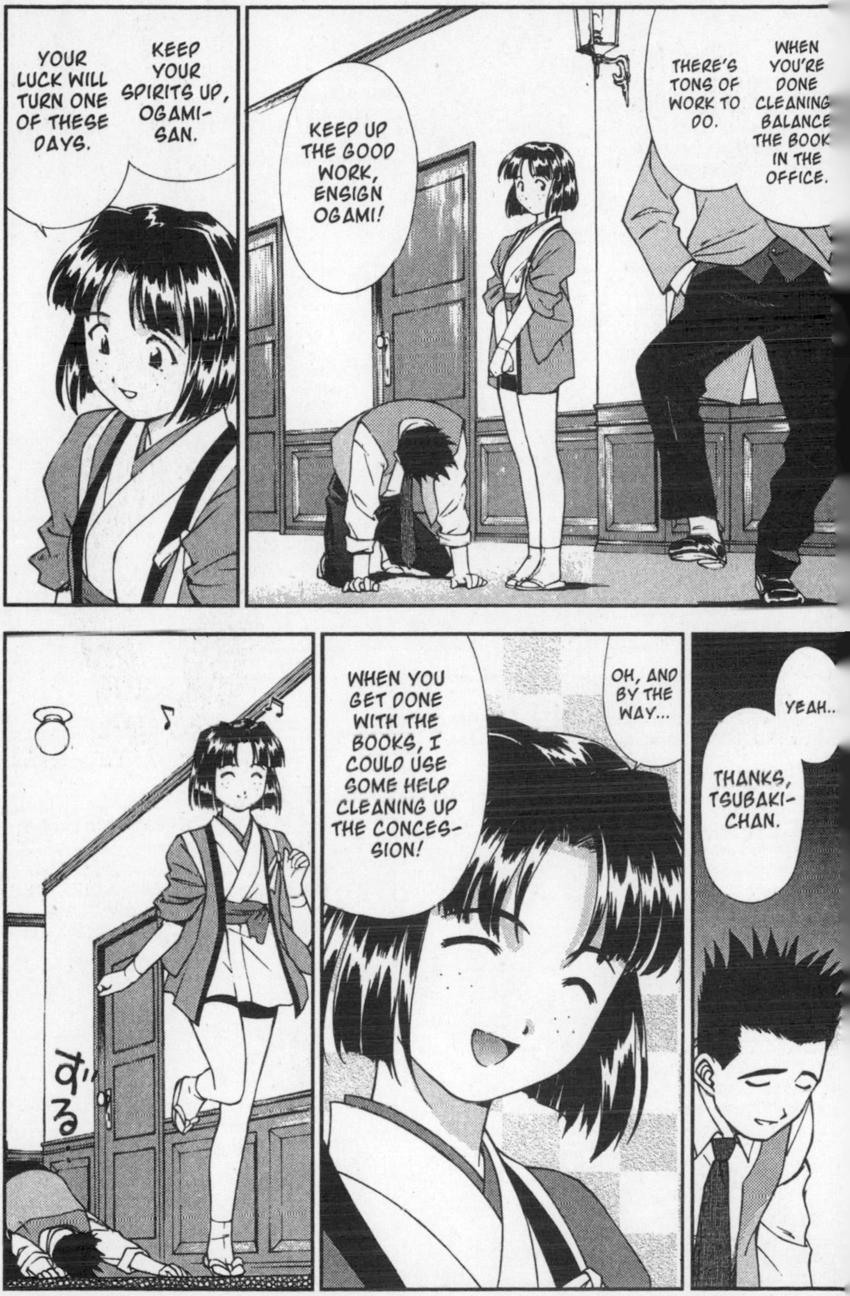
WHEN YOU'RE DONE CLEANING BALANCE THE BOOK IN THE OFFICE.
THERE'S TONS OF WORK TO DO.
KEEP UP THE GOOD WORK, ENSIGN OGAMI!
KEEP YOUR SPIRITS UP, OGAMI-SAN.
YOUR LUCK WILL TURN ONE OF THESE DAYS.
YEAH..
THANKS, TSUBAKI-CHAN.
OH, AND BY THE WAY...
WHEN YOU GET DONE WITH THE BOOKS, I COULD USE SOME HELP CLEANING UP THE CONCES-SION!
ずる

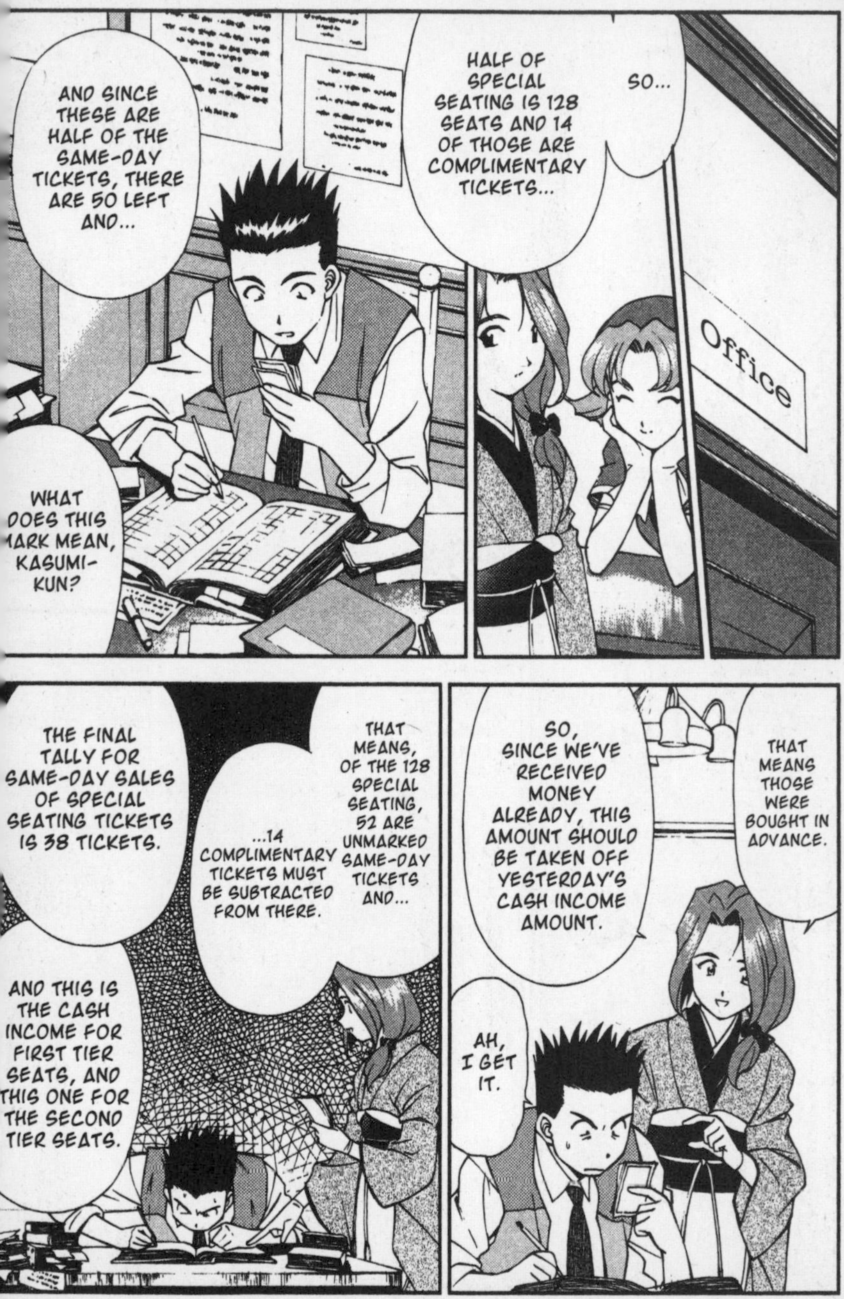

SO...
HALF OF SPECIAL SEATING IS 128 SEATS AND 14 OF THOSE ARE COMPLIMENTARY TICKETS...
AND SINCE THESE ARE HALF OF THE SAME-DAY TICKETS, THERE ARE 50 LEFT AND...
WHAT DOES THIS MARK MEAN, KASUMI-KUN?
THAT MEANS THOSE WERE BOUGHT IN ADVANCE.
SO, SINCE WE'VE RECEIVED MONEY ALREADY, THIS AMOUNT SHOULD BE TAKEN OFF YESTERDAY'S CASH INCOME AMOUNT.
AH, I GET IT.
THAT MEANS, OF THE 128 SPECIAL SEATING, 52 ARE UNMARKED SAME-DAY TICKETS AND...
...14 COMPLIMENTARY TICKETS MUST BE SUBTRACTED FROM THERE.
THE FINAL TALLY FOR SAME-DAY SALES OF SPECIAL SEATING TICKETS IS 38 TICKETS.
AND THIS IS THE CASH INCOME FOR FIRST TIER SEATS, AND THIS ONE FOR THE SECOND TIER SEATS.

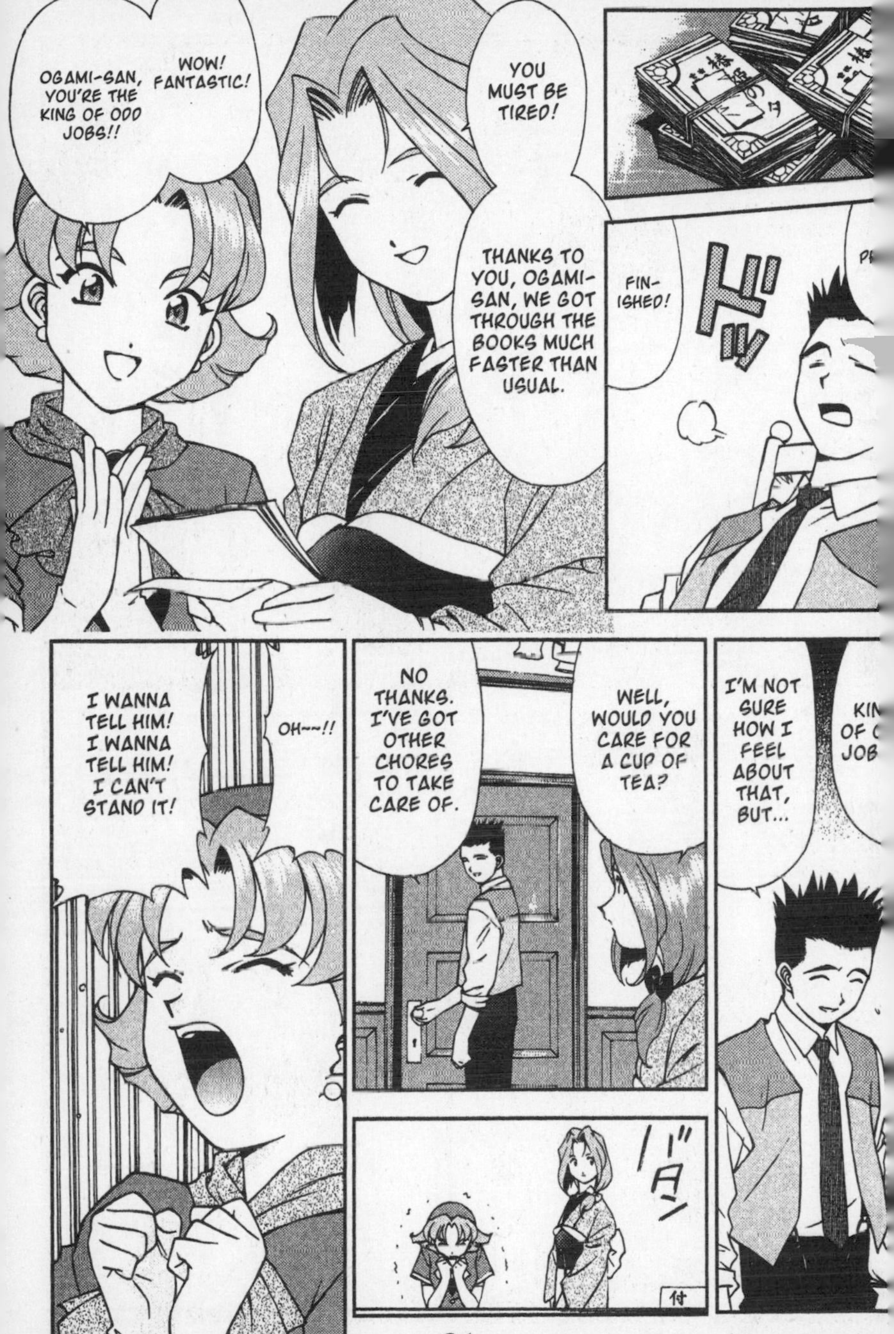
FIN- ISHED!
ドッ
THANKS TO YOU, OGAMI-SAN, WE GOT THROUGH THE BOOKS MUCH FASTER THAN USUAL.
YOU MUST BE TIRED!
WOW! FANTASTIC!
OGAMI-SAN, YOU'RE THE KING OF ODD JOBS!!
I'M NOT SURE HOW I FEEL ABOUT THAT, BUT...
WELL, WOULD YOU CARE FOR A CUP OF TEA?
NO THANKS. I'VE GOT OTHER CHORES TO TAKE CARE OF.
バタン
OH~~!!
I WANNA TELL HIM! I WANNA TELL HIM! I CAN'T STAND IT!

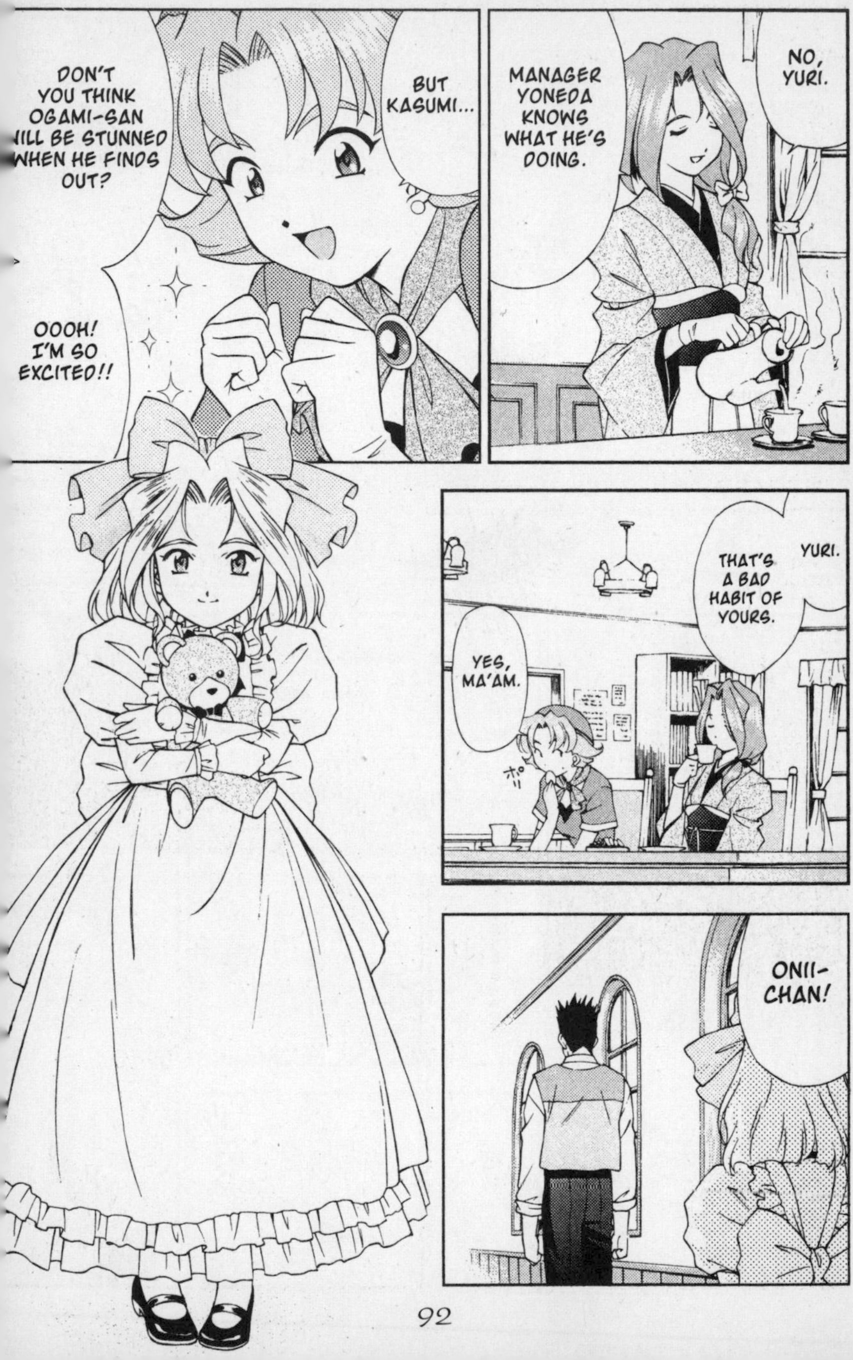
DON'T YOU THINK OGAMI-SAN WILL BE STUNNED WHEN HE FINDS OUT?
OOOH! I'M SO EXCITED!!
BUT KASUMI...
NO, YURI.
MANAGER YONEDA KNOWS WHAT HE'S DOING.
YURI.
THAT'S A BAD HABIT OF YOURS.
YES, MA'AM.
ONII-CHAN!

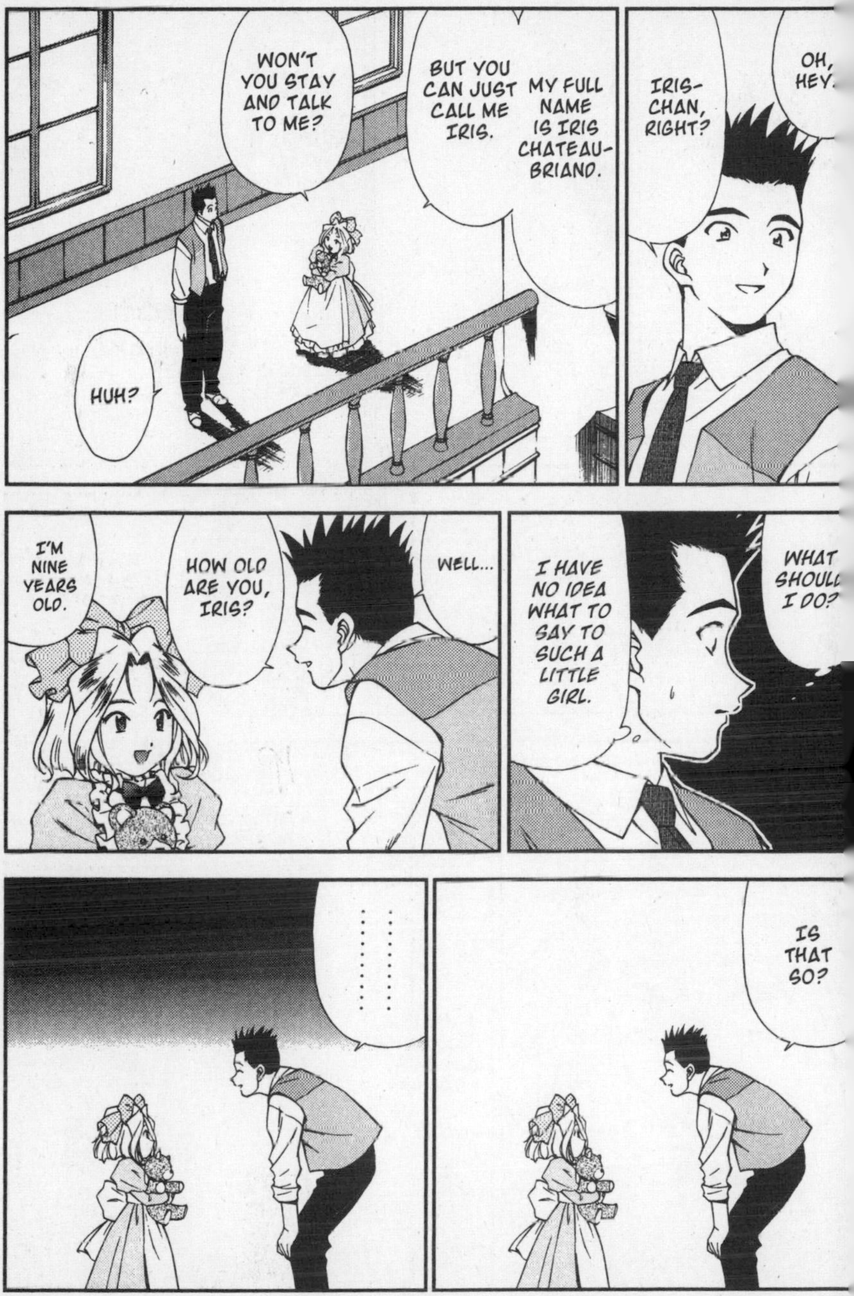

OH, HEY.
IRIS-CHAN, RIGHT?
MY FULL NAME IS IRIS CHATEAUBRIAND.
BUT YOU CAN JUST CALL ME IRIS.
WON'T YOU STAY AND TALK TO ME?
HUH?
WHAT SHOULD I DO?
I HAVE NO IDEA WHAT TO SAY TO SUCH A LITTLE GIRL.
WELL...
HOW OLD ARE YOU, IRIS?
I'M NINE YEARS OLD.
IS THAT SO?
......

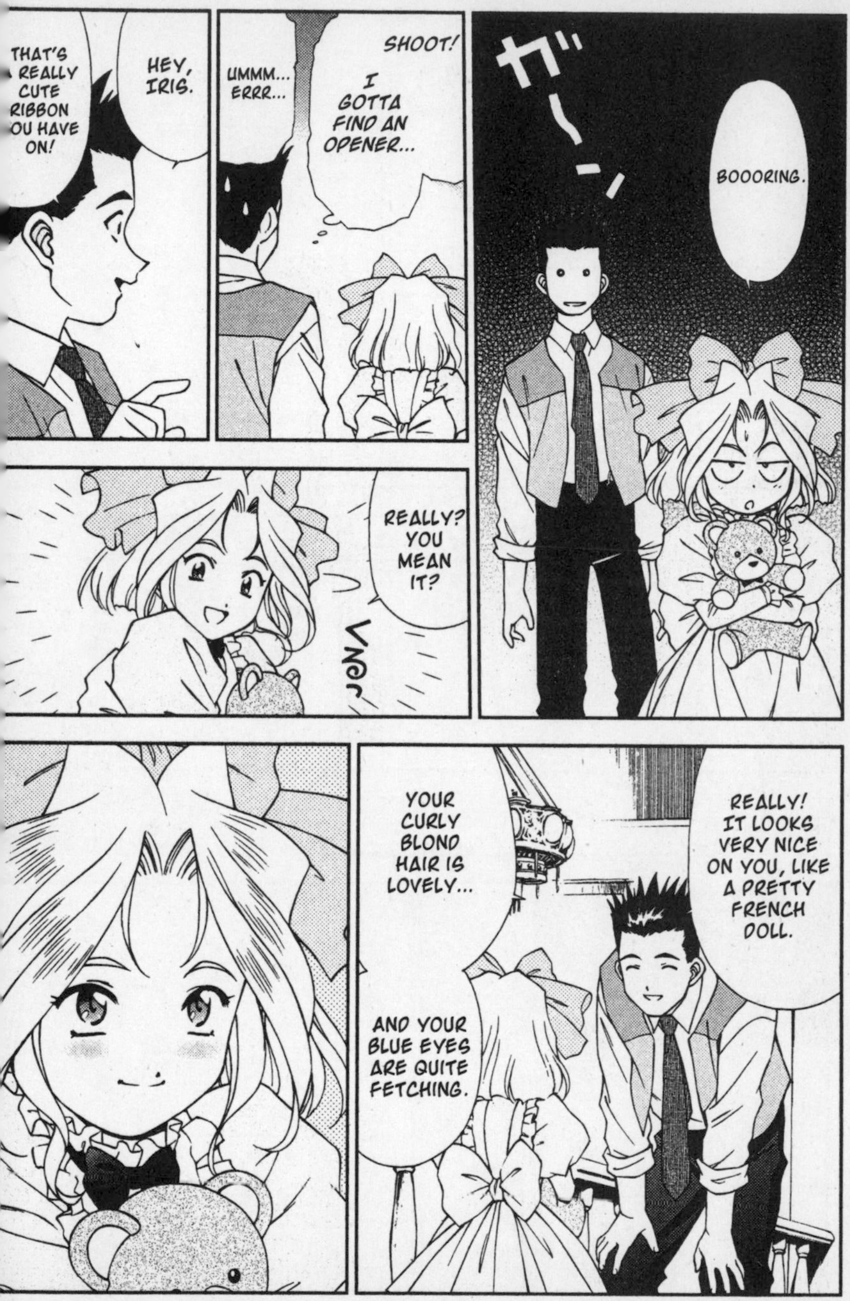
BOOORING.
SHOOT!
I GOTTA FIND AN OPENER...
UMMM... ERRR...
HEY, IRIS.
THAT'S REALLY CUTE RIBBON OU HAVE ON!
REALLY? YOU MEAN IT?
REALLY! IT LOOKS VERY NICE ON YOU, LIKE A PRETTY FRENCH DOLL.
YOUR CURLY BLOND HAIR IS LOVELY...
AND YOUR BLUE EYES ARE QUITE FETCHING.

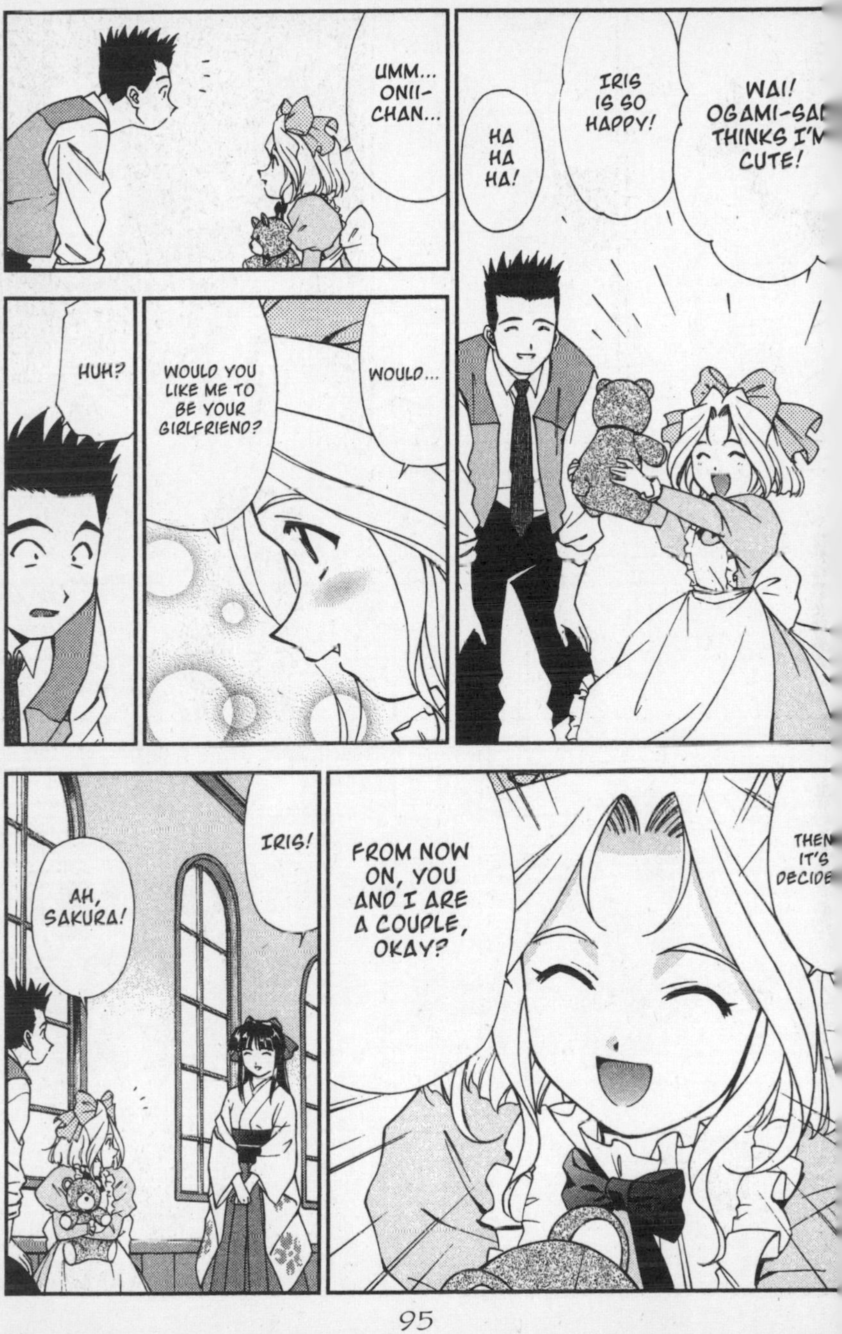

WAI! OGAMI-SA
THINKS I'M CUTE!
IRIS IS SO HAPPY!
HA HA HA!
UMM... ONII-CHAN...
WOULD...
WOULD YOU LIKE ME TO BE YOUR GIRLFRIEND?
HUH?
THEN IT'S DECIDE
FROM NOW ON, YOU AND I ARE A COUPLE, OKAY?
IRIS!
AH, SAKURA!

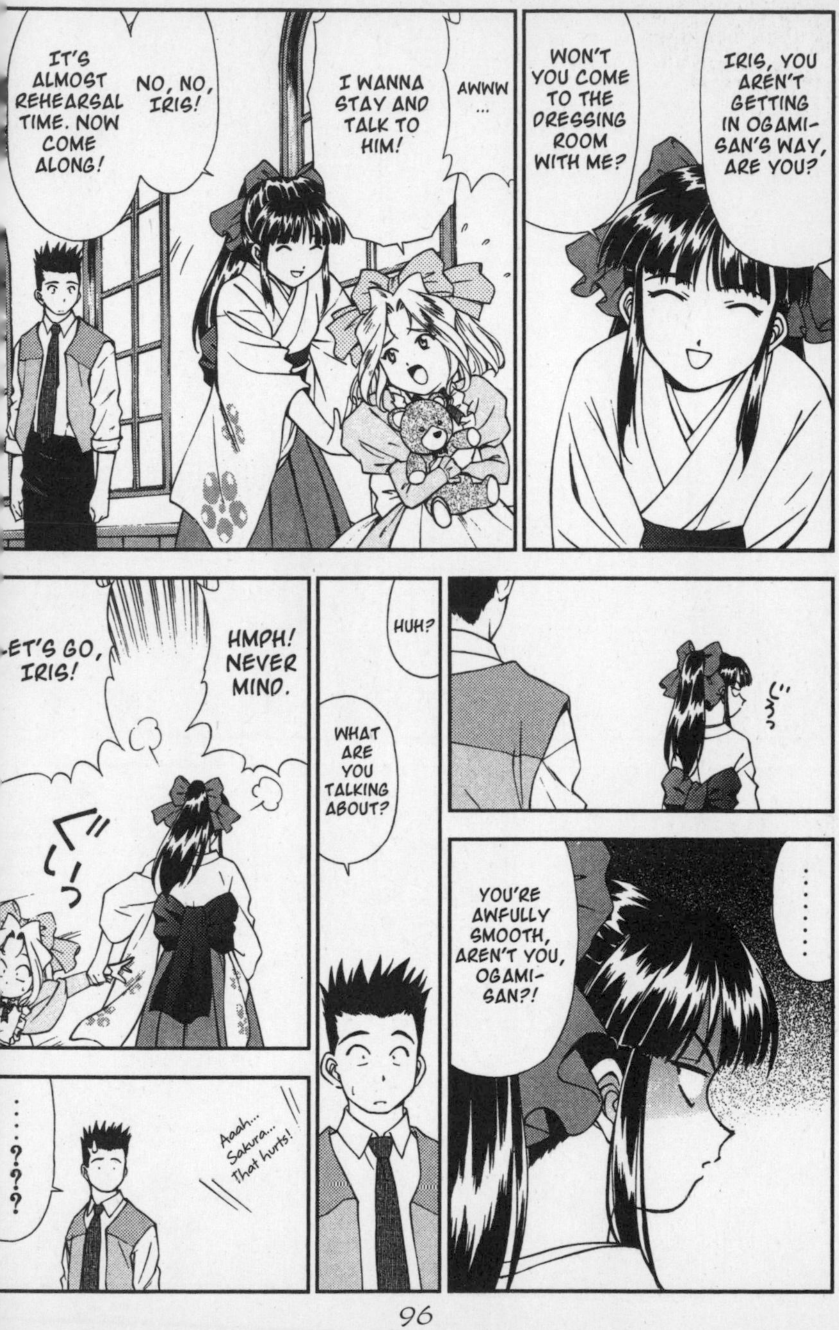
IRIS, YOU AREN'T GETTING IN OGAMI-SAN'S WAY, ARE YOU?
WON'T YOU COME TO THE DRESSING ROOM WITH ME?
AWWW ...
I WANNA STAY AND TALK TO HIM!
NO, NO, IRIS!
IT'S ALMOST REHEARSAL TIME. NOW COME ALONG!
......
YOU'RE AWFULLY SMOOTH, AREN'T YOU, OGAMI-SAN?!
HUH?
WHAT ARE YOU TALKING ABOUT?
HMPH! NEVER MIND.
ET'S GO, IRIS!
...???
Aaah... Sakura... That hurts!

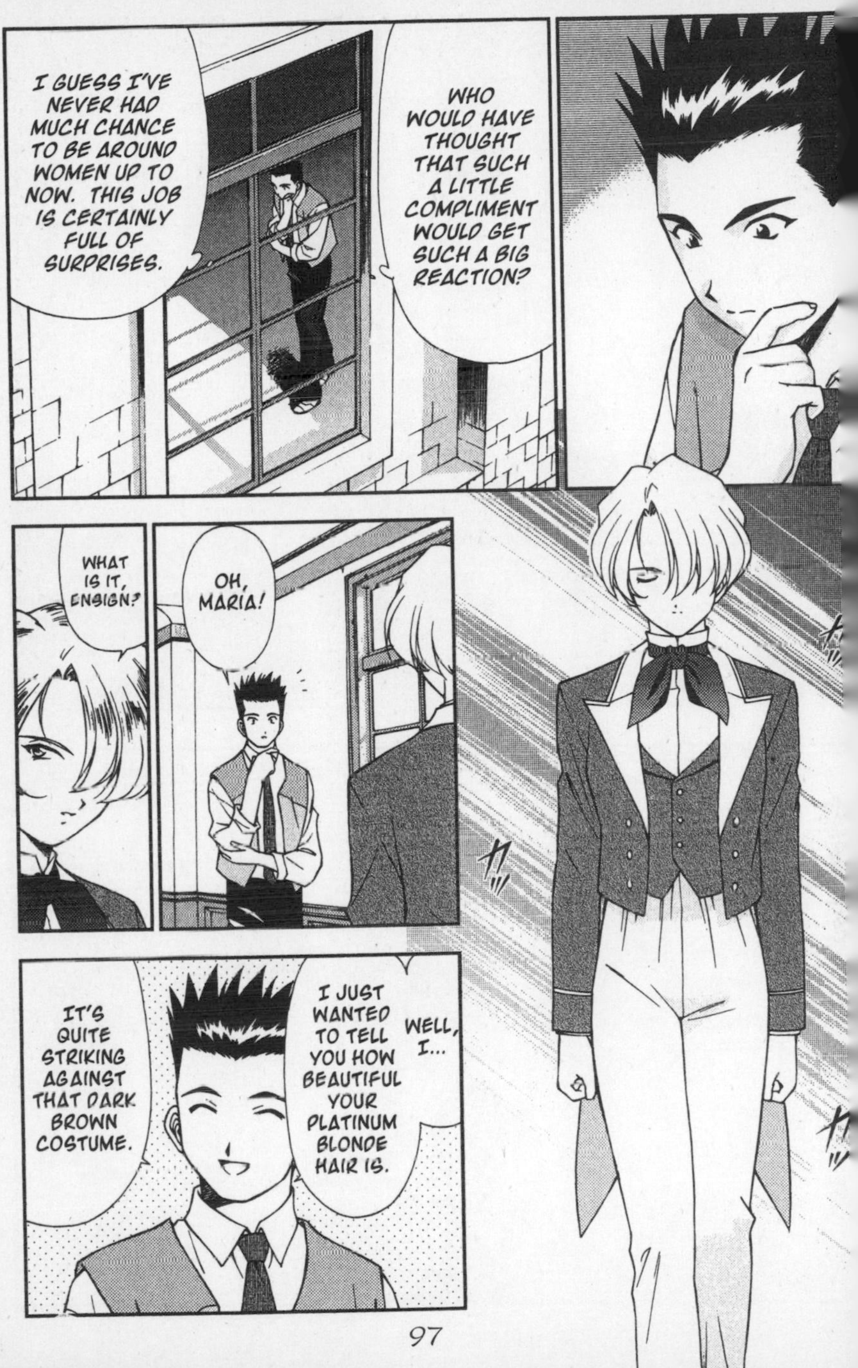
WHO WOULD HAVE THOUGHT THAT SUCH A LITTLE COMPLIMENT WOULD GET SUCH A BIG REACTION?
I GUESS I'VE NEVER HAD MUCH CHANCE TO BE AROUND WOMEN UP TO NOW. THIS JOB IS CERTAINLY FULL OF SURPRISES.
OH, MARIA!
WHAT IS IT, ENSIGN?
WELL, I...
I JUST WANTED TO TELL YOU HOW BEAUTIFUL YOUR PLATINUM BLONDE HAIR IS.
IT'S QUITE STRIKING AGAINST THAT DARK BROWN COSTUME.

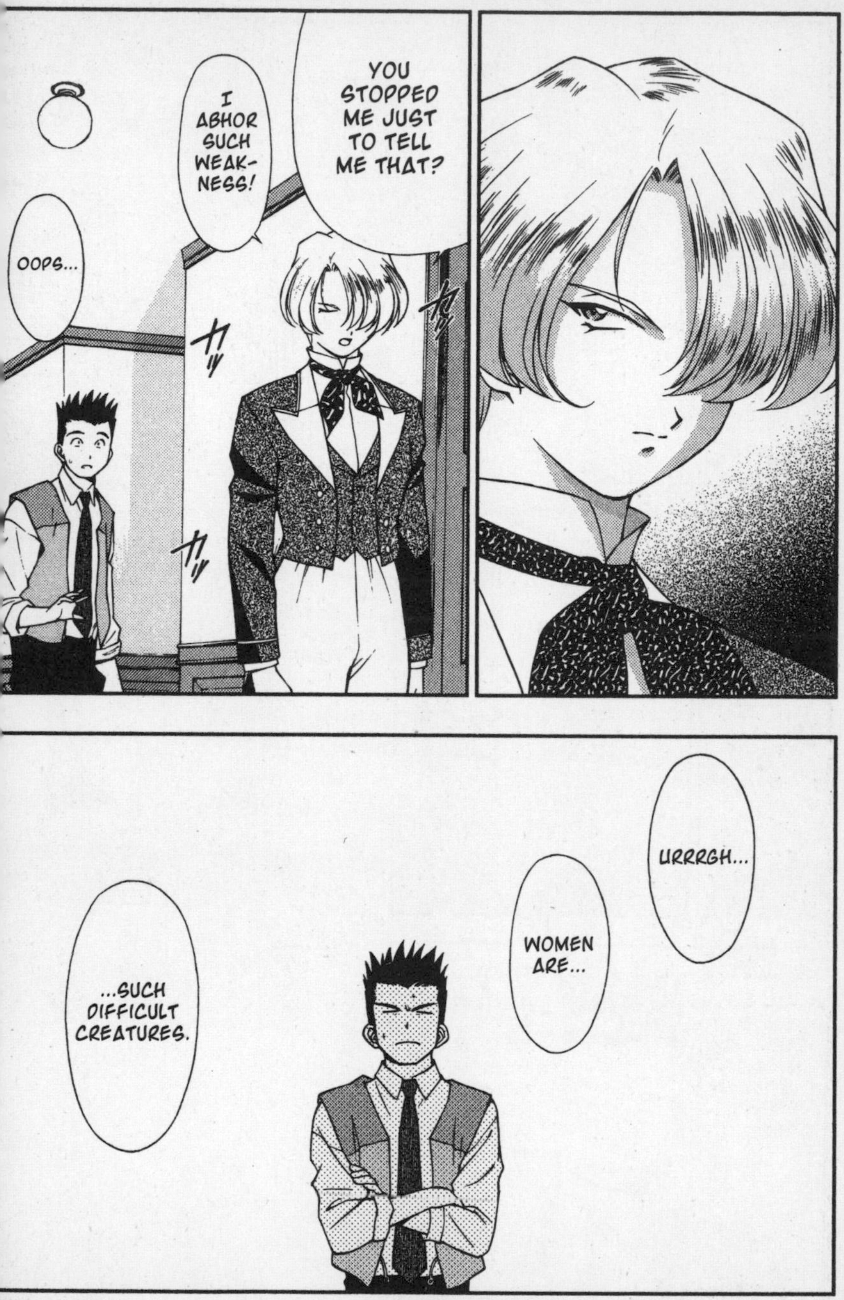
YOU STOPPED ME JUST TO TELL ME THAT?
I ABHOR SUCH WEAK-NESS!
OOPS...
URRRGH...
WOMEN ARE...
...SUCH DIFFICULT CREATURES.

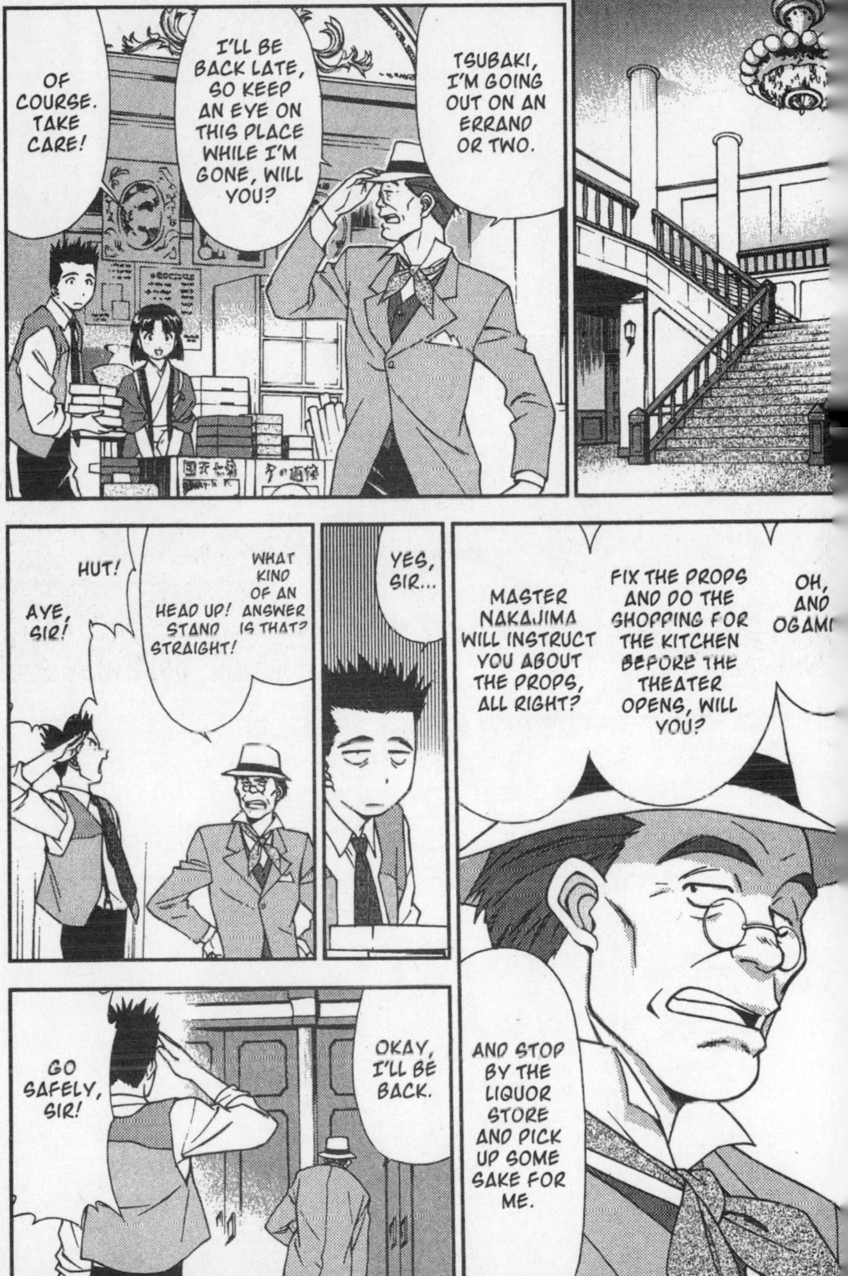
TSUBAKI, I'M GOING OUT ON AN ERRAND OR TWO.
I'LL BE BACK LATE, SO KEEP AN EYE ON THIS PLACE WHILE I'M GONE, WILL YOU?
OF COURSE. TAKE CARE!
OH, AND OGAMI
FIX THE PROPS AND DO THE SHOPPING FOR THE KITCHEN BEFORE THE THEATER OPENS, WILL YOU?
MASTER NAKAJIMA WILL INSTRUCT YOU ABOUT THE PROPS, ALL RIGHT?
AND STOP BY THE LIQUOR STORE AND PICK UP SOME SAKE FOR ME.
YES, SIR...
WHAT KIND OF AN ANSWER IS THAT?
HEAD UP! STAND STRAIGHT!
HUT!
AYE, SIR!
OKAY, I'LL BE BACK.
GO SAFELY, SIR!

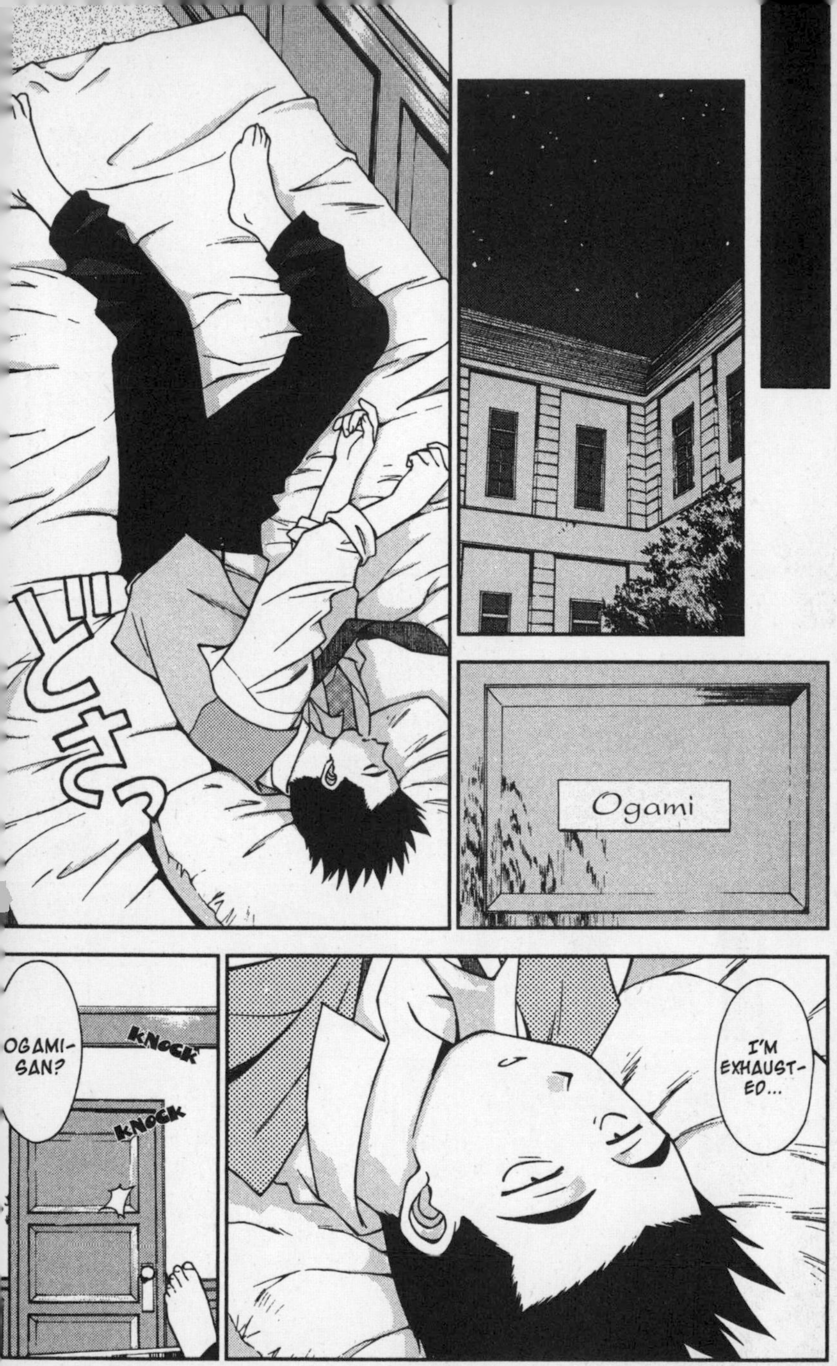
Ogami
どさっ
I'M EXHAUST-ED...
KNOCK
OGAMI-SAN?
KNOCK

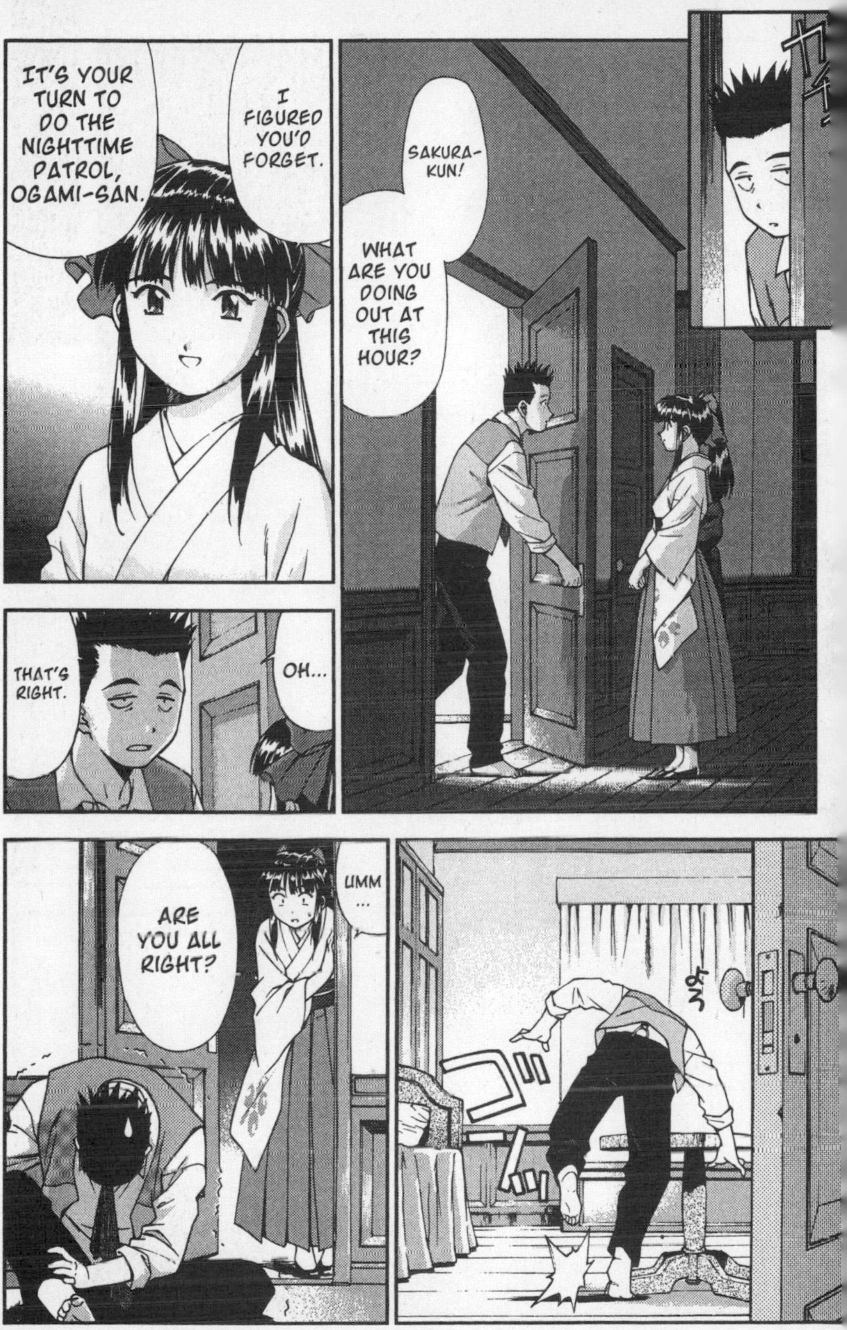
SAKURA-KUN!
WHAT ARE YOU DOING OUT AT THIS HOUR?
I FIGURED YOU'D FORGET.
IT'S YOUR TURN TO DO THE NIGHTTIME PATROL, OGAMI-SAN.
OH...
THAT'S RIGHT.
UMM ...
ARE YOU ALL RIGHT?

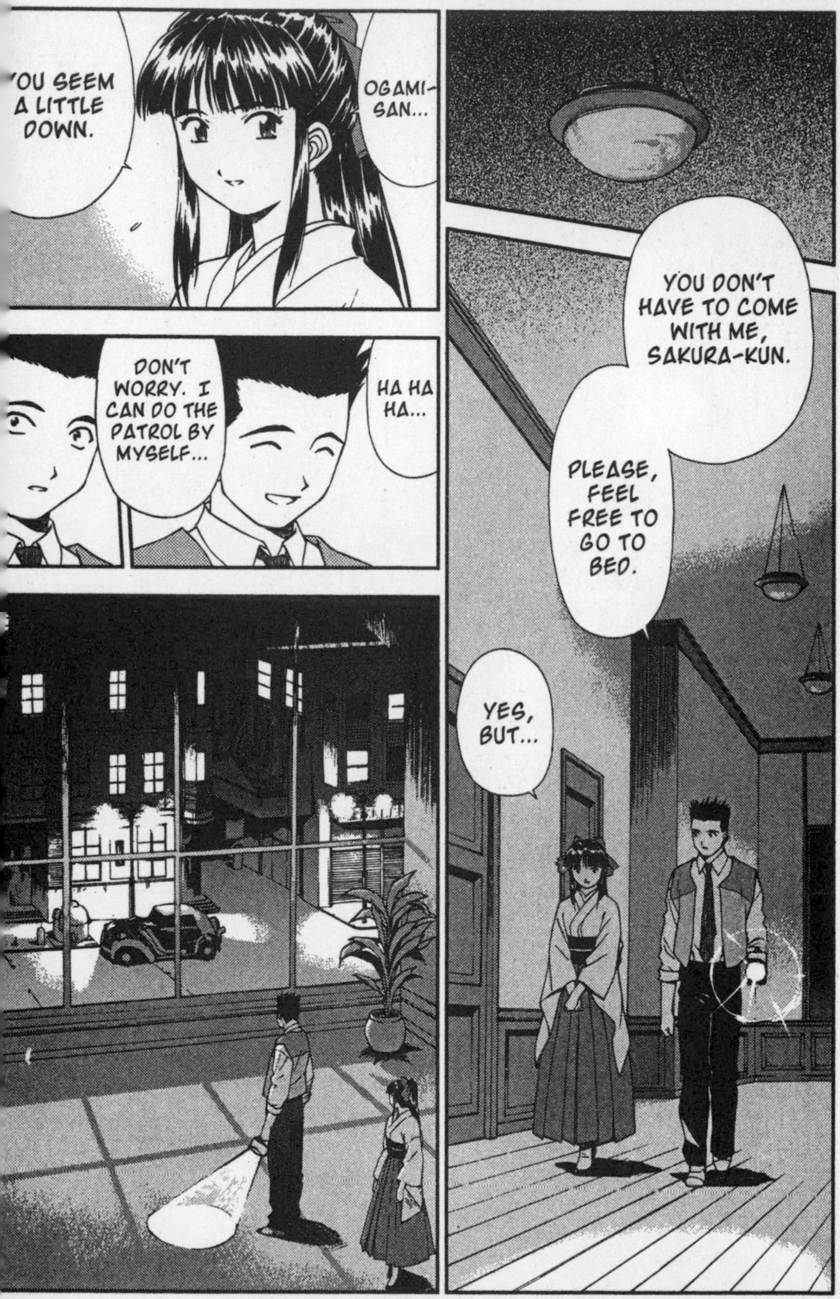
YOU DON'T HAVE TO COME WITH ME, SAKURA-KUN.
PLEASE, FEEL FREE TO GO TO BED.
YES, BUT...
OGAMI-SAN...
YOU SEEM A LITTLE DOWN.
HA HA HA...
DON'T WORRY. I CAN DO THE PATROL BY MYSELF...

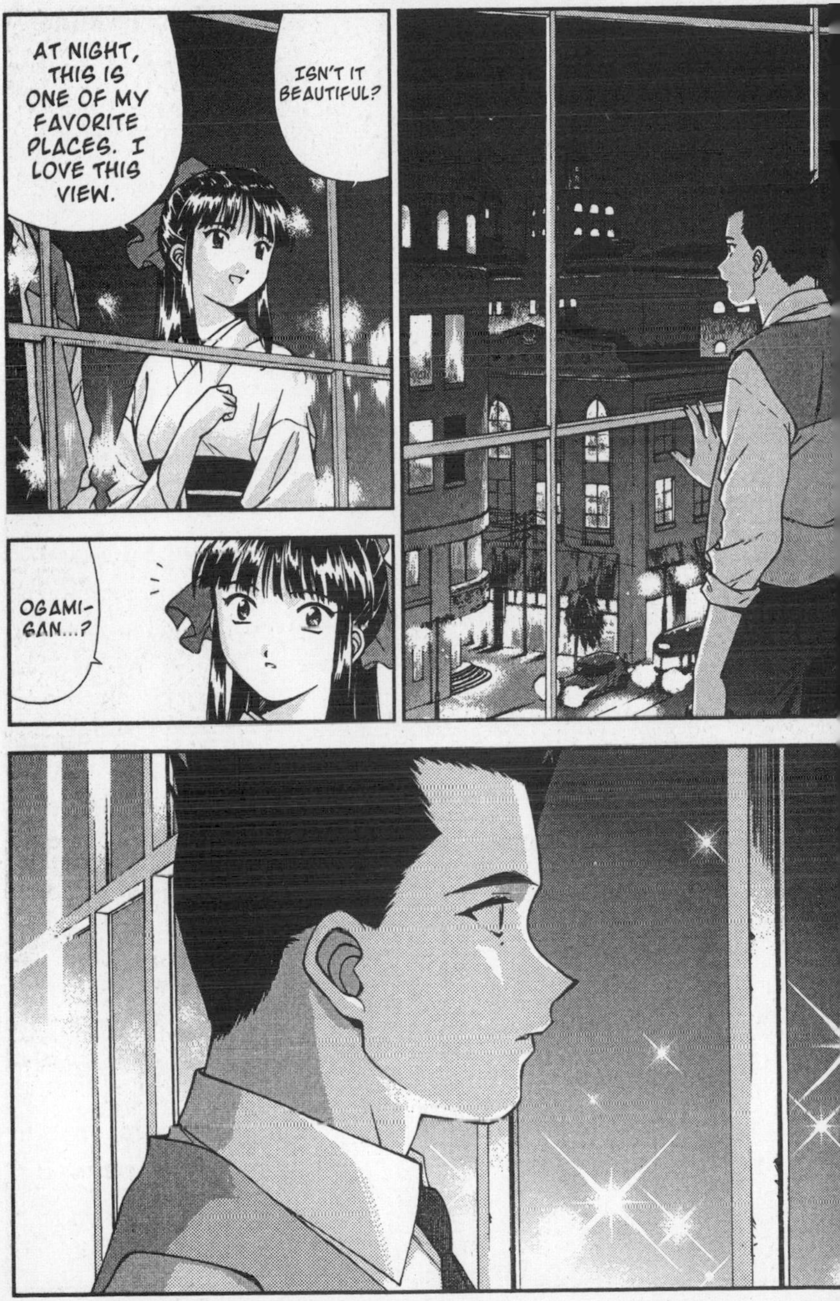
AT NIGHT, THIS IS ONE OF MY FAVORITE PLACES. I LOVE THIS VIEW.
ISN'T IT BEAUTIFUL?
OGAMI-SAN...?

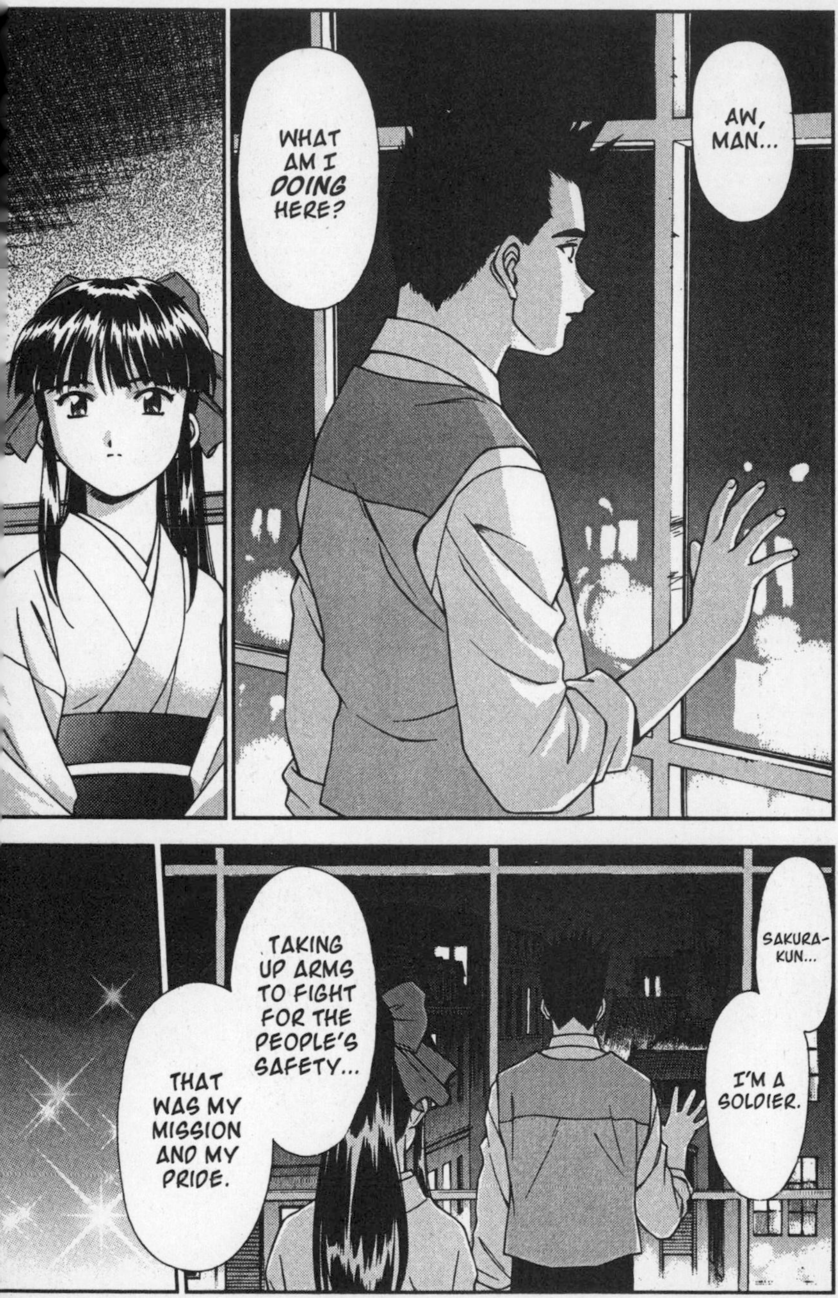
AW, MAN...
WHAT AM I DOING HERE?
SAKURA-KUN...
I'M A SOLDIER.
TAKING UP ARMS TO FIGHT FOR THE PEOPLE'S SAFETY...
THAT WAS MY MISSION AND MY PRIDE.

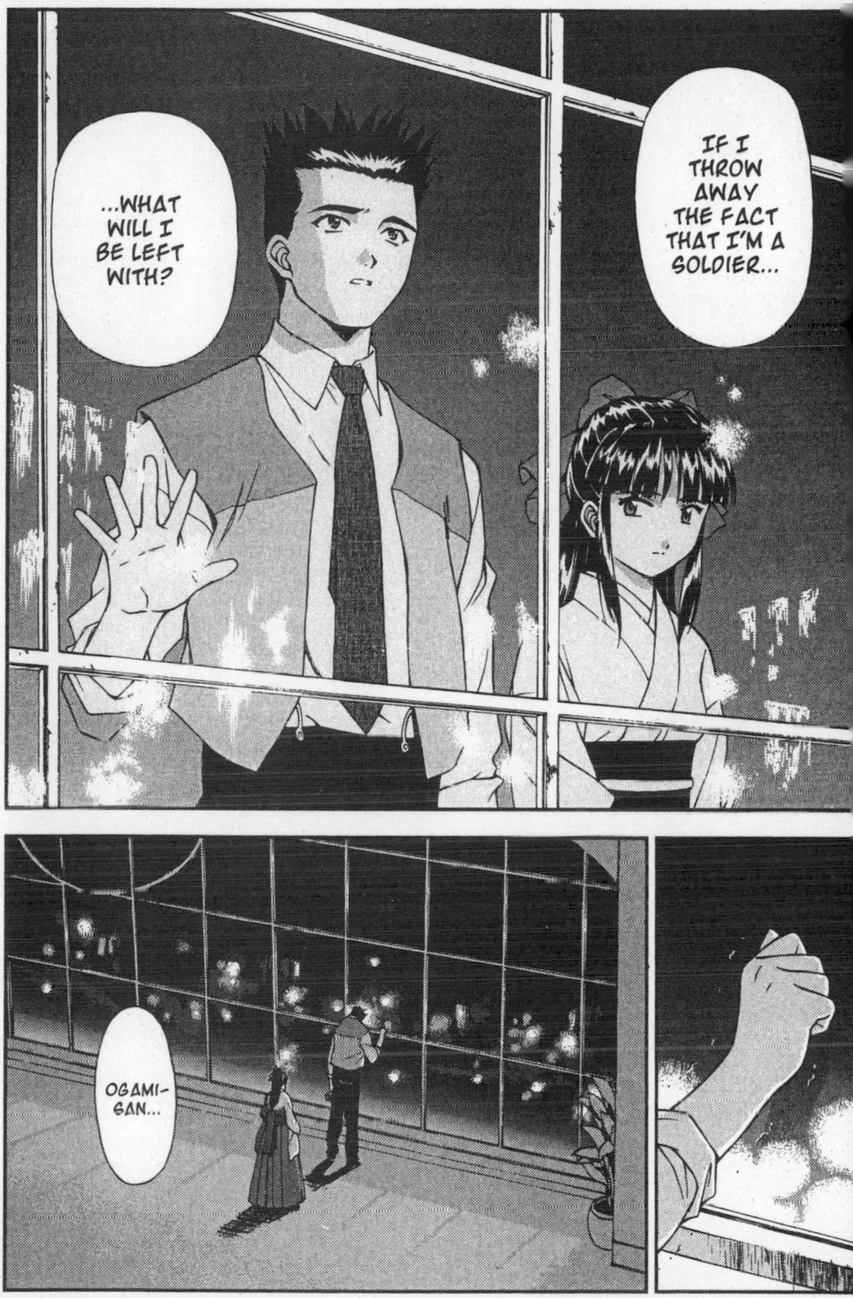
IF I THROW AWAY THE FACT THAT I'M A SOLDIER...
...WHAT WILL I BE LEFT WITH?
OGAMI-SAN...

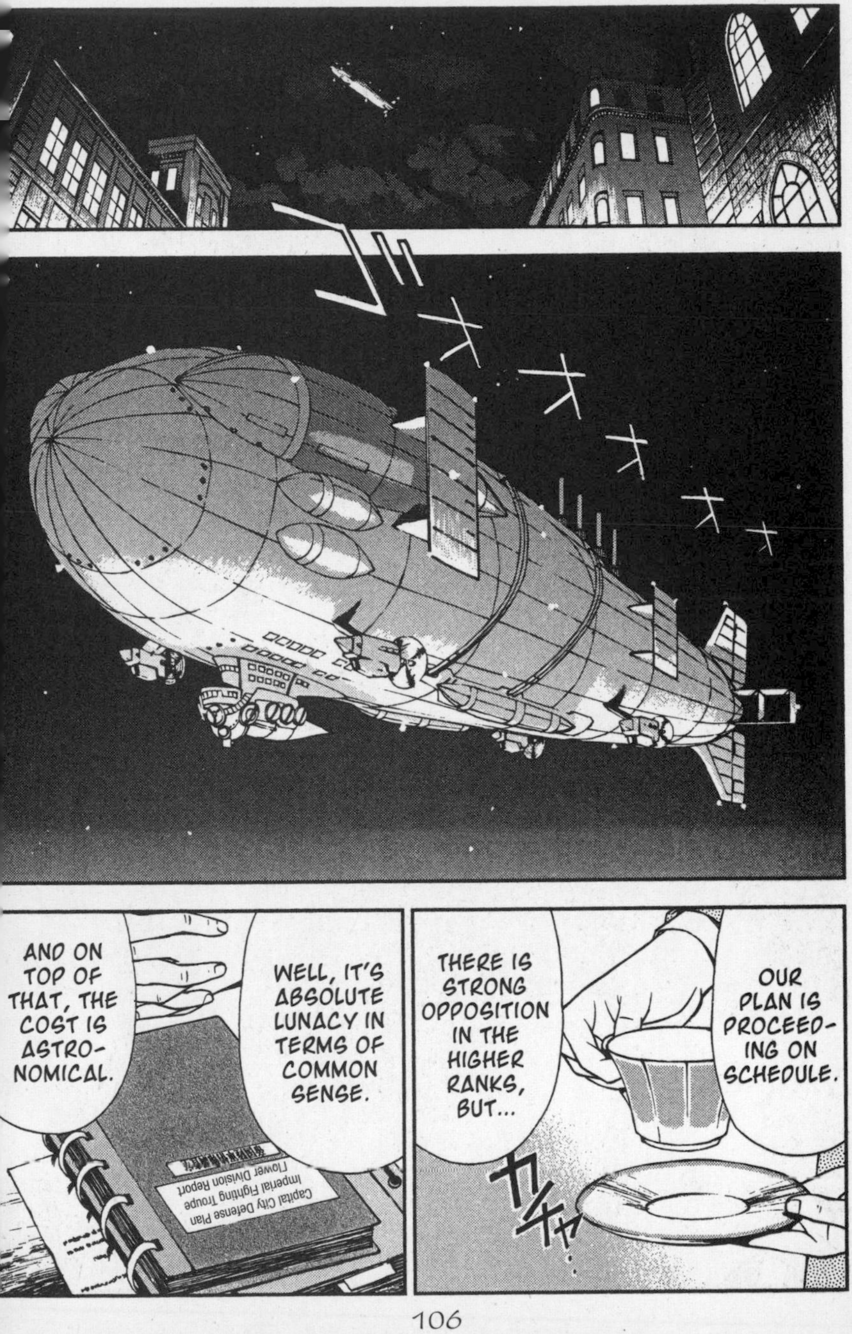
OUR PLAN IS PROCEEDING ON SCHEDULE.
THERE IS STRONG OPPOSITION IN THE HIGHER RANKS, BUT...
WELL, IT'S ABSOLUTE LUNACY IN TERMS OF COMMON SENSE.
AND ON TOP OF THAT, THE COST IS ASTRONOMICAL.
Capital City Defense Plan
Imperial Fighting Troupe
Flower Division Report

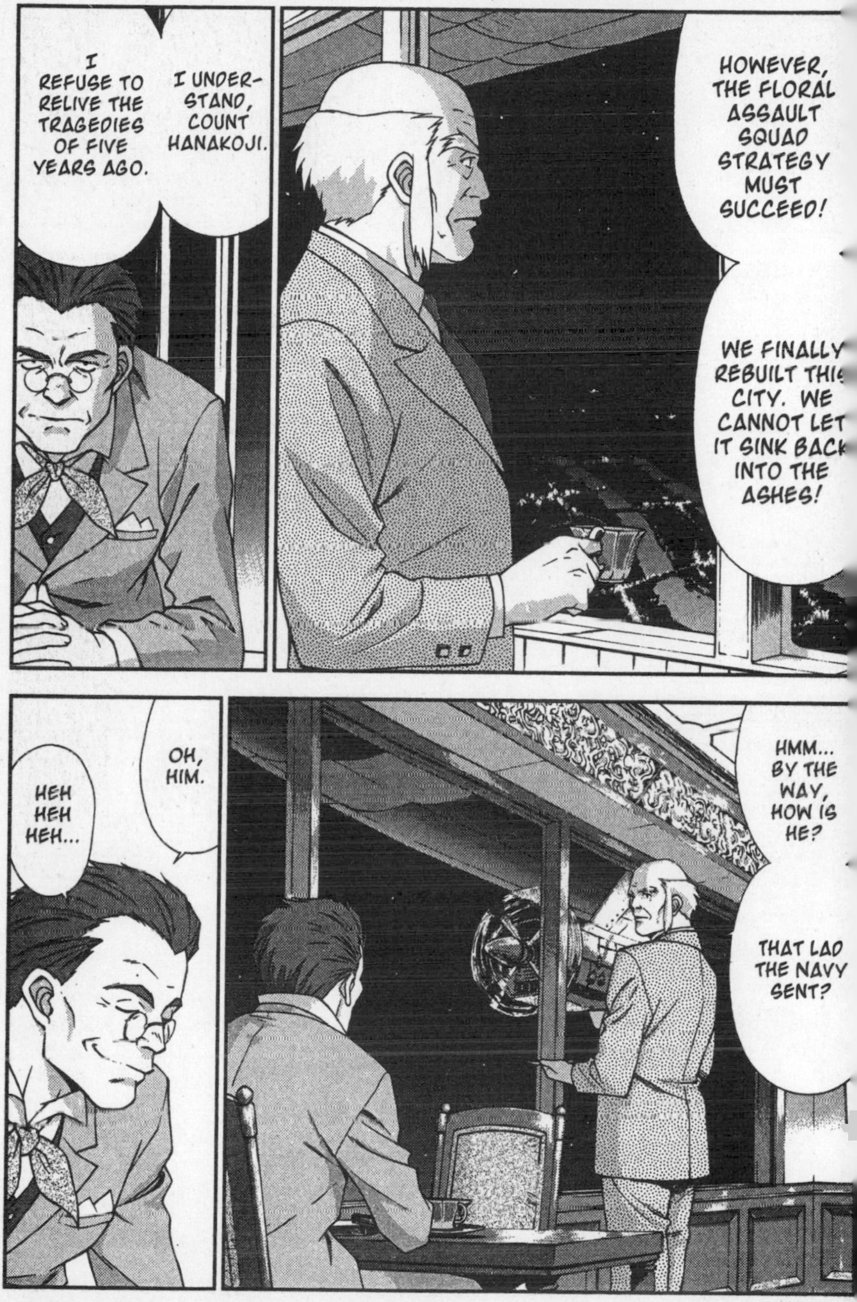
HOWEVER, THE FLORAL ASSAULT SQUAD STRATEGY MUST SUCCEED!
WE FINALLY REBUILT THIS CITY. WE CANNOT LET IT SINK BACK INTO THE ASHES!
I REFUSE TO RELIVE THE TRAGEDIES OF FIVE YEARS AGO.
I UNDER-STAND, COUNT HANAKOJI.
HMM... BY THE WAY, HOW IS HE?
THAT LAD THE NAVY SENT?
OH, HIM.
HEH HEH HEH...

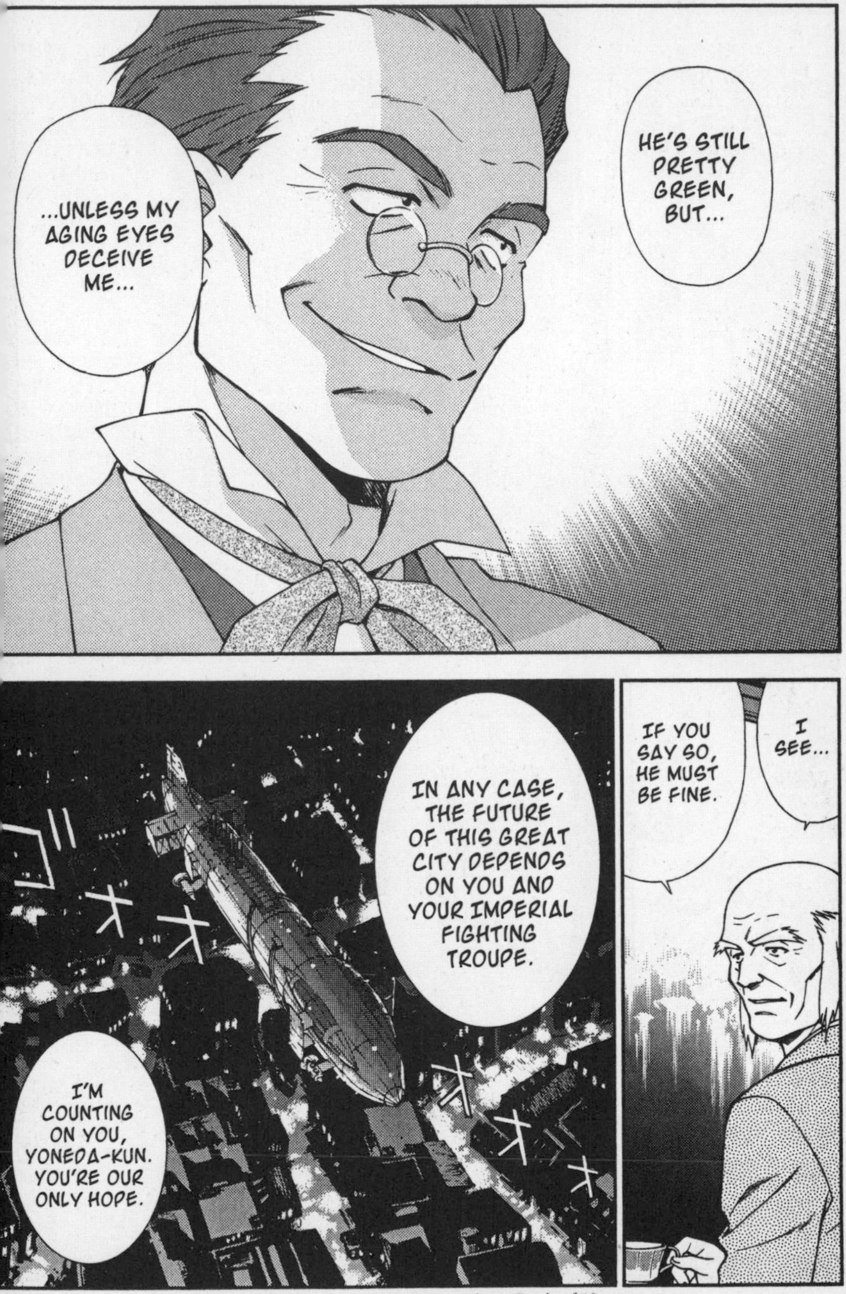
HE'S STILL PRETTY GREEN, BUT...
...UNLESS MY AGING EYES DECEIVE ME...
I SEE...
IF YOU SAY SO, HE MUST BE FINE.
IN ANY CASE, THE FUTURE OF THIS GREAT CITY DEPENDS ON YOU AND YOUR IMPERIAL FIGHTING TROUPE.
I'M COUNTING ON YOU, YONEDA-KUN. YOU'RE OUR ONLY HOPE.

The Meaningless Busywork--End of Act

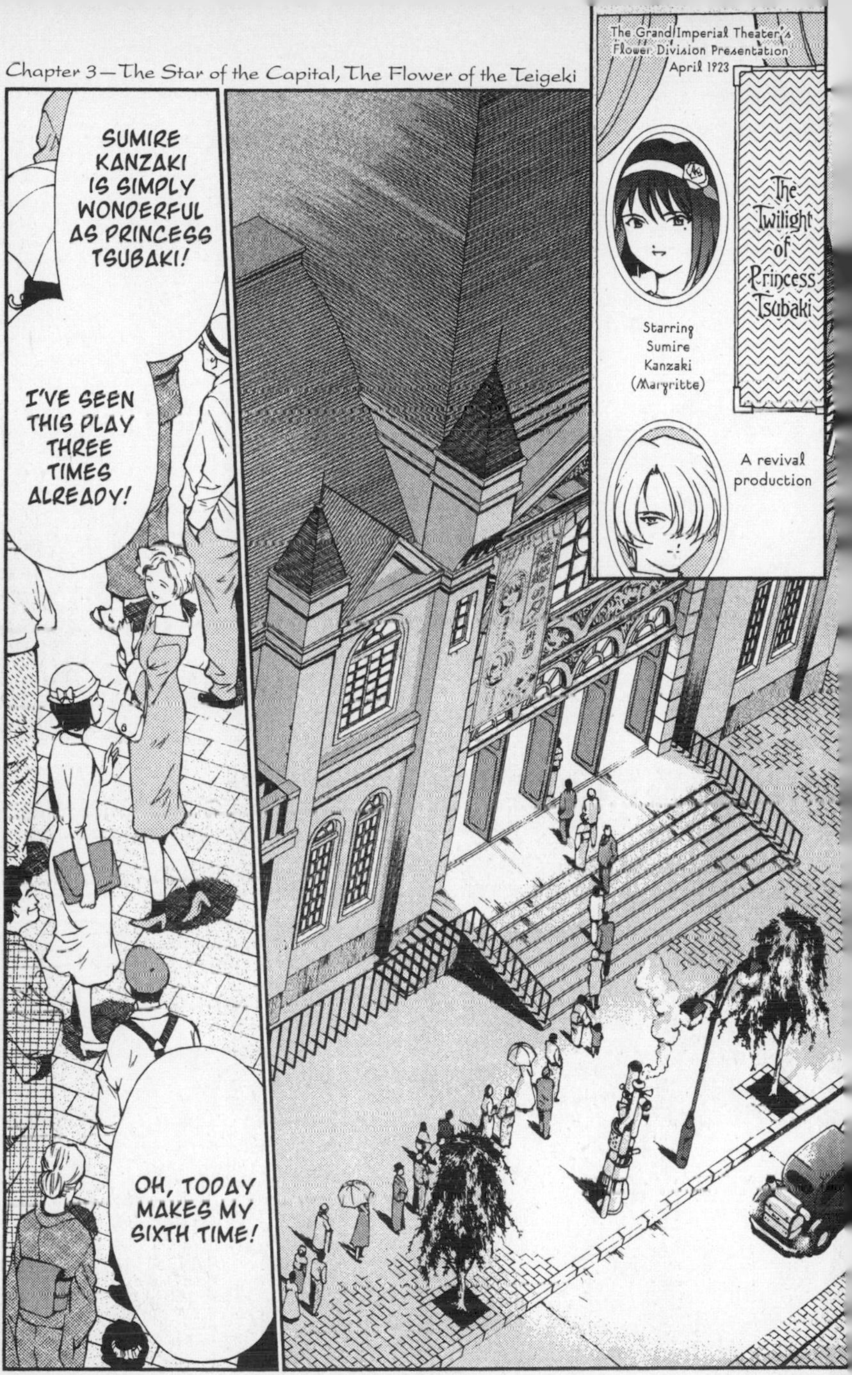
The Grand Imperial Theater's Flower Division Presentation
April 1923
The Twilight of Princess Tsubaki
Starring Sumire Kanzaki (Margritte)
A revival production
SUMIRE KANZAKI IS SIMPLY WONDERFUL AS PRINCESS TSUBAKI!
I'VE SEEN THIS PLAY THREE TIMES ALREADY!
OH, TODAY MAKES MY SIXTH TIME!

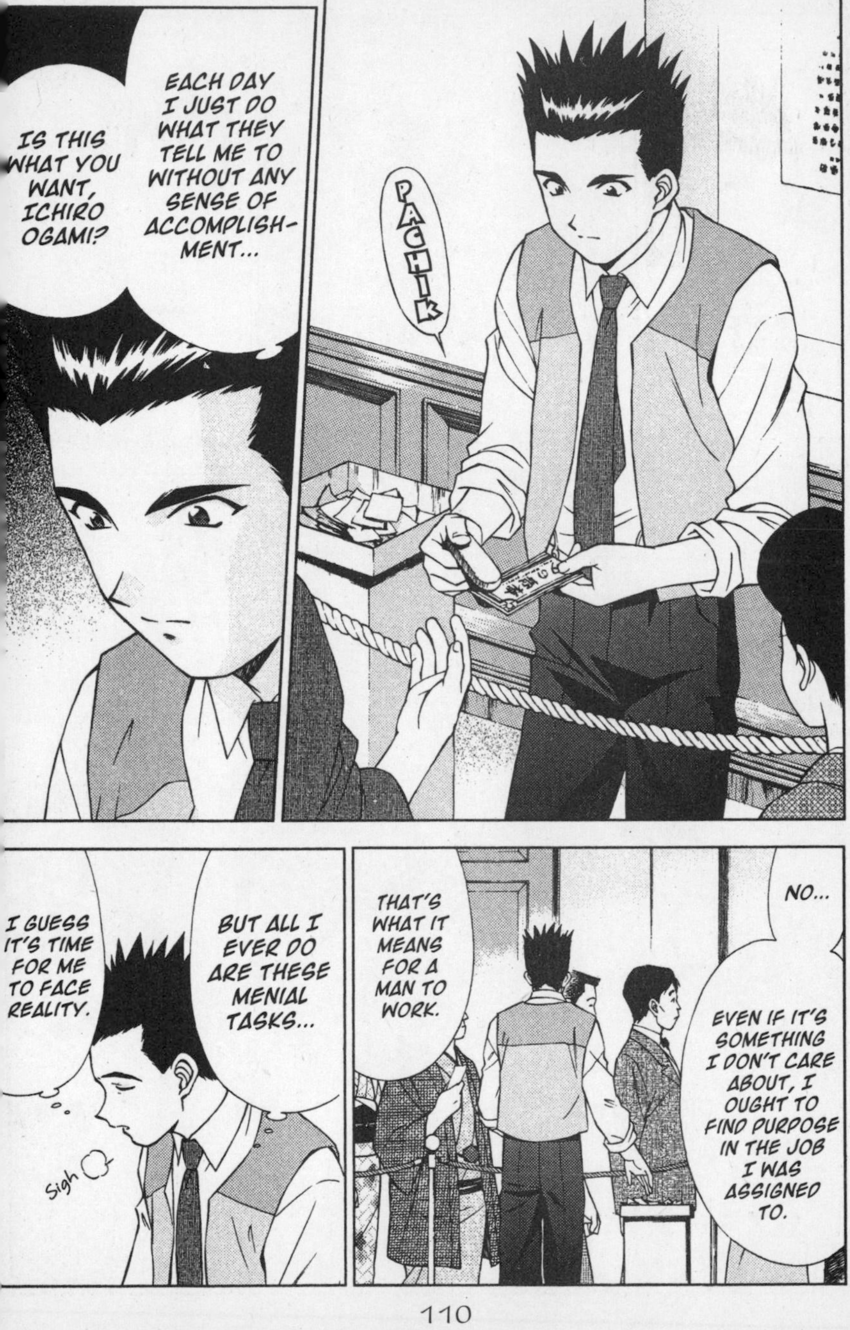
PACHIK
EACH DAY I JUST DO WHAT THEY TELL ME TO WITHOUT ANY SENSE OF ACCOMPLISHMENT...
IS THIS WHAT YOU WANT, ICHIRO OGAMI?
NO...
EVEN IF IT'S SOMETHING I DON'T CARE ABOUT, I OUGHT TO FIND PURPOSE IN THE JOB I WAS ASSIGNED TO.
THAT'S WHAT IT MEANS FOR A MAN TO WORK.
BUT ALL I EVER DO ARE THESE MENIAL TASKS...
I GUESS IT'S TIME FOR ME TO FACE REALITY.
Sigh

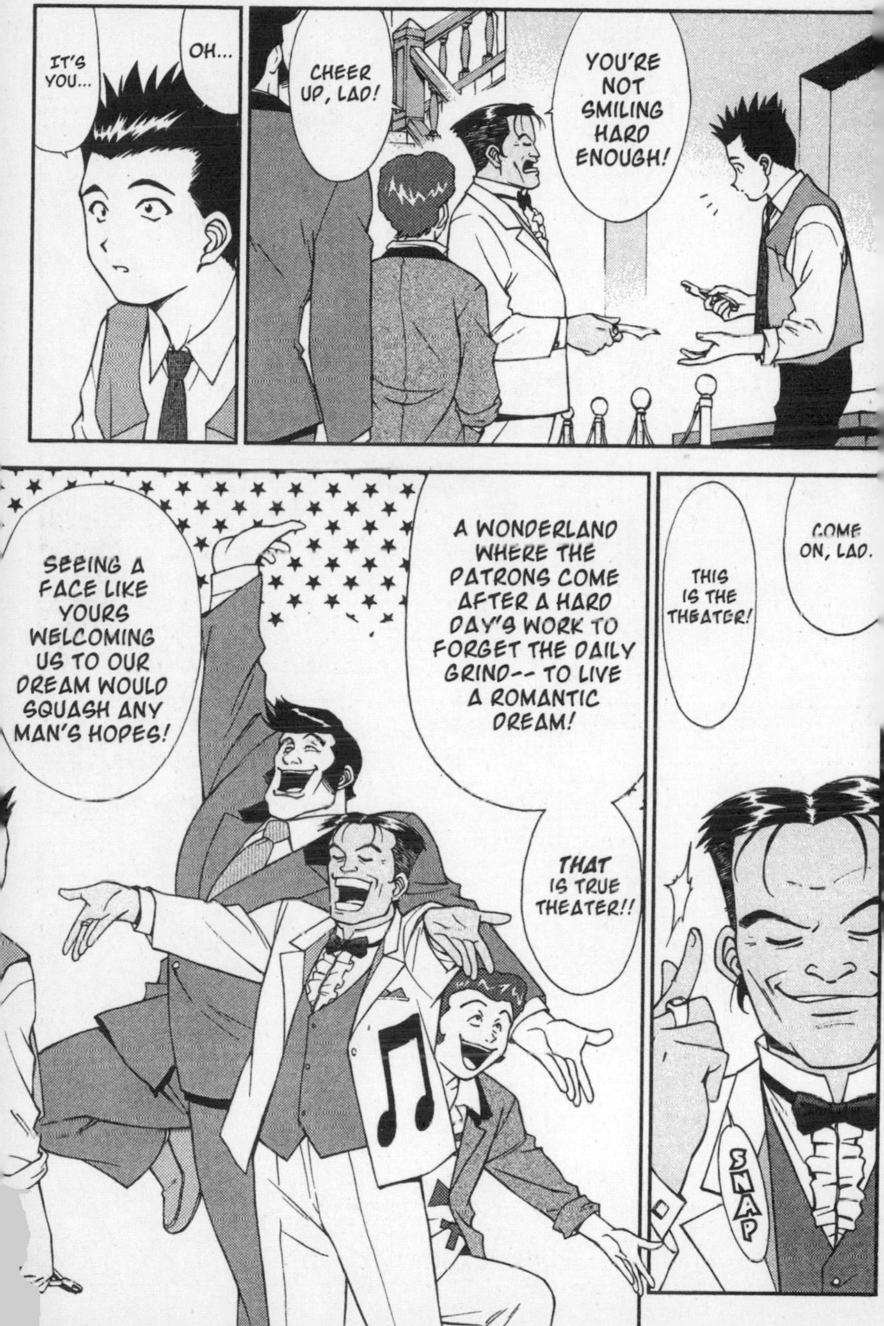
YOU'RE NOT SMILING HARD ENOUGH!
CHEER UP, LAD!
OH...
IT'S YOU...
COME ON, LAD.
THIS IS THE THEATER!
SNAP
A WONDERLAND WHERE THE PATRONS COME AFTER A HARD DAY'S WORK TO FORGET THE DAILY GRIND-- TO LIVE A ROMANTIC DREAM!
THAT IS TRUE THEATER!!
SEEING A FACE LIKE YOURS WELCOMING US TO OUR DREAM WOULD SQUASH ANY MAN'S HOPES!

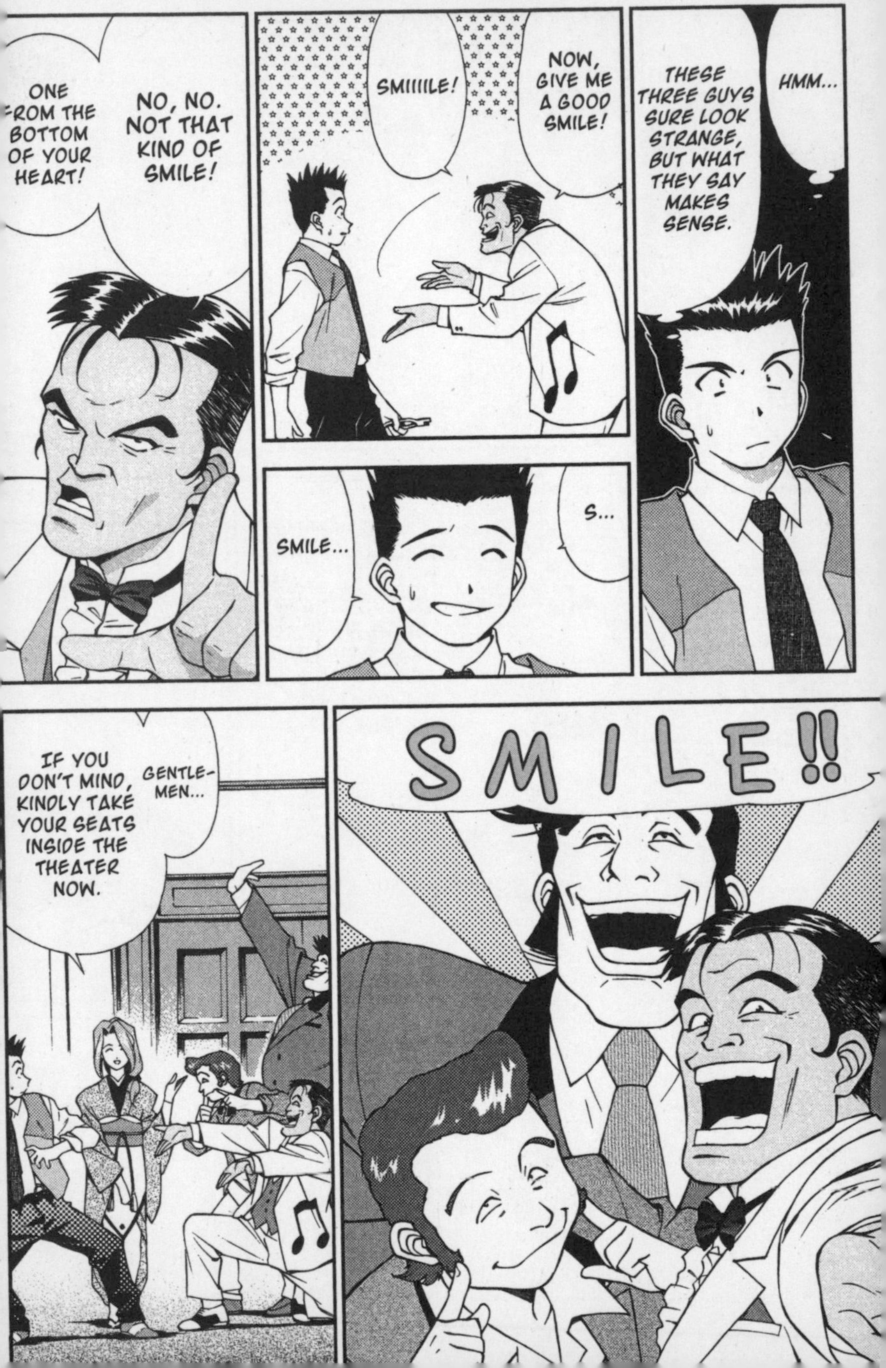
HMM...
THESE THREE GUYS SURE LOOK STRANGE, BUT WHAT THEY SAY MAKES SENSE.
NOW, GIVE ME A GOOD SMILE!
SMIIIILE!
S...
SMILE...
NO, NO. NOT THAT KIND OF SMILE!
ONE FROM THE BOTTOM OF YOUR HEART!
SMILE!!
GENTLE-MEN...
IF YOU DON'T MIND, KINDLY TAKE YOUR SEATS INSIDE THE THEATER NOW.

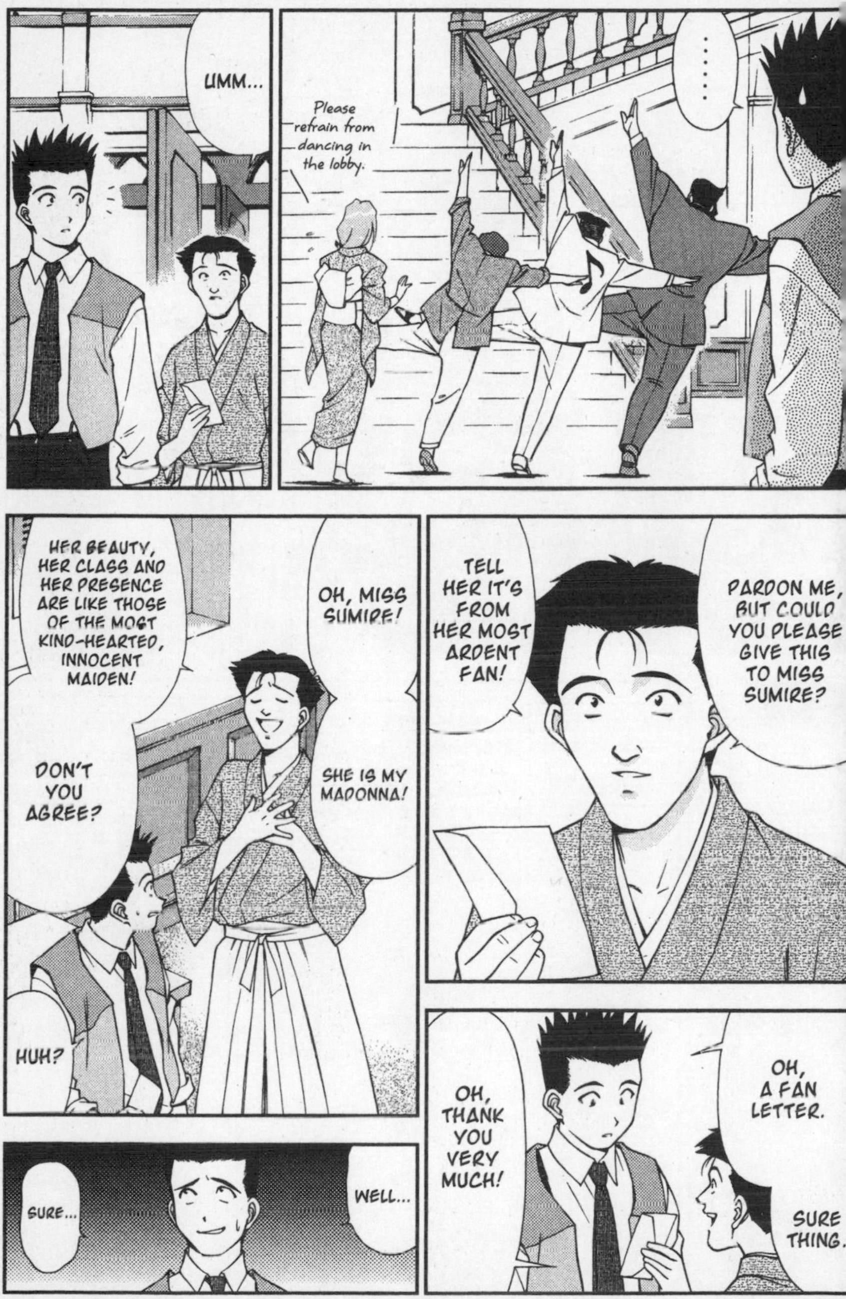
......
Please refrain from dancing in the lobby.
UMM...
PARDON ME, BUT COULD YOU PLEASE GIVE THIS TO MISS SUMIRE?
TELL HER IT'S FROM HER MOST ARDENT FAN!
OH, A FAN LETTER.
SURE THING.
OH, THANK YOU VERY MUCH!
OH, MISS SUMIRE!
HER BEAUTY, HER CLASS AND HER PRESENCE ARE LIKE THOSE OF THE MOST KIND-HEARTED, INNOCENT MAIDEN!
SHE IS MY MADONNA!
DON'T YOU AGREE?
HUH?
WELL...
SURE...

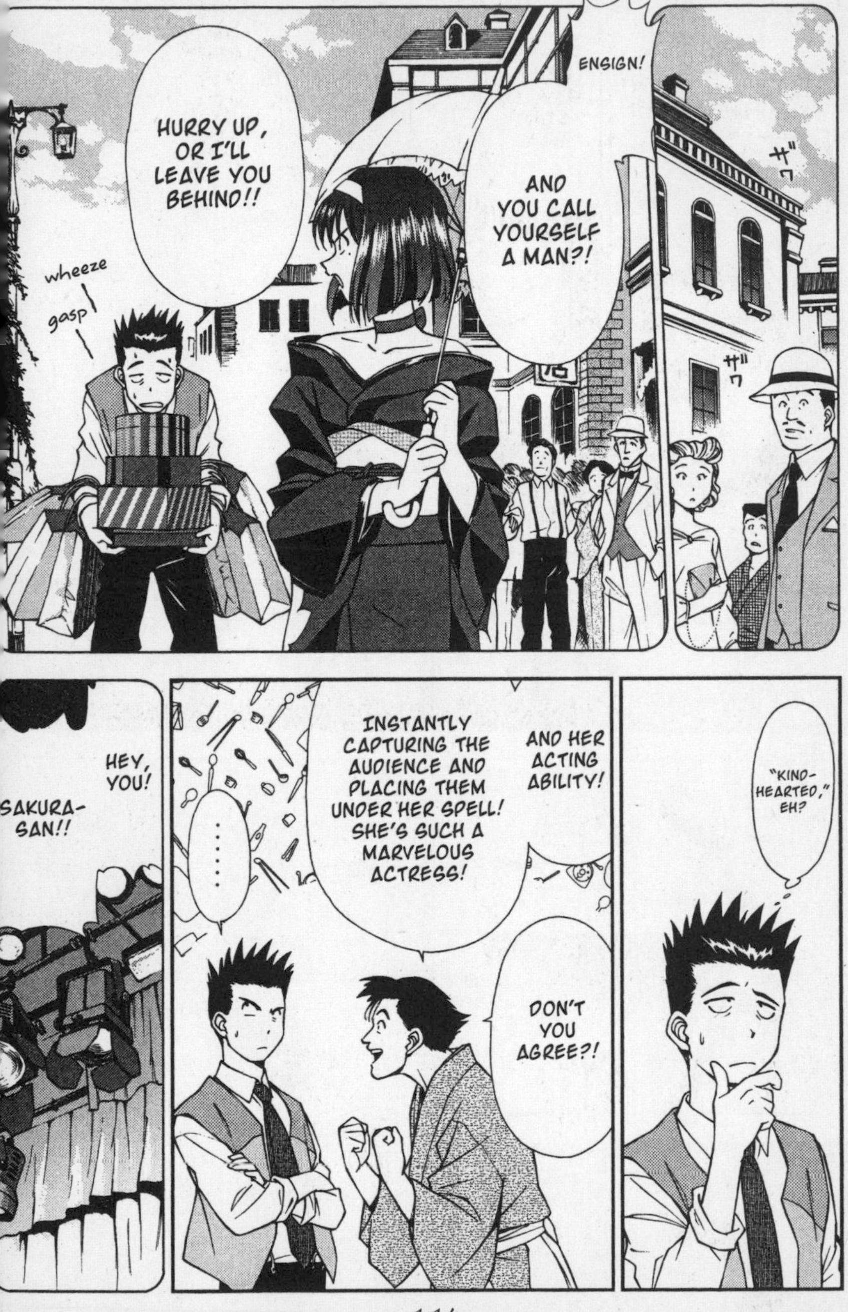
ENSIGN!
AND YOU CALL YOURSELF A MAN?!
ザワ
ザワ
HURRY UP, OR I'LL LEAVE YOU BEHIND!!
wheeze
gasp
"KIND-HEARTED," EH?
AND HER ACTING ABILITY!
INSTANTLY CAPTURING THE AUDIENCE AND PLACING THEM UNDER HER SPELL! SHE'S SUCH A MARVELOUS ACTRESS!
DON'T YOU AGREE?!
......
HEY, YOU!
SAKURA-SAN!!

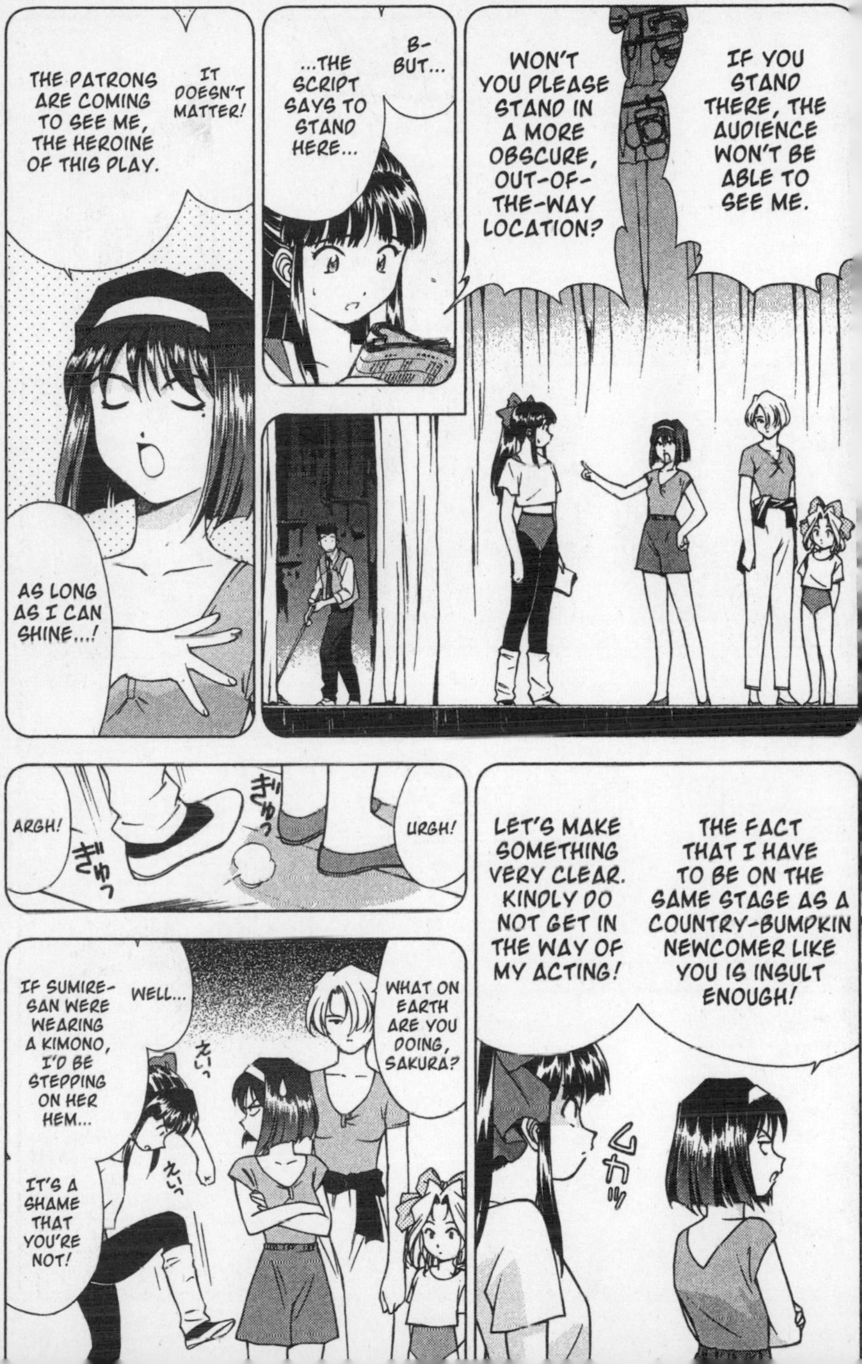
IF YOU STAND THERE, THE AUDIENCE WON'T BE ABLE TO SEE ME.
WON'T YOU PLEASE STAND IN A MORE OBSCURE, OUT-OF-THE-WAY LOCATION?
B-BUT...
...THE SCRIPT SAYS TO STAND HERE...
IT DOESN'T MATTER!
THE PATRONS ARE COMING TO SEE ME, THE HEROINE OF THIS PLAY.
AS LONG AS I CAN SHINE...!
THE FACT THAT I HAVE TO BE ON THE SAME STAGE AS A COUNTRY-BUMPKIN NEWCOMER LIKE YOU IS INSULT ENOUGH!
LET'S MAKE SOMETHING VERY CLEAR. KINDLY DO NOT GET IN THE WAY OF MY ACTING!
ムカッ
URGH!
ぎゅっ
ARGH!
ぎゅっ
WHAT ON EARTH ARE YOU DOING, SAKURA?
WELL...
IF SUMIRE-SAN WERE WEARING A KIMONO, I'D BE STEPPING ON HER HEM...
えいっ
えいっ
IT'S A SHAME THAT YOU'RE NOT!

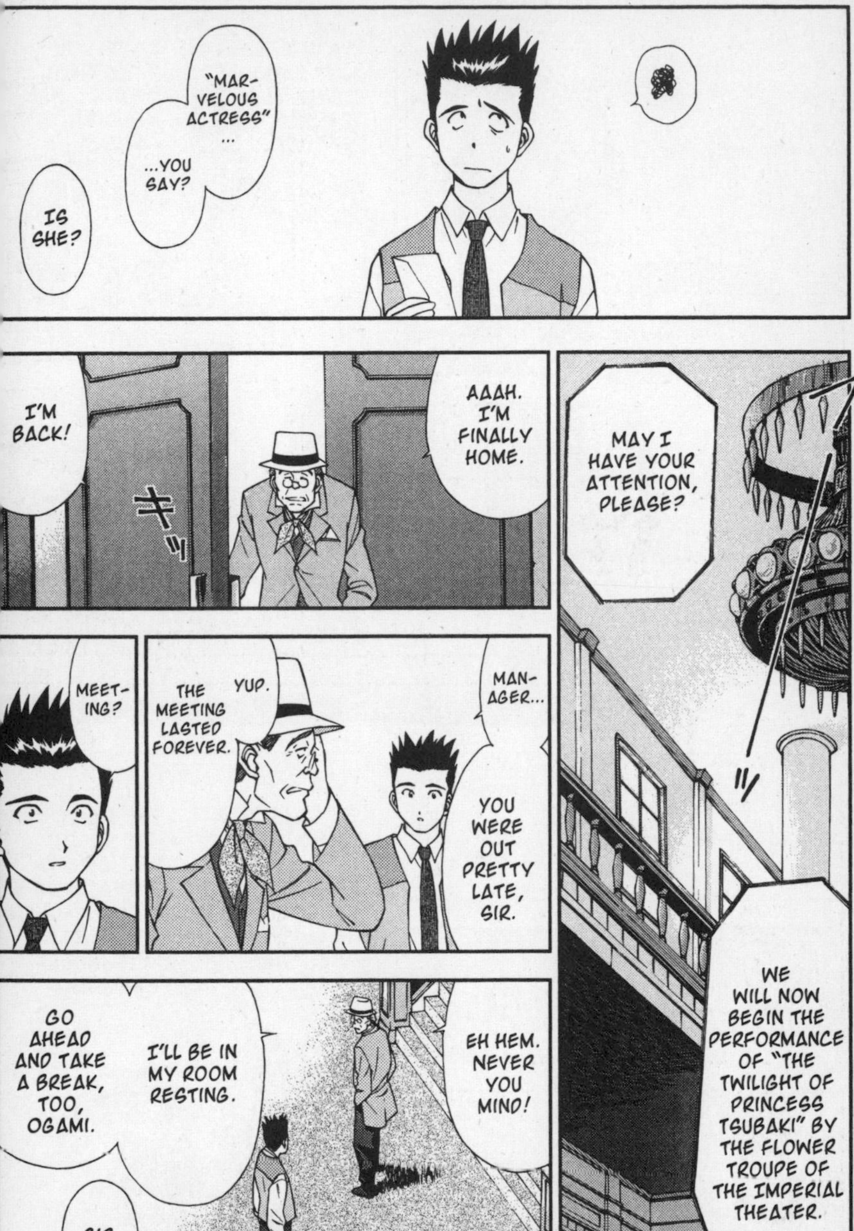
"MARVELOUS ACTRESS" ...
...YOU SAY?
IS SHE?
MAY I HAVE YOUR ATTENTION, PLEASE?
WE WILL NOW BEGIN THE PERFORMANCE OF "THE TWILIGHT OF PRINCESS TSUBAKI" BY THE FLOWER TROUPE OF THE IMPERIAL THEATER.
AAAH. I'M FINALLY HOME.
キッ
I'M BACK!
MANAGER...
YOU WERE OUT PRETTY LATE, SIR.
YUP.
THE MEETING LASTED FOREVER.
MEETING?
EH HEM. NEVER YOU MIND!
I'LL BE IN MY ROOM RESTING.
GO AHEAD AND TAKE A BREAK, TOO, OGAMI.
SIR.

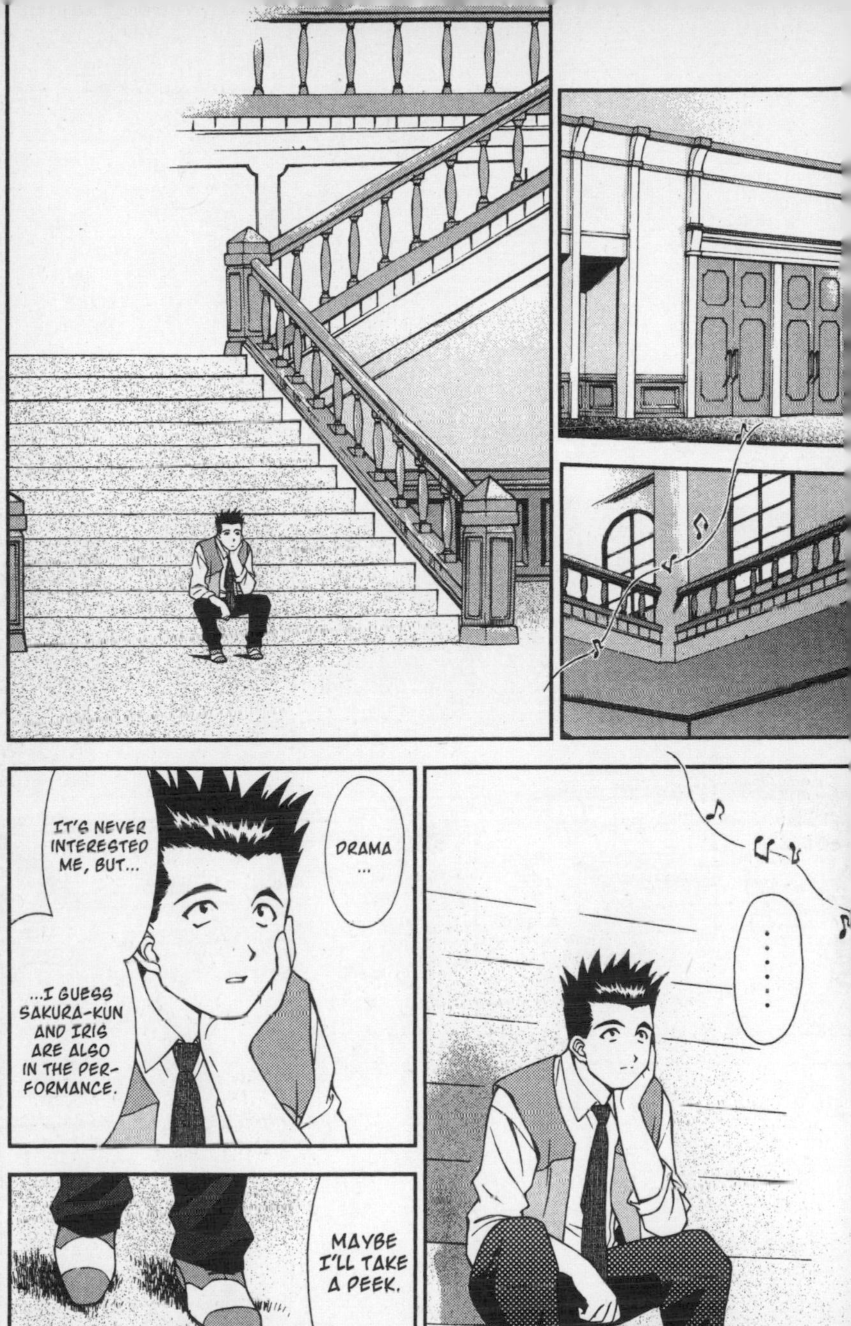
......
DRAMA ...
IT'S NEVER INTERESTED ME, BUT...
...I GUESS SAKURA-KUN AND IRIS ARE ALSO IN THE PERFORMANCE.
MAYBE I'LL TAKE A PEEK.

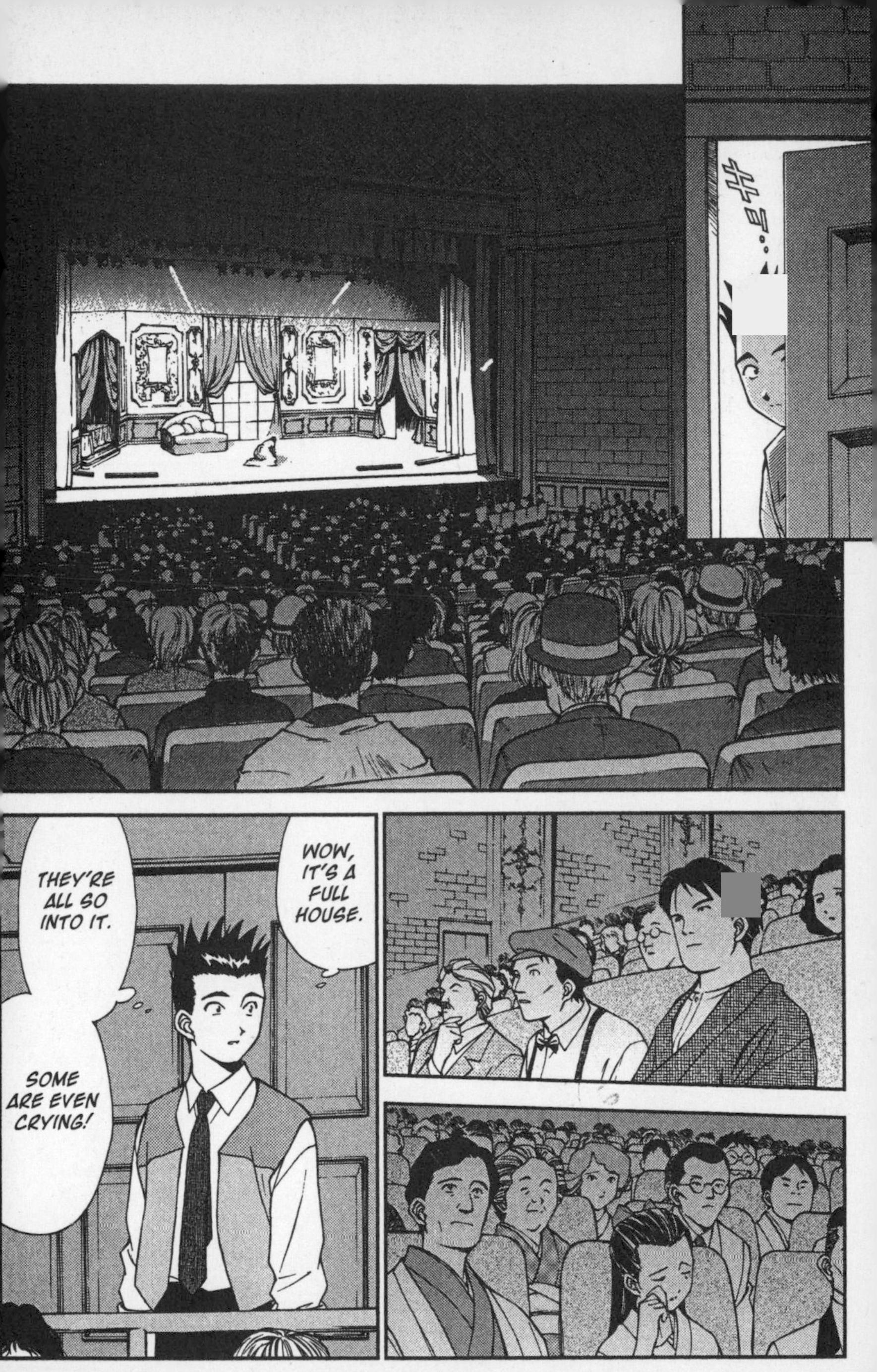
WOW, IT'S A FULL HOUSE.
THEY'RE ALL SO INTO IT.
SOME ARE EVEN CRYING!

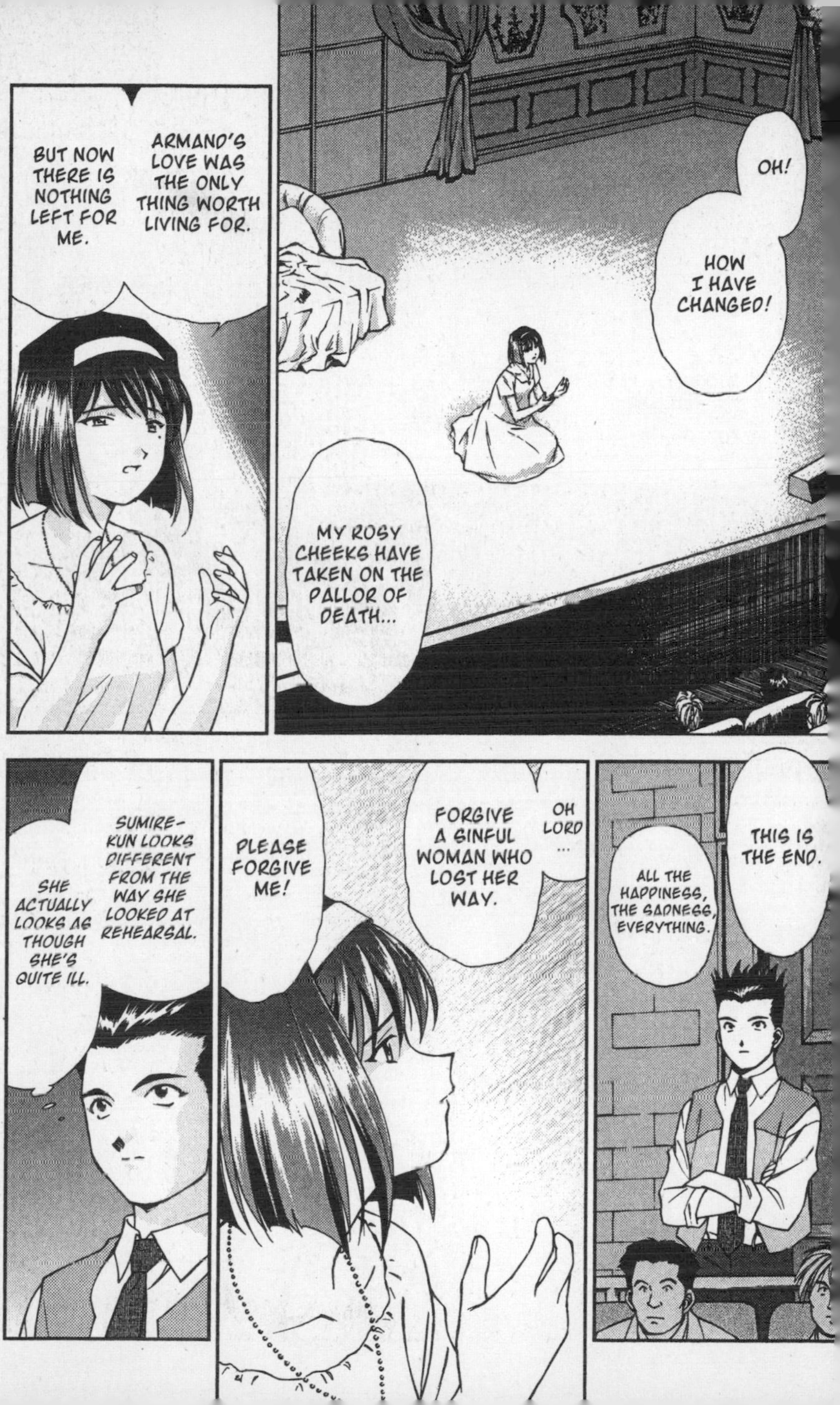
OH!
HOW I HAVE CHANGED!
MY ROSY CHEEKS HAVE TAKEN ON THE PALLOR OF DEATH...
ARMAND'S LOVE WAS THE ONLY THING WORTH LIVING FOR.
BUT NOW THERE IS NOTHING LEFT FOR ME.
THIS IS THE END.
ALL THE HAPPINESS, THE SADNESS, EVERYTHING.
OH LORD ...
FORGIVE A SINFUL WOMAN WHO LOST HER WAY.
PLEASE FORGIVE ME!
SUMIRE-KUN LOOKS DIFFERENT FROM THE WAY SHE LOOKED AT REHEARSAL.
SHE ACTUALLY LOOKS AS THOUGH SHE'S QUITE ILL.

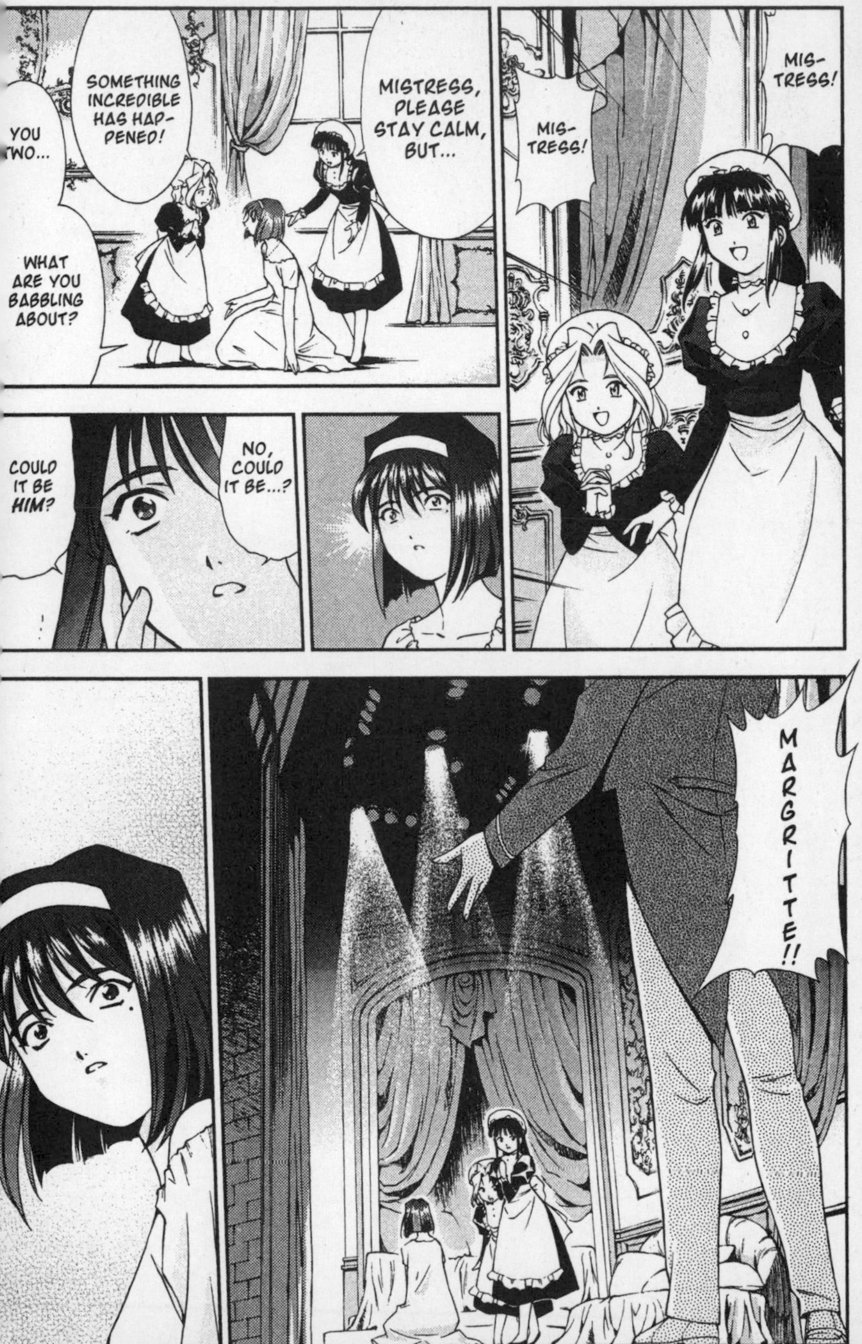

MIS-TRESS!
MIS-TRESS!
MISTRESS, PLEASE STAY CALM, BUT...
SOMETHING INCREDIBLE HAS HAP-PENED!
YOU TWO...
WHAT ARE YOU BABBLING ABOUT?
NO, COULD IT BE...?
COULD IT BE *HIM*?
MARGRITTE!!

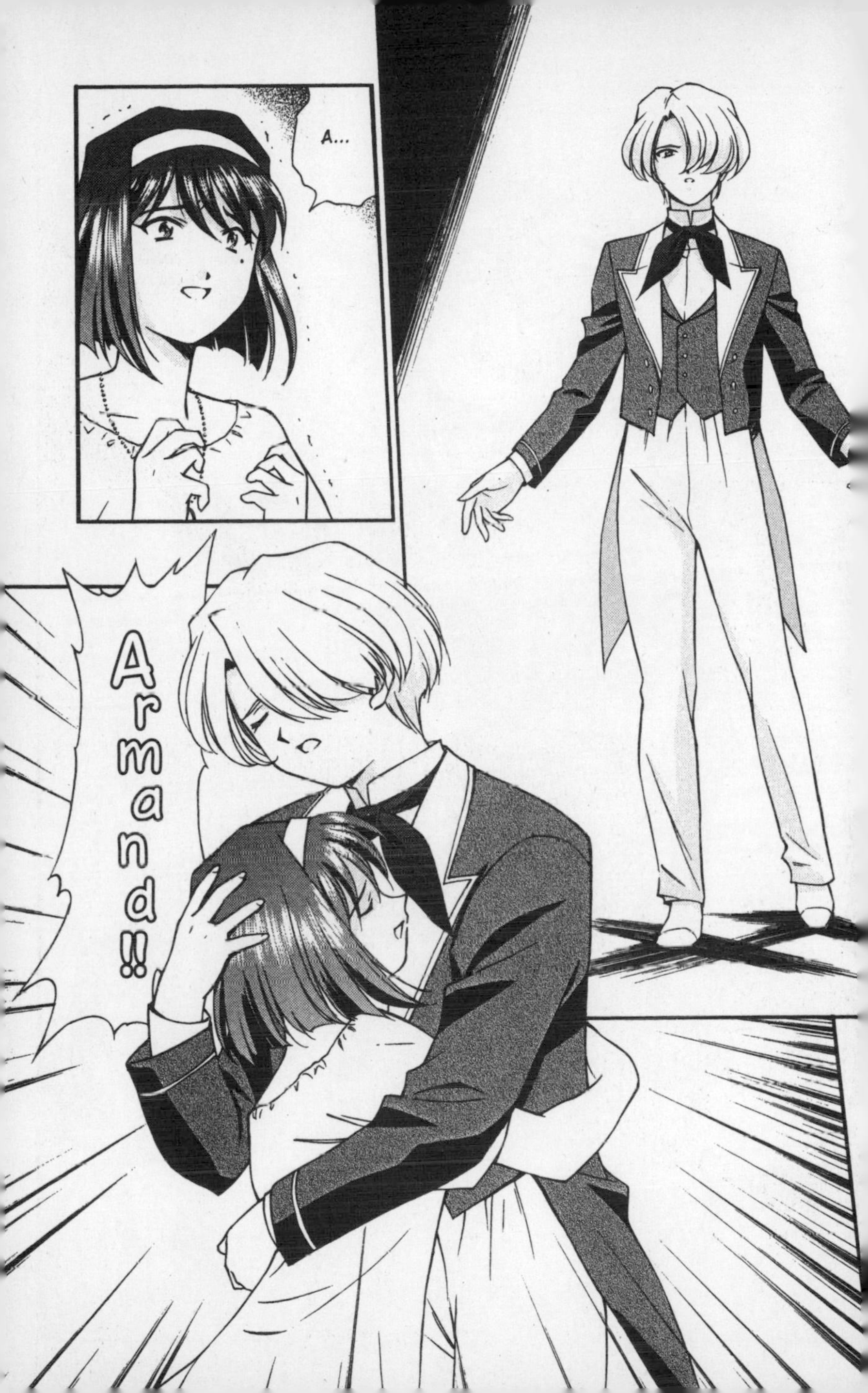
A...
Armand!!

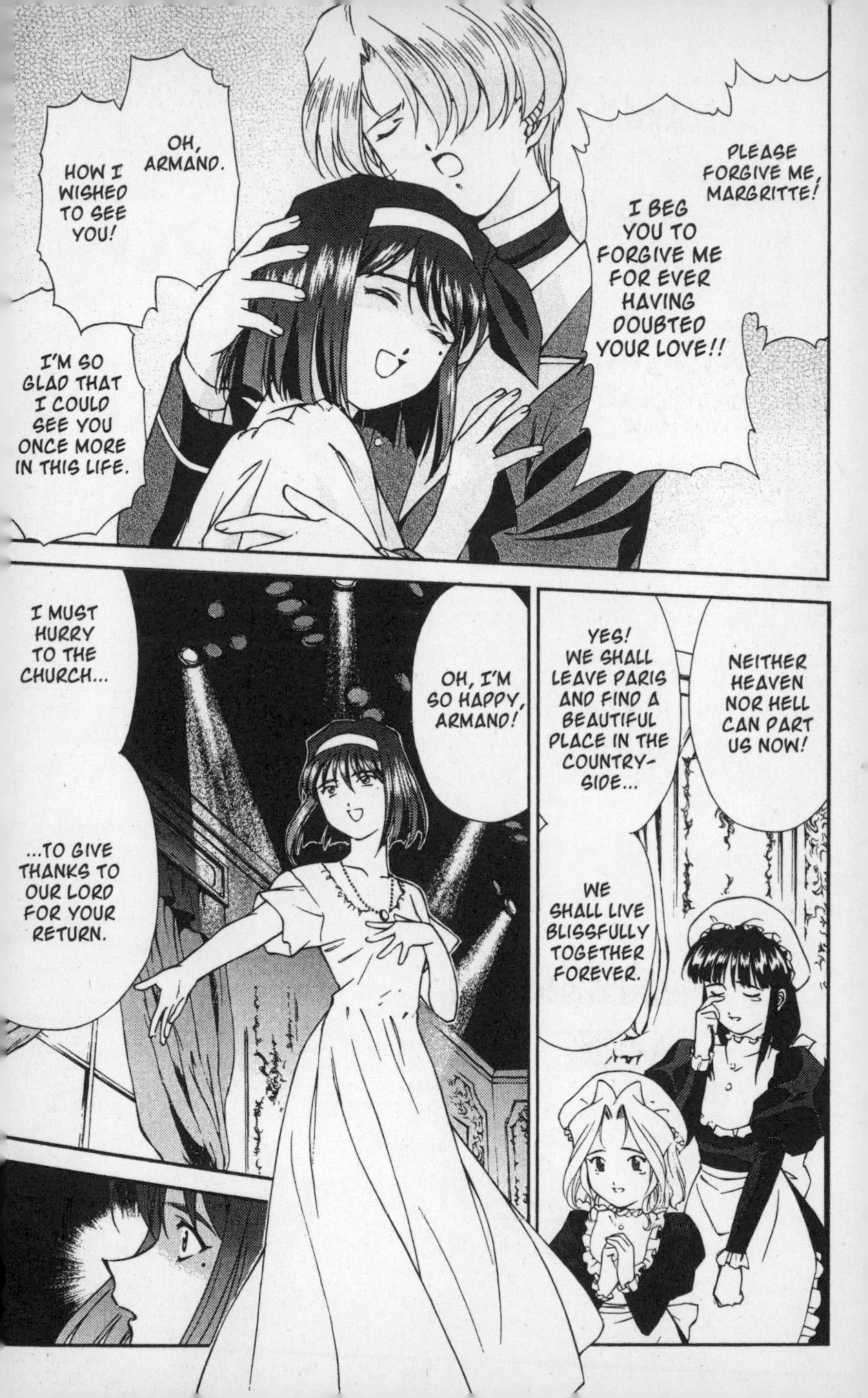
PLEASE FORGIVE ME, MARGRITTE!
I BEG YOU TO FORGIVE ME FOR EVER HAVING DOUBTED YOUR LOVE!!
OH, ARMAND.
HOW I WISHED TO SEE YOU!
I'M SO GLAD THAT I COULD SEE YOU ONCE MORE IN THIS LIFE.
NEITHER HEAVEN NOR HELL CAN PART US NOW!
YES! WE SHALL LEAVE PARIS AND FIND A BEAUTIFUL PLACE IN THE COUNTRY-SIDE...
WE SHALL LIVE BLISSFULLY TOGETHER FOREVER.
OH, I'M SO HAPPY, ARMAND!
I MUST HURRY TO THE CHURCH...
...TO GIVE THANKS TO OUR LORD FOR YOUR RETURN.

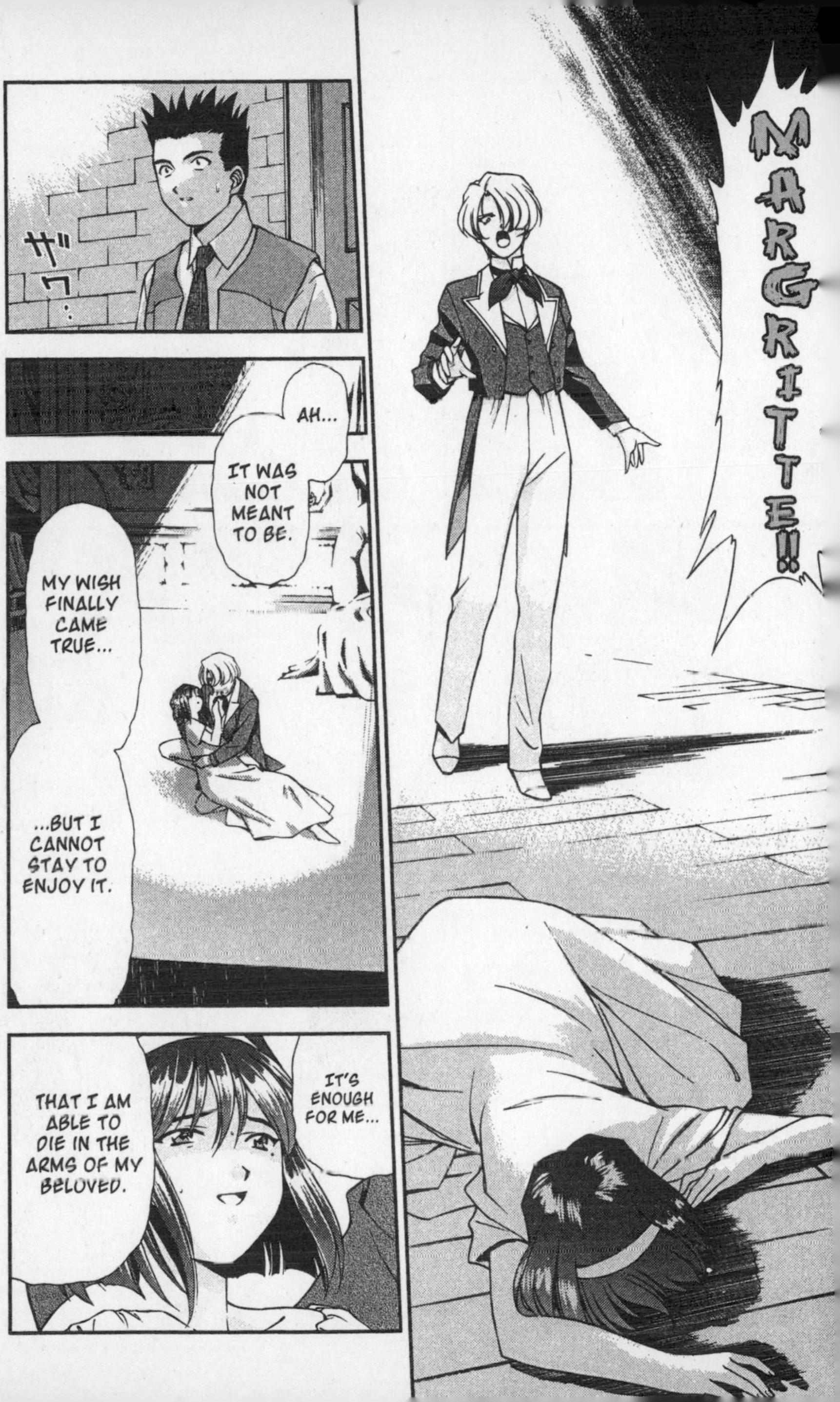
MARGRITTE!!
ザワ…
AH...
IT WAS NOT MEANT TO BE.
MY WISH FINALLY CAME TRUE...
...BUT I CANNOT STAY TO ENJOY IT.
IT'S ENOUGH FOR ME...
THAT I AM ABLE TO DIE IN THE ARMS OF MY BELOVED.

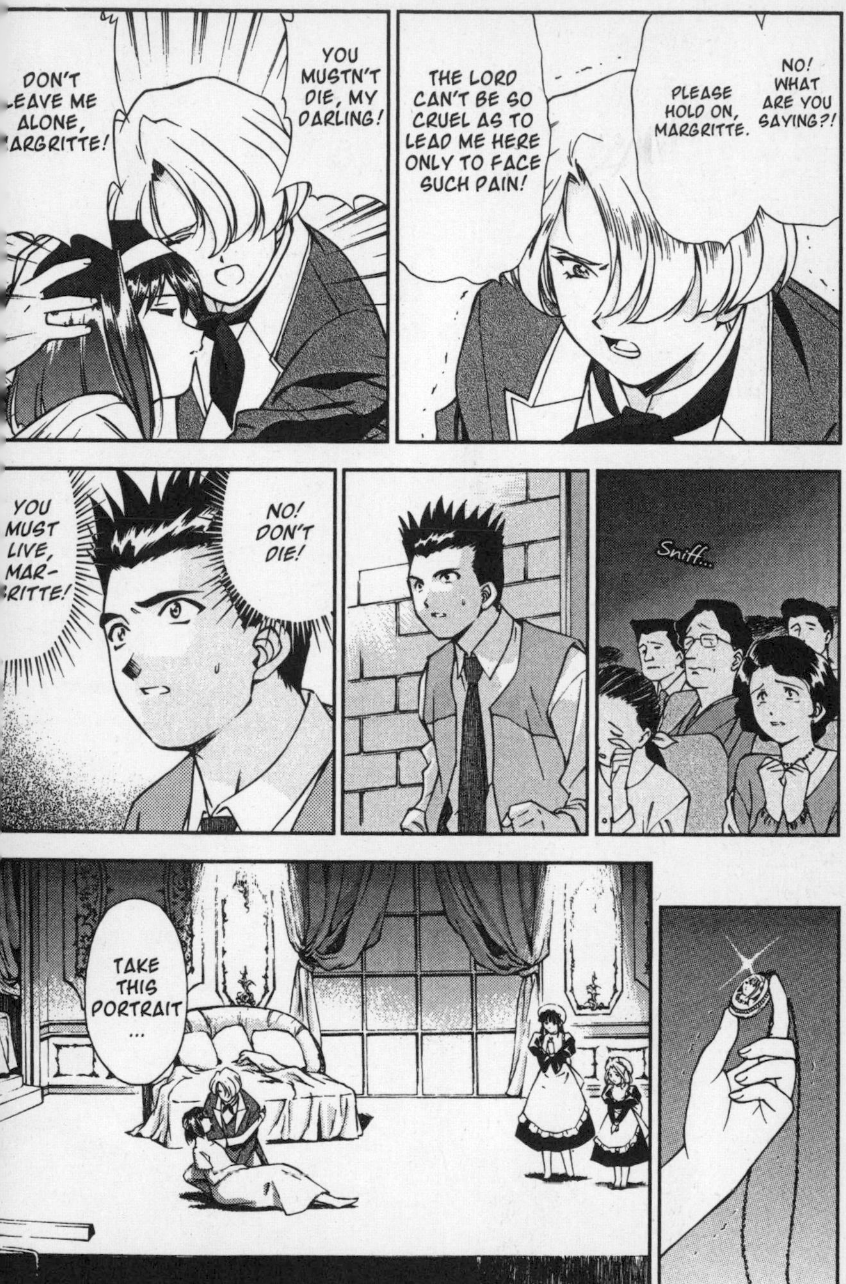
NO! WHAT ARE YOU SAYING?!
PLEASE HOLD ON, MARGRITTE.
THE LORD CAN'T BE SO CRUEL AS TO LEAD ME HERE ONLY TO FACE SUCH PAIN!
YOU MUSTN'T DIE, MY DARLING!
DON'T LEAVE ME ALONE, MARGRITTE!
Sniff...
NO! DON'T DIE!
YOU MUST LIVE, MAR-GRITTE!
TAKE THIS PORTRAIT ...

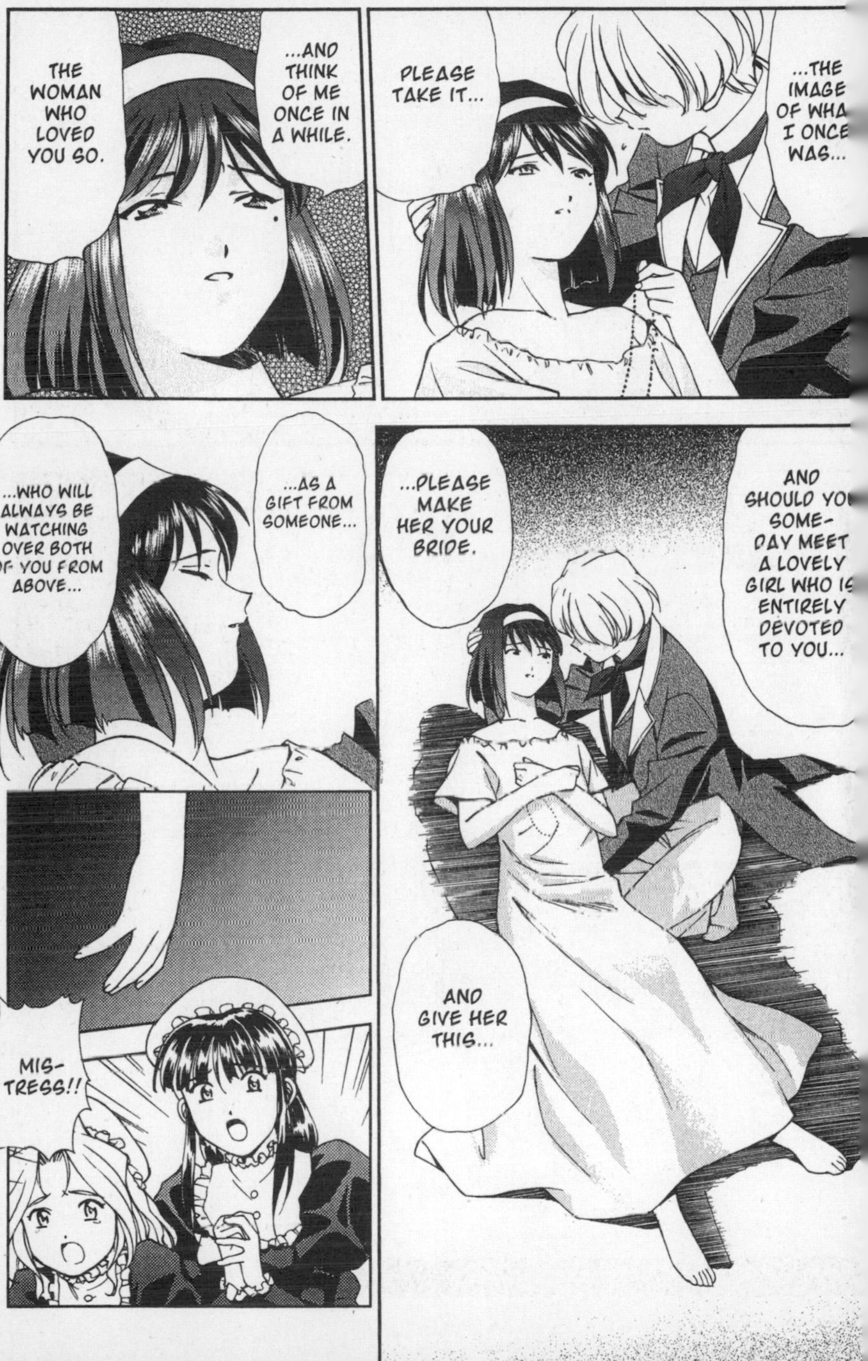
...THE IMAGE OF WHA I ONCE WAS...
PLEASE TAKE IT...
...AND THINK OF ME ONCE IN A WHILE.
THE WOMAN WHO LOVED YOU SO.
AND SHOULD YOU SOME-DAY MEET A LOVELY GIRL WHO IS ENTIRELY DEVOTED TO YOU...
...PLEASE MAKE HER YOUR BRIDE.
AND GIVE HER THIS...
...AS A GIFT FROM SOMEONE...
...WHO WILL ALWAYS BE WATCHING OVER BOTH OF YOU FROM ABOVE...
MIS-TRESS!!

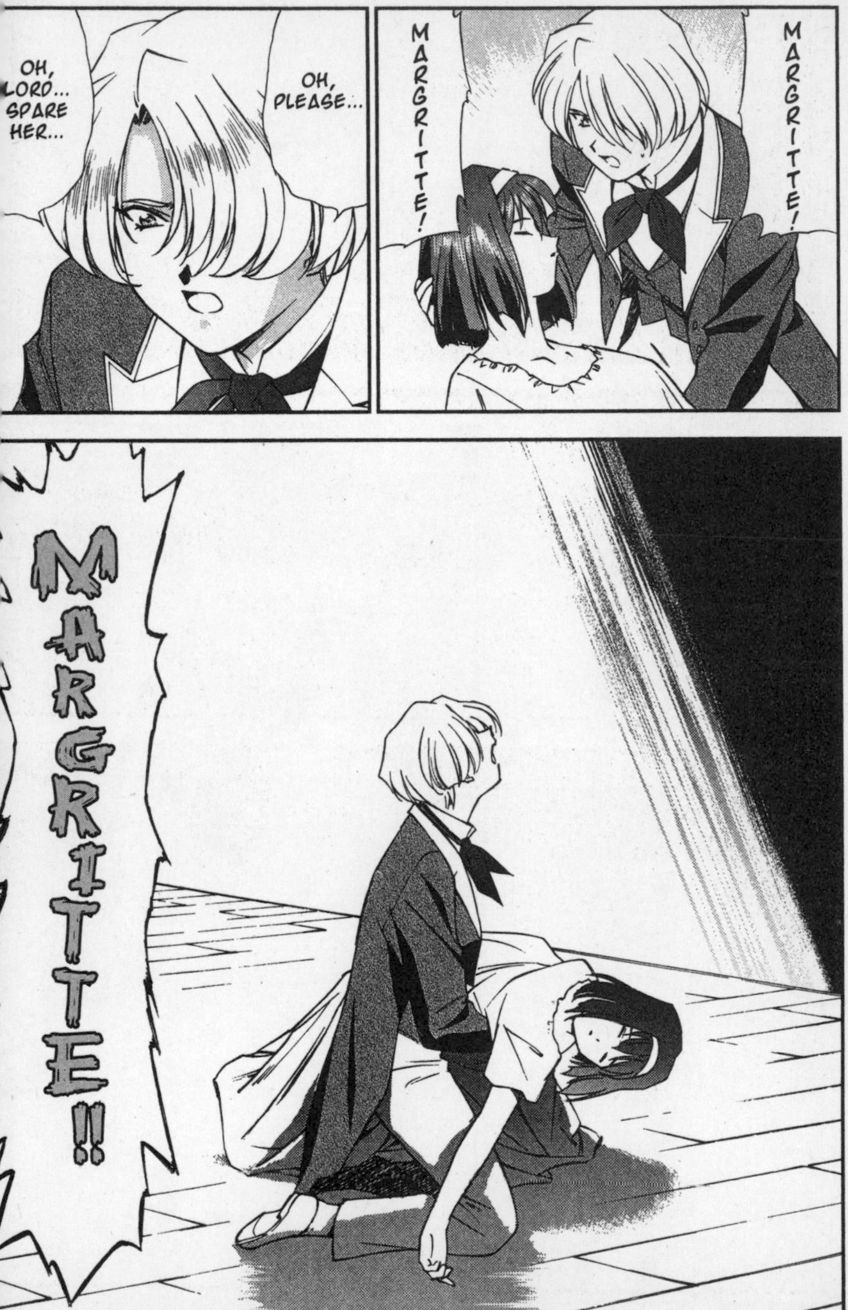
MARGRITTE!
MARGRITTE!
OH, PLEASE...
OH, LORD... SPARE HER...
MARGRITTE!!

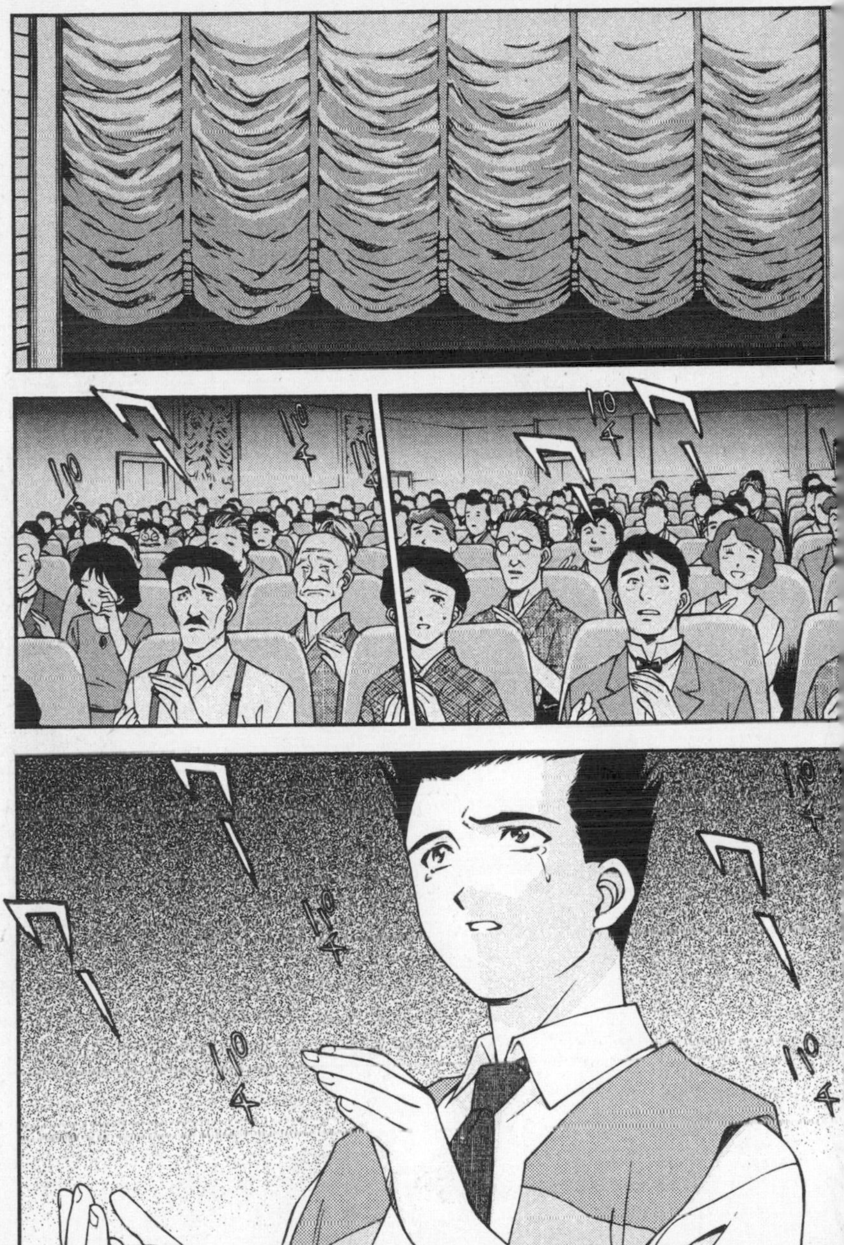

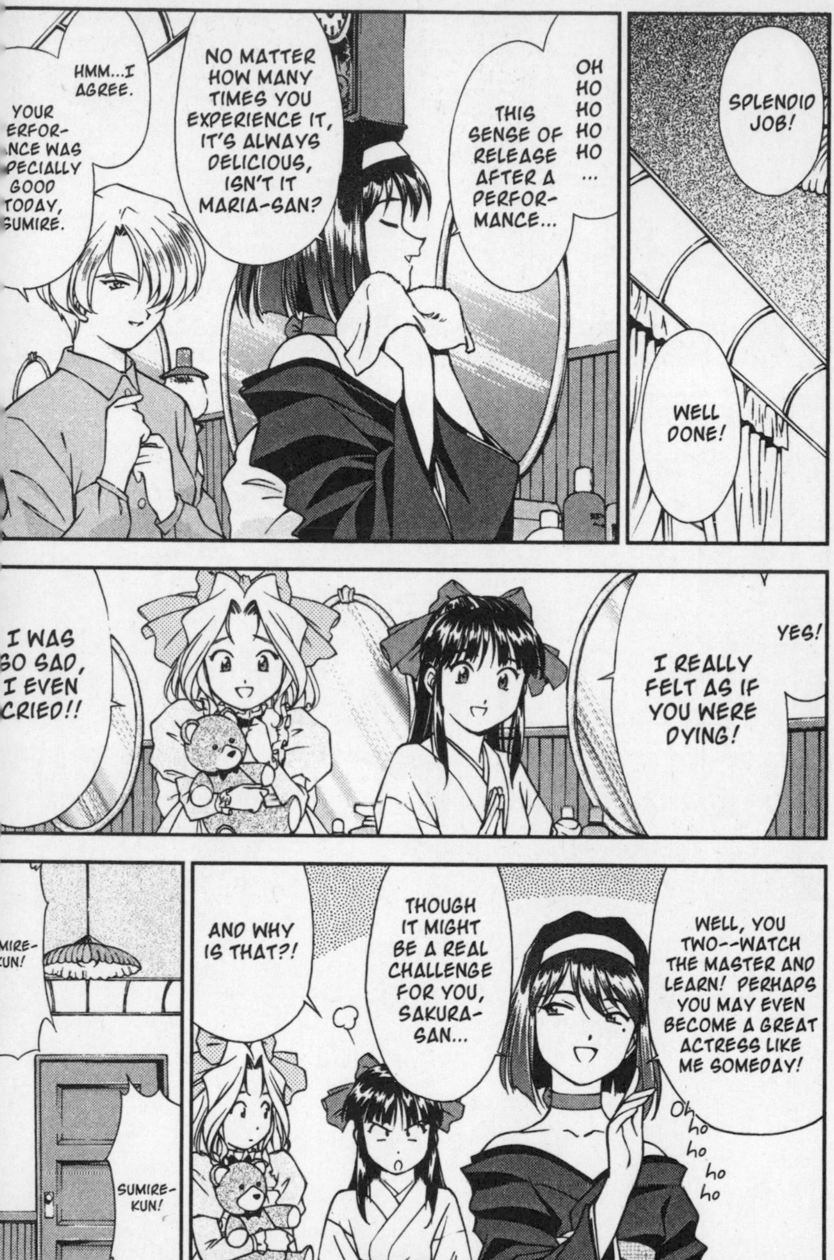
SPLENDID JOB!
WELL DONE!
OH HO HO HO HO ...
THIS SENSE OF RELEASE AFTER A PERFORMANCE...
NO MATTER HOW MANY TIMES YOU EXPERIENCE IT, IT'S ALWAYS DELICIOUS, ISN'T IT MARIA-SAN?
HMM...I AGREE.
YOUR ERFOR-ANCE WAS PECIALLY GOOD TODAY, SUMIRE.
YES!
I REALLY FELT AS IF YOU WERE DYING!
I WAS SO SAD, I EVEN CRIED!!
WELL, YOU TWO--WATCH THE MASTER AND LEARN! PERHAPS YOU MAY EVEN BECOME A GREAT ACTRESS LIKE ME SOMEDAY!
Oh ho ho ho ho
THOUGH IT MIGHT BE A REAL CHALLENGE FOR YOU, SAKURA-SAN...
AND WHY IS THAT?!
MIRE-KUN!
SUMIRE-KUN!

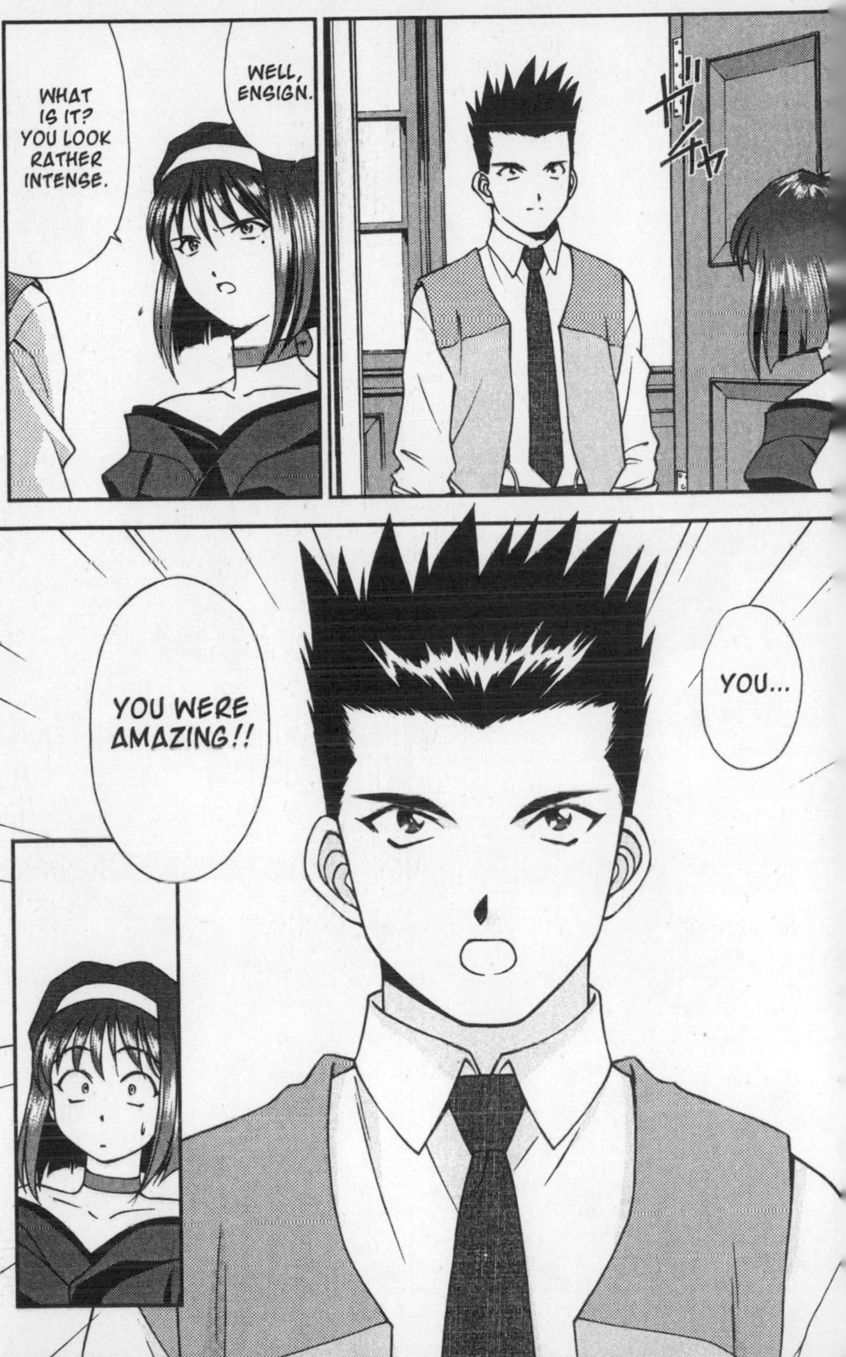
ガチャ
WELL, ENSIGN.
WHAT IS IT? YOU LOOK RATHER INTENSE.
YOU...
YOU WERE AMAZING!!

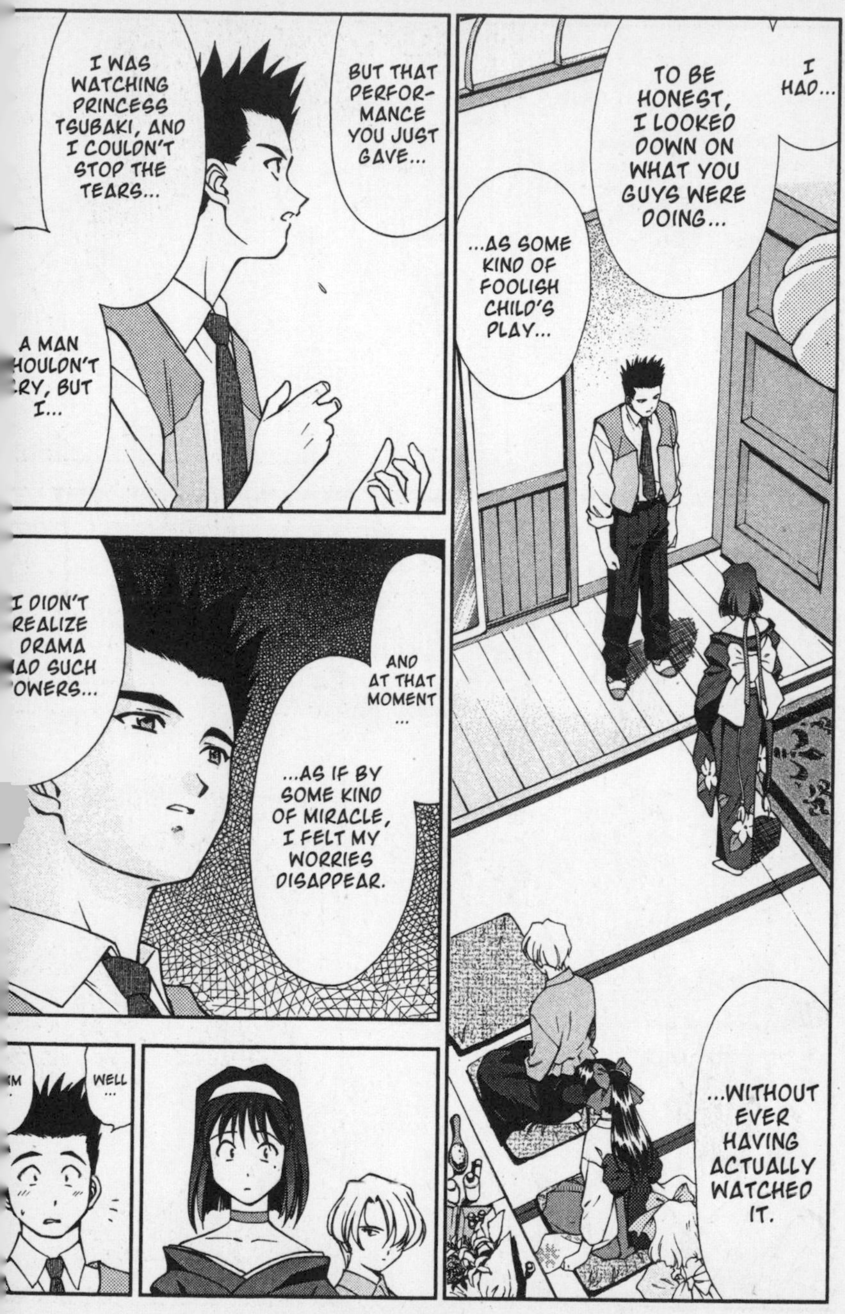
I HAD...
TO BE HONEST, I LOOKED DOWN ON WHAT YOU GUYS WERE DOING...
...AS SOME KIND OF FOOLISH CHILD'S PLAY...
...WITHOUT EVER HAVING ACTUALLY WATCHED IT.
BUT THAT PERFORMANCE YOU JUST GAVE...
I WAS WATCHING PRINCESS TSUBAKI, AND I COULDN'T STOP THE TEARS...
A MAN HOULDN'T RY, BUT I...
I DIDN'T REALIZE DRAMA AD SUCH OWERS...
AND AT THAT MOMENT...
...AS IF BY SOME KIND OF MIRACLE, I FELT MY WORRIES DISAPPEAR.
WELL...

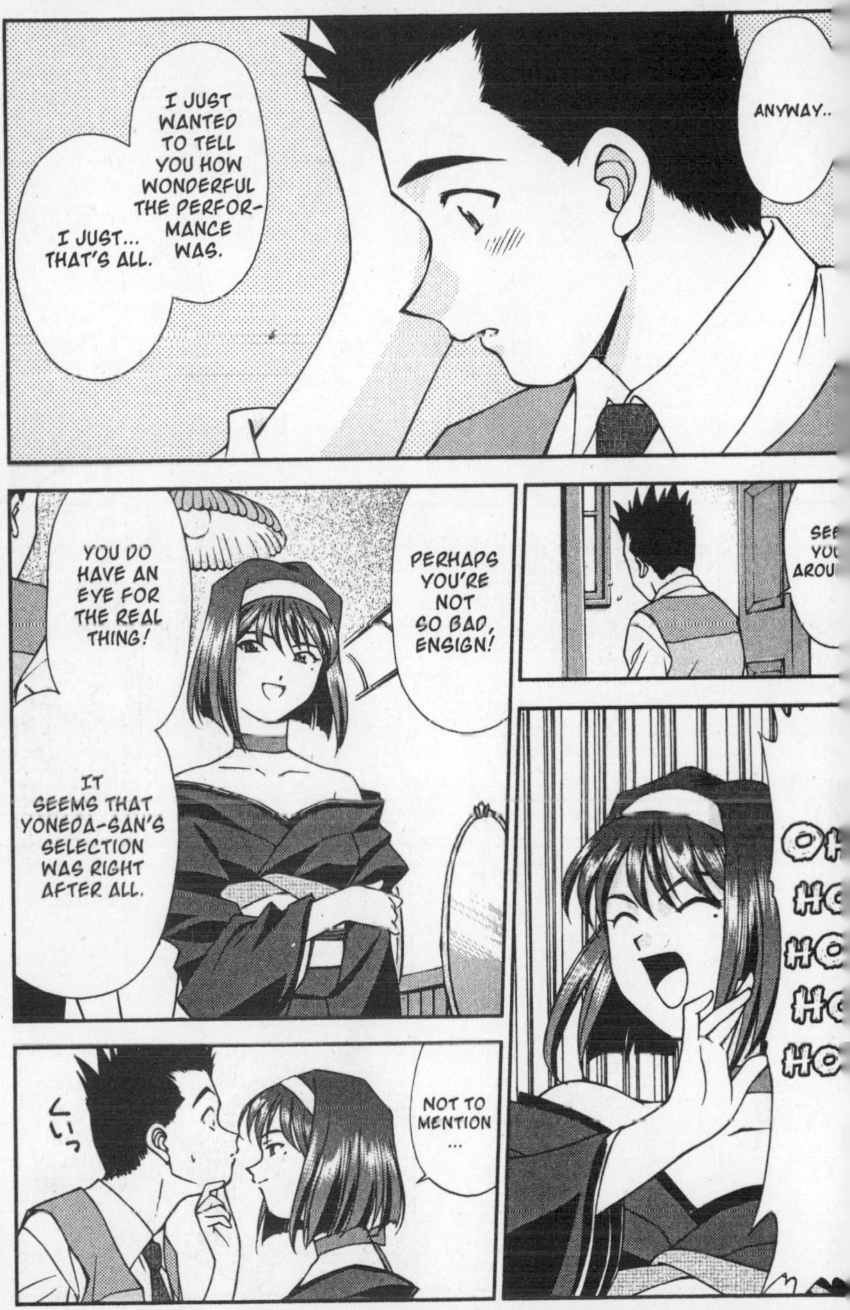
ANYWAY..
I JUST WANTED TO TELL YOU HOW WONDERFUL THE PERFORMANCE WAS.
I JUST... THAT'S ALL.
SEE YOU AROU
OH HO HO HO HO
PERHAPS YOU'RE NOT SO BAD, ENSIGN!
YOU DO HAVE AN EYE FOR THE REAL THING!
IT SEEMS THAT YONEDA-SAN'S SELECTION WAS RIGHT AFTER ALL.
NOT TO MENTION ...

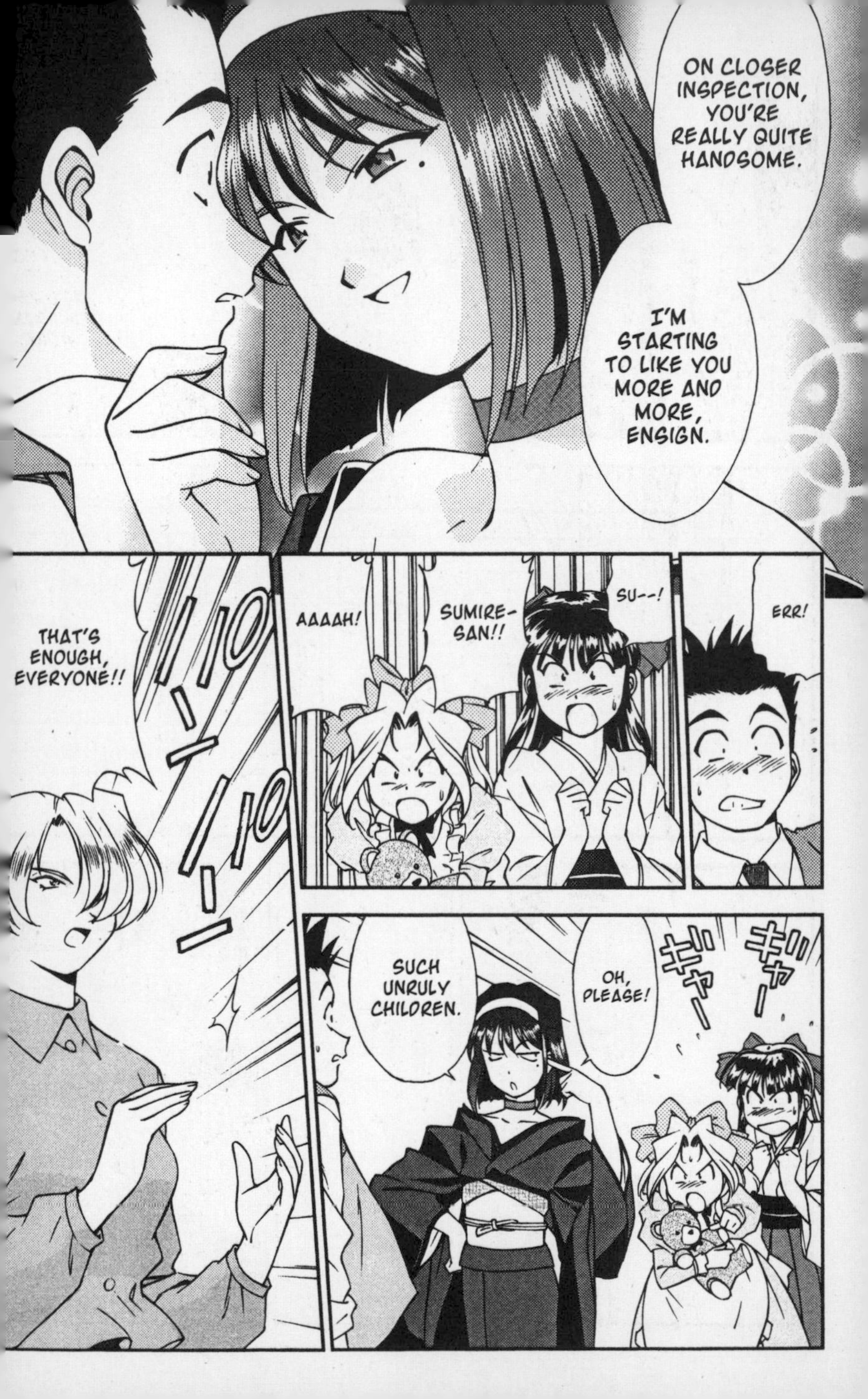
ON CLOSER INSPECTION, YOU'RE REALLY QUITE HANDSOME.
I'M STARTING TO LIKE YOU MORE AND MORE, ENSIGN.
ERR!
SU--!
SUMIRE-SAN!!
AAAAH!
ギャー
ギャー
OH, PLEASE!
SUCH UNRULY CHILDREN.
THAT'S ENOUGH, EVERYONE!!

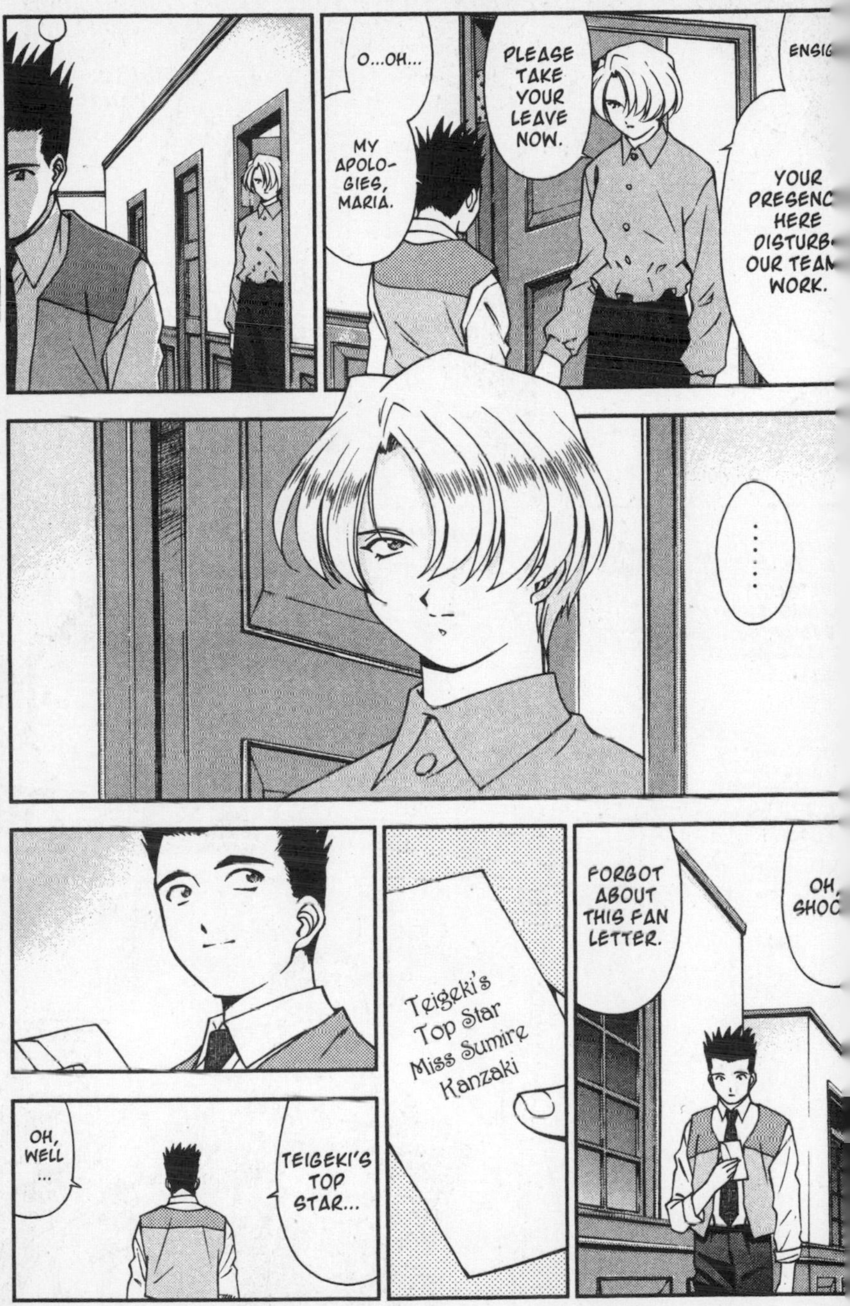
ENSIG
YOUR PRESENC HERE DISTURB OUR TEAM WORK.
PLEASE TAKE YOUR LEAVE NOW.
O...OH...
MY APOLOGIES, MARIA.
......
OH, SHOC
FORGOT ABOUT THIS FAN LETTER.
Teigeki's Top Star Miss Sumire Kanzaki
TEIGEKI'S TOP STAR...
OH, WELL ...

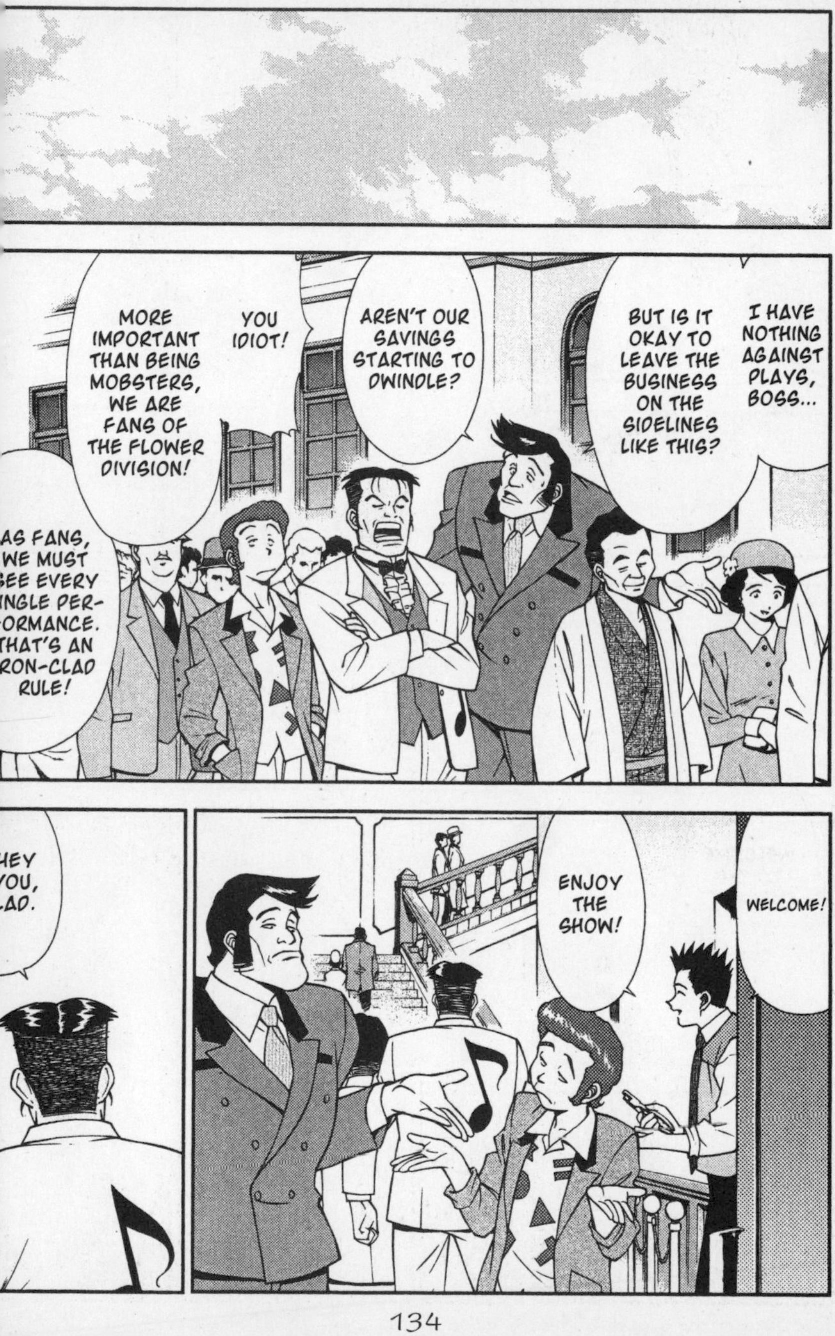
I HAVE NOTHING AGAINST PLAYS, BOSS...
BUT IS IT OKAY TO LEAVE THE BUSINESS ON THE SIDELINES LIKE THIS?
AREN'T OUR SAVINGS STARTING TO DWINDLE?
YOU IDIOT!
MORE IMPORTANT THAN BEING MOBSTERS, WE ARE FANS OF THE FLOWER DIVISION!
AS FANS, WE MUST EE EVERY INGLE PER- ORMANCE. THAT'S AN RON-CLAD RULE!
WELCOME!
ENJOY THE SHOW!
HEY YOU, LAD.

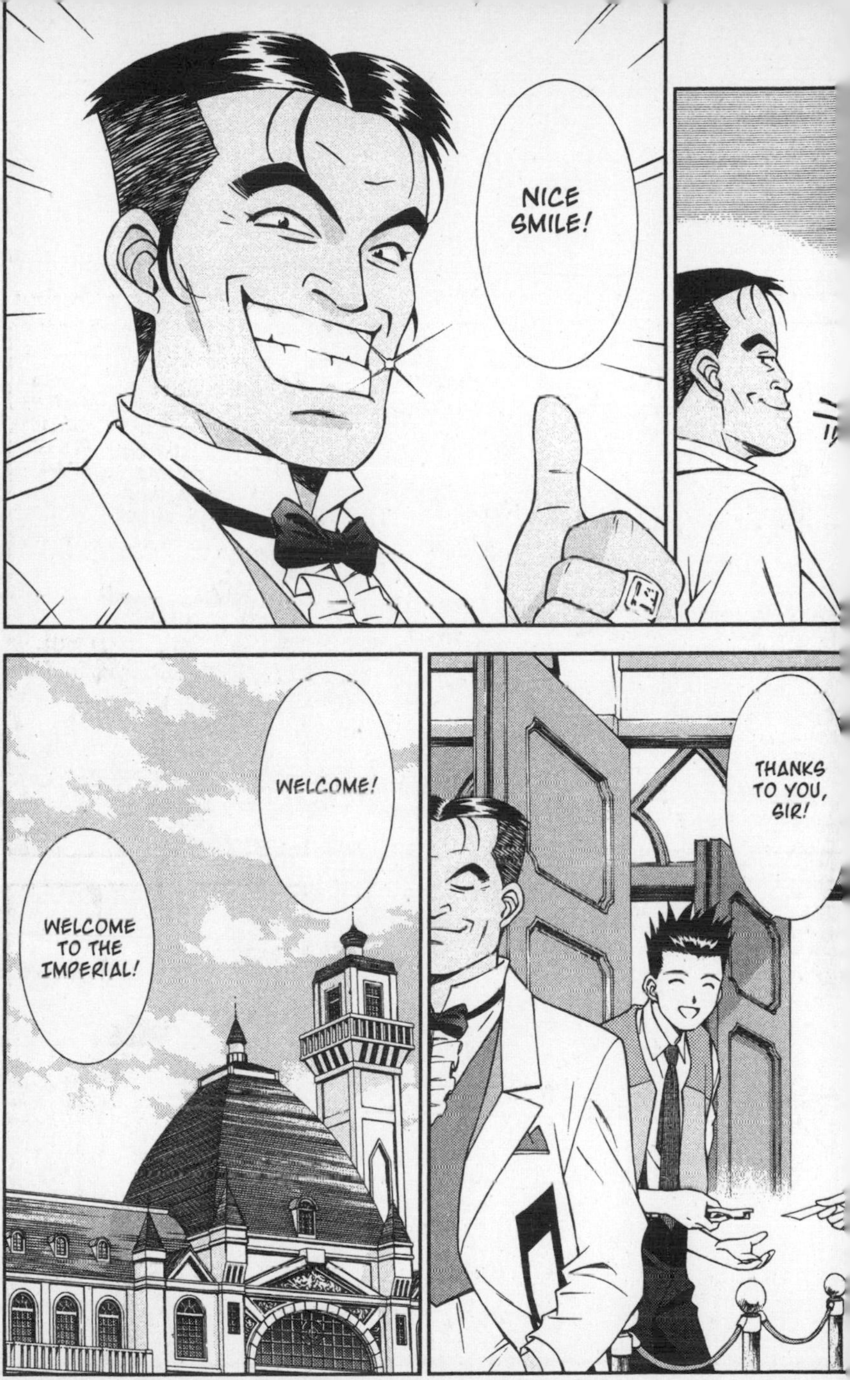
NICE SMILE!
THANKS TO YOU, SIR!
WELCOME!
WELCOME TO THE IMPERIAL!

The Star of the Capital, The Flower of the Teigeki-- End of Act

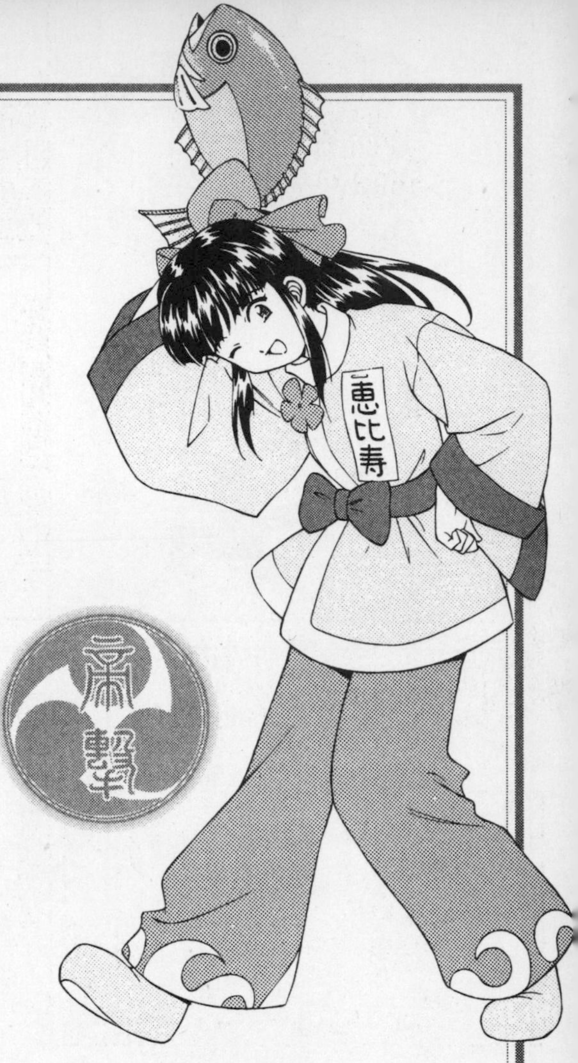
恵比寿

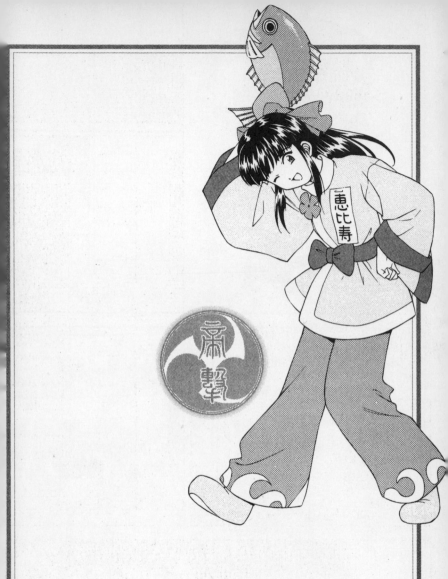

真宮寺さくら Sakura Shinguji as Ebisu.

Chapter 3—Things Get In the Way

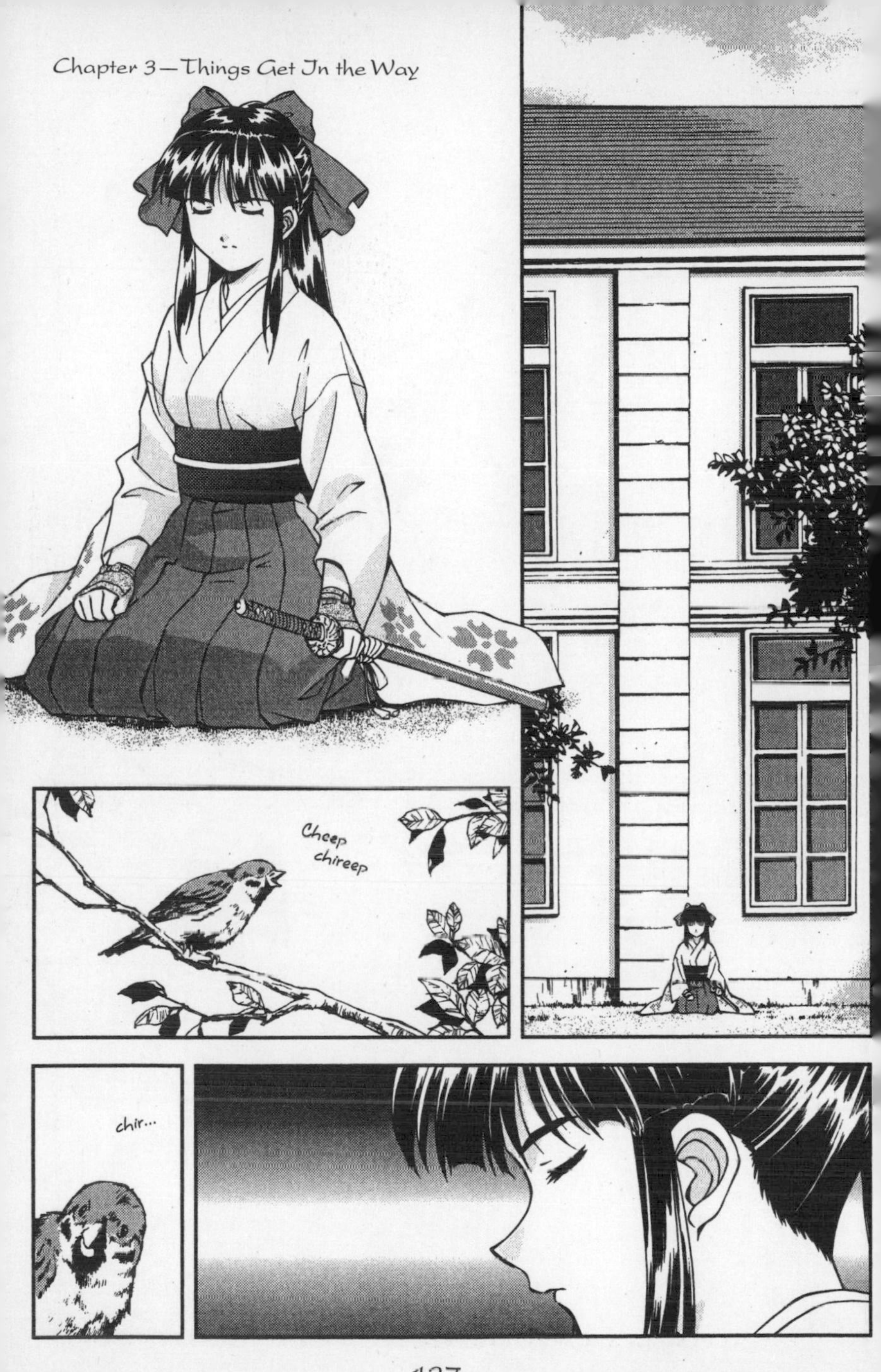
Cheep
chireep
chir...

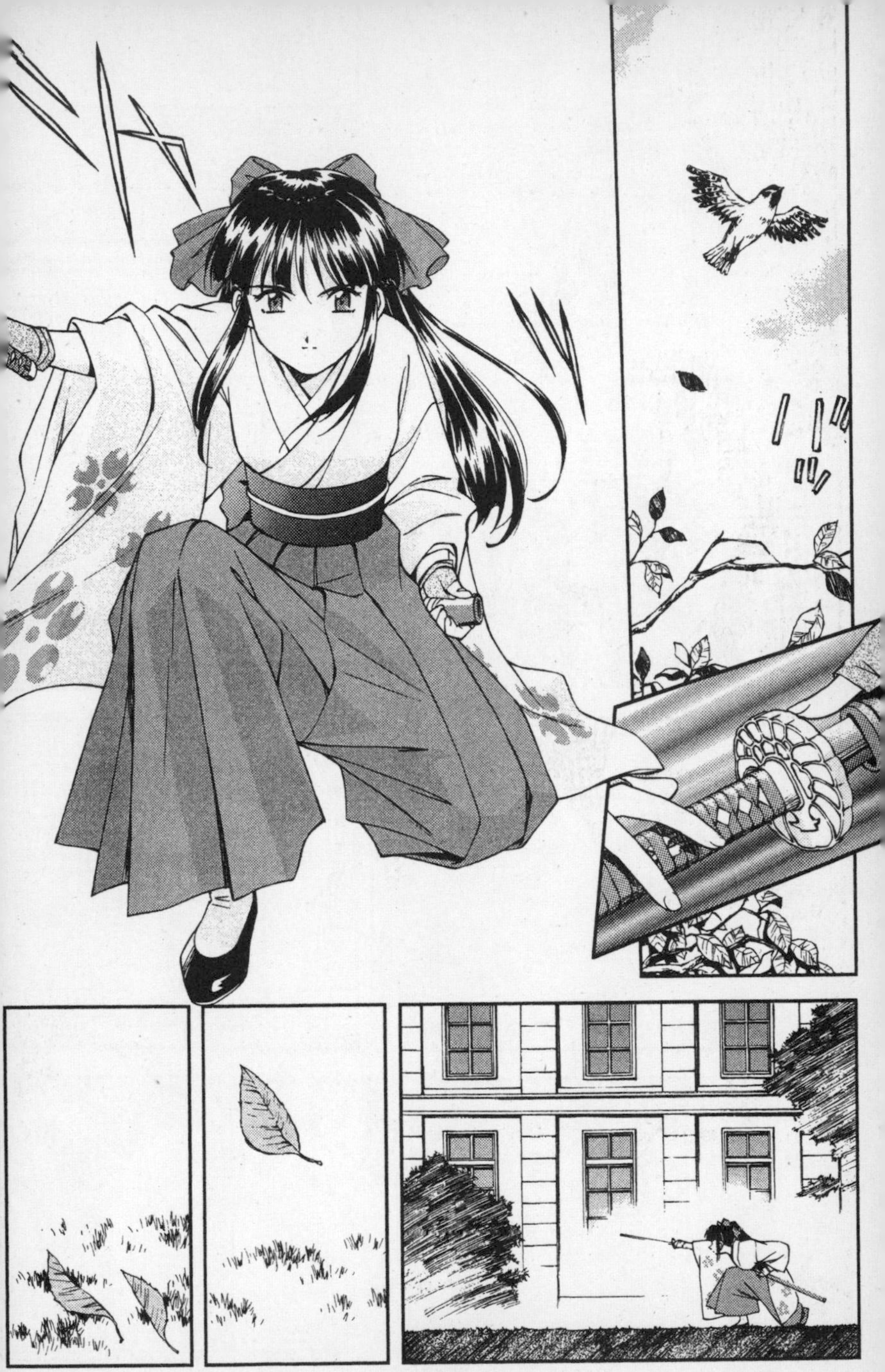

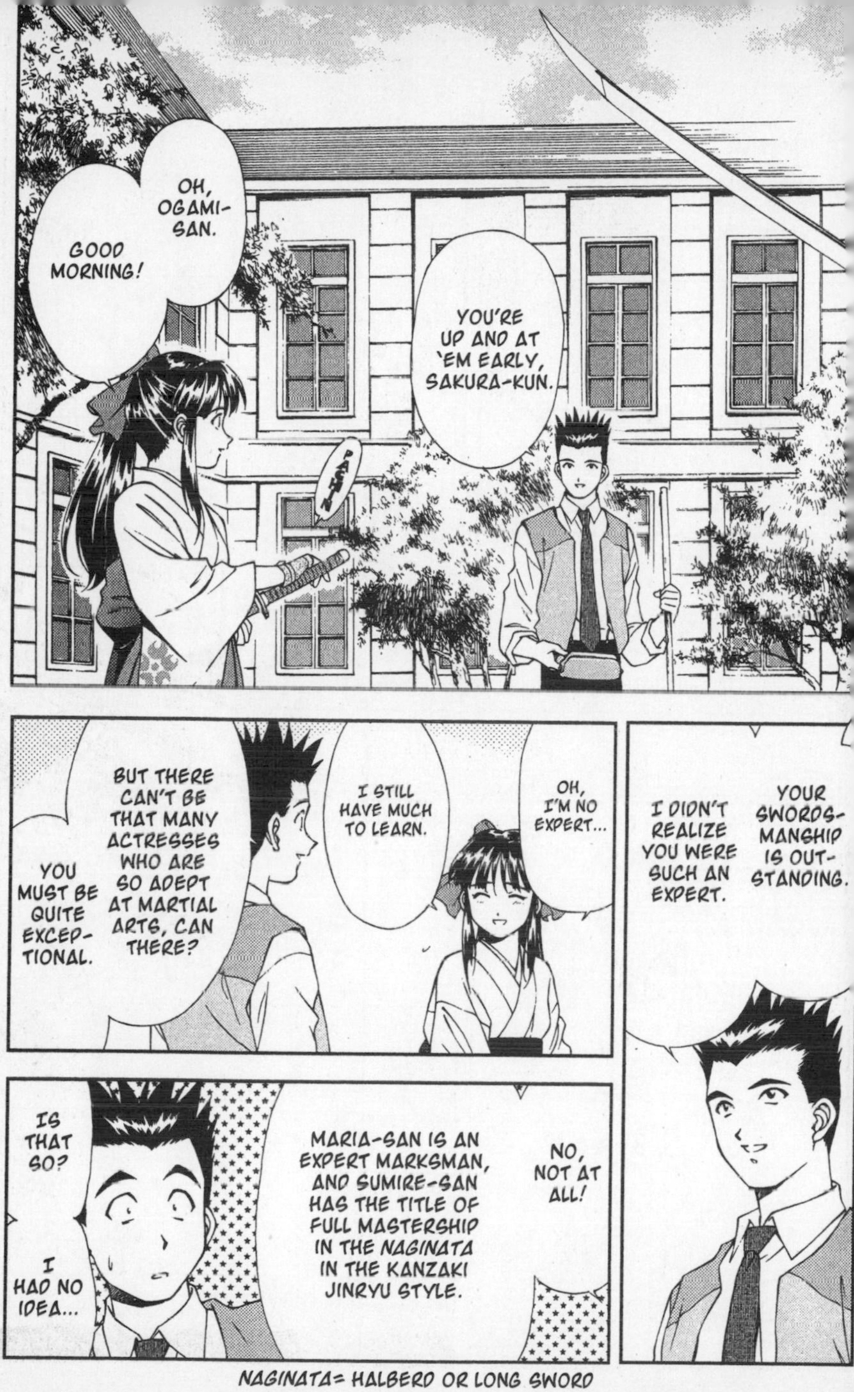
YOU'RE UP AND AT 'EM EARLY, SAKURA-KUN.
OH, OGAMI-SAN.
GOOD MORNING!
PASHIN
YOUR SWORDSMANSHIP IS OUTSTANDING.
I DIDN'T REALIZE YOU WERE SUCH AN EXPERT.
OH, I'M NO EXPERT...
I STILL HAVE MUCH TO LEARN.
BUT THERE CAN'T BE THAT MANY ACTRESSES WHO ARE SO ADEPT AT MARTIAL ARTS, CAN THERE?
YOU MUST BE QUITE EXCEPTIONAL.
NO, NOT AT ALL!
MARIA-SAN IS AN EXPERT MARKSMAN, AND SUMIRE-SAN HAS THE TITLE OF FULL MASTERSHIP IN THE NAGINATA IN THE KANZAKI JINRYU STYLE.
IS THAT SO?
I HAD NO IDEA...

NAGINATA= HALBERD OR LONG SWORD

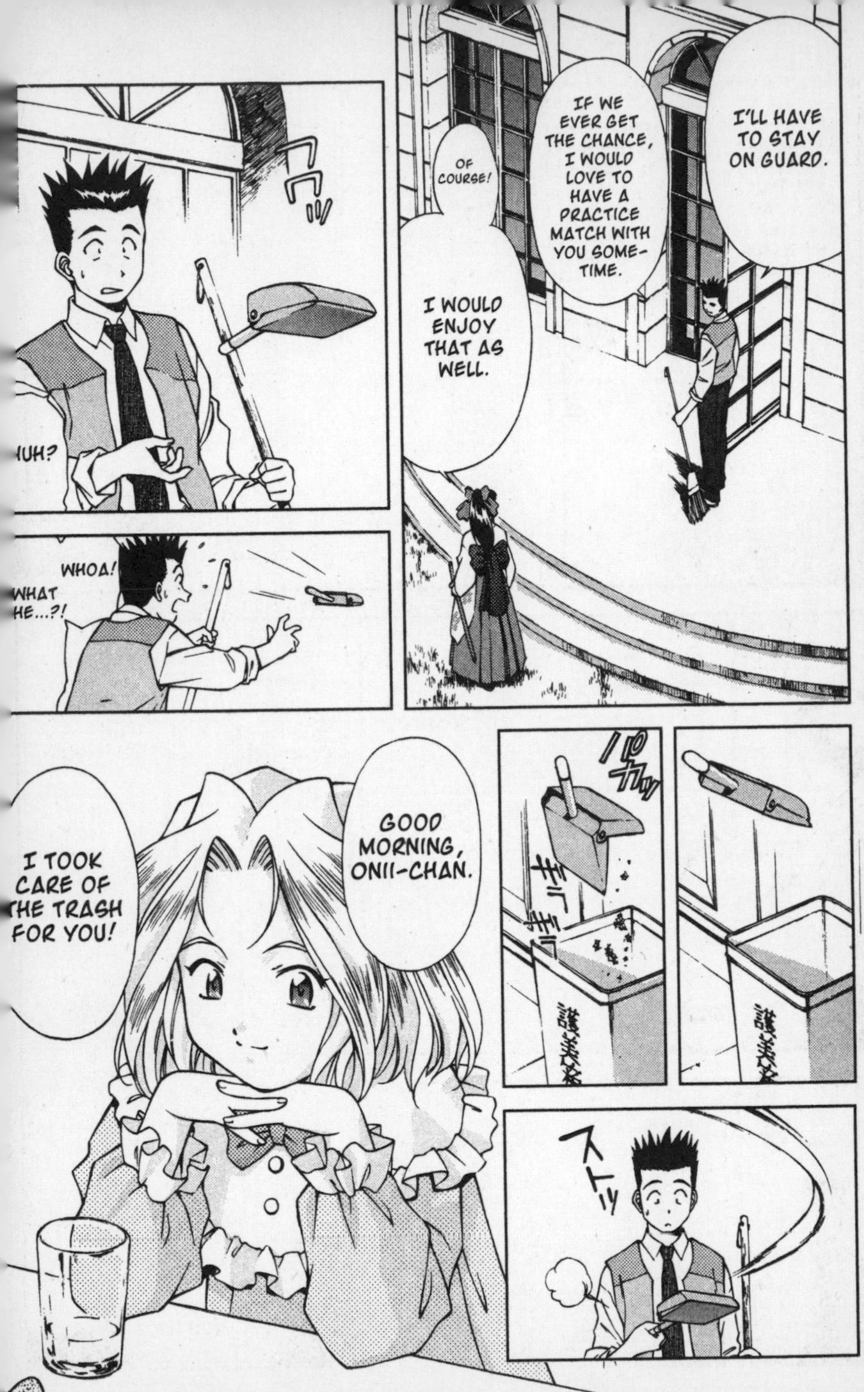

I'LL HAVE TO STAY ON GUARD.
IF WE EVER GET THE CHANCE, I WOULD LOVE TO HAVE A PRACTICE MATCH WITH YOU SOME-TIME.
OF COURSE!
I WOULD ENJOY THAT AS WELL.
HUH?
WHOA!
WHAT
HE...?!
GOOD MORNING, ONII-CHAN.
I TOOK CARE OF THE TRASH FOR YOU!

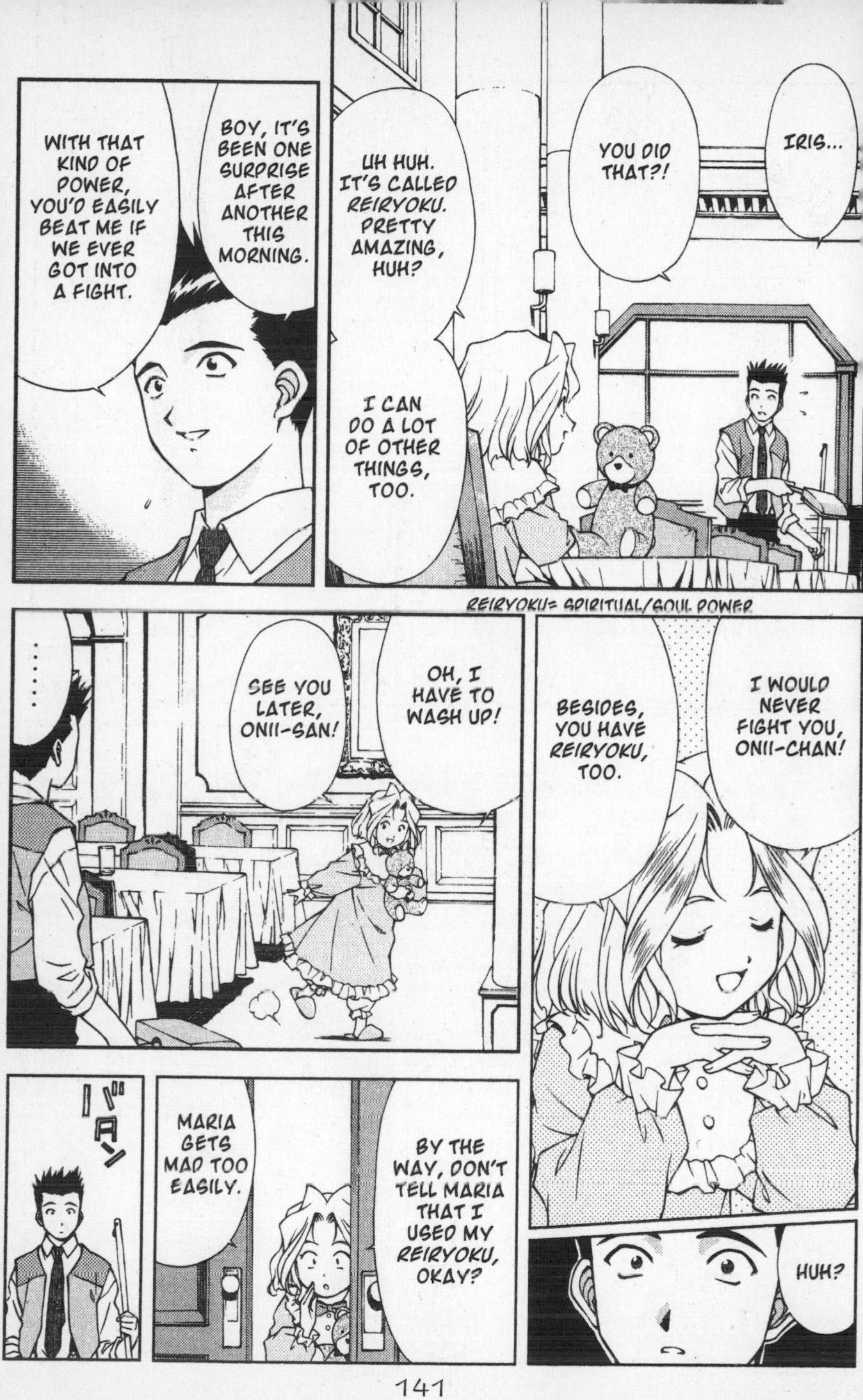
IRIS...
YOU DID THAT?!
UH HUH. IT'S CALLED REIRYOKU. PRETTY AMAZING, HUH?
I CAN DO A LOT OF OTHER THINGS, TOO.
BOY, IT'S BEEN ONE SURPRISE AFTER ANOTHER THIS MORNING.
WITH THAT KIND OF POWER, YOU'D EASILY BEAT ME IF WE EVER GOT INTO A FIGHT.
REIRYOKU= SPIRITUAL/SOUL POWER
I WOULD NEVER FIGHT YOU, ONII-CHAN!
BESIDES, YOU HAVE REIRYOKU, TOO.
OH, I HAVE TO WASH UP!
SEE YOU LATER, ONII-SAN!
......
HUH?
BY THE WAY, DON'T TELL MARIA THAT I USED MY REIRYOKU, OKAY?
MARIA GETS MAD TOO EASILY.

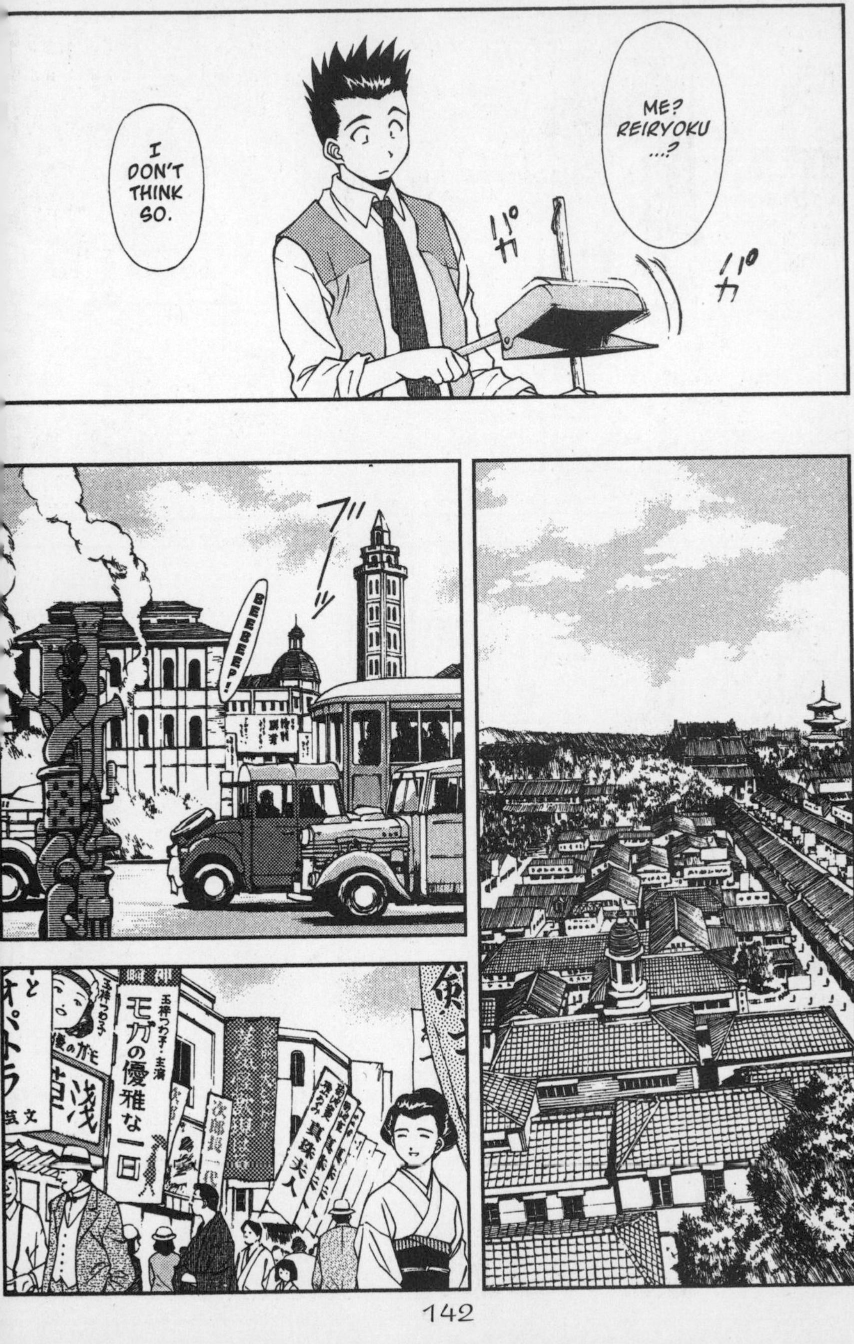
ME? REIRYOKU ...?
パカ
パカ
I DON'T THINK SO.
ブーッ
BEEEEEP!
玉梓つね子・主演
モガの優雅な一日
浅
真珠夫人

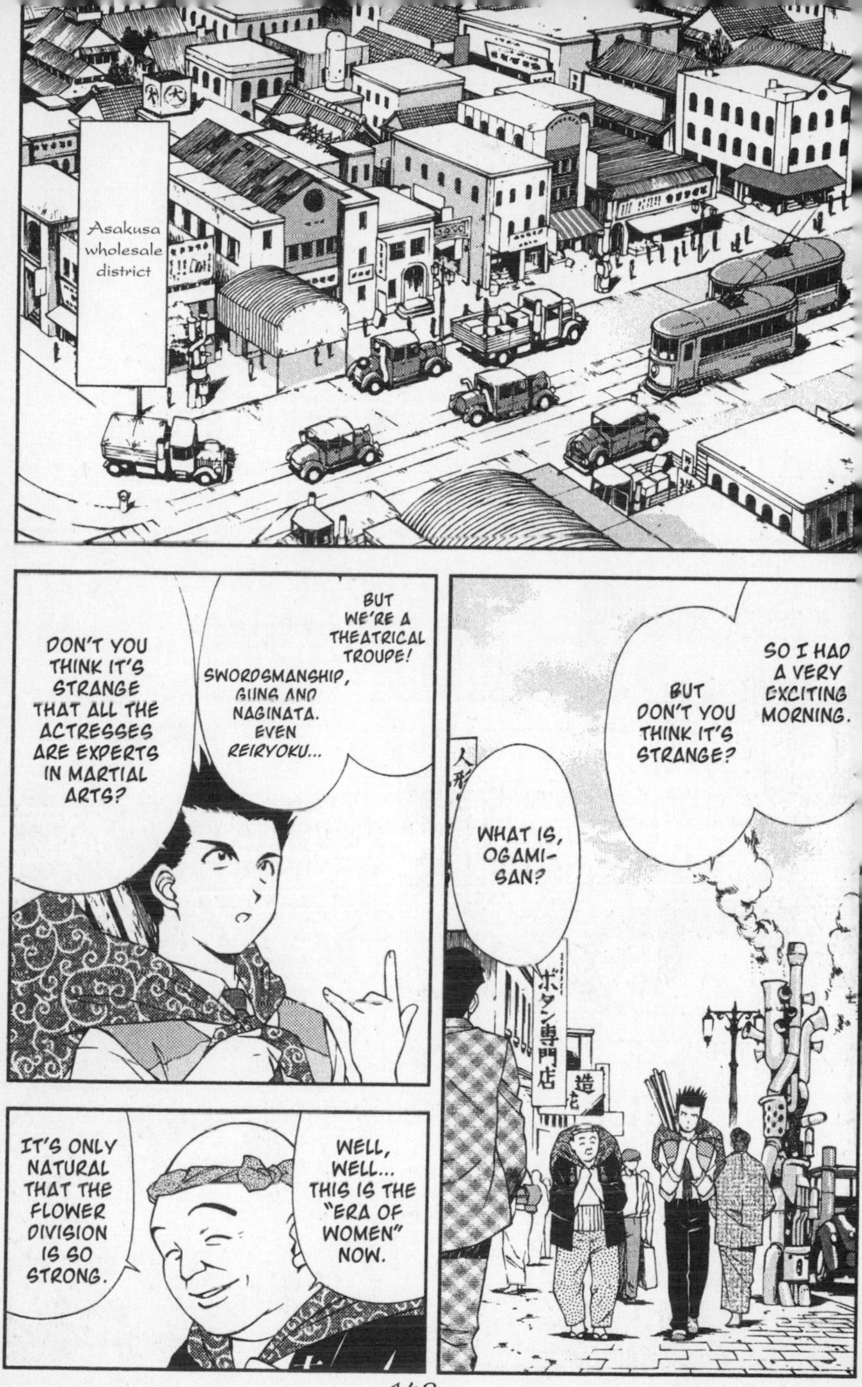
Asakusa wholesale district
SO I HAD A VERY EXCITING MORNING.
BUT DON'T YOU THINK IT'S STRANGE?
WHAT IS, OGAMI-SAN?
ボタン専門店
SWORDSMANSHIP, GUNS AND NAGINATA. EVEN REIRYOKU...
BUT WE'RE A THEATRICAL TROUPE!
DON'T YOU THINK IT'S STRANGE THAT ALL THE ACTRESSES ARE EXPERTS IN MARTIAL ARTS?
WELL, WELL... THIS IS THE "ERA OF WOMEN" NOW.
IT'S ONLY NATURAL THAT THE FLOWER DIVISION IS SO STRONG.

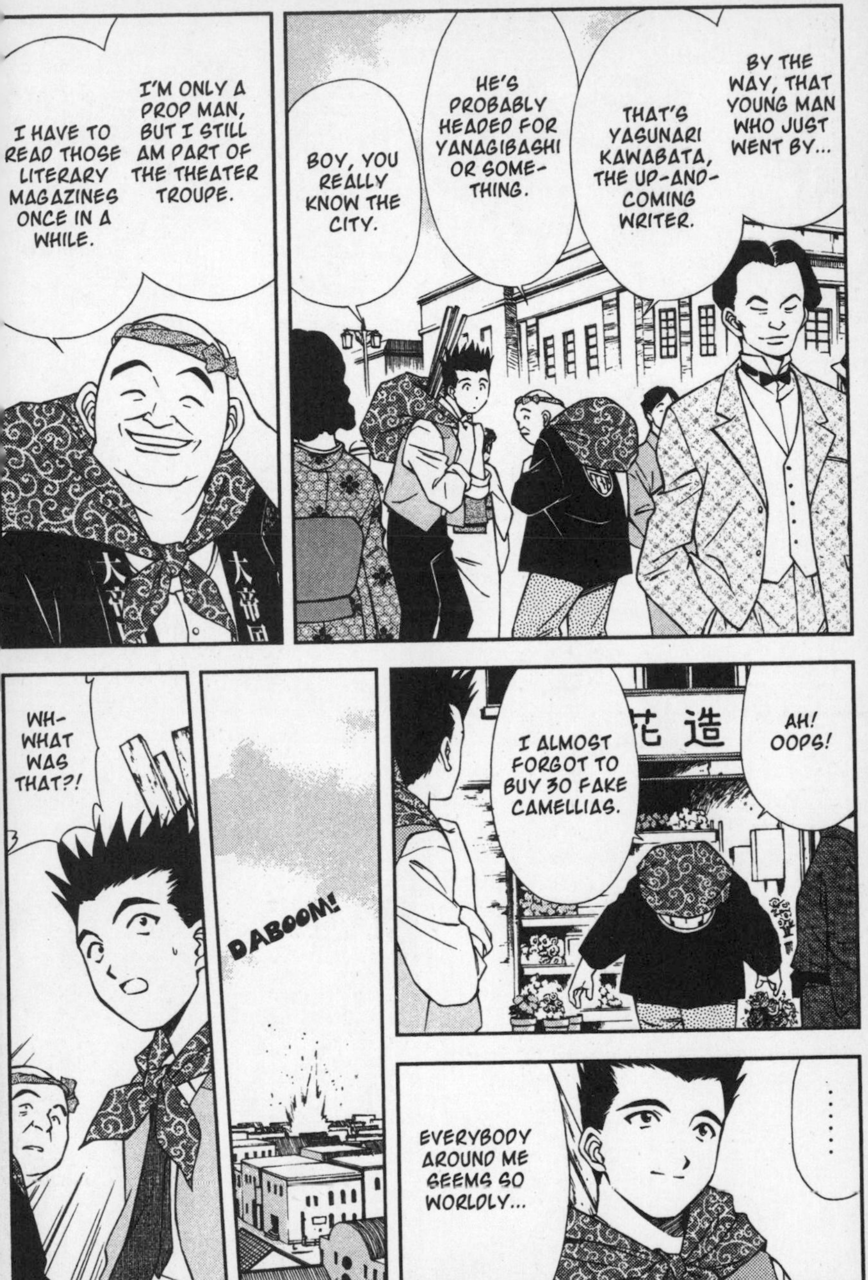

BY THE WAY, THAT YOUNG MAN WHO JUST WENT BY...
THAT'S YASUNARI KAWABATA, THE UP-AND-COMING WRITER.
HE'S PROBABLY HEADED FOR YANAGIBASHI OR SOME-THING.
BOY, YOU REALLY KNOW THE CITY.
I'M ONLY A PROP MAN, BUT I STILL AM PART OF THE THEATER TROUPE.
I HAVE TO READ THOSE LITERARY MAGAZINES ONCE IN A WHILE.
AH! OOPS!
I ALMOST FORGOT TO BUY 30 FAKE CAMELLIAS.
......
EVERYBODY AROUND ME SEEMS SO WORLDLY...
DABOOM!
WH- WHAT WAS THAT?!

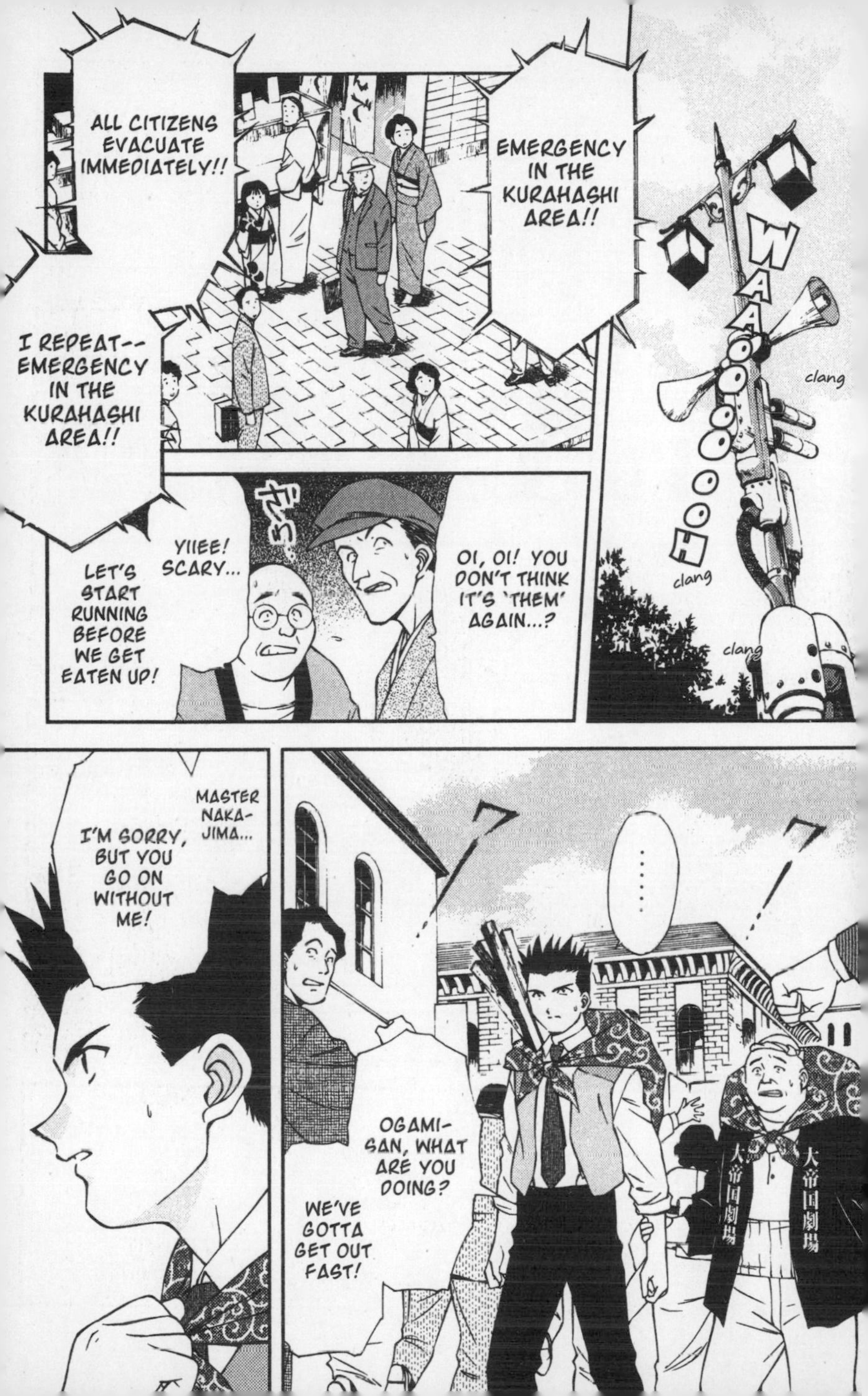
WAAOOOOOOOH
clang
clang
clang
EMERGENCY IN THE KURAHASHI AREA!!
ALL CITIZENS EVACUATE IMMEDIATELY!!
I REPEAT-- EMERGENCY IN THE KURAHASHI AREA!!
OI, OI! YOU DON'T THINK IT'S 'THEM' AGAIN...?
YIIEE! SCARY...
LET'S START RUNNING BEFORE WE GET EATEN UP!
......
!
!
OGAMI-SAN, WHAT ARE YOU DOING?
WE'VE GOTTA GET OUT FAST!
大帝国劇場
大帝国劇場
MASTER NAKAJIMA...
I'M SORRY, BUT YOU GO ON WITHOUT ME!

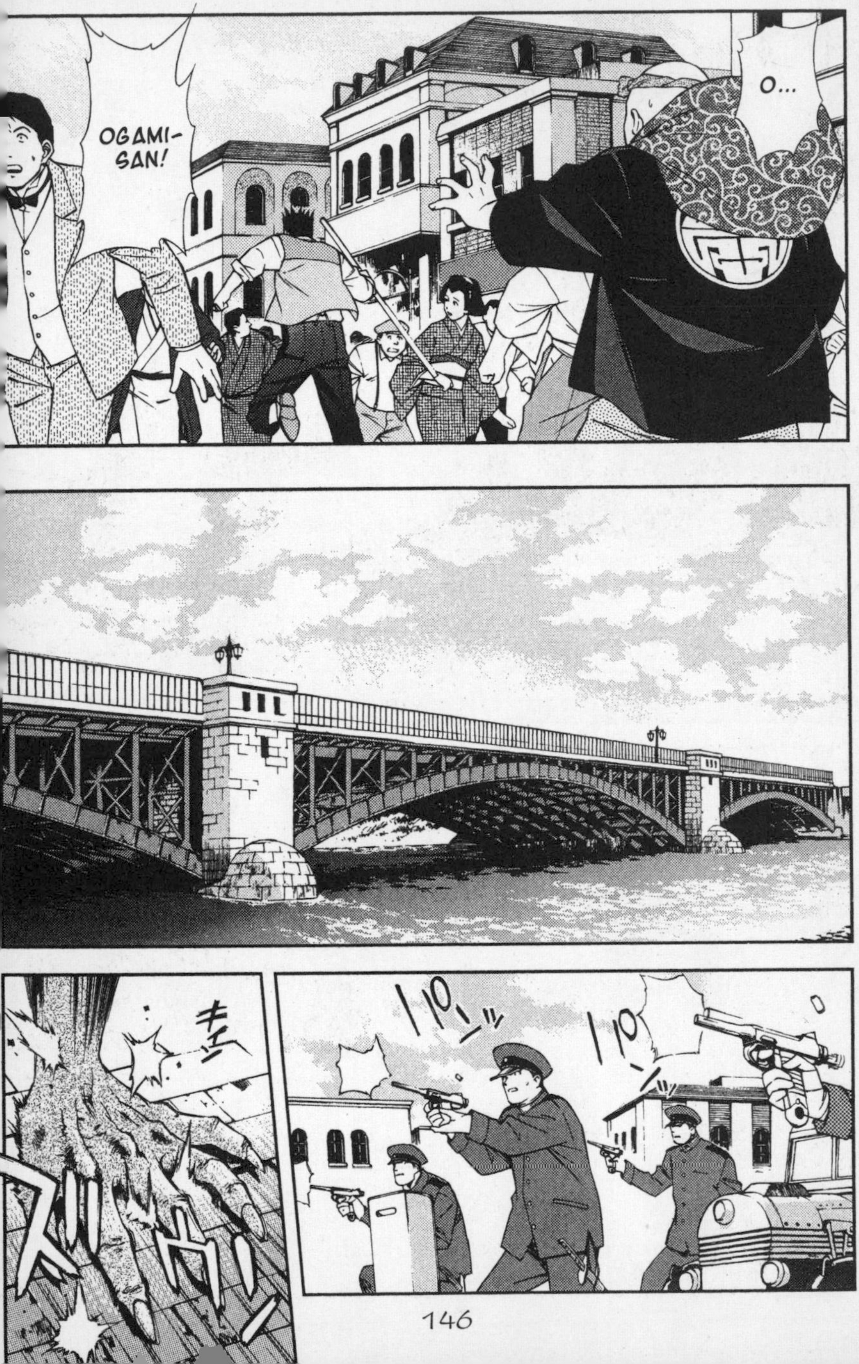
O...
OGAMI-SAN!

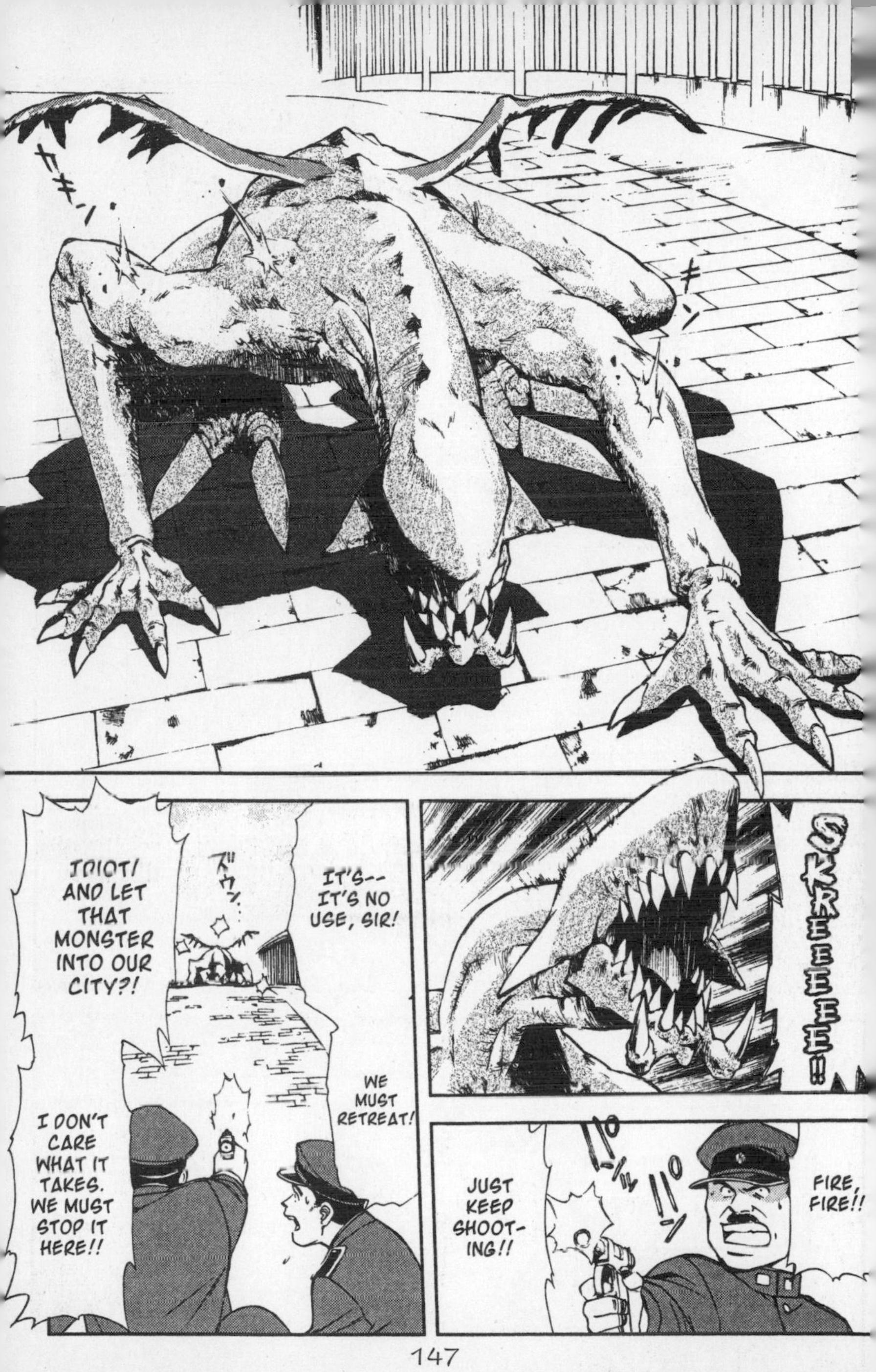
SKREEEEEE!!
FIRE, FIRE!!
JUST KEEP SHOOTING!!
IT'S-- IT'S NO USE, SIR!
IDIOT! AND LET THAT MONSTER INTO OUR CITY?!
WE MUST RETREAT!
I DON'T CARE WHAT IT TAKES. WE MUST STOP IT HERE!!

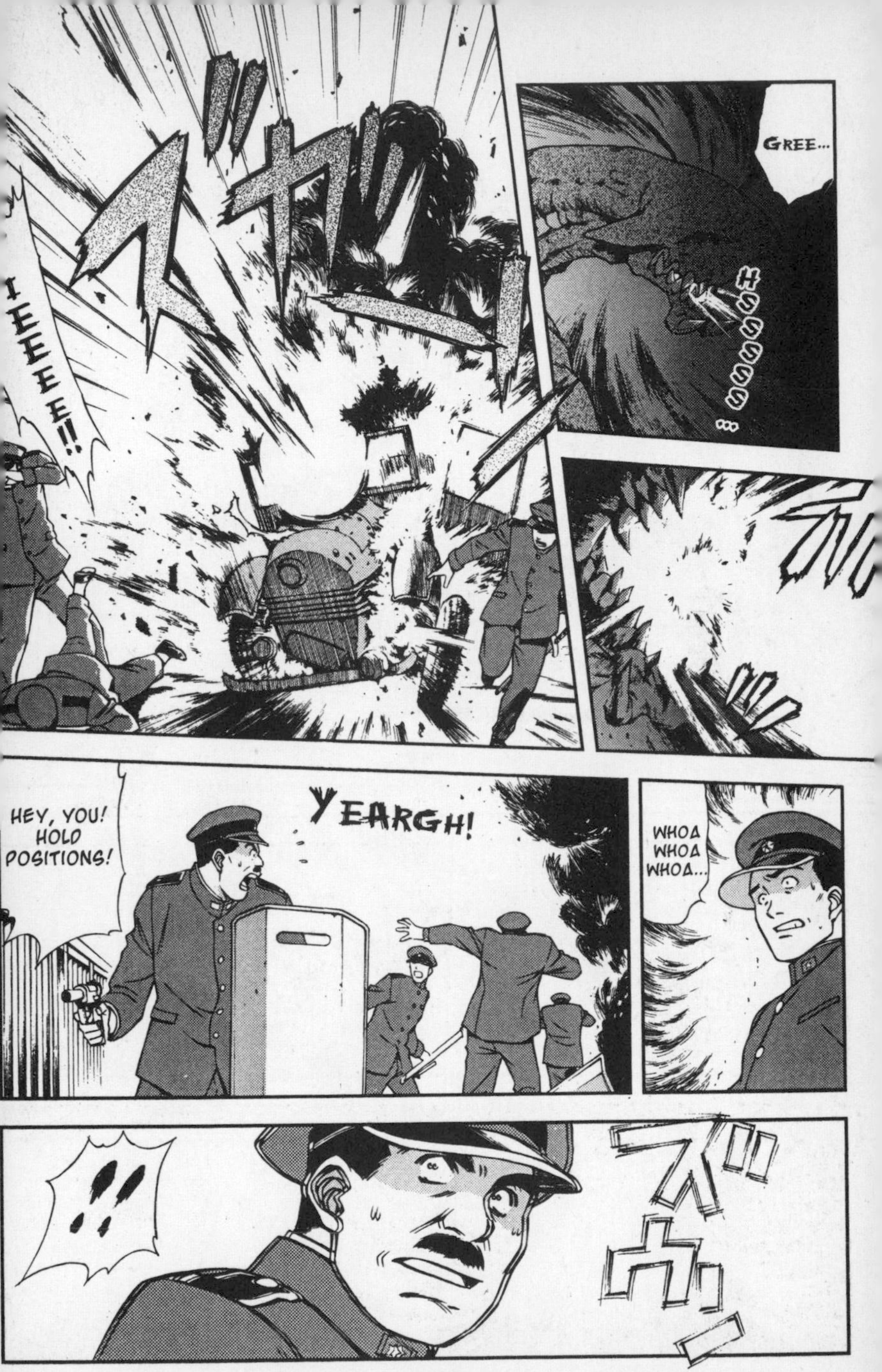
GREE...
HSSSSSS...
IEEEEEE!!
HEY, YOU! HOLD POSITIONS!
YEARGH!
WHOA WHOA WHOA...
!!

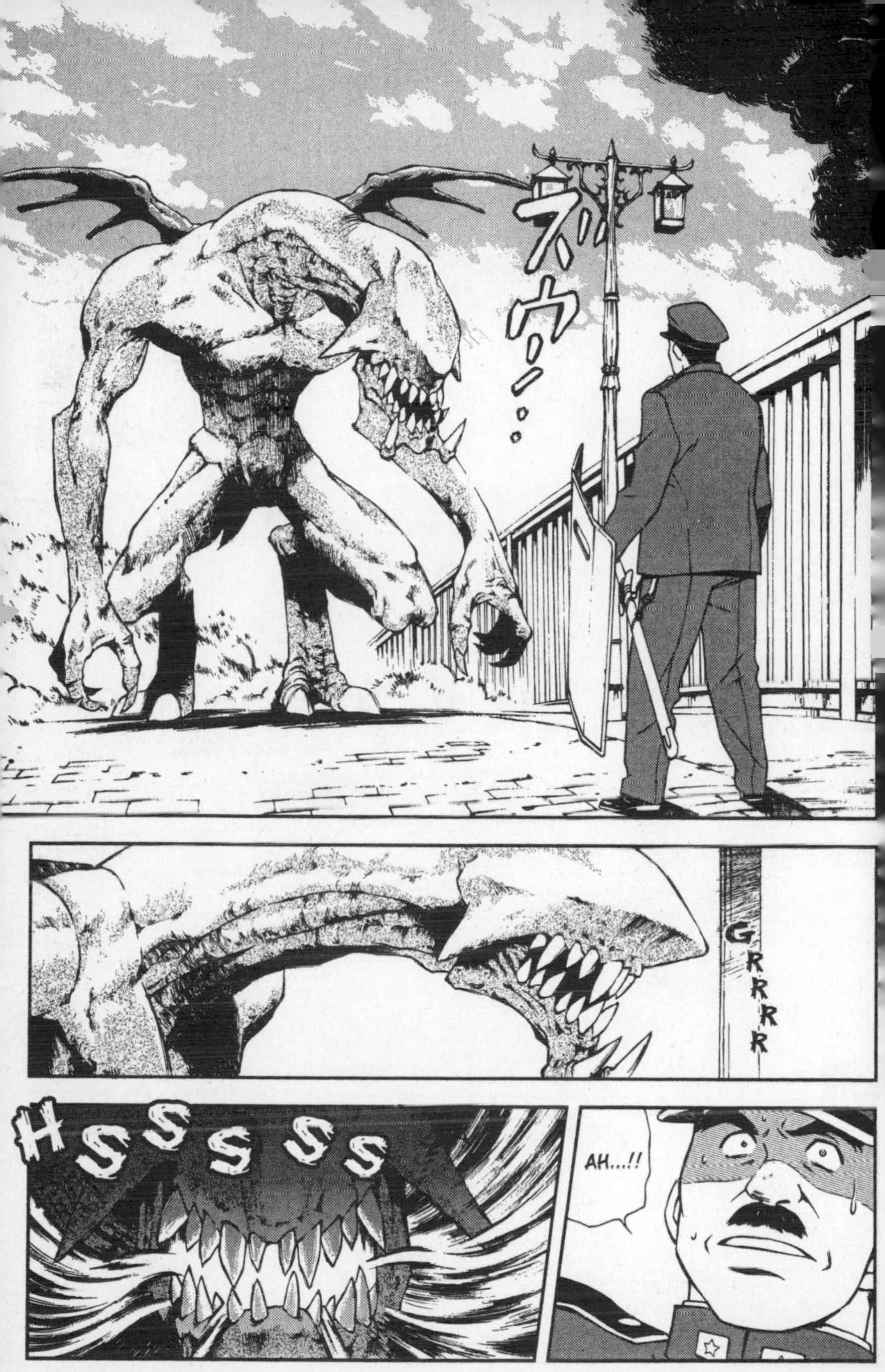
ズウ…
GRRRR
HSSSSS
AH...!!

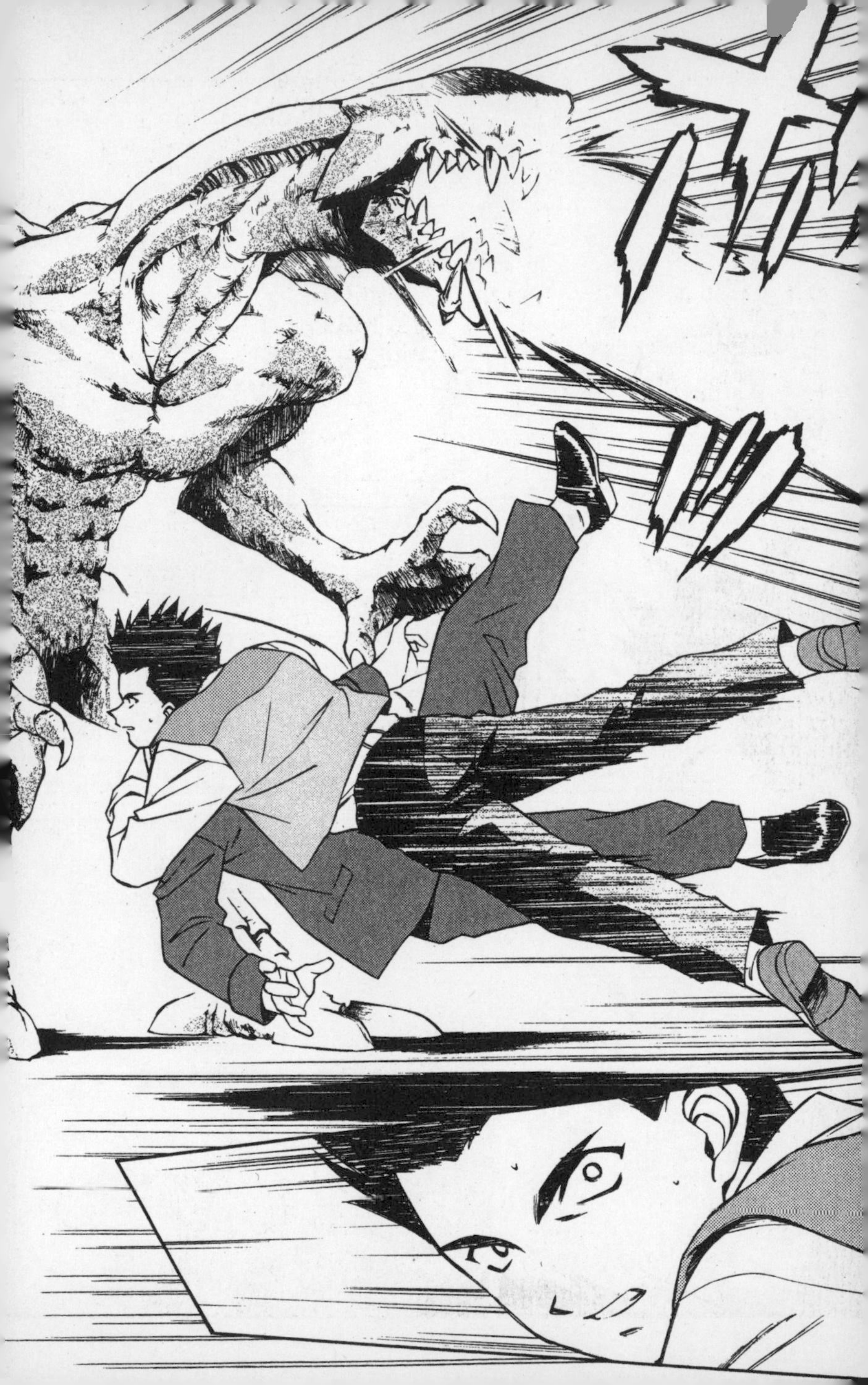

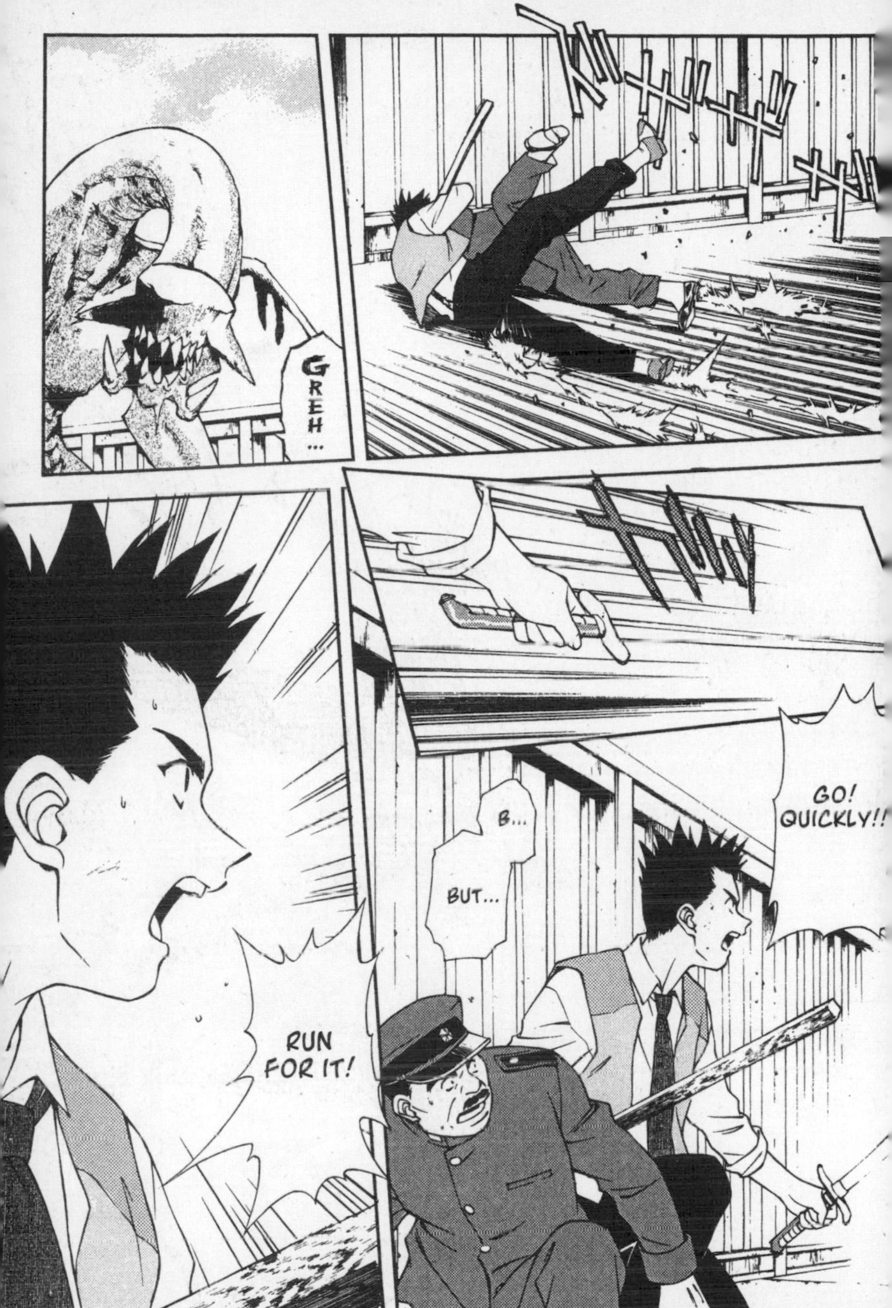
GREH...
GO! QUICKLY!!
B...
BUT...
RUN FOR IT!

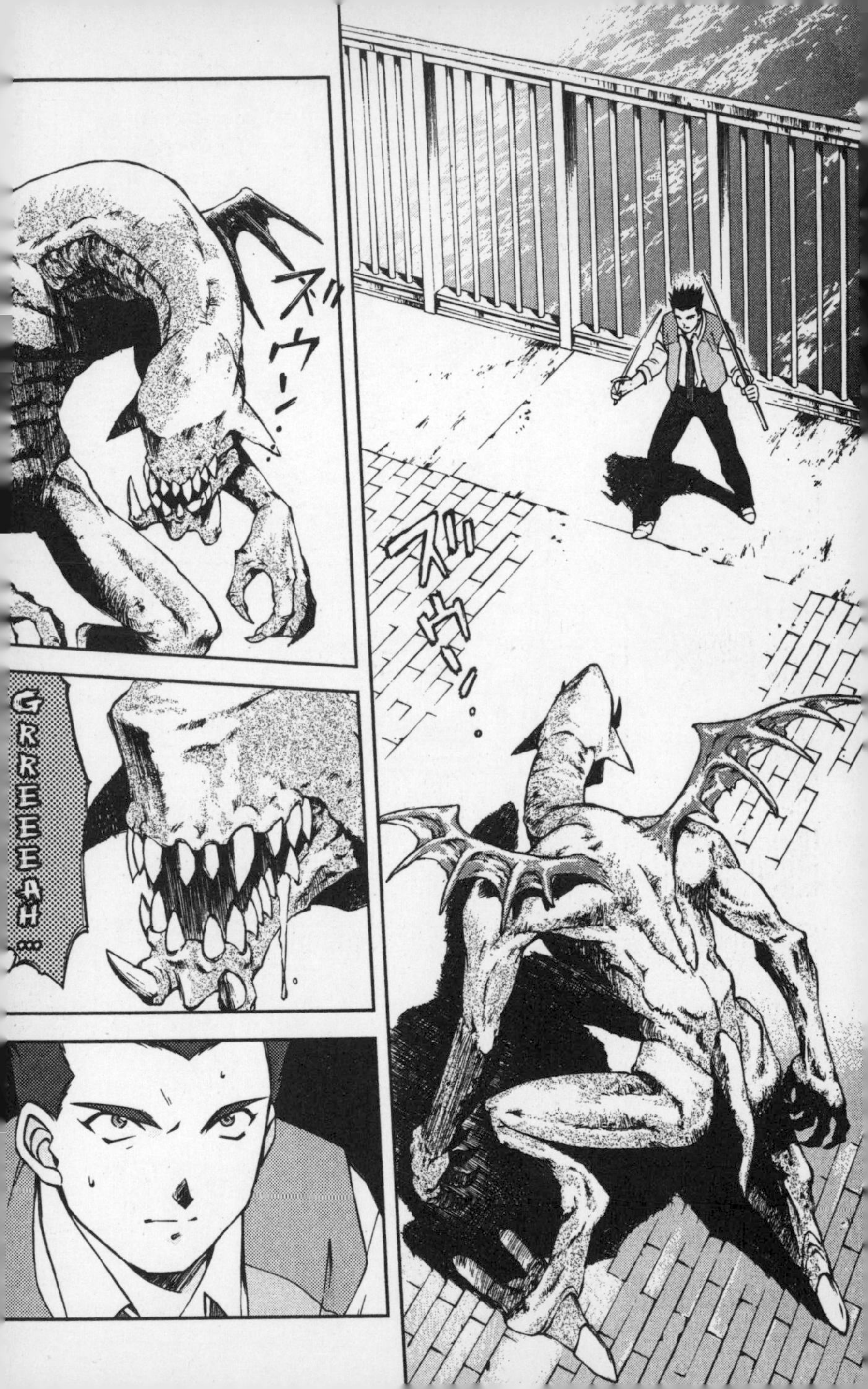
ズゥーー…
ヌゥーー…
GRREEEAH…

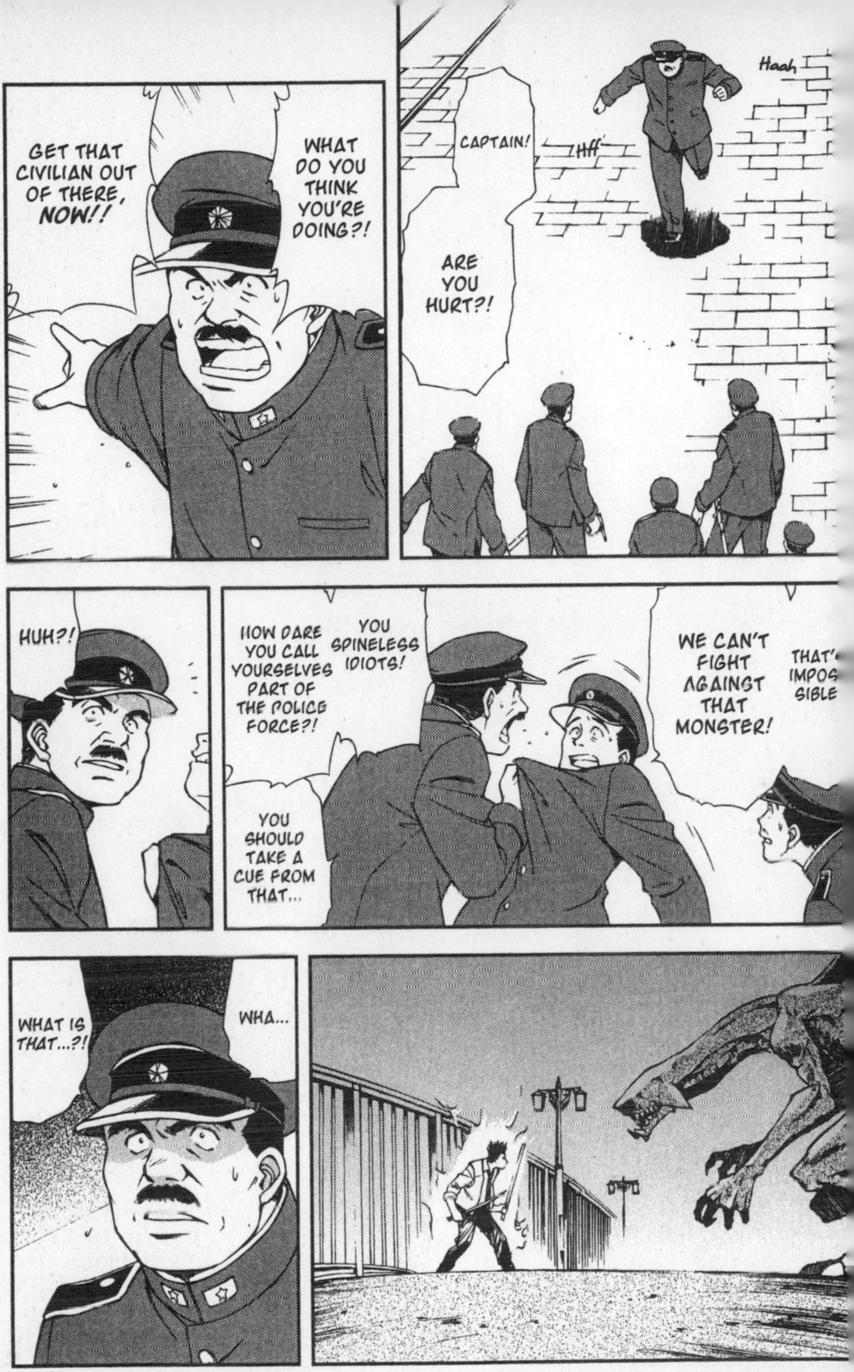
Haah
CAPTAIN!
Hff
ARE YOU HURT?!
WHAT DO YOU THINK YOU'RE DOING?!
GET THAT CIVILIAN OUT OF THERE, NOW!!
THAT'S IMPOSSIBLE
WE CAN'T FIGHT AGAINST THAT MONSTER!
YOU SPINELESS IDIOTS!
HOW DARE YOU CALL YOURSELVES PART OF THE POLICE FORCE?!
YOU SHOULD TAKE A CUE FROM THAT...
HUH?!
WHA...
WHAT IS THAT...?!

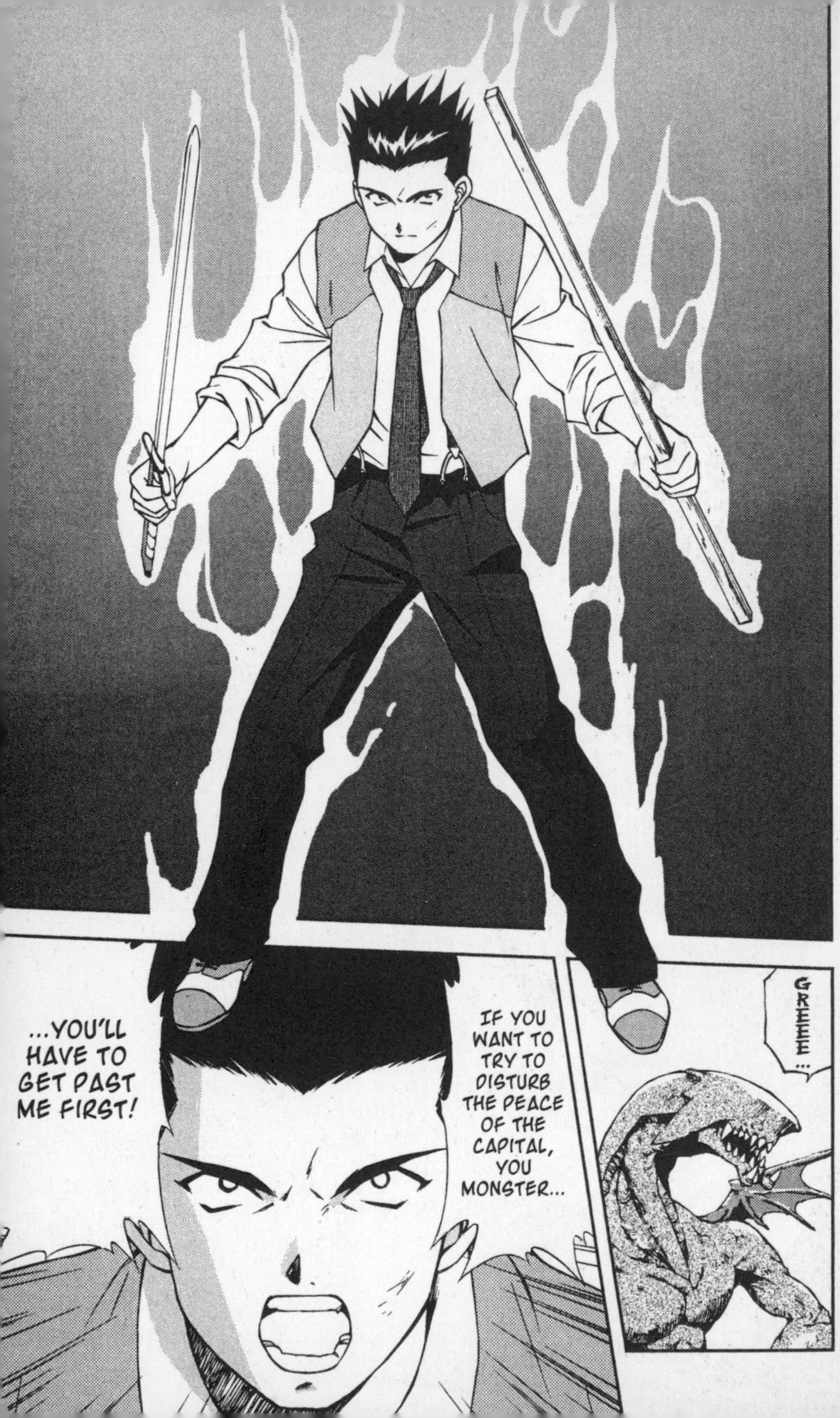
GREEE...
IF YOU WANT TO TRY TO DISTURB THE PEACE OF THE CAPITAL, YOU MONSTER...
...YOU'LL HAVE TO GET PAST ME FIRST!

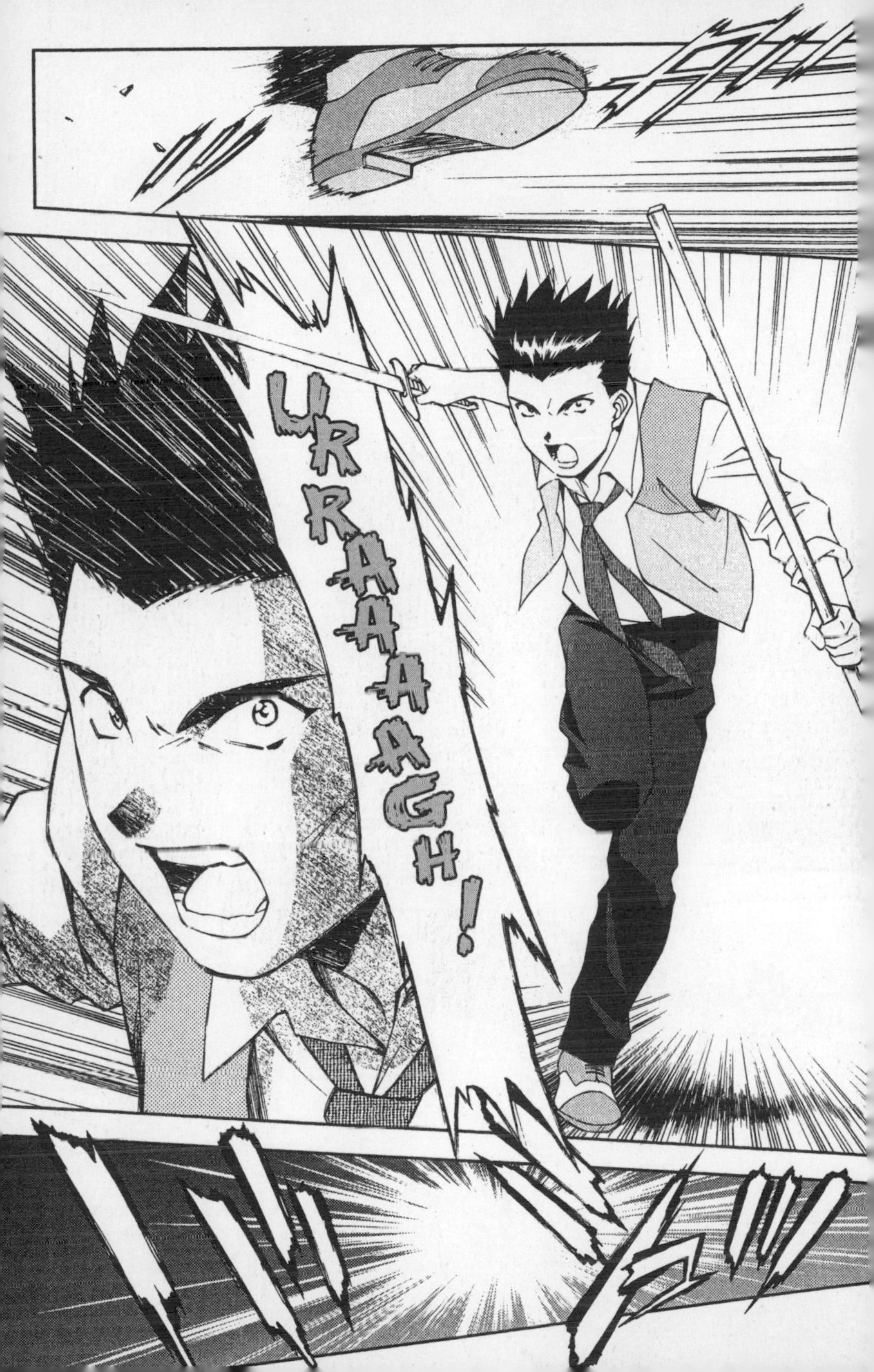
URRAAAGH!

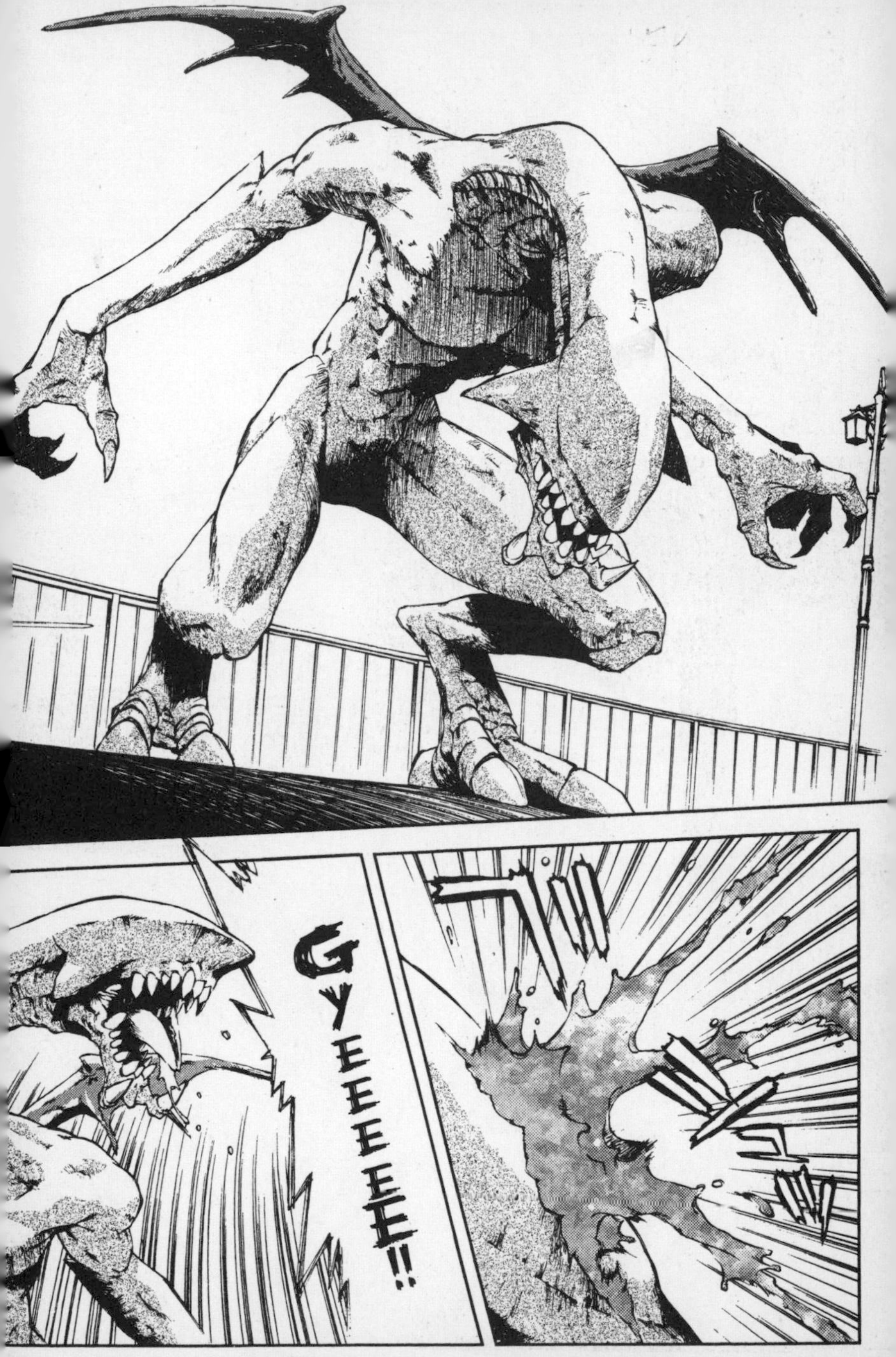
GYEEEEE!!

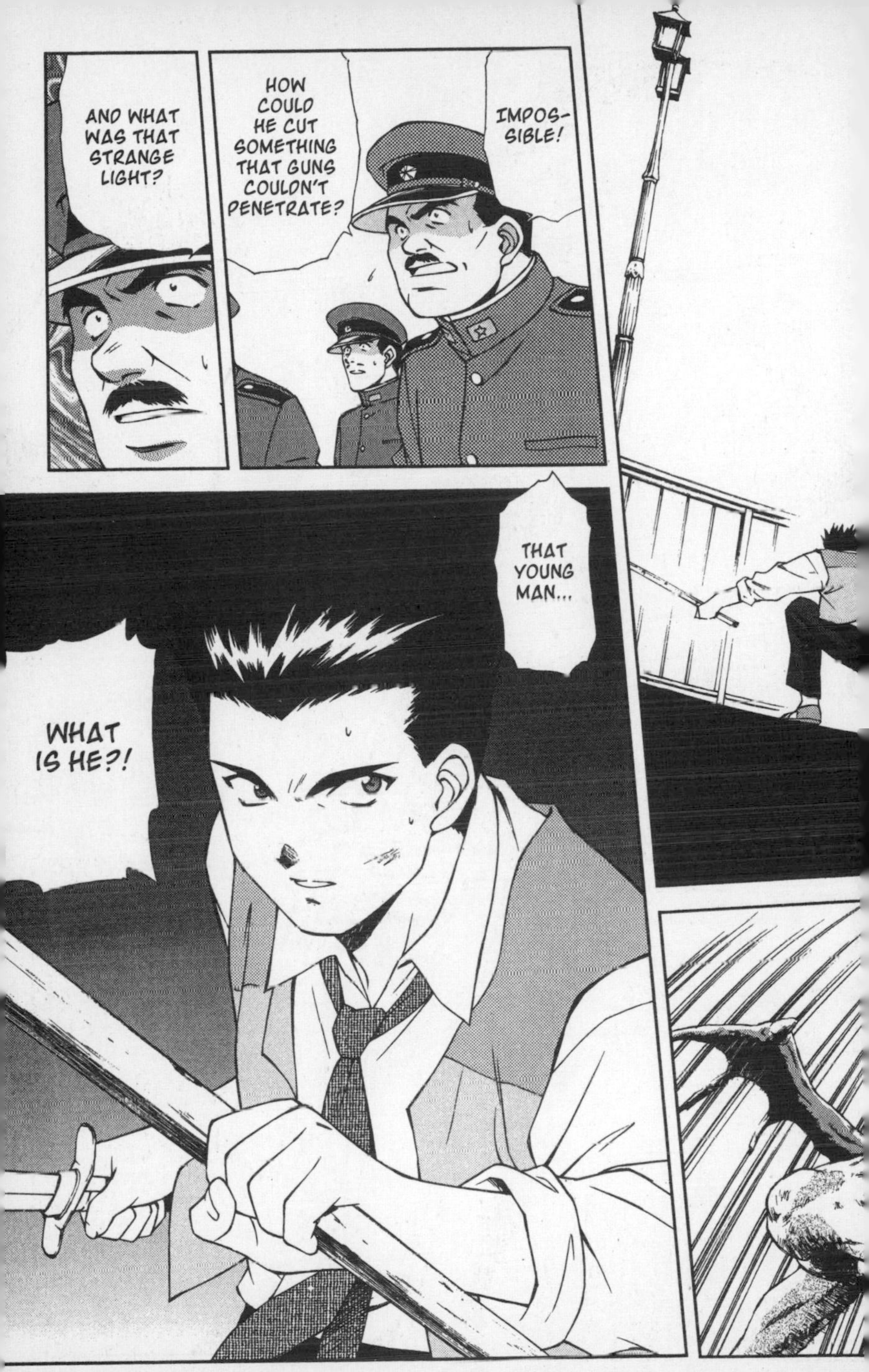
IMPOS-SIBLE!
HOW COULD HE CUT SOMETHING THAT GUNS COULDN'T PENETRATE?
AND WHAT WAS THAT STRANGE LIGHT?
THAT YOUNG MAN...
WHAT IS HE?!

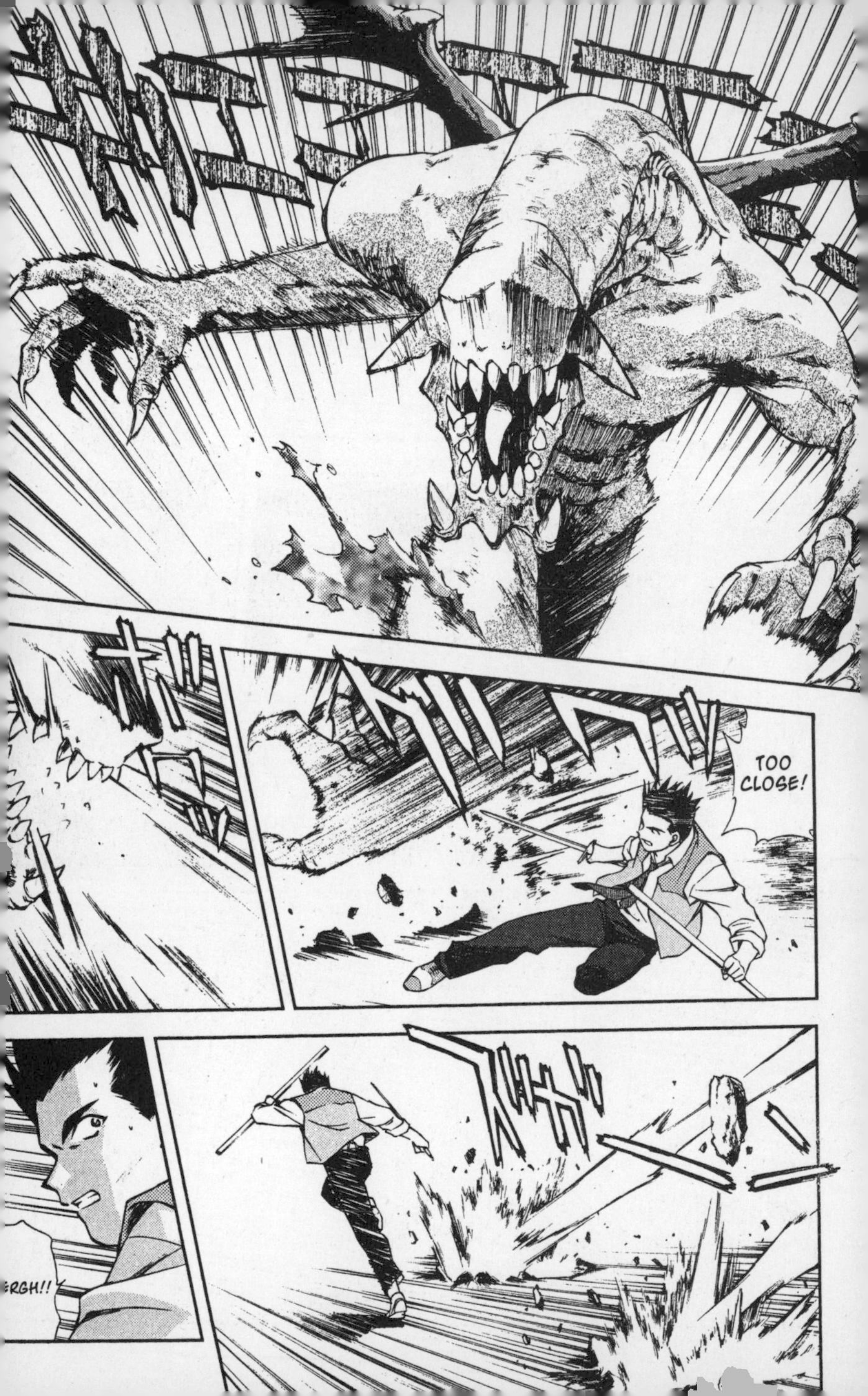
TOO CLOSE!
ERGH!!

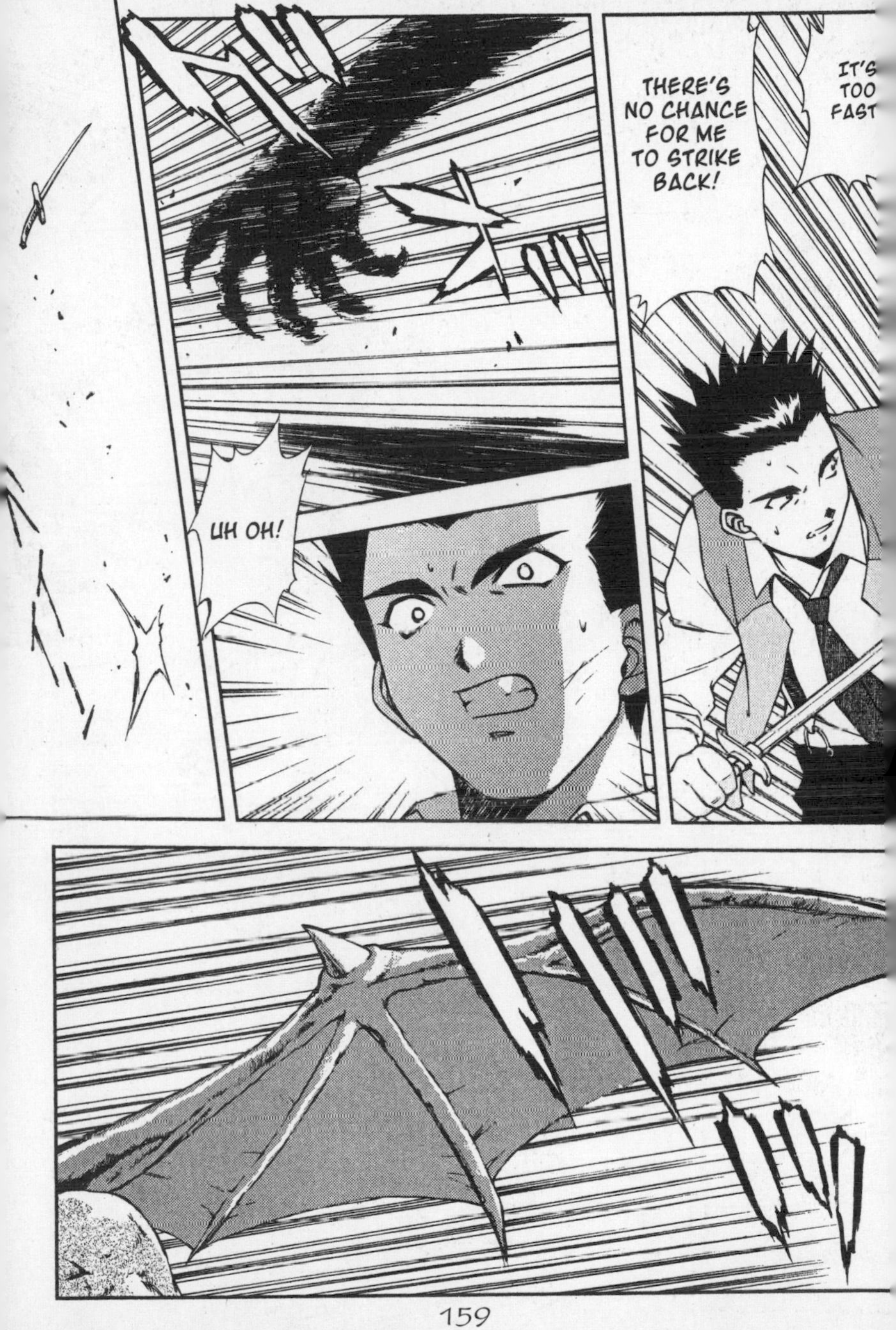
IT'S TOO FAST
THERE'S NO CHANCE FOR ME TO STRIKE BACK!
UH OH!

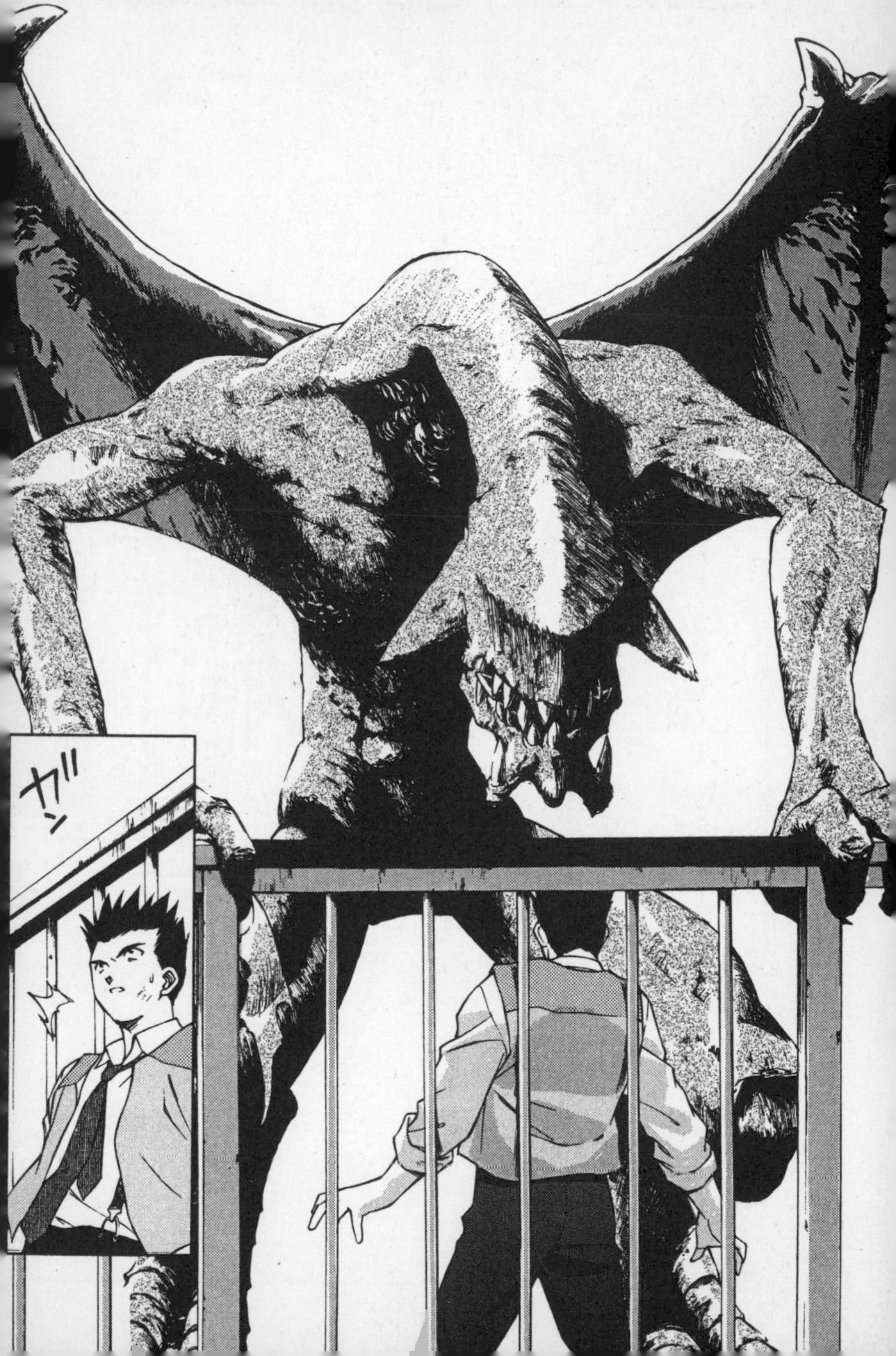
ガン

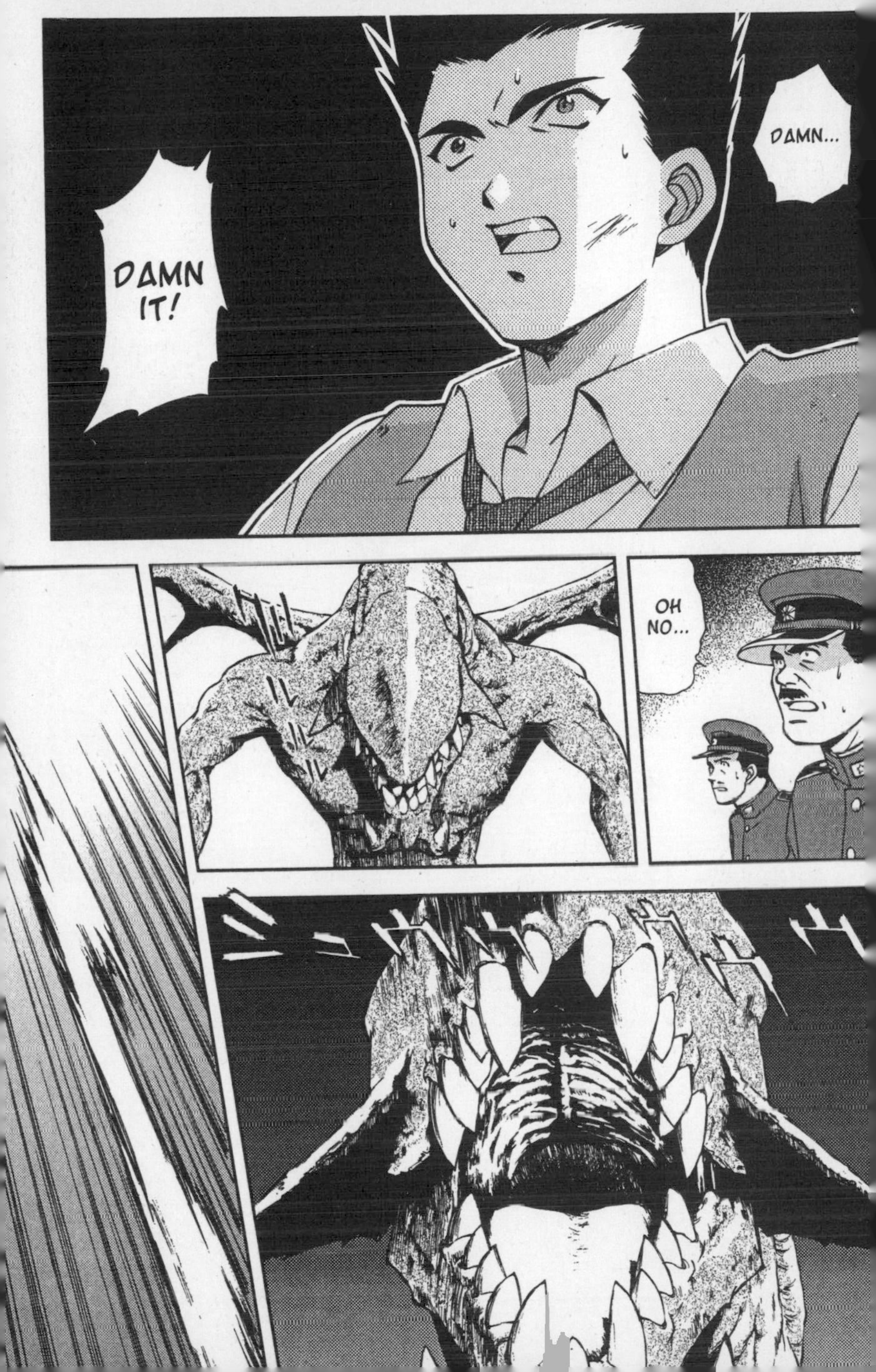
DAMN...
DAMN IT!
OH NO...

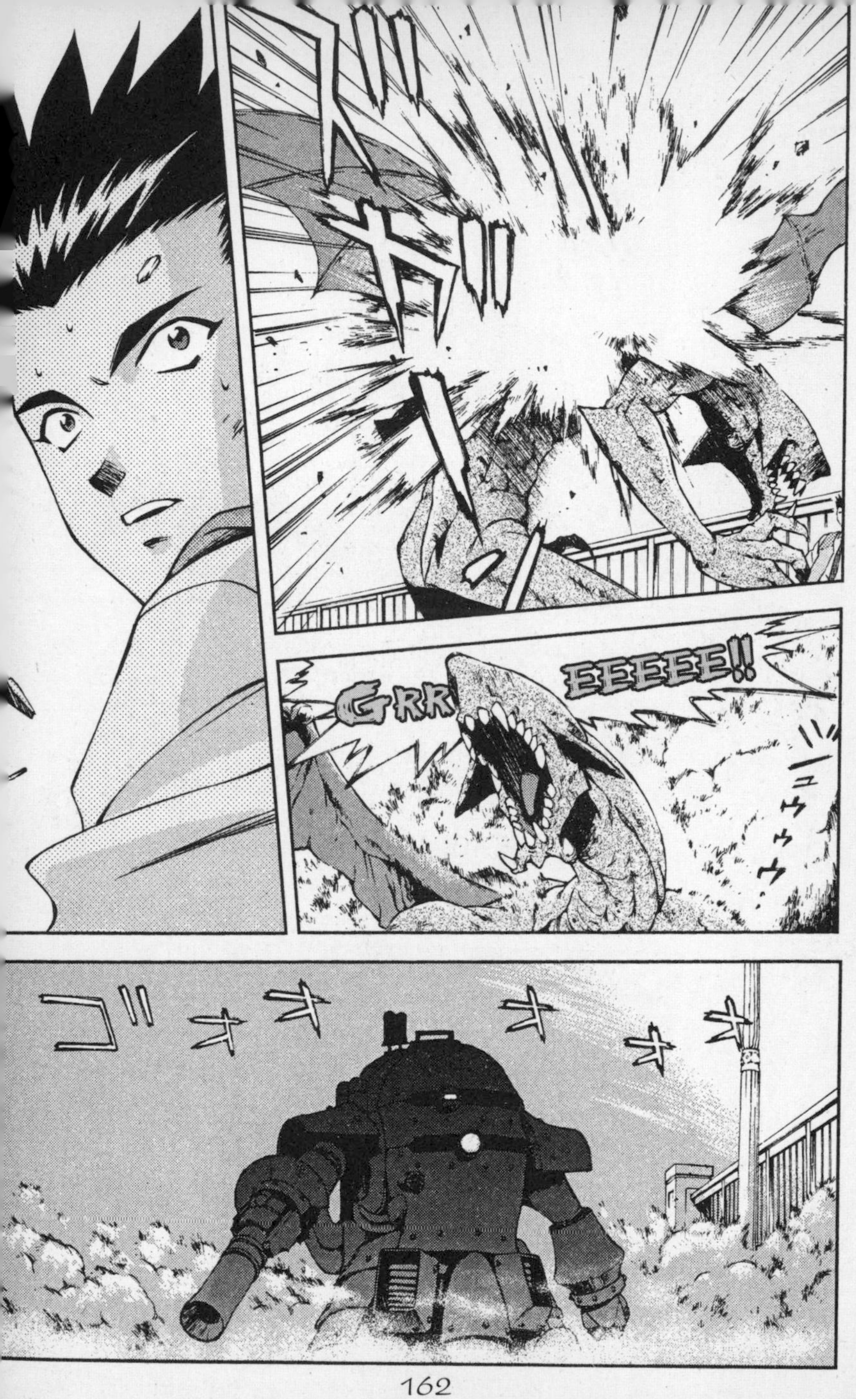
GRR
EEEEEE!!

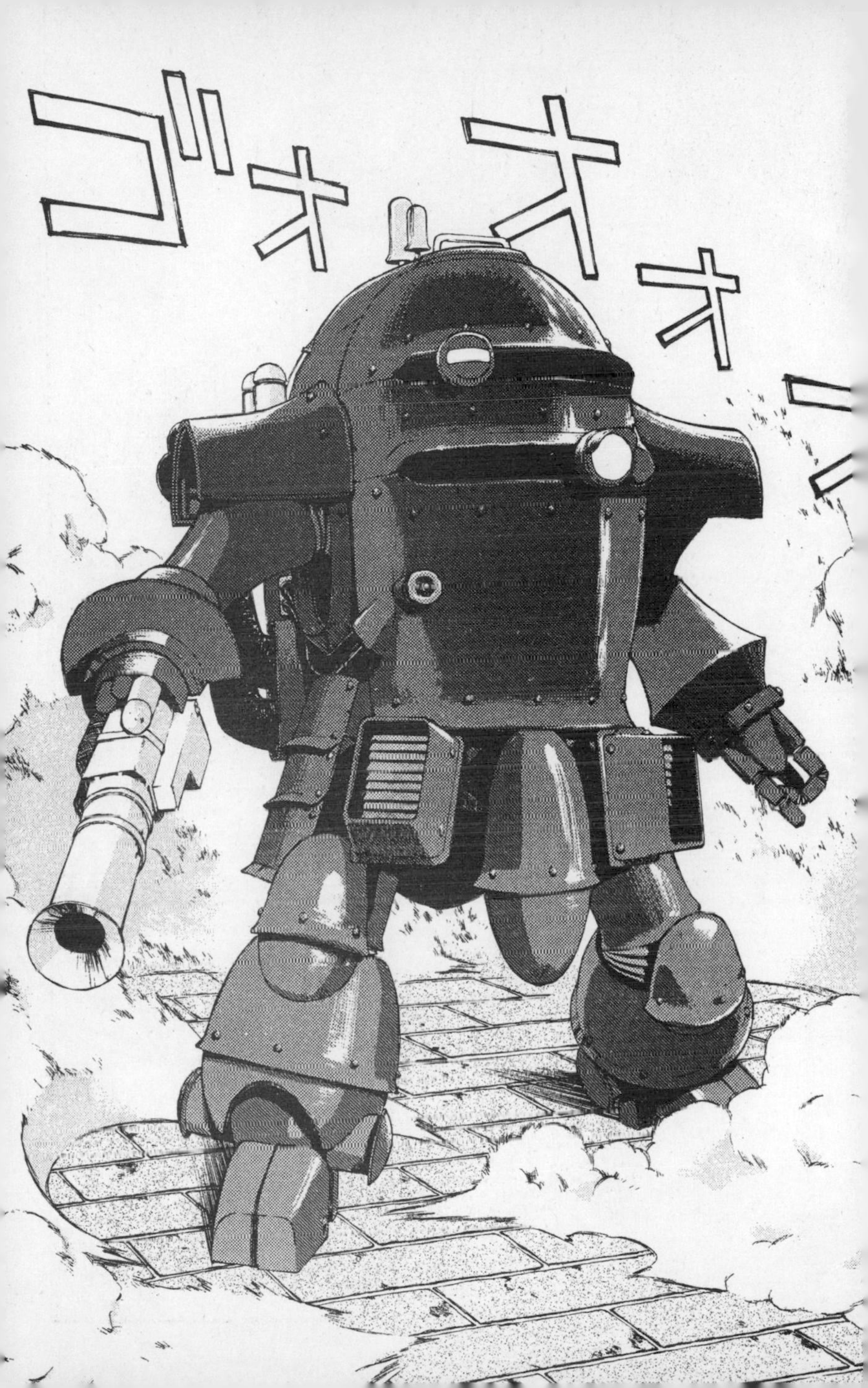
ゴォオォー

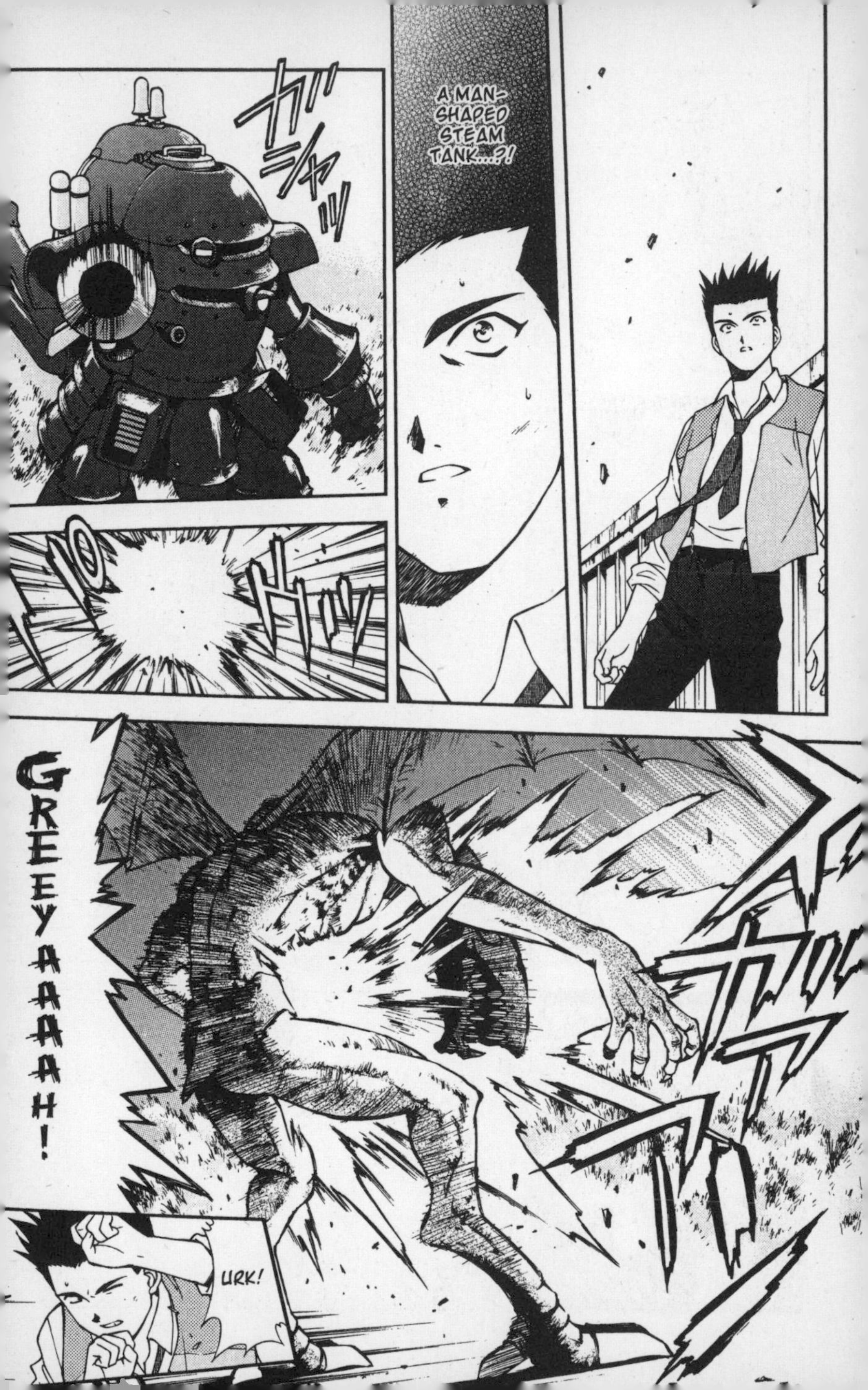
A MAN-SHAPED STEAM TANK...?!
GREEEYAAAAAAH!
URK!

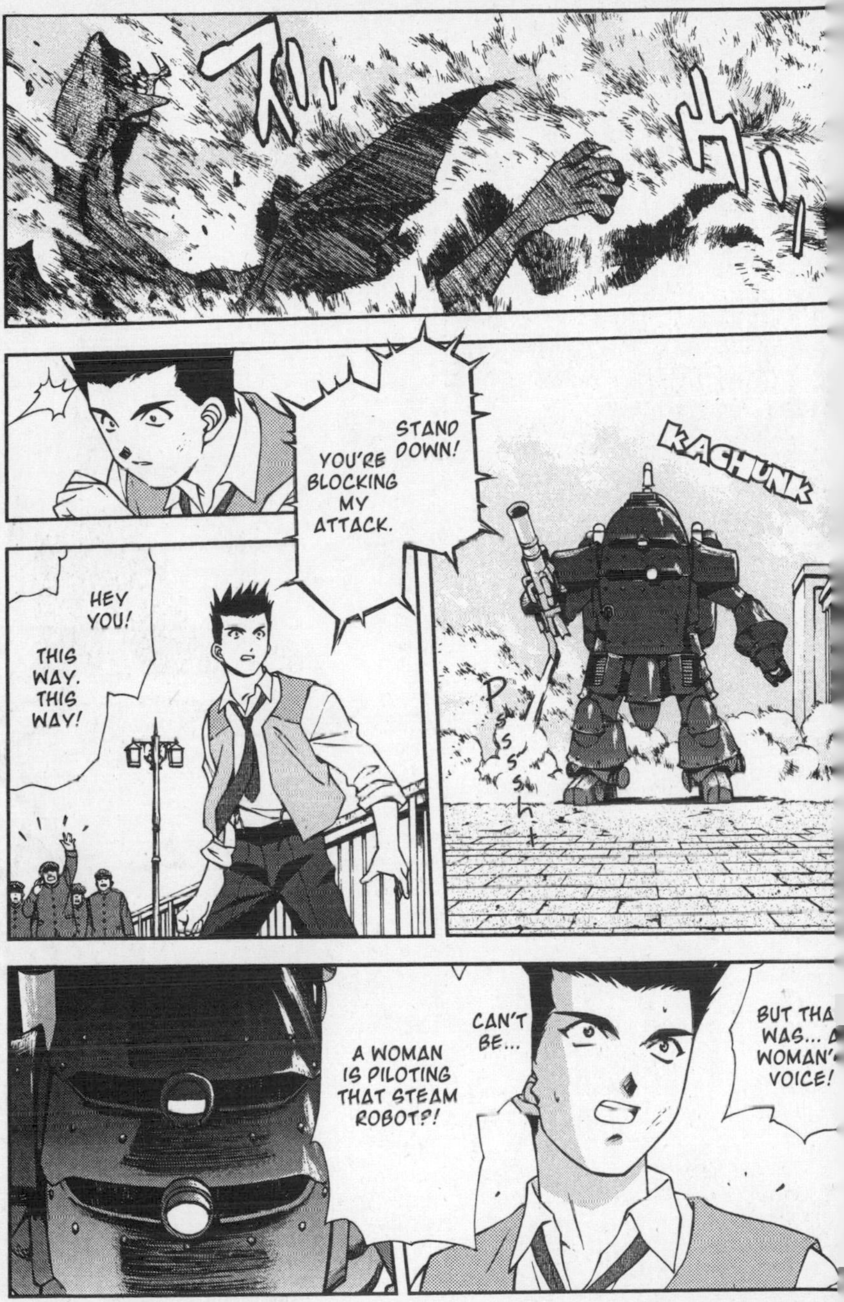
KACHUNK
PSSSSH
STAND DOWN! YOU'RE BLOCKING MY ATTACK.
HEY YOU!
THIS WAY. THIS WAY!
BUT THA WAS... A WOMAN' VOICE!
CAN'T BE...
A WOMAN IS PILOTING THAT STEAM ROBOT?!

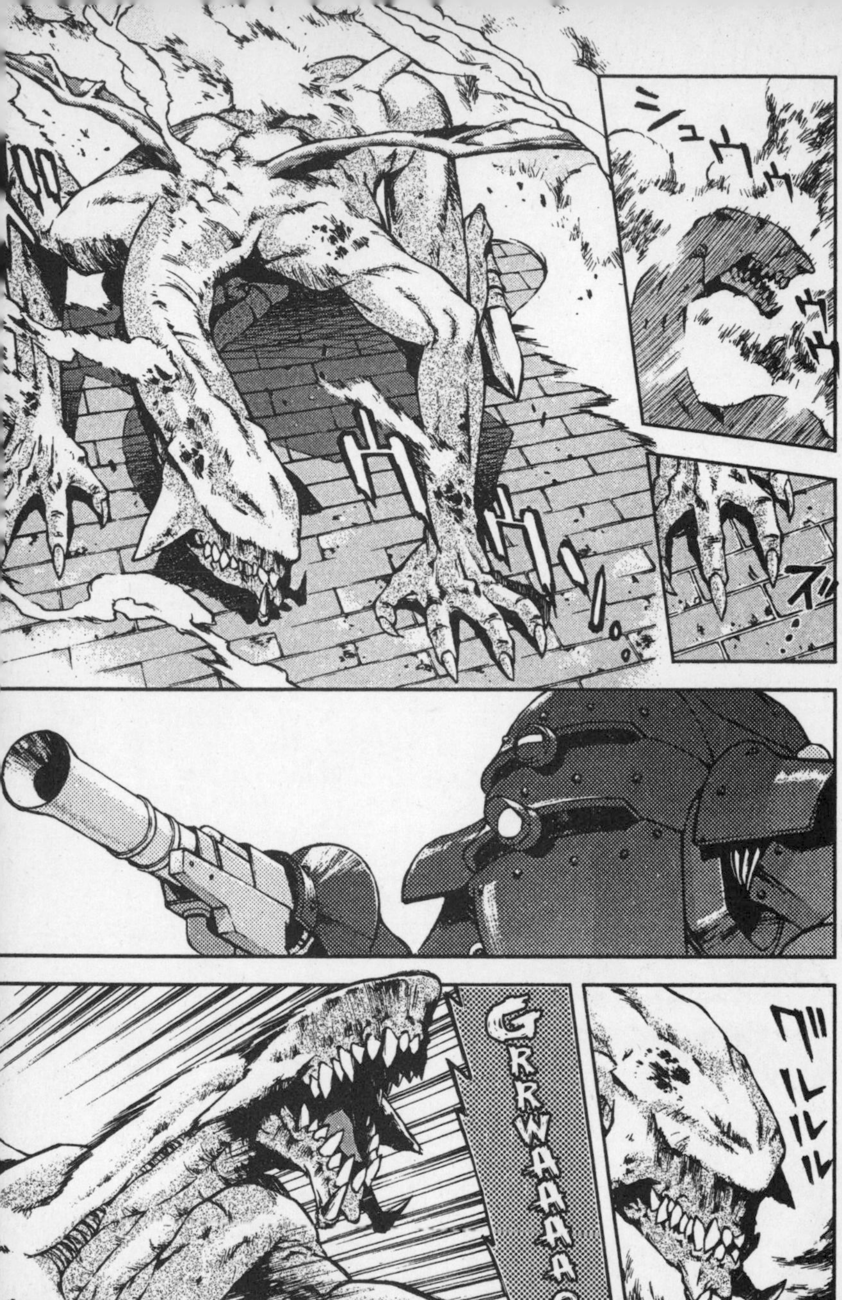
GRRWAAAAOH

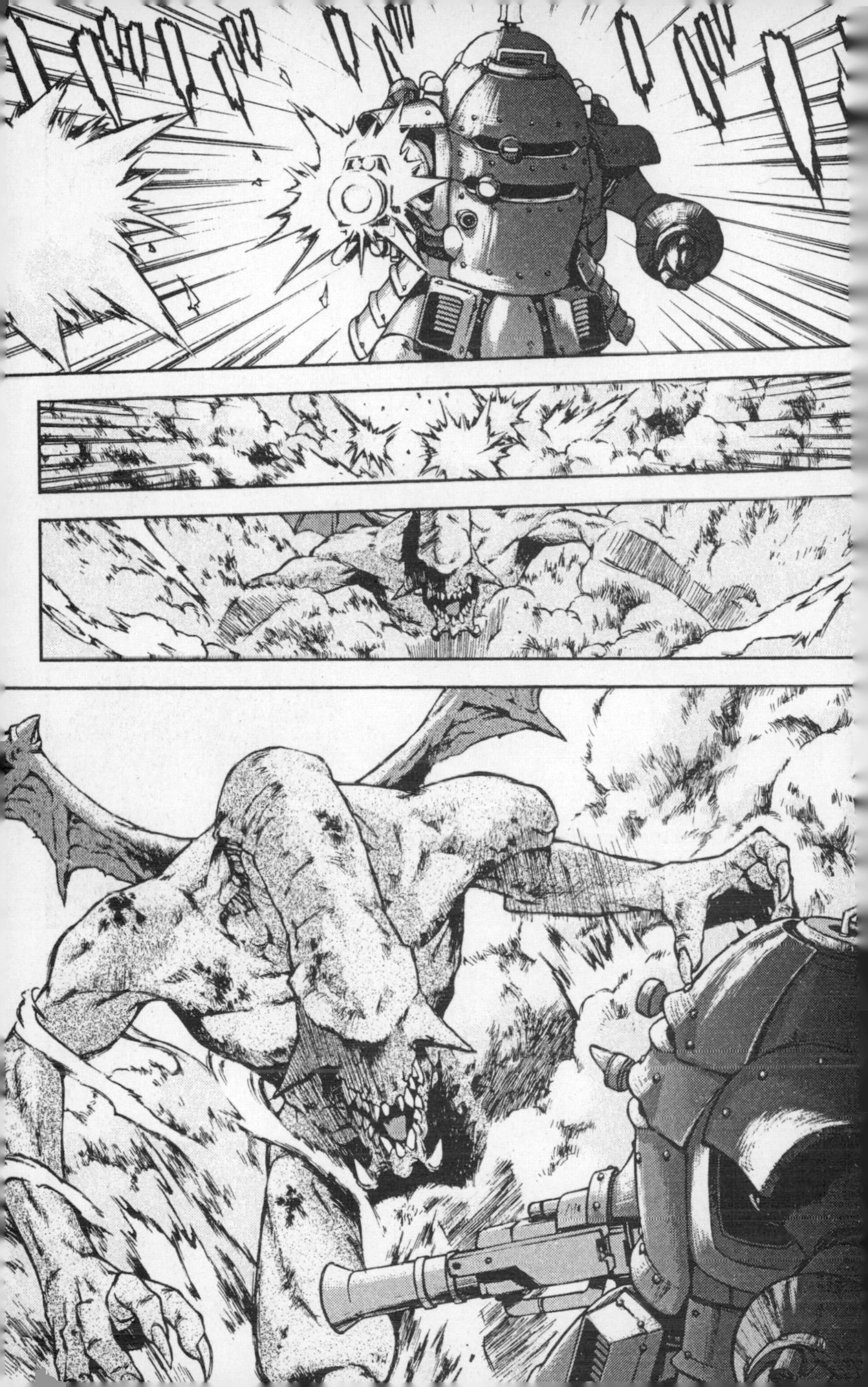

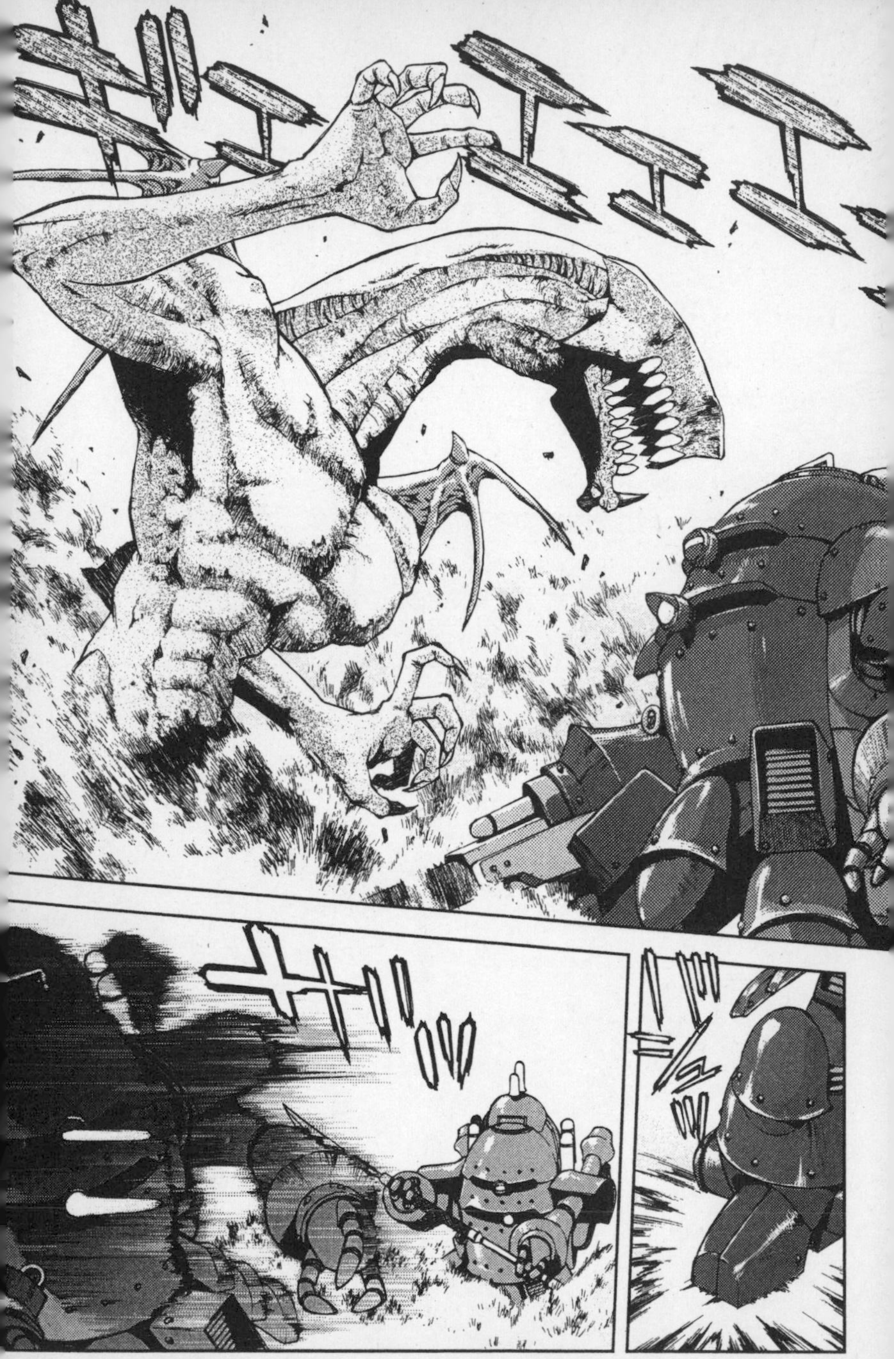

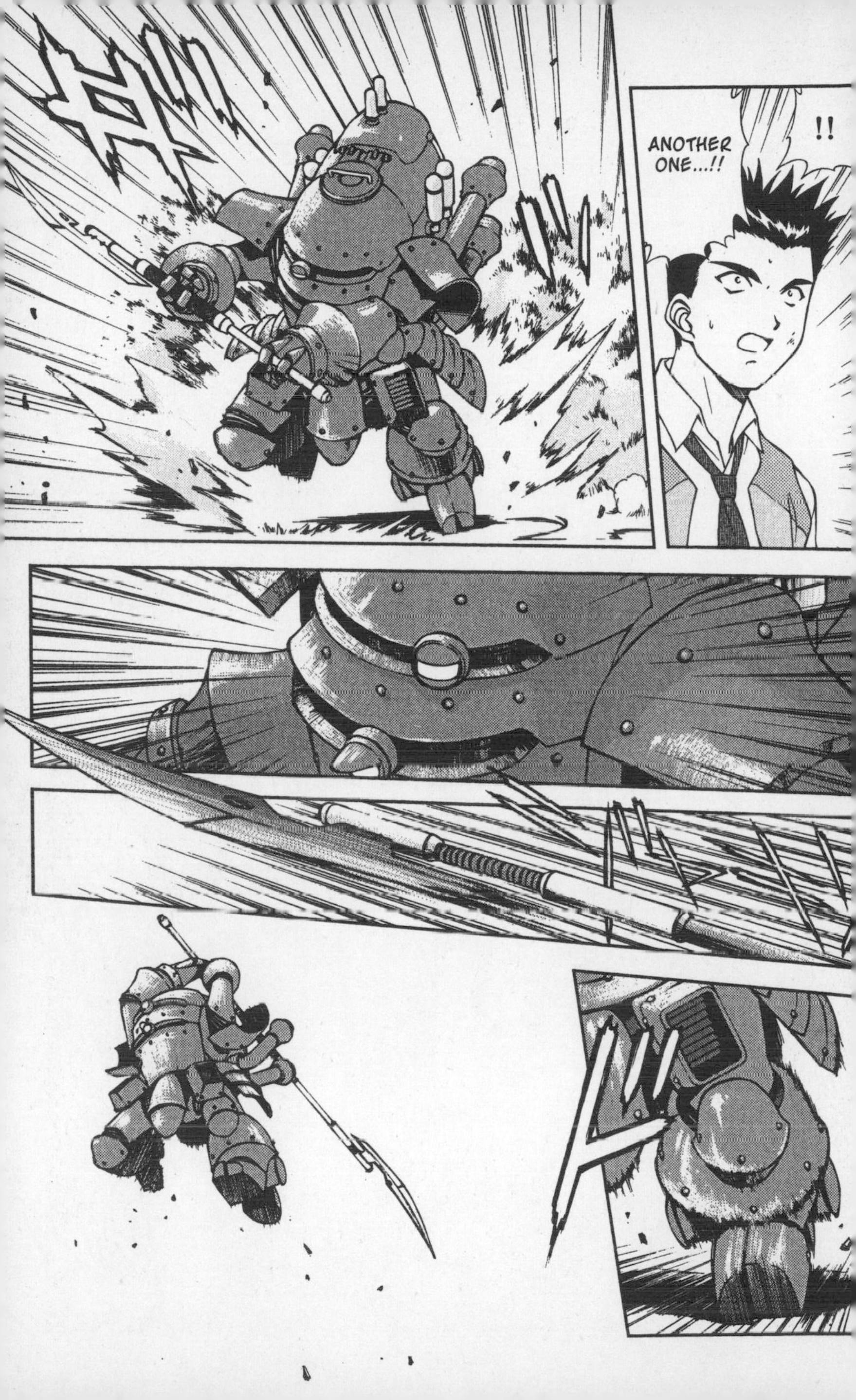
!!
ANOTHER ONE...!!

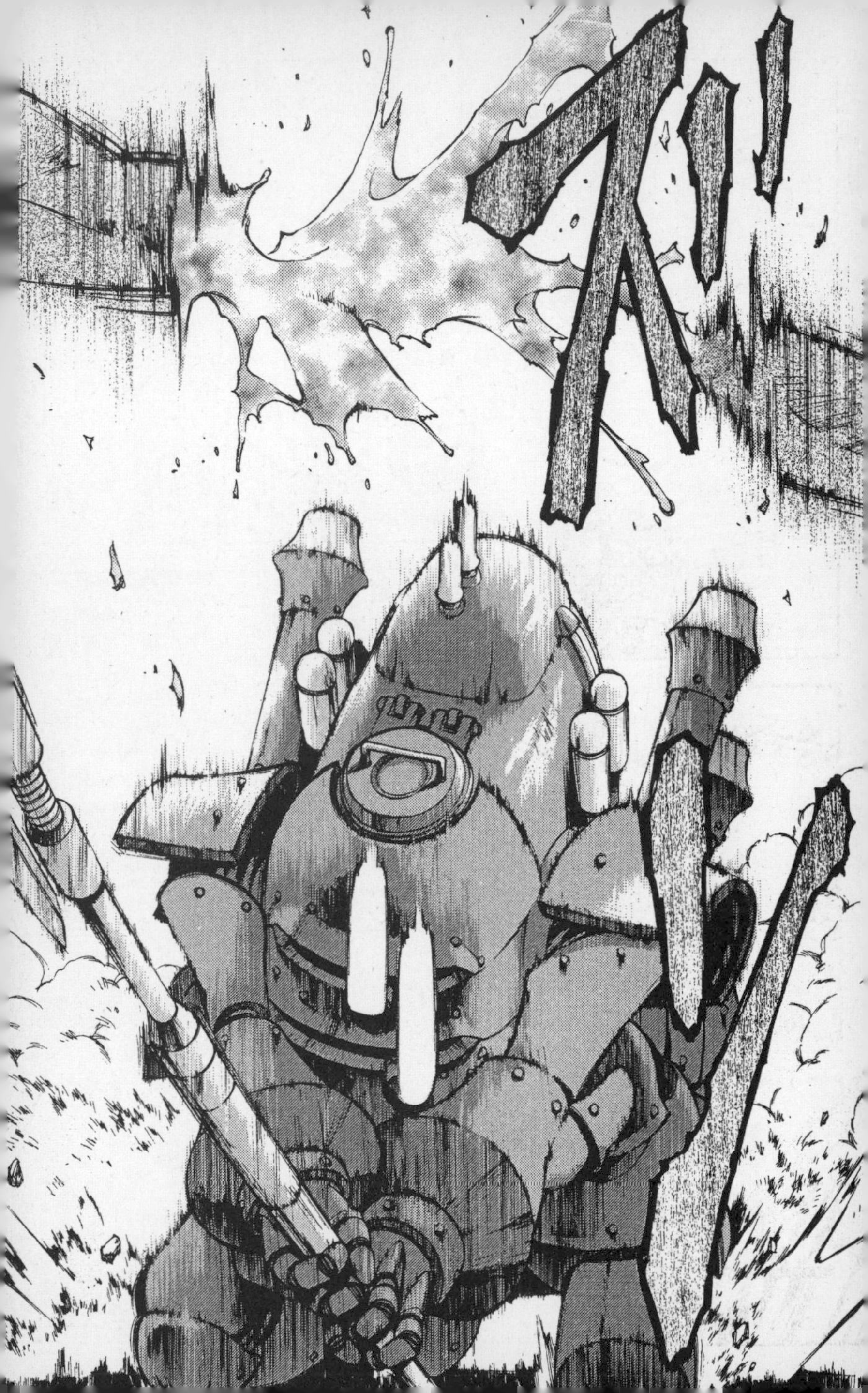
ズン

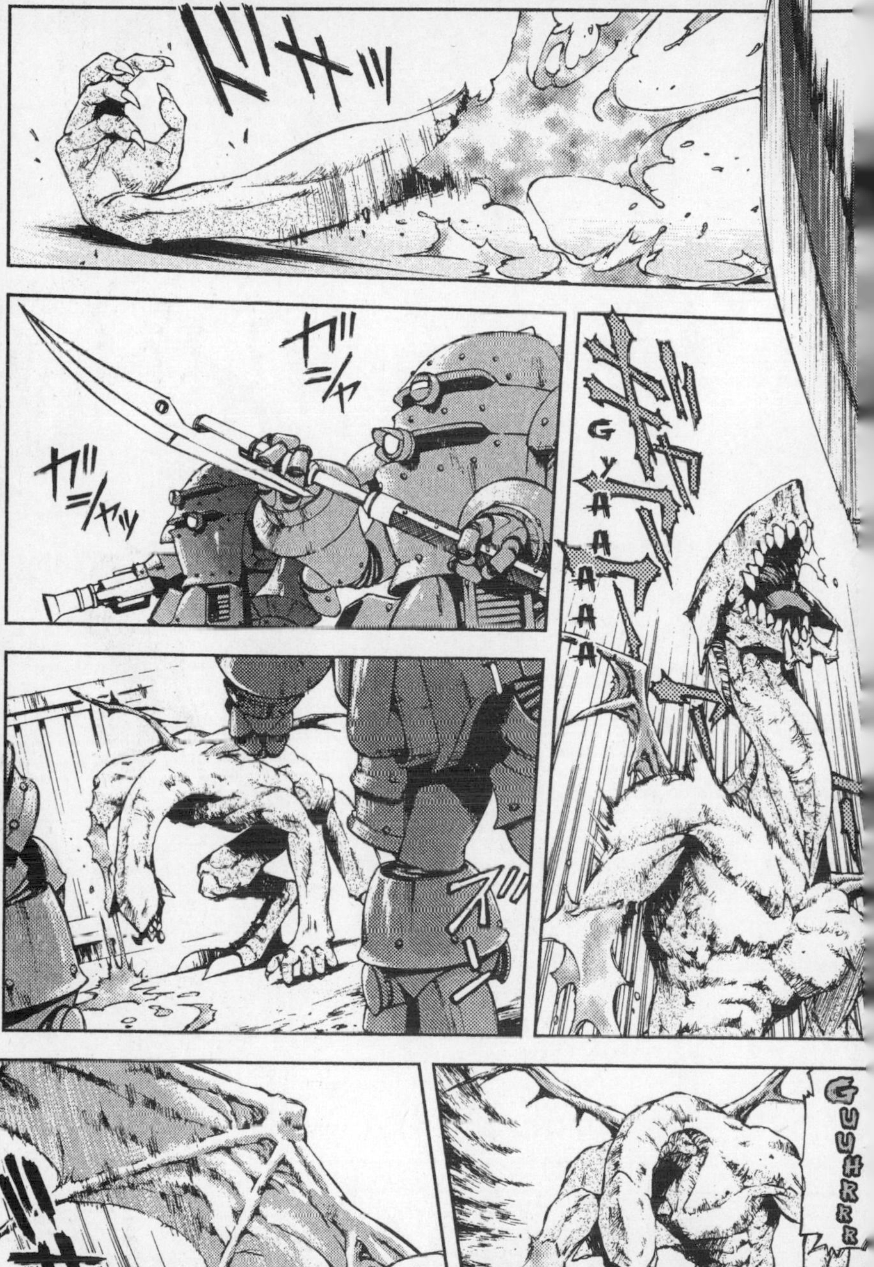

ドォォッ
ギャッ
GYAAAAAAA
ガシャ
ガシャッ
ズー
GUHRRR
バッ

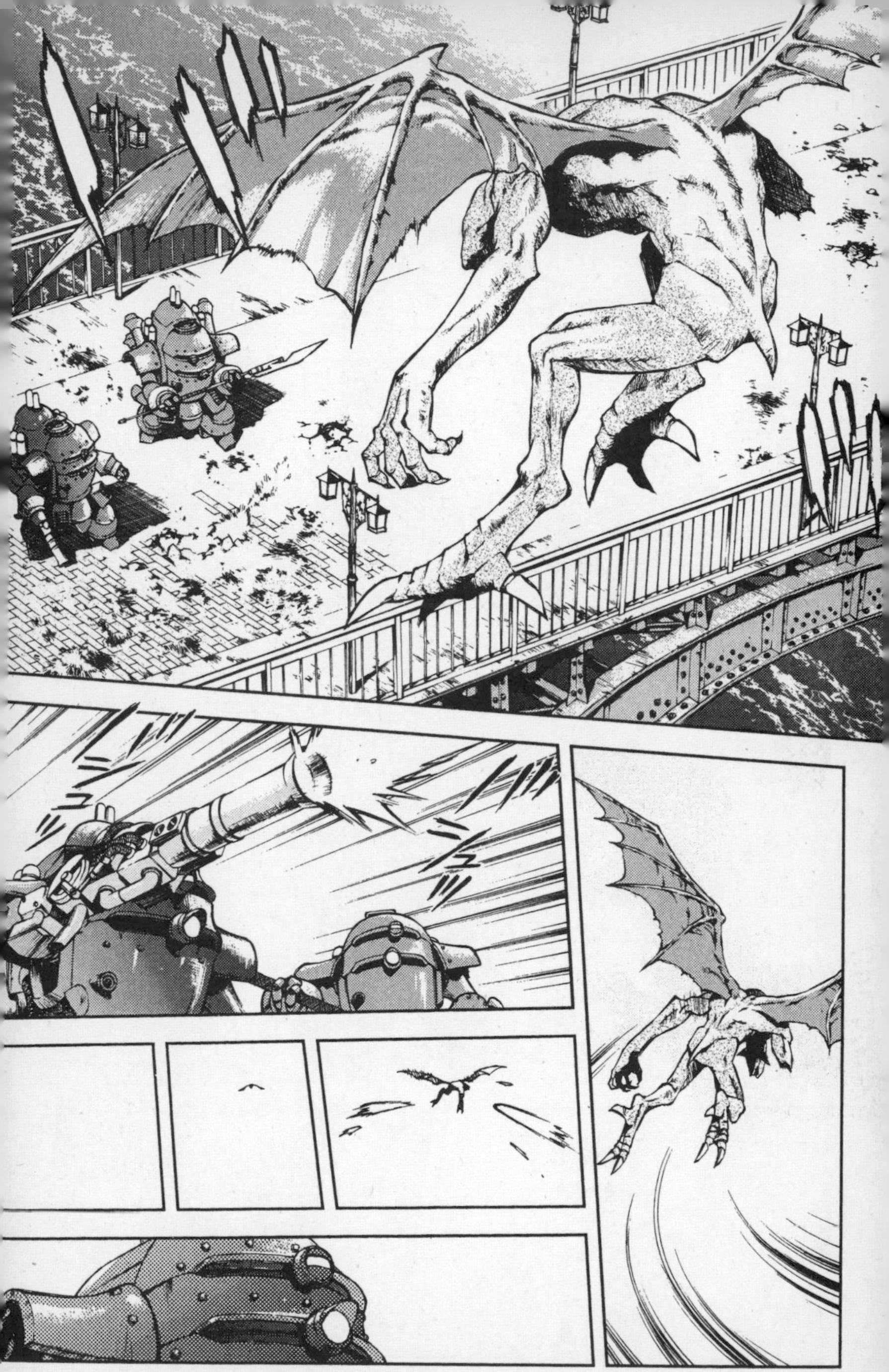

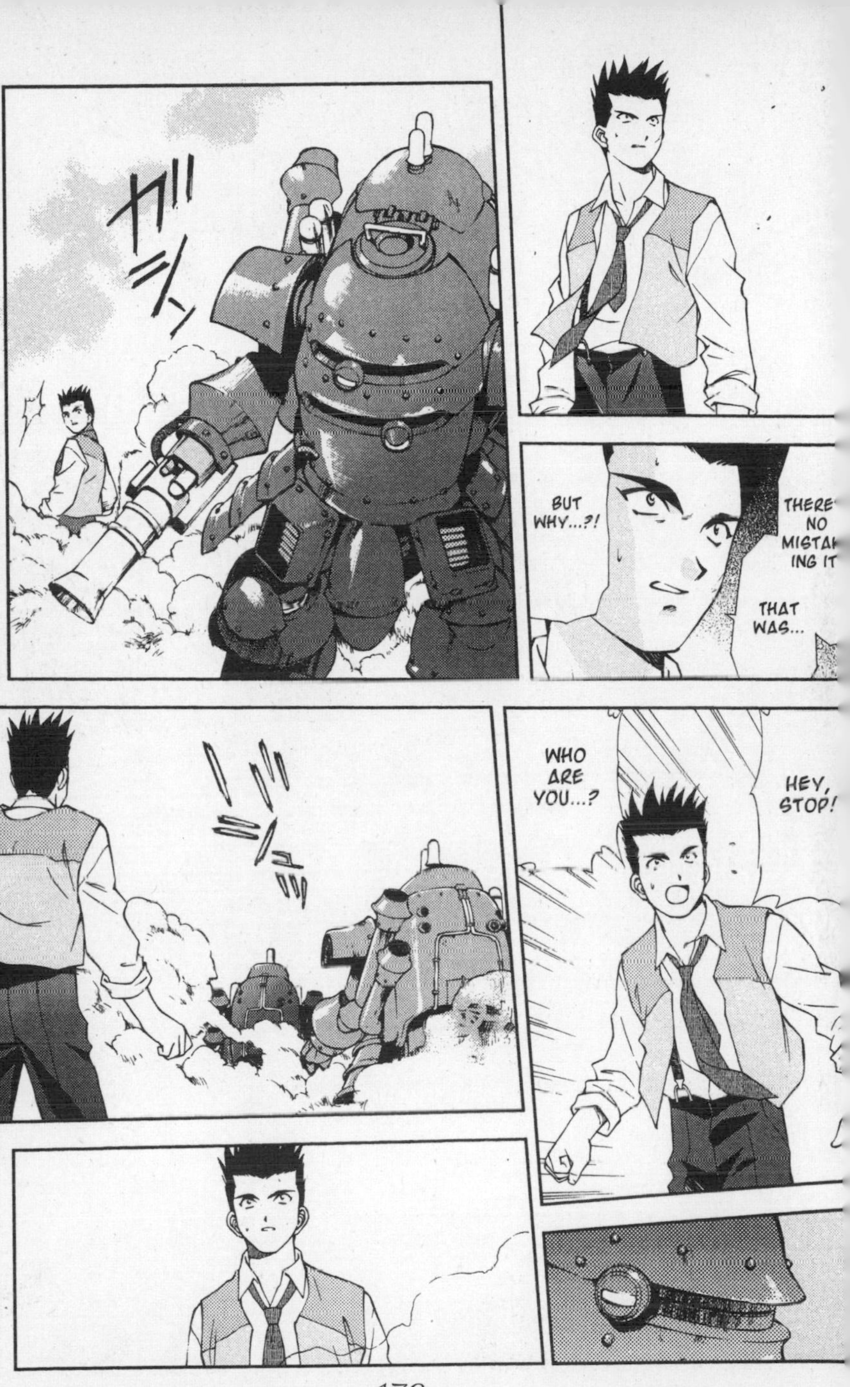
THERE' NO MISTAK ING IT
BUT WHY...?!
THAT WAS...
HEY, STOP!
WHO ARE YOU...?

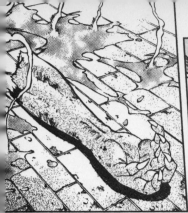

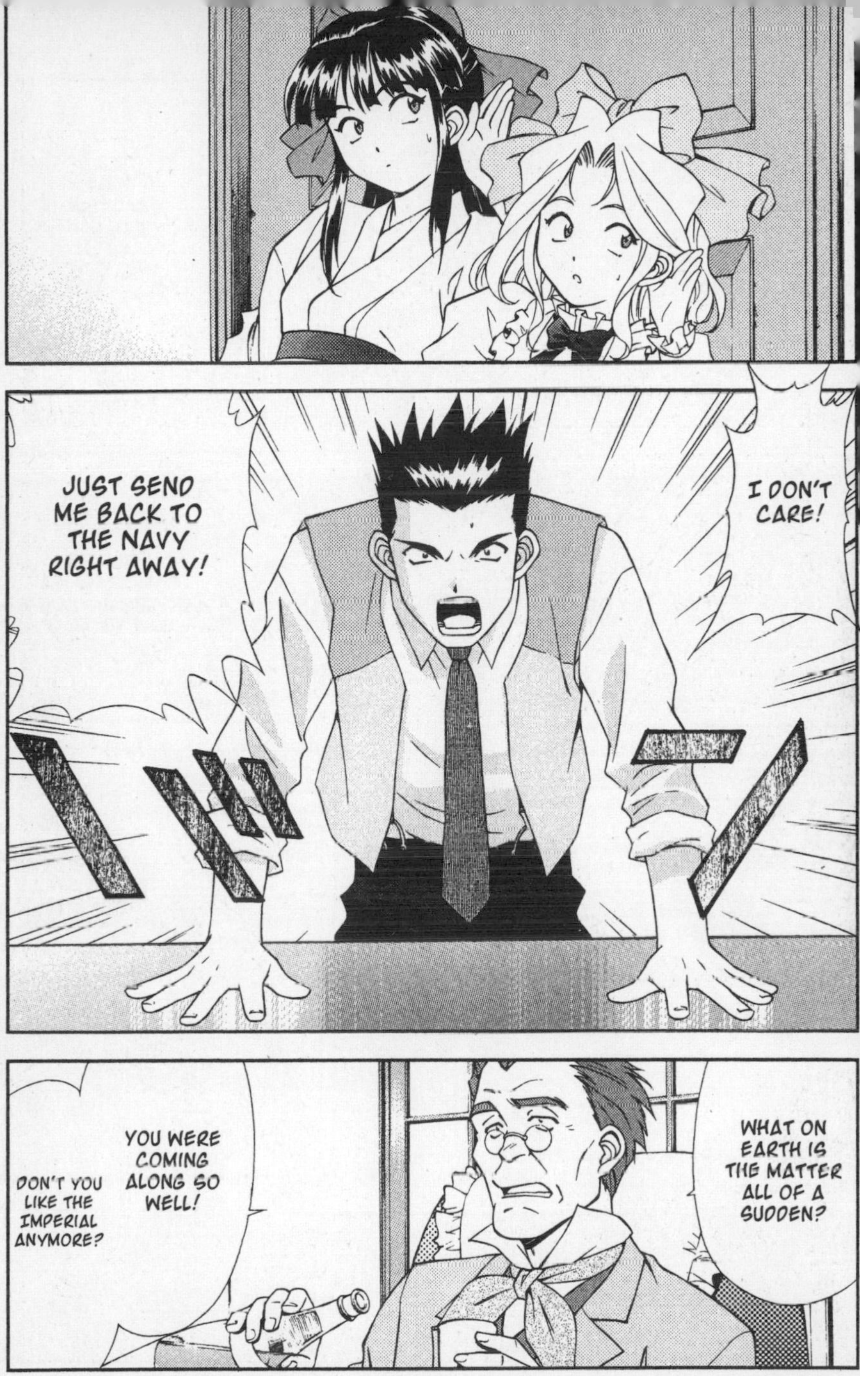
I DON'T CARE!
JUST SEND ME BACK TO THE NAVY RIGHT AWAY!
WHAT ON EARTH IS THE MATTER ALL OF A SUDDEN?
YOU WERE COMING ALONG SO WELL!
DON'T YOU LIKE THE IMPERIAL ANYMORE?

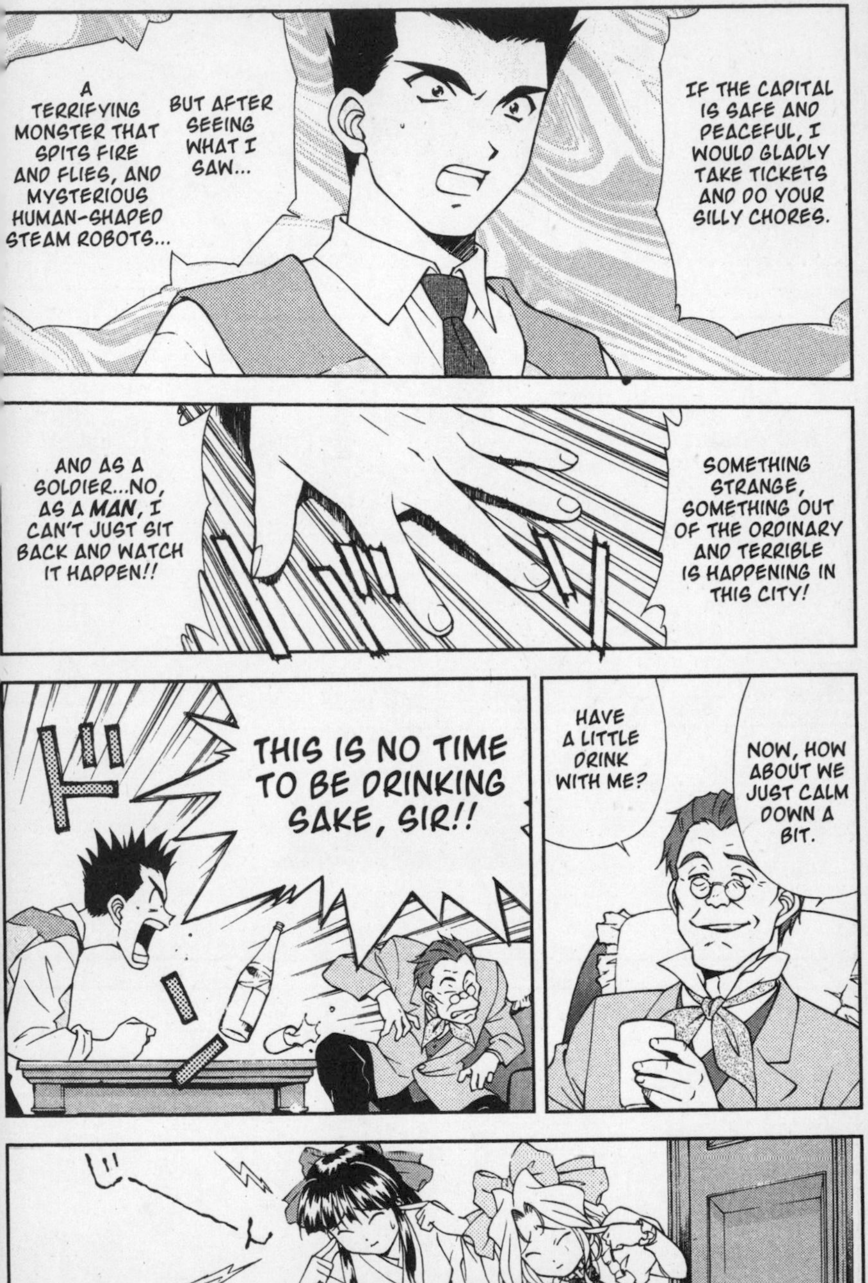
IF THE CAPITAL IS SAFE AND PEACEFUL, I WOULD GLADLY TAKE TICKETS AND DO YOUR SILLY CHORES.
BUT AFTER SEEING WHAT I SAW...
A TERRIFYING MONSTER THAT SPITS FIRE AND FLIES, AND MYSTERIOUS HUMAN-SHAPED STEAM ROBOTS...
SOMETHING STRANGE, SOMETHING OUT OF THE ORDINARY AND TERRIBLE IS HAPPENING IN THIS CITY!
AND AS A SOLDIER...NO, AS A *MAN*, I CAN'T JUST SIT BACK AND WATCH IT HAPPEN!!
NOW, HOW ABOUT WE JUST CALM DOWN A BIT.
HAVE A LITTLE DRINK WITH ME?
THIS IS NO TIME TO BE DRINKING SAKE, SIR!!

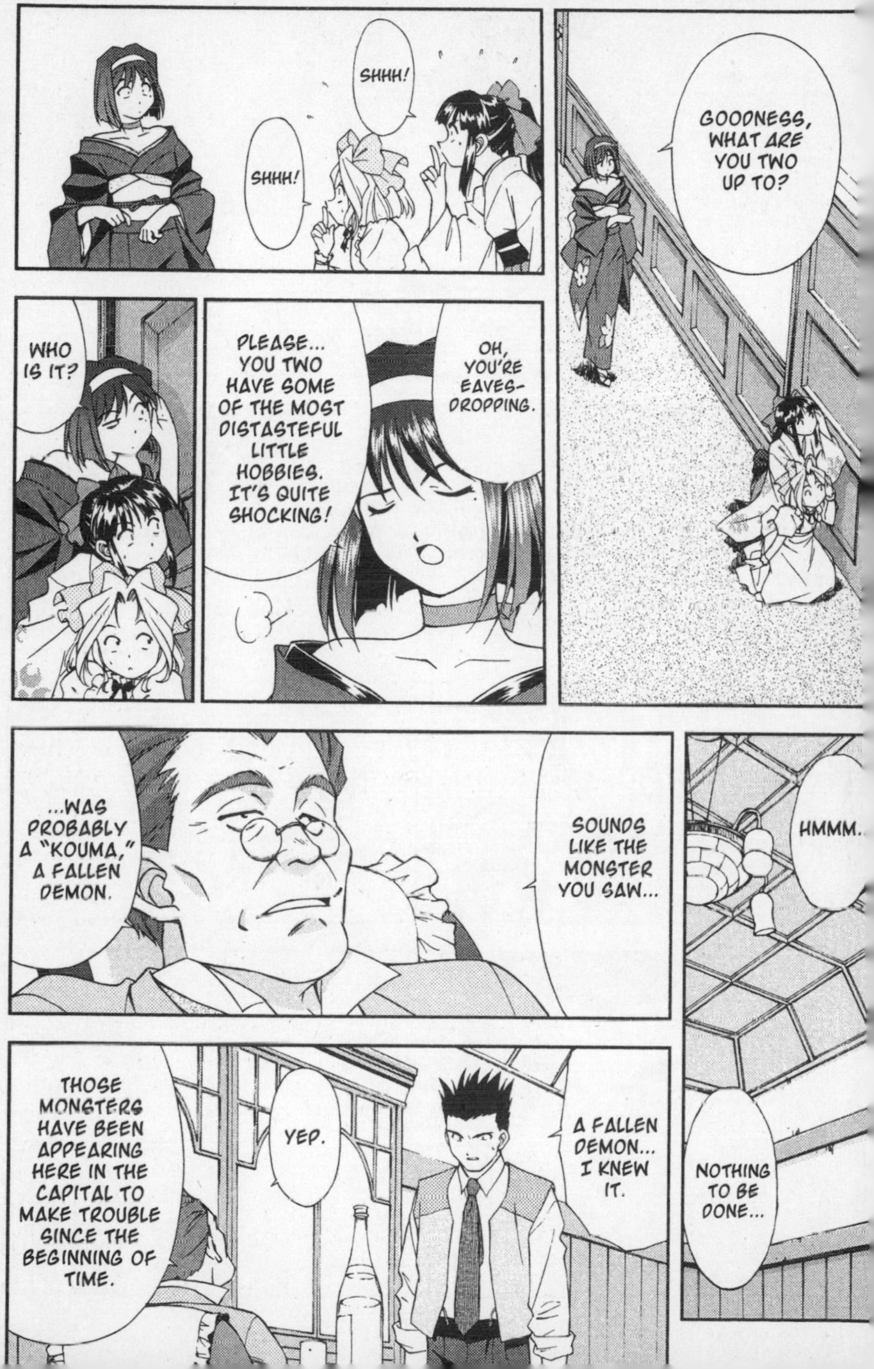
GOODNESS, WHAT ARE YOU TWO UP TO?
SHHH!
SHHH!
OH, YOU'RE EAVES-DROPPING.
PLEASE... YOU TWO HAVE SOME OF THE MOST DISTASTEFUL LITTLE HOBBIES. IT'S QUITE SHOCKING!
WHO IS IT?
HMMM.
NOTHING TO BE DONE...
SOUNDS LIKE THE MONSTER YOU SAW...
...WAS PROBABLY A "KOUMA," A FALLEN DEMON.
A FALLEN DEMON... I KNEW IT.
YEP.
THOSE MONSTERS HAVE BEEN APPEARING HERE IN THE CAPITAL TO MAKE TROUBLE SINCE THE BEGINNING OF TIME.

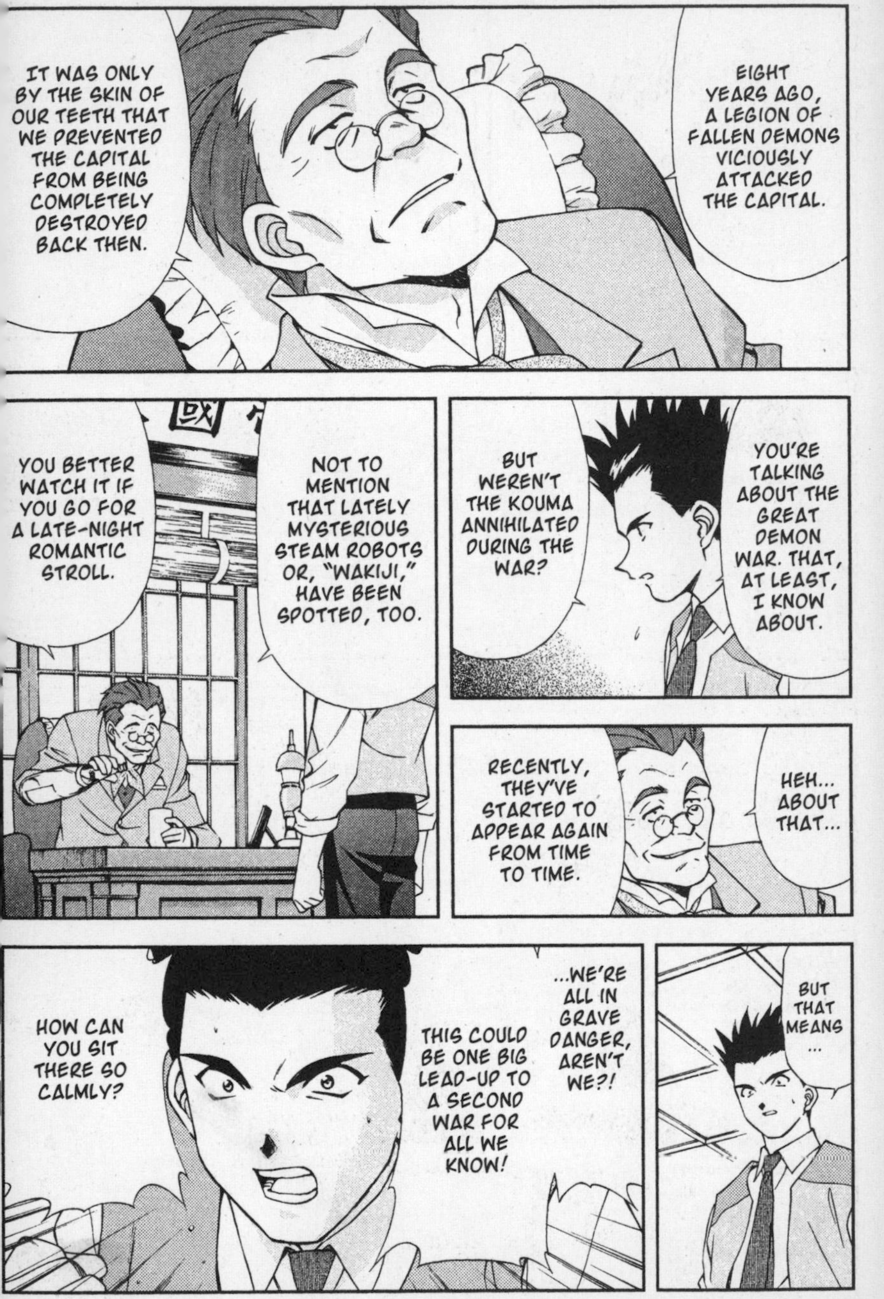
EIGHT YEARS AGO, A LEGION OF FALLEN DEMONS VICIOUSLY ATTACKED THE CAPITAL.
IT WAS ONLY BY THE SKIN OF OUR TEETH THAT WE PREVENTED THE CAPITAL FROM BEING COMPLETELY DESTROYED BACK THEN.
YOU'RE TALKING ABOUT THE GREAT DEMON WAR. THAT, AT LEAST, I KNOW ABOUT.
BUT WEREN'T THE KOUMA ANNIHILATED DURING THE WAR?
HEH... ABOUT THAT...
RECENTLY, THEY'VE STARTED TO APPEAR AGAIN FROM TIME TO TIME.
NOT TO MENTION THAT LATELY MYSTERIOUS STEAM ROBOTS OR, "WAKIJI," HAVE BEEN SPOTTED, TOO.
YOU BETTER WATCH IT IF YOU GO FOR A LATE-NIGHT ROMANTIC STROLL.
BUT THAT MEANS ...
...WE'RE ALL IN GRAVE DANGER, AREN'T WE?!
THIS COULD BE ONE BIG LEAD-UP TO A SECOND WAR FOR ALL WE KNOW!
HOW CAN YOU SIT THERE SO CALMLY?

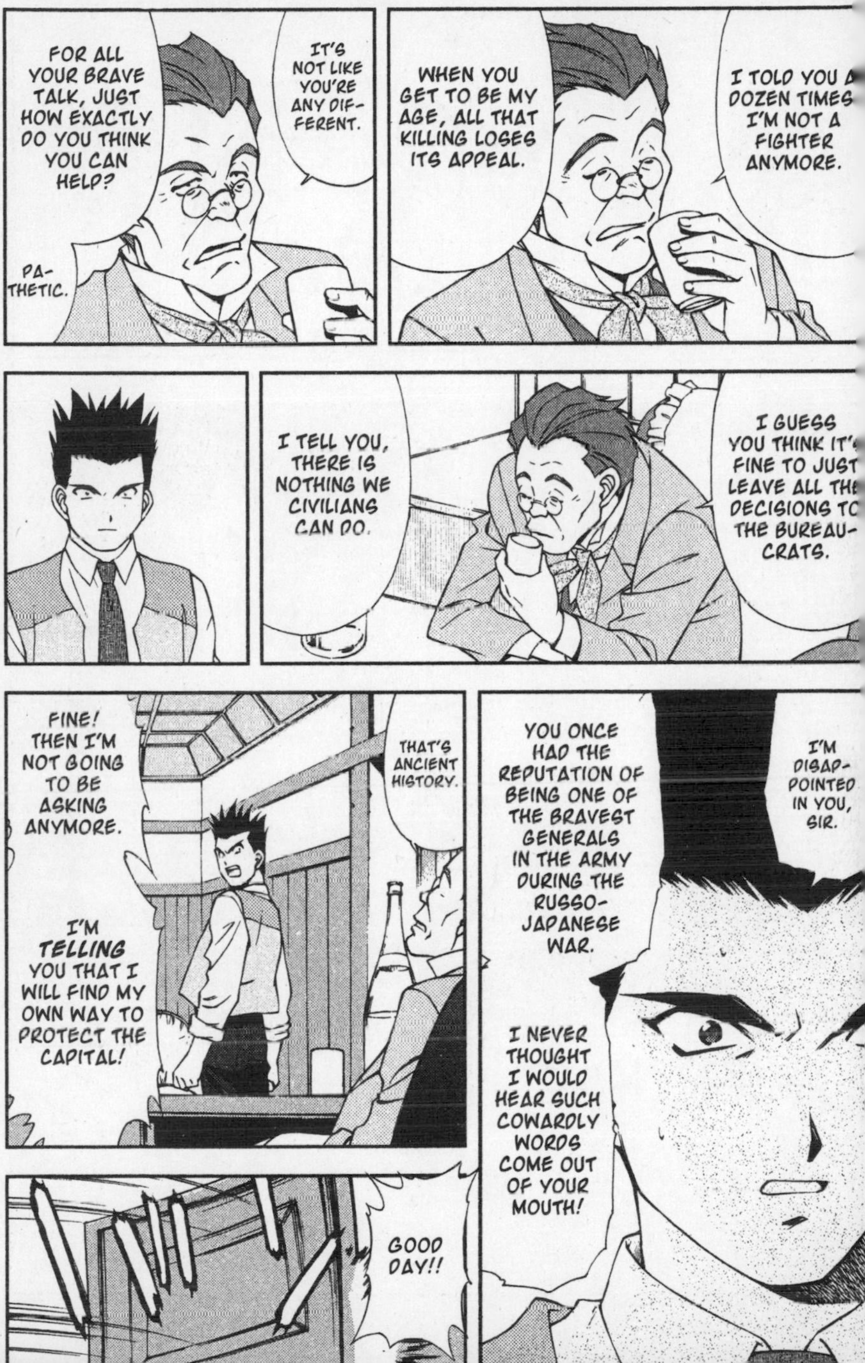
I TOLD YOU A DOZEN TIMES I'M NOT A FIGHTER ANYMORE.
WHEN YOU GET TO BE MY AGE, ALL THAT KILLING LOSES ITS APPEAL.
IT'S NOT LIKE YOU'RE ANY DIF-FERENT.
FOR ALL YOUR BRAVE TALK, JUST HOW EXACTLY DO YOU THINK YOU CAN HELP?
PA-THETIC.
I GUESS YOU THINK IT'S FINE TO JUST LEAVE ALL THE DECISIONS TO THE BUREAU-CRATS.
I TELL YOU, THERE IS NOTHING WE CIVILIANS CAN DO.
I'M DISAP-POINTED IN YOU, SIR.
YOU ONCE HAD THE REPUTATION OF BEING ONE OF THE BRAVEST GENERALS IN THE ARMY DURING THE RUSSO-JAPANESE WAR.
I NEVER THOUGHT I WOULD HEAR SUCH COWARDLY WORDS COME OUT OF YOUR MOUTH!
THAT'S ANCIENT HISTORY.
FINE! THEN I'M NOT GOING TO BE ASKING ANYMORE.
I'M *TELLING* YOU THAT I WILL FIND MY OWN WAY TO PROTECT THE CAPITAL!
GOOD DAY!!

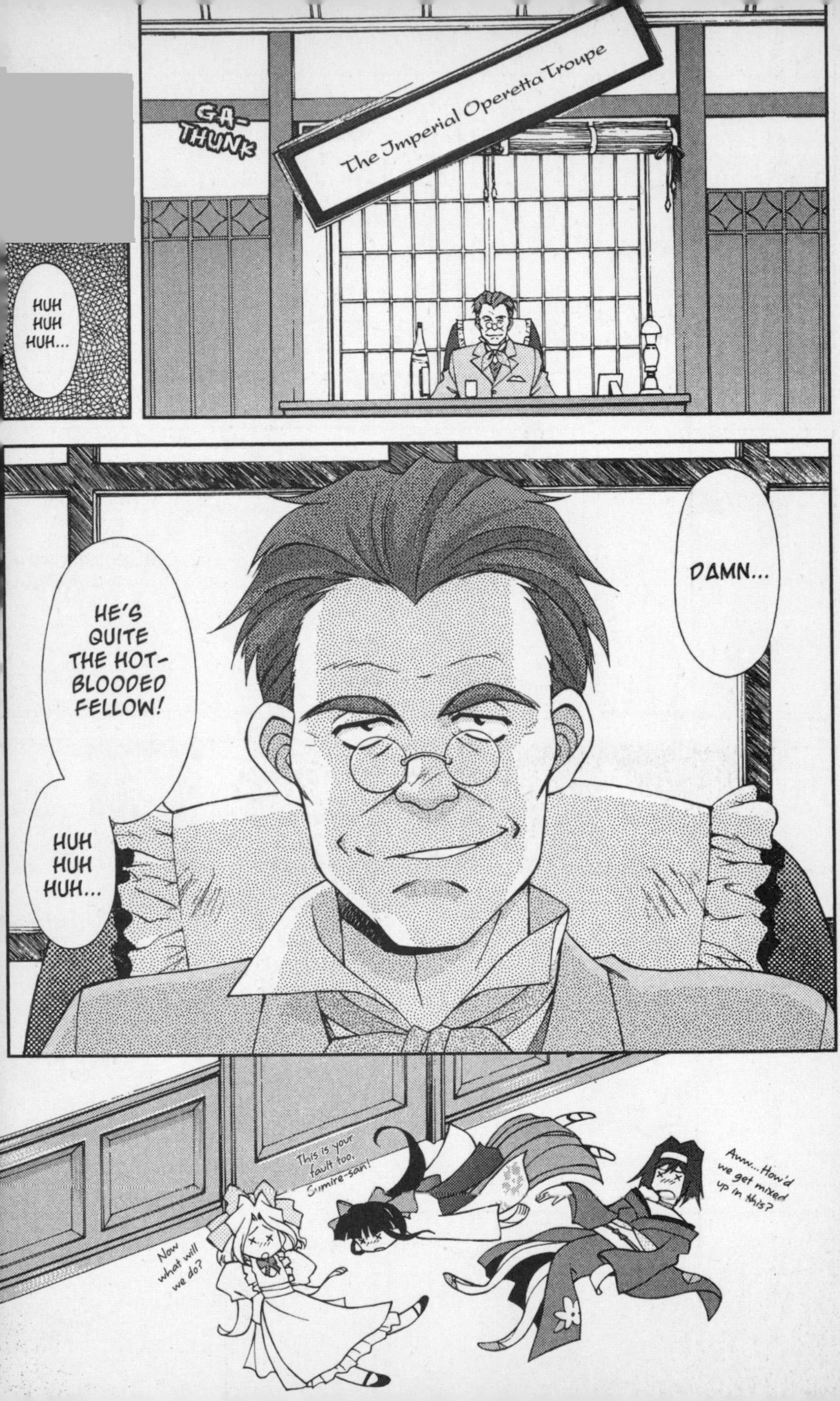
The Imperial Operetta Troupe
GA-THUNK
HUH HUH HUH...
DAMN...
HE'S QUITE THE HOT-BLOODED FELLOW!
HUH HUH HUH...
Aww...How'd we get mixed up in this?
This is your fault too, Sumire-san!
Now what will we do?

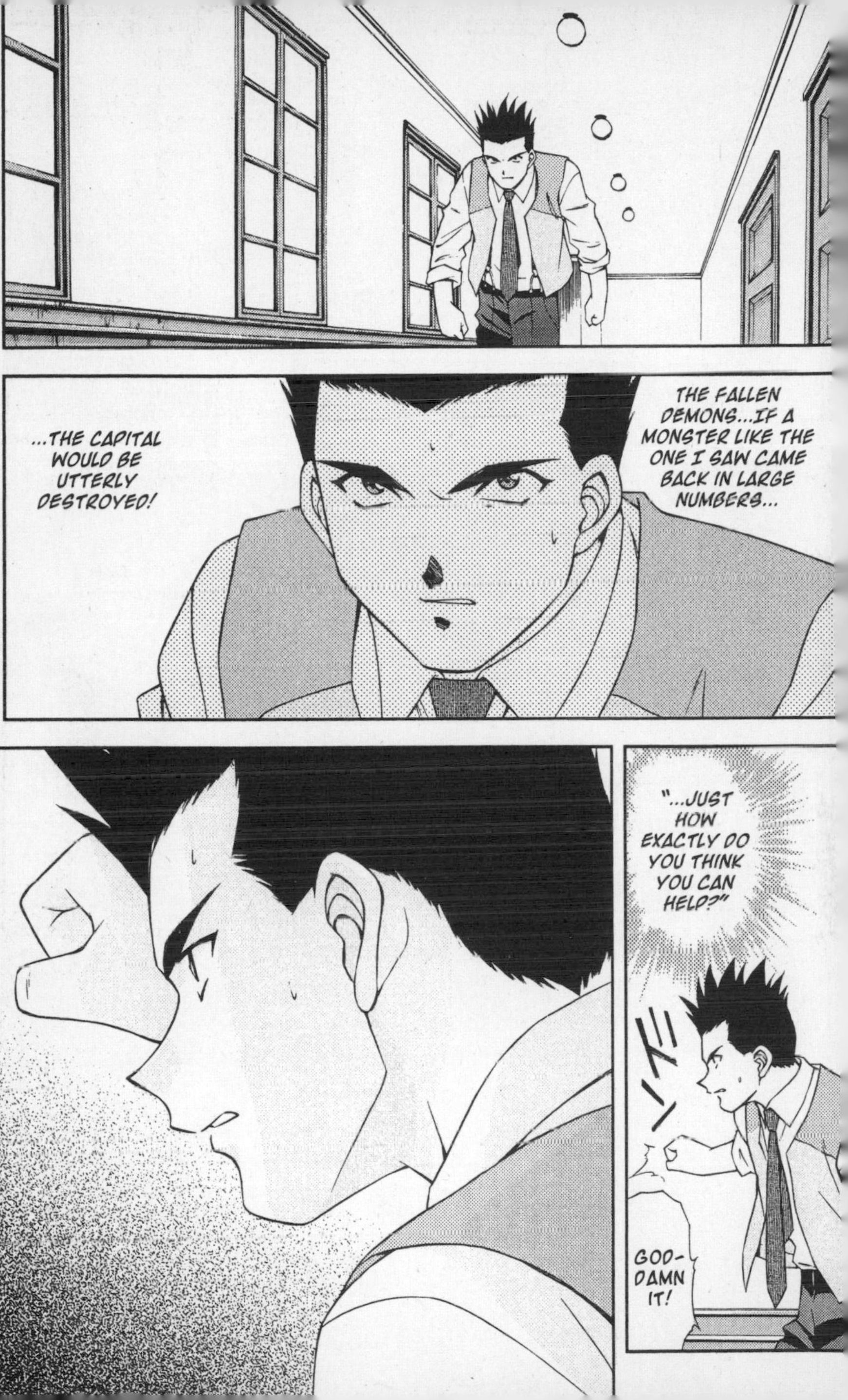
THE FALLEN DEMONS...IF A MONSTER LIKE THE ONE I SAW CAME BACK IN LARGE NUMBERS...
...THE CAPITAL WOULD BE UTTERLY DESTROYED!
"...JUST HOW EXACTLY DO YOU THINK YOU CAN HELP?"
GOD-DAMN IT!

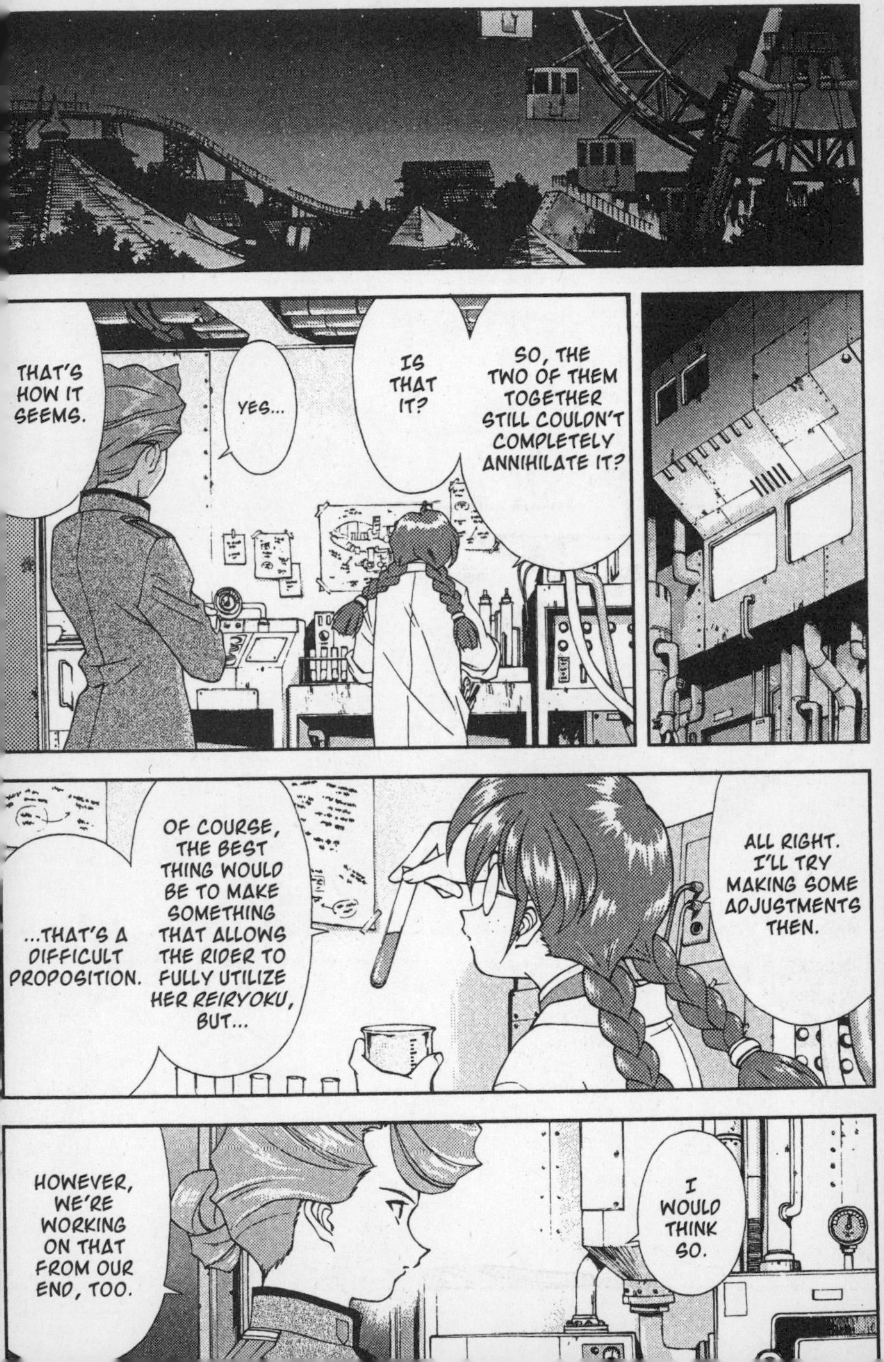

SO, THE TWO OF THEM TOGETHER STILL COULON'T COMPLETELY ANNIHILATE IT?
IS THAT IT?
YES...
THAT'S HOW IT SEEMS.
ALL RIGHT. I'LL TRY MAKING SOME ADJUSTMENTS THEN.
OF COURSE, THE BEST THING WOULD BE TO MAKE SOMETHING THAT ALLOWS THE RIDER TO FULLY UTILIZE HER *REIRYOKU*, BUT...
...THAT'S A DIFFICULT PROPOSITION.
I WOULD THINK SO.
HOWEVER, WE'RE WORKING ON THAT FROM OUR END, TOO.

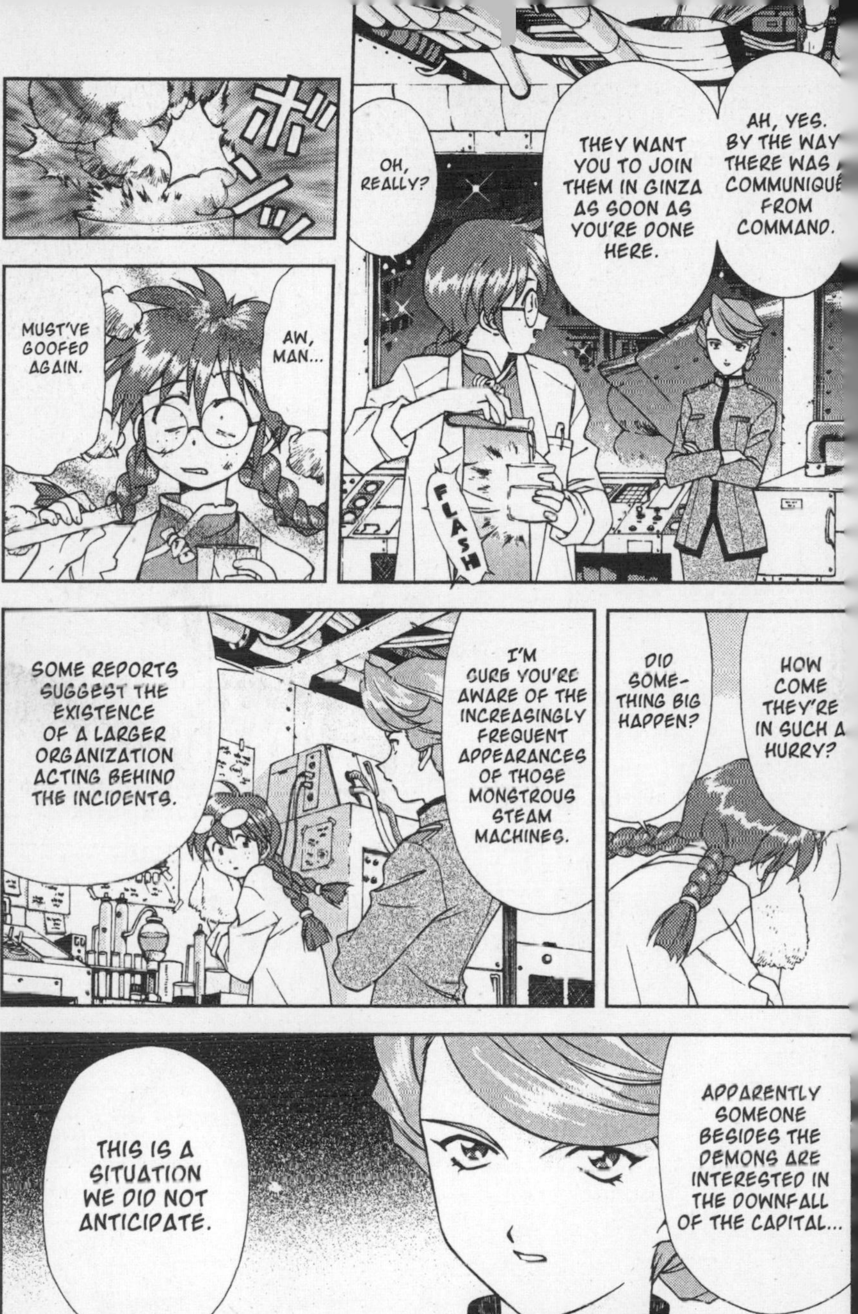

AH, YES. BY THE WAY THERE WAS A COMMUNIQUÉ FROM COMMAND.
THEY WANT YOU TO JOIN THEM IN GINZA AS SOON AS YOU'RE DONE HERE.
OH, REALLY?
FLASH
AW, MAN...
MUST'VE GOOFED AGAIN.
HOW COME THEY'RE IN SUCH A HURRY?
DID SOME-THING BIG HAPPEN?
I'M SURE YOU'RE AWARE OF THE INCREASINGLY FREQUENT APPEARANCES OF THOSE MONSTROUS STEAM MACHINES.
SOME REPORTS SUGGEST THE EXISTENCE OF A LARGER ORGANIZATION ACTING BEHIND THE INCIDENTS.
APPARENTLY SOMEONE BESIDES THE DEMONS ARE INTERESTED IN THE DOWNFALL OF THE CAPITAL...
THIS IS A SITUATION WE DID NOT ANTICIPATE.

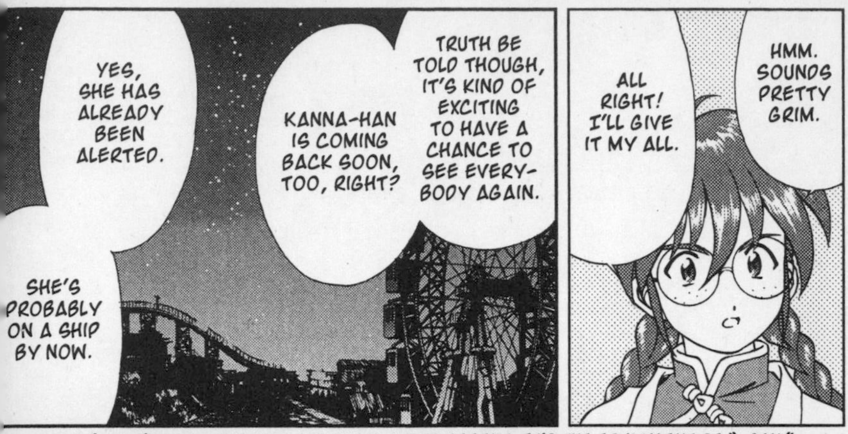
HMM. SOUNDS PRETTY GRIM.
ALL RIGHT! I'LL GIVE IT MY ALL.
TRUTH BE TOLD THOUGH, IT'S KIND OF EXCITING TO HAVE A CHANCE TO SEE EVERY-BODY AGAIN.
KANNA-HAN IS COMING BACK SOON, TOO, RIGHT?
YES, SHE HAS ALREADY BEEN ALERTED.
SHE'S PROBABLY ON A SHIP BY NOW.

NOTE: "-HAN" INDICATES THAT SHE HAS A KYOTO ACCENT. IT'S THE EQUIVALENT OF "-SAN."

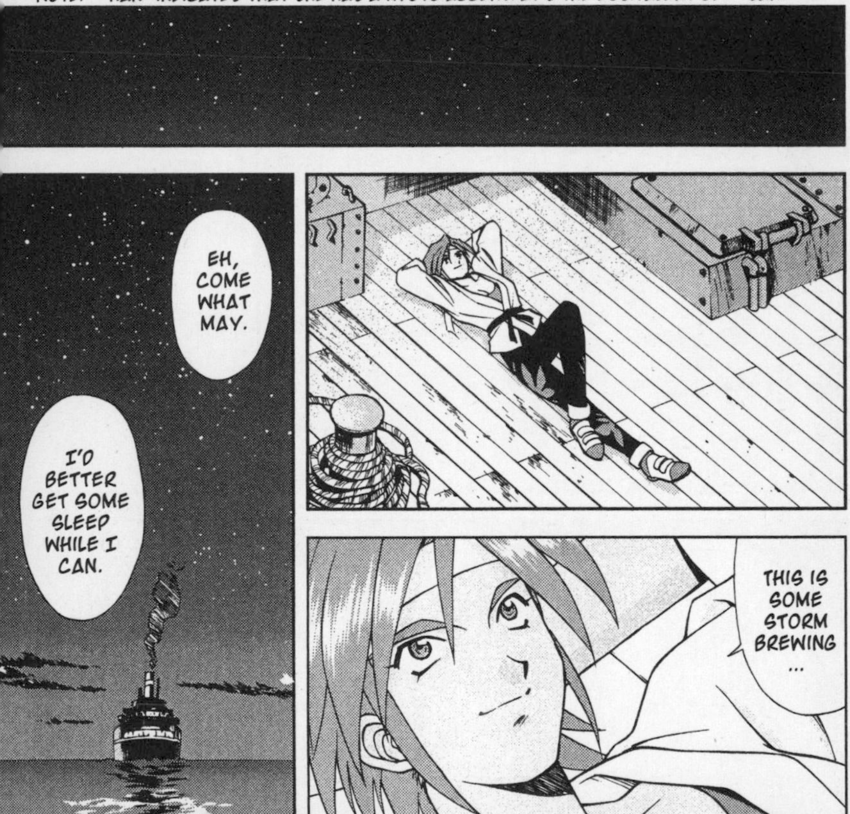
THIS IS SOME STORM BREWING ...
EH, COME WHAT MAY.
I'D BETTER GET SOME SLEEP WHILE I CAN.

Sakura Taisen Volume 1—End of Performance

From Sakura to Ogami

Everybody has a period when they are new to things. Reading this manga featuring poor, hapless Ogami (who is drawn so wonderfully with so many different expressions!) and seeing his bewilderment so clearly made me remember the first time I auditioned for anime when I was sixteen. The large empty studio was like the cockpit of a Koubu that made me feel faint from nerves and intensified my sense of being wholly alone. The inorganic microphone was like a Kouma, quietly waiting to attack. I hated it! Everything was so grand and impressive that I felt very small and depressed. The only thing that kept me going was the hope that I would be recognized one day. It was exactly the same as Ogami-san just after he was posted to the Grand Imperial Theater. People must endure many trials, but when they get past them they acquire strength and kindness. As I watch Ogami-san perform and grow, I think of my youth and my strong-headed ways back then, and smile from afar.

**Chisa Yokoyama playing
Sakura Shinguji**

Bonus Section

First Installment

Cherry Blossoms Flourish in Otowa

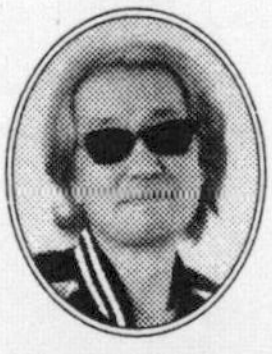

By Ohji Hiroi

ıen you peel back the three leaves, you can ell sweet cherry through the slightly wet and nslucent thin skin of mochi. It was an elegant, endid sakura mochi. When I took a bite, the ntle sweetness danced around my mouth, filling with joy.

the first flush of spring at the beginning of the st Century, two men from Kodansha came with ne sakura mochi from Choumei Temple. One s a country-samurai type, Yamamoto, the other obviously geeky Nomura.

offered the sweets that they had brought me, cusing myself for my "rudeness" as all Japanese

ıen I reached out for the second mochi, mamoto said with a heavy overtone, "Magazine would like to do a manga version of *Sakura* isen..."

lot possible," I said as I grabbed the second ochi.

on't say that. Would you please just have a look, ease?" Yamamoto spread out a series of penciled ges on the table.

/hat the hell's this?" I said.

e is a new manga artist."

put the sakura mochi down and looked over the eshly drawn pages.

mazing. It looks just like Fujishima-sensei's ork."

ou see? You see?" Nomura said gaily as he ınched his way through some mochi of his own.

ut you know..."

lo, I understand. I understand your feeling that u want it to be Fujishima-sensei's manga, but u know, we've gotten an okay from Fujishima-nsei, and Sega's already given approval...We ent to Haneda many, many times and begged. 'm not saying this 'cause I'm drunk or insane. just like Sakura so much! I want to see more her! **Waah! Sniffle!**" Nomura started his aggerated cry.

d. Note: Mochi is a form of Japanese candy, ade from rice flour that is pounded into a dough d wrapped around a tasty filling. Yum!]

Yamamoto began talking slowly as he rubbed Nomura's back as if to soothe him. "[...] we need is your O.K. for the series to begin. Of course I understand your feeling th[...] Sakura Taisen should always be the real thing. That is why Kodansha has pleaded w[...] you many times suggesting different manga writers and editors. And many times we hit the thick wall created by Fujishima-sensei, Sega and you, causing people to get fire[...] develop neuroses, defect overseas... Why don't we stop this already? It's not good for y[...] to resist any longer."

The way he put it was interesting. He put on a front of compassion and understanding, b[...] it was really a threat.

I knew. Mr. Kosuke Fujishima is a manga writer of Kodansha's. When we were fi[...] planning Sakura Taisen, I begged and got to borrow him. Yamamoto was saying that [...] was time to repay the debt. Country-samurai-type Yamamoto was just as iron-armed [...] he looked.

"So, it's okay with Fujishima sensei...?" I asked.
"Yes."
"I'm the only one left..."
"Yes."
"And if I say no?"
"You've worked long enough to know how big this industry is. We are Kodansha, after all."
"Is that a threat?"
"Yes." Yamamoto smiled coldly.

At that moment I remembered that several prominent writers had disappeared aft[...] refusing work from Kodansha. I didn't want to end up in the bottom of Tokyo Bay.

"Boy, this manga artist is quite good. His name is Ikku Masa, is it? He's good. But can h[...] handle a whole series?"
"Don't worry about that. We have a Series Reinforcement Isolation Apartment behir[...] Kodansha. We'll have him live there. We'll do our best, 24/7."
"I see."
"So, what do you say?"
"Let's do it. Everyone's been waiting for Sakura's manga." I hated myself at this point.
"Then you'll do the script?"
"What? I have to write it?" In my mind, I was yelling, "You dirty, old con-man, Yamamot[...]
"Yes, Akahori-san says you ought to." I was completely trapped.
"But I'm kinda busy at the moment." I wanted out somehow.
"Igarashi says hello."

When I heard that name, a cold shiver ran down my spine. Everyone in the industry know[...] of the "Cold-blooded Igarashi." Women go into labor, politicians bow and Yakuza ask [...] shake hands. He is the sharpest of the sharp at Kodansha, the boss of publishing.
"Okay, let's do it! I'll write!"
"Great! Banzai!!"

My mind was a rain storm, threatening to drown my heart. Thus began my tribulations wi[...] Sakura Taisen's manga.

Ensign Ogami has only just begun his first assignment, and he's already considering handing in his resignation! Punching tickets at the theater doesn't seem to be furthering his goal of defending Tokyo from demonic invaders, but the employees of the Imperial Theater are more than they seem, and Manager Yoneda is no exception. The secret mission of the Flower Troupe is revealed, and Ogami's part in it turns out to be a lot more than he ever could have imagined! However, when the girls suit up for their first major battle against the demon steam suits, they will find that their enemies are quite a bit tougher than expected. Will Ogami's leadership (and budding spiritual powers?!) and the teamwork of the Flower Troupe, honed through many a stage show, be enough to fend off the Kuronosu Council and their demonic hordes?

Find out in Sakura Taisen, Vol. 2!

TOKYOPOP SHOP

.HACK//AI BUSTER – NOVEL
BY TATSUYA HAMAZAKI

In the epic prequel to *.hack*, the avatar Albireo is a solo adventurer in The World, the most advanced online fantasy game ever created. When he comes across Lycoris, a strange little girl in a dungeon, he soon comes to realize that she may hold a very deadly secret—a secret that could unhinge everything in cyberspace... and beyond!

Discover the untold origins of the phenomenon known as *.hack*!

© Tatsuya Hamazaki © Rei Izumi

CHRONO CODE
BY EUI-CHEOL SHIN & IL-HO CHOI

Time flows like a river, without changing its course. This is an escape from the river's flow...

Three people must cross time and space to find each other and change their destinies. However, a powerful satellite, a secret code and the future police impede their progress, and their success hinges on an amnesiac who must first uncover the true nature of her past in order to discover who her friends are in the future.

T TEEN AGE 13+

© IL-HO CHOI & EUI-CHEOL SHIN, DAIWON C.I. Inc.

SAIYUKI RELOAD
BY KAZUYA MINEKURA

Join Sanzo, Gojyo, Hakkai, Goku and their updated wardrobe as they continue their journey west toward Shangri-La, encountering new challenges and new adventures along the way. But don't be fooled by their change in costume: The fearsome foursome is just as ferocious and focused as before...if not more so.

The hit manga that inspired the anime, and the sequel to TOKYOPOP's hugely popular *Saiyuki*!

OT OLDER TEEN AGE 16+

© Kazuya Minekura

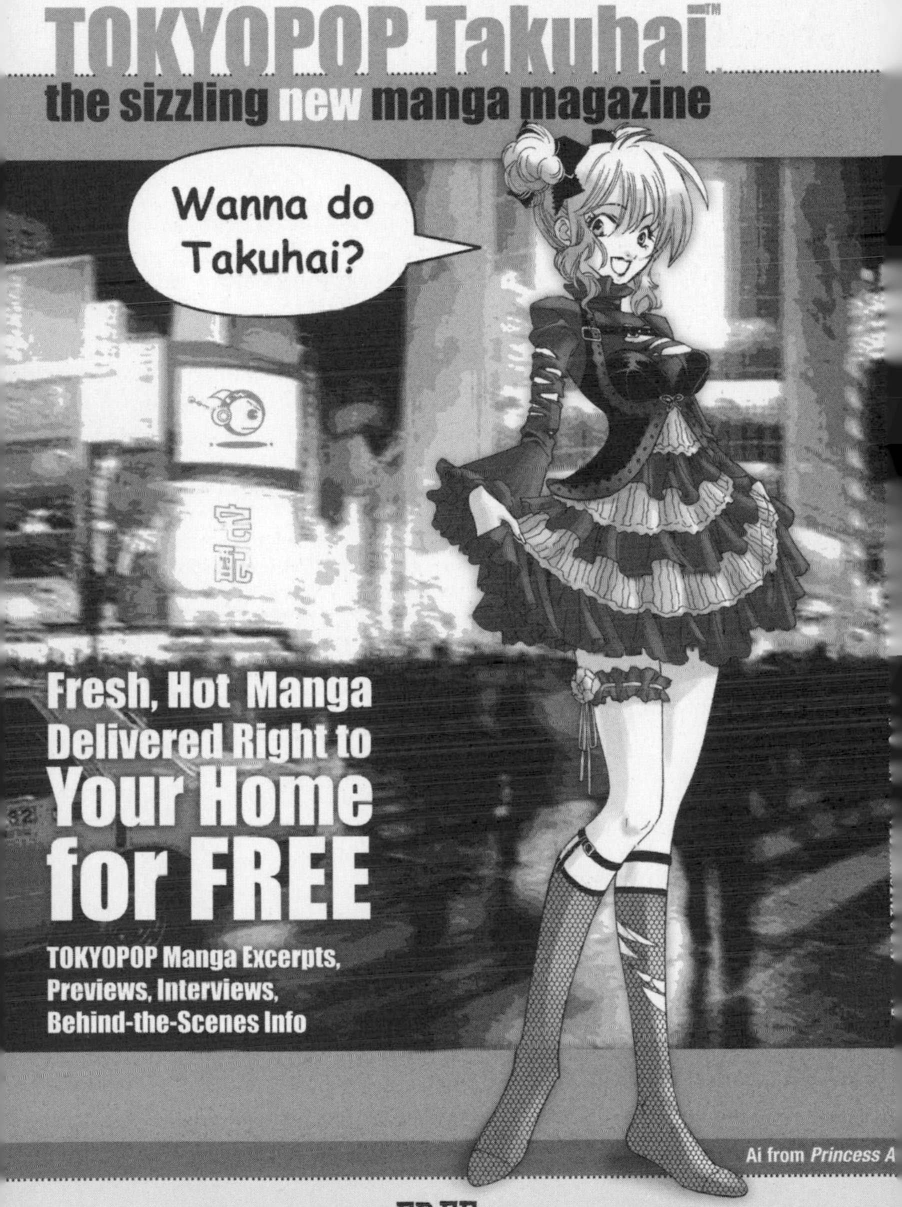
TOKYOPOP Takuhai
the sizzling new manga magazine
Wanna do Takuhai?
Fresh, Hot Manga Delivered Right to Your Home for FREE
TOKYOPOP Manga Excerpts, Previews, Interviews, Behind-the-Scenes Info
Ai from Princess A

STOP!

This is the back of the book.
You wouldn't want to spoil a great ending!

This book is printed "manga-style," in the authentic Japanese right-to-left format. Since none of the artwork has been flipped or altered, readers get to experience the story just as the creator intended. You've been asking for it, so TOKYOPOP® delivered: authentic, hot-off-the-press, and far more fun!

DIRECTIONS

If this is your first time reading manga-style, here's a quick guide to help you understand how it works.

It's easy... just start in the top right panel and follow the numbers. Have fun, and look for more 100% authentic manga from TOKYOPOP®!